ONE WEEK LO

SHELLEY AND THE
REVOLUTIONARY SUBLIME

A major new study of Percy Shelley's intellectual life and poetic career, *Shelley and the Revolutionary Sublime* identifies Shelley's fascination with sublime natural phenomena as a key element in his understanding of the way ideas like 'nature' and 'imagination' informed the social and political structures of the Romantic period. Offering a genuinely fresh set of perspectives on Shelley's texts and contexts, Cian Duffy argues that Shelley's engagement with the British and French discourse on the sublime had a profound influence on his writing about political change in that age of revolutionary crisis. Examining Shelley's extensive use of sublime imagery and metaphor, Duffy offers not only a substantial reassessment of Shelley's work but also a significant re-appraisal of the role of the sublime in the cultural history of Britain during the Romantic period.

CIAN DUFFY is a Postdoctoral Research Fellow in the Centre for Eighteenth-Century Studies at the University of York.

CAMBRIDGE STUDIES IN ROMANTICISM

This series aims to foster the best new work in one of the most challenging fields within English literary studies. From the early 1780s to the early 1830s a formidable array of talented men and women took to literary composition, not just in poetry, which some of them famously transformed, but in many modes of writing. The expansion of publishing created new opportunities for writers, and the political stakes of what they wrote were raised again by what Wordsworth called those 'great national events' that were 'almost daily taking place': the French Revolution, the Napoleonic and American wars, urbanisation, industrialisation, religious revival, an expanded empire abroad and the reform movement at home. This was an enormous ambition, even when it pretended otherwise. The relations between science, philosophy, religion and literature were reworked in texts such as *Frankenstein* and *Biographia Literaria*; gender relations in *A Vindication of the Rights of Woman* and *Don Juan*; journalism by Cobbett and Hazlitt; poetic form, content and style by the Lake School and the Cockney School. Outside Shakespeare studies, probably no body of writing has produced such a wealth of response or done so much to shape the responses of modern criticism. This indeed is the period that saw the emergence of those notions of 'literature' and of literary history, especially national literary history, on which modern scholarship in English has been founded.

The categories produced by Romanticism have also been challenged by recent historicist arguments. The task of the series is to engage both with a challenging corpus of Romantic writings and with the changing field of criticism they have helped to shape. As with other literary series published by Cambridge, this one will represent the work of both younger and more established scholars, on either side of the Atlantic and elsewhere.

For a complete list of titles published see end of book.

SHELLEY AND THE
REVOLUTIONARY SUBLIME

CIAN DUFFY

CAMBRIDGE
UNIVERSITY PRESS

CAMBRIDGE UNIVERSITY PRESS
Cambridge, New York, Melbourne, Madrid, Cape Town, Singapore, São Paulo

CAMBRIDGE UNIVERSITY PRESS
The Edinburgh Building, Cambridge CB2 2RU, UK
Published in the United States of America by Cambridge University Press, New York

www.cambridge.org
Information on this title: www.cambridge.org/9780521854009

First published 2005

Printed in the United Kingdom at the University Press, Cambridge

A catalogue record for this book is available from the British Library

ISBN-13 978-0-521-85400-9 hardback
ISBN-10 0-521-85400-8 hardback

for my family

Contents

Acknowledgements

Many people have contributed to the writing of this book. *Shelley and the Revolutionary Sublime* began life as a doctoral thesis in the Faculty of English at Cambridge University, and my greatest debt is to my supervisor, Nigel Leask, who expertly fanned its 'fading coals'. Thanks also to Jennifer Wallace, who supervised me during Nigel's sabbatical term in Michaelmas 1998, and to Peter de Bolla, whose comments on my first year's work gave it an invaluable early sense of direction. My examiners – Michael O'Neill and Neil Vickers – gave enormous assistance in moving the book beyond its original, doctoral conception. Likewise, it would not have achieved its present scope without the comments of my two anonymous readers at Cambridge University Press. Sincere thanks, too, to Linda Bree and Maartje Scheltens, my editors at Cambridge, for providing such sure guidance throughout the publication process. All contemporary Shelley scholars owe an incalculable debt to the efforts of the Garland Manuscript Facsimile series editors, and to editorial projects in progress on both sides of the Atlantic, and it is my pleasure to acknowledge that debt here. I am deeply grateful to the trustees of the Leslie Wilson Memorial fund at Magdalene College Cambridge, without whose generous financial assistance the original doctoral thesis would not have been written. Equally, I am indebted to the Robert Gardiner Memorial fund at Cambridge, and to the Cambridge European Trust, for their generous financial support throughout my doctoral work. I want to thank my parents, Luan and Mary, and my grandmother, Sarcy, for their continuing love, support and encouragement. And I want to thank Lisbet, for those days 'under the eye of Mont Blanc' and for all the other days.

Parts of this book have already appeared elsewhere and are republished here by permission of the editors of the respective publications. Material from chapters 1 and 3 was published as 'Mont Blanc's revolutionary "Voice": Shelley and Archibald Alison', in *The Bulletin of the British Association for Romantic Studies* 17 (March 2000), and as 'Shelley and the

Discourse on the Sublime', in Fiona Price and Scott Masson (eds.), *Silence, Sublimity and Suppression* (Lampeter: Edwin Mellen Press, 2001); part of chapter 2 appeared as 'Revolution or Reaction?: Shelley's *Assassins* and the Politics of Necessity', in *Keats-Shelley Journal* 52 (September 2003); a further portion of chapter 1 was published as '"One draught from Snowdon's ever-sacred spring": Shelley's Welsh Sublime', in Lynda Pratt and Damian Walford-Davies (eds.), *Wales and the Romantic Imagination* (Cardiff: University of Wales Press, 2005). I am grateful to the editors of these volumes for permission to use this material.

Note on texts

All dates for Shelley's works are dates of composition. All other dates are dates of publication. Where possible, Shelley's poetry is quoted from *The Poems of Shelley*, ed. Kelvin Everest and G. M. Matthews, 2 vols. to date (London: Longman, 1989, 2000–). Hereafter cited in the text as *Poems*. Similarly, where possible, Shelley's prose is quoted from *The Prose Works of Percy Bysshe Shelley*, ed. E. B. Murray, 1 vol. to date (Oxford: Clarendon Press, 1993–). Hereafter cited in the text as *Murray*.

Abbreviations

H6WT,	Percy Bysshe Shelley and Mary Wollstonecraft Shelley, *History of a Six Weeks' Tour through a Part of France, Switzerland, Germany and Holland* . . . (London, 1817).
Letters	*The Letters of Percy Bysshe Shelley*, ed. F. L. Jones, 2 vols. (Oxford: Clarendon, 1964).
MWSJ,	*The Journals of Mary Shelley: 1814–1844*, ed. Paula R. Feldman and Diana Scott-Kilvert, Softshell edition, 1 vol. (London: Johns Hopkins University Press, 1987).
MYRS	*Manuscripts of the Younger Romantics: Shelley*, ed. D. H. Reiman et al., 9 vols. (New York, Garland: 1985–1996).
Poetry & Prose	*Shelley's Poetry and Prose*, ed. D. H. Reiman and N. Fraistat, second edition (New York: Norton, 2002).
Prose	*Shelley's Prose, or, the Trumpet of a Prophecy*, ed. David Lee Clark, corrected edition (Albuquerque: University of New Mexico Press, 1966).
PW	*The Prose Works of Percy Bysshe Shelley*, ed. E. B. Murray, 1 vol. to date (Oxford: Clarendon Press, 1993, –).
Rousseau	Jean Jacques Rousseau, *The Collected Writings of Rousseau*, ed. C. Kelley, R. Masters, and P. Stillman, 8 vols. to date (London: University of New England Press, 1990–).
Ruins	C. F. Volney, *A New Translation of Volney's Ruins; or Meditations on the Revolution of Empires: Made under the Inspection of the Author*, 2 vols. (Paris, 1802).
Wordsworth	*The Poetical Works of William Wordsworth*, ed. E. De Selincourt and Helen Darbishire, rev. Helen Darbishire, 5 vols. (Oxford: Oxford University Press, 1952–59).

Journals

ELH	*English Literary History*
ELN	*English Language Notes*
K-SJ	*Keats-Shelley Journal*
K-SMB	*Keats-Shelley Memorial Bulletin*
MLQ	*Modern Language Quarterly*
MLR	*Modern Language Review*
PMLA	*Publications of the Modern Language Association of America*

N&Q   Notes and Queries
PQ   Philological Quarterly
RES   Review of English Studies
SiR   Studies in Romanticism

Introduction: Approaching the 'Shelleyan sublime'

It has become something of a commonplace to begin a study of Percy Shelley by noting the extraordinary fluctuation in his posthumous standing, personal no less than literary. In the years since his death, critics and commentators have given us a range of different Shelleys. It is fair to say that many of these portraits are radically misconceived, and often patronisingly reductive. From the nineteenth century, we inherit the Satanic Shelley, Shelley the 'lunatic angel', Shelley the 'beautiful and ineffectual angel', Shelley 'the eternal child'.[1] And while such ad hominem accounts were largely abandoned in the early twentieth century, critical appraisal of Shelley's work frequently remained condemnatory and dismissive. The New Critics and their followers gave us the vague and incomprehensible Shelley, the philosophically confused Shelley, the politically naive Shelley. More recent criticism has effectively refuted these charges, and Shelley's epistemological and political maturity is no longer in any serious doubt.[2] But one important aspect of his work has yet to benefit from this critical renaissance. Shelley's engagement with the 'discourse on the sublime' remains relatively unexplored and largely misunderstood, and this despite 'all those glaciers and winds and volcanoes' that Paul Foot and others have noted in his 'great revolutionary poetry'.[3] This book explores the relationship between the sublime and the revolutionary in Shelley's work.

Critical investigation of Shelley's interest in the natural sublime has laboured under persistent misconceptions about the development of his thought – and, indeed, about the nature of the 'romantic sublime' *per se*.[4] These misconceptions can best be illustrated by reference to the only full-length study of the subject to date, Angela Leighton's *Shelley and the Sublime*.[5] Leighton reads Shelley's career as a 'shift' 'from reliance on empirical arguments, which support his radicalism and atheism, to an interest in the sublime, as a theory and language of creativity which is congenial to his own imaginative temperament'.[6] There are a number of

I

significant problems with this reading, not the least of which is the extent to which it echoes New Critical claims that Shelley 'progressively' abandoned his early radicalism and atheism in favour of an 'aesthetic ... of inspiration or vision'.[7] Leighton does not actually go so far as to repeat this claim; she accepts that Shelley remained 'an atheist and a radical throughout his life'.[8] However, she does locate Shelley's interest in the natural sublime within a perceived 'shift in emphasis in [his] thinking': a supposed movement towards an 'imaginative temperament' that 'consistently' conflicts with his empirically grounded politics.[9] There is thus, according to Leighton, a sustained ontological 'tension' between Shelley's radical politics and his 'imaginative' interest in the natural sublime.[10] And this formulation has been largely retained by the two most recent accounts of the subject: Paul Endo's articles on *Mont Blanc* (1816) and *The Cenci* (1819), both of which similarly locate the 'Shelleyan sublime' within a perceived 'shift' towards an increasingly apolitical philosophical idealism.[11]

The problem with this reading is the fact that it wholly elides the obvious political overtones of Shelley's engagement with the discourse on the natural sublime. Put simply, by identifying the 'Shelleyan sublime' as an idealising and largely apolitical discourse, Leighton and Endo either blindly or wilfully fail to acknowledge – still less to explain or to account for – the recurrent appearance of 'glaciers, and winds, and volcanoes' in Shelley's 'great revolutionary poetry'.

This failure stems in no small measure from the fact that both Leighton and Endo assume the existence of a generic British 'romantic' discourse on the sublime that is both uncomplicatedly idealising and largely apolitical, an assumption that has long governed critical engagements with the subject. To put it more precisely, it seems to me that their accounts of the 'Shelleyan sublime' amply reflect what Peter De Bolla has identified as the persistent 'misreading and misunderstanding' of the British discourse on the sublime.[12]

In both *The Discourse of the Sublime* and his later *Reader*, co-edited with Andrew Ashfield, De Bolla has shown how scholarly descriptions of the eighteenth-century British discourse on the sublime have been persistently distorted by a tendency to read that discourse, without any sensitivity to historical context, through the transcendental-idealist paradigms set out in Immanuel Kant's *Critique of Judgement* (1790).[13] 'Kant's critical philosophy', De Bolla concludes, 'has become sublimated within our perceptions of the sublime'.[14] Ashfield and De Bolla correctly trace this tendency to Samuel Holt Monk's highly influential 1935 study *The Sublime*, the first study to argue 'with some scholarly authority' that eighteenth-century

British speculation about the sublime ought to be read as an 'inexorable movement' towards the paradigms of the third *Critique*.[15] De Bolla's work seeks to replace Monk's distorting, Kantian perspective on British aesthetics with an 'historical account' of the role of the sublime in British cultural development during the eighteenth century.[16] While he and Ashfield allow that Monk's narrative provides a 'general trajectory' for that role, it is clear that the widespread acceptance of this trajectory has not only sidelined texts which fall outside the epistemological scope of Monk's teleology, but has also led to a situation whereby commentators routinely read and assess pre-Kantian texts in broadly Kantian terms.[17]

My re-appraisal of the 'Shelleyan sublime' here takes a hint from De Bolla's consequent insistence upon the need to re-historicise the eighteenth-century British discourse on the sublime, to untie the Gordian knot that has for so long inextricably bound British speculation about the sublime up with the Kantian analytic. Indeed, although De Bolla's work is concerned only with the eighteenth-century British discourse on the sublime, it would be difficult to overstate its importance for our understanding of the 'romantic sublime', although that importance has yet to be elaborated, and has not been developed by De Bolla himself. The key factor here is De Bolla's emphasis on the extent to which Kant's philosophical paradigms have come to dominate scholarly descriptions of the British discourse on the sublime, on what he calls the 'widely unexamined Kantian appropriation of sublimity'.[18] Once again, Ashfield and De Bolla's concern is that this appropriation has led to a situation whereby pre-Kantian texts are routinely read and assessed in Kantian terms. But, by extension, it seems to me that the widespread acceptance of Monk's thesis has also created an unexamined consensus amongst students of British Romanticism that the British 'romantic' discourse on the sublime – as the culmination of the eighteenth-century tradition – effectively *coincides* with the transcendental-idealist paradigms of the *Critique of Judgement*. That consensus will be subject to scrutiny throughout the following pages.

The dominance of Kantian paradigms over scholarly descriptions of the 'romantic sublime' began with Thomas Weiskel's seminal *Romantic Sublime*, which, drawing explicitly on Monk, describes a generic 'romantic sublime' in post-Kantian, Freudian terminology. 'Monk found in the *Critique of Judgement* "the unconscious goal" of eighteenth-century aesthetic', Weiskel asserts, 'and we can easily discern in Kant the unconscious origins or radical forms of nineteenth-century speculation'.[19] Weiskel's formerly influential study is now seldom invoked directly, mainly because of its heavy reliance upon psychoanalytical terminology. But Weiskel's concept of a 'romantic sublime' that coincides with the paradigms of the third *Critique* has effectively been enshrined as an orthodoxy of romantic-period criticism. Neil Hertz's *End of the Line*, for example, takes exclusively Freudian and Kantian paradigms for its enquiry into 'the literature of the sublime'.[20] Indeed, even De Bolla accepts a distinction between the eighteenth-century discourse on the sublime and the 'romantic sublime', which he sees as 'less a variant of the eighteenth-century enquiry than a completely distinct discourse which borrows many terms from it'.[21]

Once again, it is important to remember that De Bolla's work is not intended to challenge Weiskel's Kantian–Freudian topography of the 'romantic sublime'; rather, it critiques the tendency to reduce eighteenth-century British speculation about the sublime to a 'pre-text' for that topography.[22] And yet, more than a decade after De Bolla first identified the need for re-historicising the eighteenth-century British discourse on the sublime, Weiskel's Kantian topography of the 'romantic sublime' remains largely unchallenged. Frances Ferguson's work on the sublime, for example – and I am thinking of her studies of Edmund Burke in particular – marked a crucial move towards recovering an historical and political context for the eighteenth-century discourse.[23] However, her otherwise highly perceptive readings in *Solitude and the Sublime* still take 'Burke and Kant as virtually the exclusive exemplars of the eighteenth-century and Romantic discussion of the philosophical issues' surrounding the discourse on the sublime.[24] 'Briefly stated', Ferguson writes, 'the view of this book is that the aesthetics of the sublime, as staked out principally by Edmund Burke and Immanuel Kant at the end of the eighteenth century, resolves itself into two basic positions – empiricism and idealism'.[25] Her aim is 'to represent' what she tellingly identifies as 'the claims of *Romantic and specifically Kantian idealism* in current critical debates'.[26]

Let me not be misunderstood here: I have no wish to slight the contribution of these critics to our understanding of the literature of the sublime. However, I am pointing towards the need to challenge the pervasive 'Kantian appropriation' of the 'romantic sublime' that their work both exemplifies and perpetuates – to challenge indeed the very notion of a generic 'romantic sublime' that does not develop out of its eighteenth-century predecessor – and I want to identify this book as part of such a project. Hence, while first and foremost a book about Shelley, my exploration of the relationship between the sublime and the revolutionary in Shelley's work is also concerned to test the limits of the 'romantic sublime'.

We can now return to that exploration by re-stating the claim with which this survey of critical engagements with the discourse on the sublime began: namely, that the standard account of the 'Shelleyan sublime' is premised upon mistaken notions about the British Romantic discourse on the natural sublime *per se*. We are now in a position to refine that claim considerably. The standard approach to the 'Shelleyan sublime' is premised upon a critical orthodoxy which assumes not only that there is such a thing as a generic 'romantic sublime', but also that this 'sublime' rehearses the transcendentalist paradigms of the *Critique of Judgement*. Ferguson's 1984 article on *Mont Blanc*, for example, is guided by the assumption that Shelley, like Kant, 'identifies the sublime as the aesthetic operation through which one makes an implicit argument for the transcendent existence of man', that '*Mont Blanc* discovers the same assertion of human power that Kant did'.[27] Leighton similarly bases her readings on the paradigms of the third *Critique*, which she – following Monk and Weiskel – identifies as 'Kant's comprehensive systematisation of the eighteenth-century sublime'.[28] Paul Endo's work, too, follows suit: 'the sublime can be read', he affirms, 'following the model of Kant's mathematical sublime, as a *negative* comprehension, as the *indeterminate* conception of a magnitude'.[29]

I am suggesting, then, that the standard account of the 'Shelleyan sublime' not only bears out De Bolla's claim that 'Kant's critical philosophy has become sublimated within our perceptions of the sublime', but amply vindicates his consequent insistence upon the need to re-historicise the British discourse. After all, while both Leighton and Endo confidently assume Kantian paradigms for their readings of the 'Shelleyan sublime', neither makes the slightest effort to demonstrate Shelley's access to those paradigms. Indeed, such an effort would be unlikely to succeed. As early as 1931, René Wellek felt that 'there is no evidence for any real acquaintance of Shelley with Kant's philosophy', and no substantial evidence has since emerged to contradict his claim.[30] Hence, by following orthodox notions about the 'romantic sublime' and basing their enquiries upon largely irrelevant Kantian paradigms, Leighton and Endo effectively ignore the actual discourse on the natural sublime available to Shelley in the early nineteenth century: a British discourse that had become heavily politicised in the wake of the French Revolution. In short, their idealising accounts of the 'Shelleyan sublime' are premised less upon attention to Shelley's texts and their historical contexts than upon what I have identified as received (and mistaken) twentieth-century notions about the 'romantic sublime'. It is hardly surprising, then, that these critics elide the historical and political dimensions of Shelley's engagement with the discourse on the natural sublime. After all, as Ashfield and De Bolla put it, 'the aesthetic, at least since Kant, has been understood as without political or ethical motivation since its *affective* registers are, according to the Kantian model, disinterested'.[31]

As I have already suggested, however, the standard critical approach to the 'Shelleyan sublime' is not only premised upon mistaken notions about the 'romantic sublime'. Rather, it is also intimately bound up with a misreading of Shelley's own philosophical thought: namely, the claim that he 'moves progressively' from a radical empiricism to an increasingly apolitical idealism.[32] Nor indeed is this claim particularly new: critics have long read *Mont Blanc* – in despite of its ostensible subject matter – less as a statement about the natural sublime *per se* than as an 'ambiguous' philosophical manifesto, a 'great transitional poem' supposedly recording Shelley's movement from empiricism to idealism.[33] Hence, again, Ferguson's claim that *Mont Blanc* argues for the 'transcendent existence of man' and 'discovers the same assertion of human power that Kant did'. I challenge this account of Shelley's best-known statement about the natural sublime in chapter 3, where I re-contextualise *Mont Blanc* in relation to the complex, early nineteenth-century discourse on the alpine sublime. For now, however, it is sufficient to recognise that while Leighton's deconstructive agenda certainly questions the *ease* of the transition described by Kapstein and his followers, her reading unquestioningly retains their basic assumption about Shelley's philosophical development.

As long ago as 1962, however, serious questions were asked about the accuracy of that assumption. In his seminal account of 'Shelley's poetic skepticism', Pulos argues persuasively that Shelley's exposure to sceptical philosophy was 'largely responsible for those modifications in his thought which critics have long recognised as distinguishing the mature from the young Shelley'.[34] 'Due attention to Shelley's scepticism', Pulos suggests, 'disposes not only of the alleged inconsistency between [Shelley's] idealism and necessarianism, but also of his alleged pseudo-Platonism'.[35] 'There is not the slightest evidence', he notes, 'that Berkeley had any significant influence on Shelley's rejection of materialism'.[36] Hence, according to Pulos, Shelley's philosophical career needs to be read not as a movement towards an apolitical idealism, but rather as an attempt to *re-ground* his politics in terms of a sceptical epistemology derived from David Hume and William Drummond. 'Shelley's scepticism is important', Pulos concludes, 'because it provides us with a possible clue to the unity of his thought in all its variety'.[37]

This book bears out Pulos' claims. I argue that the connection between the sublime and the revolutionary in Shelley's work is the product of a lifelong, sceptical engagement with the eighteenth-century British discourse on the natural sublime. More precisely, I argue that Shelley was concerned to revise the standard, pious or theistic configuration of that discourse along secular and politically progressive lines, and that epistemological scepticism was central to the attempt. By the time that Shelley completed his first major poem – *Queen Mab*, in 1813 – the idea that natural grandeur was evidence, by design, for the existence of a creator-God had long been a commonplace of the discourse on the sublime in Britain.[38] In the second of his 'long and philosophical' Notes to the poem, Shelley makes a claim about the natural sublime that explicitly contradicts this commonplace (*Letters*, i, p. 354). 'The plurality of worlds', he writes, 'the indefinite immensity of the universe is a most awful subject of contemplation. He who rightly feels its mystery and grandeur, is in no danger of seduction from the falsehoods of religious systems, or of deifying the principle of the universe' (*Poems*, i, p. 360).[39] The passage reveals two things. First, Shelley's awareness that the 'contemplation' of the 'mystery' and 'grandeur' of the 'awful' in nature *has* led, or at least *can* lead to the repressive 'falsehoods of religious systems'. Second, his conviction that this 'deifying' response to the natural sublime is an error, an error arising specifically from the failure to 'rightly' feel the 'mystery' of natural 'grandeur'. In sum, then, the passage reveals Shelley's dissatisfaction with the pious configuration of the British discourse on the natural sublime, and implies a concern on his part to re-write that discourse along secular, libertarian lines, and away from a belief in the creator-God whom *Queen Mab* denigrates as the legitimating 'prototype of human misrule' (*Queen Mab*, vi, 105). That concern is the object of my enquiry here.

The major focal point of Shelley's engagement with the eighteenth-century British discourse on the sublime was, of course, the imagination, long acknowledged as the agency of the mind's response to natural 'grandeur'.[40] By the time that Shelley wrote *Queen Mab*, there were any number of conflicting models of the faculty available: indeed, it is fair to say that from Addison right up to Dugald Stewart's 1810 *Philosophical Essays*, the imagination was a major pre-occupation of British philosophy.[41] Nor indeed was this pre-occupation merely a matter of epistemology. In the wake of the French Revolution, conservative theorists like Burke linked the faculty directly with the impetus to violent revolution, with the dangerously excessive sensibilities of Rousseau and the 'frenzy' of his supposed Jacobin 'scholars'.[42] However, the imagination had also long been suspected by the rational-empiricist tradition deriving from Hobbes and Locke, and Shelley's radical forebears – the *philosophes* and *idéologues*, Paine, Wollstonecraft, and Godwin – similarly linked the faculty to primitivism and political reaction. The key concept here is 'enthusiasm'. 'Enthusiasm' as a source of revolution or 'enthusiasm' as a source of reaction: chapters 1 and 2 show that Shelley's early exploration of the imaginative response to the natural sublime treads a thin – and often blurred – line between these conflicting accounts of the faculty.[43]

The pious or theistic configuration of the eighteenth-century British discourse on the natural sublime prioritises the imagination as the only faculty capable of intuiting the divine presence supposedly immanent in 'awful' natural phenomena. In his Notes to *Queen Mab*, Shelley confidently marshals materialist arguments – drawn principally from Baron d'Holbach's 1770 *Système de la Nature* – against this 'vulgar', *enthusiastic* 'mistake', the product of fear and ignorance of nature (*Poems*, i, p. 379). However, as I show in chapter 1, his little-discussed early letters and poems reveal a rather more ambiguous attitude to the rival claims – and, in particular, to the rival *political* affiliations – of the rational / scientific and the imaginative / enthusiastic responses to the natural sublime. This ambiguity is the source of Angela Leighton's rational–politics versus imaginative–aesthetics schema, but she fails to recognise both the complexity of the problem faced by Shelley and the extent to which he works through this early hurdle.[44] After all, *Queen Mab's* claim that it is possible to 'rightly' *feel* the 'mystery' of natural 'grandeur' argues for an imaginative response to the natural sublime that *accords* with the rational, scientific understanding of 'awful' natural phenomena: an accordance that reflects the poem's utopian insistence that 'Reason and passion' should 'cease to combat' (*Queen Mab*, viii, 231).

In point of fact, this claim marks the beginning of Shelley's redemption of the imagination from decades of philosophical and political distrust within the radical and empirical traditions. As I show in chapter 2, vital epistemological support for that redemption would later come from the sceptical philosophy of David Hume, mediated – at least in part – through Sir William Drummond's *Academical Questions* (1805).[45] But Shelley's early confidence in the imagination also came from his own re-theorisation of the faculty, albeit a re-theorisation owing much – as argued in chapter 1 – to one of the (then) most famous of the *idéologue* writings: Constantin Volney's *Les Ruines, ou, Méditations sur les Révolutions des Empires* (1791). The imagination that *Mab* claims can 'rightly' feel the 'mystery' of natural 'grandeur' is not the primitive, reactionary imagination critiqued by

Godwin et al. Nor is it the enthusiastic imagination derided by Burke. Rather it is an *educated* imagination, an imagination acting in concert with a rational / scientific understanding of 'awful' natural phenomena (and hence I repeatedly emphasise Shelley's debts to contemporary science).[46] It is an imagination – as Shelley will put it in his approximately contemporary *Refutation of Deism* – 'considerably tinctured with science, and enlarged by cultivation' (*PW*, p. 120; emphasis added).[47] This innovative concept of an *educated* or *cultivated* imagination forms the central tenet of Shelley's attempt to revise the eighteenth-century British discourse on the natural sublime along politically radical lines – and arguably, of much of his thought. A major corollary of this study, then, is the claim that the concept of the politically and scientifically potent imagination that informs Shelley's *Defence of Poetry* was worked out – and can only be fully under-stood – within the context of his engagement with the pious configuration of the discourse on the natural sublime.

For all its undoubted achievements, however, that engagement was far from being a comfortable or unambiguous success. Shelley's revision of the theistic discourse on the natural sublime turns upon the ability of the cultivated imagination to seize politically potent truths from the landscape of the natural sublime: the revolutionary 'voice' of nature that *Mont Blanc* insists is 'not understood / By all, but which the wise, and great, and good / Interpret, or make felt, or deeply feel' (*Mont Blanc*, 80–3). In brief, the cultivated imagination reads the landscape of the natural sublime not as evidence of God's presence in creation, but as evidence of systematic natural processes. These processes expose the artificiality, the *un-naturalness* of contemporary social structures – we think, for example, of *Queen Mab*'s contention that 'Nature rejects the monarch, not the man; / The subject, not the citizen' – a politically potent revelation, and one that explicitly attacks Burke's attempt to justify the current political order in England as 'the happy effect of following nature' (*Queen Mab*, iii, 170–1).[48]

The 'Shelleyan sublime' can therefore be (re)defined as – to borrow Furniss's phrase – an 'aesthetic ideology': as a discourse concerned not only to regulate and politicise the affective response to the natural sublime, but also to emphasise the historical and political implications of the landscape per se.[49] As such, Shelley's engagement with the discourse on the sublime repeatedly resists what Chloe Chard has identified as the tendency of early nineteenth-century tourist writing to *de-contextualise* the sites of the sub-lime.[50] While I have echoed Furniss's use of the concept of 'aesthetic ideology' in its contemporary, post-de Manian sense here, however, I also want to register the fact that this formula was not available to

Shelley and his generation.[51] The term 'ideology' itself has its origins in French intellectual culture of the 1790s, and for Shelley and his contemporaries it described the increasingly politically-charged study, by French philosophers in particular (the so-called *idéologues*), of the nature and status of human ideas.[52] This distinction bears directly upon a further corollary claim of this study: that the politicised theorisation of the imagination that arises from Shelley's revision of the discourse on the sublime marks an important moment in the development of modern notions of ideology. As I make clear in chapter 2, it is during his own foray into the 'science of mind' (or 'ideology' in the 1790s sense), that Shelley first theorises the role of the imagination in articulating – and, therefore, in potentially *re-articulating* – the conventions upon which social and political institutions are premised.

As an 'aesthetic ideology', Shelley's revision of the pious discourse on the natural sublime is perfectly in accord with the ostensibly gradualist, Godwinian tenor of his political thought.[53] Shelley's great revolutionary writing – works like *Queen Mab, Laon and Cythna* (1817), *Prometheus Unbound* (1818–19), and *A Philosophical View of Reform* (1819) – repeatedly insists that a systematic revolution in opinion, a *moral* and *intellectual* revolution, must precede any successful or lasting change in political institutions. Shelley clearly saw his own work – and his revision of the discourse on the sublime in particular – as participating in this vital, long-term intellectual revolution. For all its ostensible faith in gradualism, however, Shelley's great – and not so great – revolutionary writing repeatedly begs the question not only of *where* political change will come from, but also of *how* that change will come about. Chapter 5 describes at length the extent to which the ostensibly gradualist agenda of Shelley's greatest utopian narrative – *Prometheus Unbound* – is deeply problematised by the violent imagery surrounding the actual moment of political change. But in point of fact, from *Queen Mab* onwards, there is a persistent – one might go so far as to say a *defining* – tension at the heart of Shelley's political writing between gradualism and revolutionism, quietism and violence.

From the outset, this tension is intimately – and uncomfortably – bound up with Shelley's revision of the discourse on the natural sublime. The relationship can best be introduced by noting the extent to which Shelley's writing invokes the natural sublime not merely in a political context, but specifically in order to figure political violence. In the 'Preface' to *Laon and Cythna*, for example, Shelley describes the French Revolution and Napoleonic Wars as 'the *tempests* which have shaken the age in which we live' (*Poems*, ii, p. 32). Similarly, the thirteenth stanza of the *Ode to Liberty*

(1820) describes Europe's ongoing political upheaval in terms of systematic volcanic activity, while the approximately contemporary 'Liberty' (1820) compares the 'dawning' of freedom to 'the earthquake's tramp' and other catastrophic natural phenomena (*Ode to Liberty*, 181–4; 'Liberty', 19, 12). In fact, one only has to glance at Ellis's *Lexical Concordance* to see just how prevalent these image-patterns are in Shelley's poetry.[54] Out of a total of fifty-five occurrences of the word 'earthquake' and its cognates, for example, on twenty-eight occasions the term is explicitly deployed as a figure for political violence of one sort or another. Likewise, out of a total of eleven occurrences of the word 'volcano', on eight occasions the term figures revolutionary violence.[55] Nor let it be thought that these image-patterns occur mainly in lesser-known works: chapter 5 documents at length the violent – and explicitly volcanic – revolution at the heart of the gradualist *Prometheus Unbound*.[56]

These statistics clearly raise difficult questions for the standard, apolitical account of the 'Shelleyan sublime'. However, for a critic not steeped in the idealising 'Kantian appropriation of sublimity', the image-patterns are not all that surprising or even original in themselves. After all, as Ronald Paulson (amongst many others) has noted, both sides of the political divide in England – from Paine and Wollstonecraft to the propagandists of the *Anti-Jacobin Magazine* – frequently invoked the tropes of the natural sublime to figure the French Revolution and its aftermath.[57] To this extent, then, Shelley's consistent use of natural catastrophe to figure 'awful' political processes could be said to draw upon a pre-existent – and again highly politicised – discourse on the natural sublime, albeit a discourse not always compatible with his own political allegiances.

However, this study argues that Shelley's political writing takes the connection between the sublime and the revolutionary much further than the philosophers and pamphleteers of the 1790s, leading to a highly problematic intersection between his political thought and his engagement with the discourse on the sublime. While in the literature of the 'revolution controversy' the relationship between the natural sublime and the politically revolutionary is figurative, in Shelley's writing this relationship is *analogical*.[58] In other words – as I show in my readings of *Queen Mab*, *Mont Blanc*, *Laon and Cythna*, and *Prometheus Unbound* – Shelley's writing does not merely use sublime natural processes to *figure* 'awful' political processes. Rather, his writing repeatedly understands and figures political history as a *function* of natural history. And within this schema, violent revolution emerges as an 'awful' *natural* phenomenon – as a worrying instance, if you like, of the *natural* sublime. For all its confidence in the political potency of the 'cultivated' imagination, Shelley's writing comes again and again to the conclusion that 'revolution' is 'the *natural* death of all great commercial empires' (*Letters*, i, 110; emphasis added).

The defining tension in Shelley's political writing – the tension between gradualism and revolutionism – accordingly comes down to a tension between human moral agency and natural determinism. To use the terminology of the *Queen Mab* period, Shelley's engagement with the discourse on the sublime recognises that 'all-sufficing nature can chastise / Those who transgress her law' (*Queen Mab*, iii, 82–3). Oppression makes revolution inevitable, tyranny breeds tyranny, violence breeds violence in a *natural* cycle of creation and destruction: this is the 'awful' fear at the heart of Shelley's attempt to bring the British discourse on the natural sublime within the pale of political radicalism. His efforts to address and resolve this dilemma are as relevant today as they were two hundred years ago.

A few words, before beginning in earnest, about the structure and scope of the book. The chapters are arranged chronologically, each one describing a particular period in Shelley's writing life. Within this chronological structure, I have surveyed as broad as possible a range of Shelley's writing, but have inevitably had to focus on some texts at the expense of others: *Adonais* and *The Mask of Anarchy* in particular, would, I believe, reward more detailed attention than I have been able to pay them here. The reader will also have noticed that I refer, more or less exclusively, to Shelley's engagement with the discourse on the *natural* sublime. While it is undoubtedly the case that interest in the rhetorical sublime, so prominent in the early eighteenth century, had declined considerably by Shelley's day, it is no less true that much more could profitably have been said about his interest in the sublime as language and in the language of the sublime. Fascinating scholarly work continues to be done on the technical and stylistic aspects of Shelley's writing – on the *artistry* of a poet whom William Wordsworth once described as 'one of the best artists of us all ... in workmanship of style' – and I regret that I have not had the opportunity to further extend that work here. But it is a 'vacancy' that I am confident other Shelleyans will fill.

CHAPTER I

From religion to revolution, 1810–1813

On Sunday 11 October 1813, Shelley's first wife, Harriet Westbrook, wrote to her Irish friend, Catherine Nugent, from Ambleside, in the heart of the English Lake District. 'We are again', Harriet affirmed, 'among our dear mountains' (*Letters*, i, p. 378 n. 3). Her remark comes at the end of a two-year period during which she and Shelley had lived in some of Britain's most dramatic landscapes: the North Wales mountains and the Lake District. These were undoubtedly the most politically active years of Shelley's life. But they also witnessed the beginning of his lifelong engagement with the British discourse on the natural sublime, an engagement surely prompted by the grandeur of the surroundings in which he chose to live. To put it more precisely, the years 1810–12 witnessed Shelley's first attempts to revise the British discourse on the natural sublime along politically radical lines. These attempts bore fruit in *Queen Mab*'s already cited claim that it is possible to 'rightly' feel the 'mystery' of natural 'grandeur'. But this success was not won without cost. Rather, the years 1810–12 also saw the emergence of deep-rooted ambiguities, ambiguities that would not only problematise Shelley's attempt to bring the discourse on the natural sublime within the pale of radical politics, but which would ultimately call into question the entire gradualist tenor of his political thought.

IMAGINATION, RELIGION AND THE NATURAL SUBLIME

From the origins of the discourse on the sublime in the seventeenth century, the defeat of the understanding by natural grandeur had repeatedly been figured by British philosophers and aestheticians as evidence of the immanent presence of God in creation. The most sophisticated and readily available formulations of this theory in 1812 came from Thomas Reid and Archibald Alison. Shelley's early engagement with the discourse on the sublime can be usefully approached through the works of these men.

In a letter to William Godwin on 3 June 1812, Shelley mentions Reid, along with Locke and Hume, in a list of the metaphysicians whom he has read (*Letters*, i, p. 303). Reid's *Essays on the Intellectual Powers of Man* (1785) contains an extended analysis of the affective response to the natural sublime, and makes an explicit connection between this response and a belief in God.[1]

Following Addison, Reid adopts the aesthetic categories of 'novelty', 'grandeur', and 'beauty', equating 'grandeur' with the natural sublime (*EIPM*, p. 579).[2] The contemplation of 'grandeur' produces the 'awful, solemn, and serious' emotions of 'admiration', 'devotion', and 'enthusiasm', it 'raise[s] our conceptions' and 'elevate[s] the mind' (*EIPM*, p. 582). Reid rejects Burke's claim that terror is the source of the sublime, on the grounds that terror is incapable of producing such positive emotion.[3] Reid also argues against the scepticism of Hume, suggesting that aesthetic qualities do indeed have objective existence, that is, an existence independent of the mind that *perceives* them. But Reid denies that these qualities are attributes of matter *per se* (thus also rejecting the sensationist empiricism of Burke's *Enquiry*). Rather, drawing on a neo-platonic tradition deriving originally from Shaftesbury and Hutcheson, Reid claims that grandeur and beauty are 'properly the attributes of mind only', and can become attached to matter only insofar as it suggests mind (*EIPM*, p. 587).[4] 'Grandeur', Reid argues, 'is found originally and properly, in qualities of mind; [and] it is discerned in objects of sense only by reflection, as the light we perceive in the moon and planets is truly the light of the sun' (*EIPM*, p. 591). Hence, when we describe an action as brave, we properly mean that the person who acted is brave; when we call a work of art beautiful, we properly refer to the conception of the artist which is embodied in the work (*EIPM*, p. 587). 'By a figure', Reid says, 'we assign to the effect a quality which is inherent only in the cause ... we ascribe to a work that grandeur which is properly inherent in the mind of the author' (*EIPM*, p. 587). For Reid, then, the 'grandeur' of nature figures the grandeur of God in exactly the same way as the grandeur of art reflects the genius of the artist. And the agency of this figuration, for Reid, is the associative imagination. It is the 'stretch of the imagination' in response to the defeat of the understanding by natural grandeur that enables the mind to go beyond the mere perception of matter to an intuition of the higher mind that informs it (*EIPM*, p. 586).

Archibald Alison's *Essays on the Nature and Principles of Taste* (1790) expands and refines Reid's account of the affective response to the natural sublime, outlining in more detail the central role played by the imagination. The first edition of the *Essays* received little public notice. Richard Payne Knight critiqued it in passing in the second edition of his *Analytical Inquiry into the Principles of Taste* (1804), and Dugald Stewart mentions it favourably in the first edition of his *Elements of the Philosophy of the Human Mind* (1792), and again in his *Philosophical Essays* (1810). The second edition of Alison's *Essays* (1811), however, received widespread popular and critical acclaim, quickly becoming the most influential treatise on aesthetics at the time (during Shelley's lifetime, further editions were published in 1812, 1815 and 1817).[5] Although there is no direct evidence that Shelley read Alison, he did know Stewart's works and would probably have come across the favourable references there.[6] Similarly, Shelley would almost certainly have read the *Edinburgh Review*, where the *Essays* were discussed enthusiastically and at some length by Francis Jeffrey in May 1811.[7] More broadly speaking, though, it is difficult to imagine that someone with Shelley's voracious reading habits would not have been aware of so widely known a work as the second edition of the *Essays*.

Alison follows Reid in denying that matter *per se* can be sublime or beautiful, since these qualities are properly only attributes of mind. 'Matter itself is unfitted to produce any kind of emotion', he claims, 'matter [is] sublime or beautiful only as it is significant of Mind' (*ENPT*, i, p. 176; ii, p. 436). In other words, Alison argues that the affective response to the natural sublime is produced by the perception of such *material* qualities as are capable – thanks to the associative imagination – of suggesting the *mental* qualities that he considers sublime. 'The beauty and sublimity which is felt in the various appearances of matter', he writes, 'are finally to be ascribed to their expression of mind; or to their being, either directly or indirectly, the signs of those qualities of mind which are fitted, by the constitution of our nature, to affect us with pleasing or interesting emotion' (*ENPT*, ii, p. 423). As with Reid, then, Alison argues that matter becomes sublime or beautiful by a figurative association of effect with cause. And the example he gives of this figuration is taken straight from Reid: 'thus ... all the works of human art or design, are directly significant to us of the wisdom, the invention, the taste, or the benevolence of the artist; and the works of nature, of the power, the wisdom, and the beneficence of the Divine artist' (*ENPT*, ii, p. 418).

The mental qualities Alison considers sublime are 'elevation', 'power', 'vastness', and 'duration' or 'stability' (*ENPT*, i, pp. 325–7). Like Reid, Alison believes God to be the ultimate embodiment of these qualities. The material quality most capable of suggesting them is extreme 'magnitude' or immensity (*ENPT*, i, pp. 324–7). Hence objective 'magnitude', for Alison, is the index of the natural sublime – and the evidence of God's immanent presence in Creation (*ENPT*, i, pp. 325–8; ii, pp. 441–2). 'I believe there is no man of genuine taste', Alison writes, 'who has not often felt, in the lone majesty of nature, some unseen spirit to dwell' (*ENPT*, ii, p. 438).

If nature is so many 'signs' and 'expressions', then Alison argues – still following Reid – that it is the imagination that interprets these 'signs'. 'Whenever the emotions of Sublimity or Beauty are felt', he writes, 'that exercise of Imagination is produced, which consists in the indulgence of a train of thought' (*ENPT*, i, p. 69). This associative ('train of thought') 'exercise or employment of imagination' is what 'exalt[s] objects of simple and common pleasure [mere matter], into objects of Beauty or Sublimity [matter suggestive of mind]' (*ENPT*, i, xxv). 'When we feel [the] sublimity of natural scenery', he argues, 'we are conscious of a variety of images in our minds, very different from those which the objects themselves can present to the eye':

Trains ... of solemn thought arise spontaneously within our minds; our hearts swell with emotions, of which the objects before us seem to afford no adequate cause; and we are never so much satiated with delight, as when, in recalling our attention, we are unable to trace either the progress or the connection of those thoughts, which have passed with so much rapidity through our imagination (*ENPT*, i, pp. 5–6)

Alison stresses the involuntary, 'spontaneous' nature of the imagination's associative response: 'in such trains of imagery, no labour of thought, or habits of attention are required; they rise spontaneously in the mind' (*ENPT*, i, p. 21). Reid had also emphasised the involuntary nature of the imaginative response to the natural sublime: it 'is irresistible, like fire thrown into the midst of combustible matter' (*EIPM*, p. 586). The imagination, Alison argues, is 'lead ... almost insensibly along, in a kind of bewitching reverie' (*ENPT*, i, p. 21). Central to this 'leading' is the apparent suspension of reason: 'it is then, indeed, in this *powerless state of reverie*, when we are carried on by our conceptions, not guiding them, that the deepest emotions of beauty or sublimity are felt' (*ENPT*, i, pp. 58–9; emphasis added). The experience of the sublime is a 'play of fancy', 'a romantic dream' in which 'our imaginations are kindled by ... power' and 'we lose ourselves amid the number of images that pass before our minds' (*ENPT*, i, p. 6). And ultimately, Alison concludes, this involuntary and unreflective activity of the imagination leads intentionally and unavoidably to an intuition of God's presence in Creation. '[N]ature, in all its aspects around us', he writes, 'ought only to be felt as signs of ... providence, and as conducting us, by the universal language of these signs, to the throne of the Deity' (*ENPT*, ii, p. 442).

For both Reid and Alison, then, the defeat of the understanding by the natural sublime is evidence that the power and grandeur of God is imminent in His Creation. For both men, the imagination enables the mind to overcome the defeat of the understanding and read the landscape of the natural sublime as the 'signs' and 'expressions' of Deity.

It is precisely this pious, theistic configuration of the discourse on the sublime that Shelley critiques in the second Note to *Queen Mab*, calling it a failure to 'rightly feel' the 'mystery' of natural 'grandeur'. The grounds for Shelley's critique can be approached through another of his Notes to the poem, the gloss to Canto VII, line 13: 'There is no God'. In this Note, Shelley outlines various arguments against the existence of God, including a re-working of his own pamphlet, *The Necessity of Atheism* (1811), which draws heavily on Locke and Hume. Shelley points out that the idea of a creator-God does not meet Newton's standards of proof (*Poems*, i, p. 384). 'It is probable', he claims, 'that the word God was originally only an expression denoting the unknown cause of the known events which men perceived in the universe' (*Poems*, i, p. 379). Through a figurative act of imagination similar to that described by Reid and Alison, *Queen Mab* argues, this metaphorical usage of the term God became a literal usage. 'By the vulgar mistake of a metaphor for a real being, of a word for a thing', he writes, 'it became a man, endowed with human qualities and governing the universe as an earthly monarch governs his kingdom' (*Poems*, i, p. 379). In other words, the idea of God is a product of human ignorance, the result of an anthropomorphic personification of the 'unknown' causes of visible effects (*Poems*, i, p. 379). And Shelley recognises explicitly that it is the imagination that has enacted this 'vulgar mistake'. In a letter to Elizabeth Hitchener on 11 June 1811, he confirms that 'Imagination delights in personification; were it not for this embodying quality of eccentric fancy we should be to this day without a God' (*Letters*, i, p. 101).

In support of his arguments against the existence of a creator-God in the Notes to *Queen Mab*, Shelley includes a long quotation from Holbach's *Système de la Nature*, the *ne plus ultra* of eighteenth-century French Materialism. Shelley first read the *Système* in May 1812, and thought it 'a work of uncommon powers' (*Letters*, i, p. 303). The passage he cites in the Note to *Queen Mab* is taken from Holbach's analysis of the origins of the idea of God. Holbach backs up Shelley's claim that this idea originated in the fear produced by an ignorance of nature. 'In a word', he writes, 'man has always reverenced the unknown causes of extraordinary effects, which his ignorance has prevented him from discerning'.[8] Primitive man, confronted by natural forces that defied his understanding, attempted to come to terms with these forces by personifying them anthropomorphically. From this first worship of the elements, Holbach argues, God has always inhabited those terrifying aspects of nature that defied human understanding:

> it is in this darkness that [men] have set up their God; it is in this shadowy abyss that their anxious imagination labours continuously to create for itself chimeras which plague them until their knowledge of nature disabuses them of the phantoms which they have always so vainly adored (*Prose*, p. 354)[9]

In other words, Holbach confirms that the idea of God derives from an anthropomorphic response to the 'awful' in nature – that is, from a personification of the natural sublime – and that the agency of this personification is the imagination. In the gloss to 'There is no God', Shelley critiques the pious configuration of the discourse on the sublime on precisely these grounds. That discourse, he suggests, perpetuates the 'anthropomorphism of the vulgar' by continuing to personify God in the defeat of the understanding by natural grandeur: 'God is represented as infinite, eternal, incomprehensible, he is contained under every *predicate in non* that the logic of ignorance could fabricate' (*Poems*, i, p. 385).

Holbach and Shelley's materialist analysis of the idea of God has significant implications for the theistic discourse on the sublime formulated by Reid and Alison.[10] If Reid and Alison argue that the associative imagination reveals the presence of God in the 'awful' elements of nature, then materialism counters with the suggestion that the imagination actually *creates* God by personifying those elements. Put differently, Alison and Reid do not discover the lineaments of the divine mind in the landscape of the natural sublime; rather they resolve the existential anxiety that landscape produces by personifying the incomprehensible and calling it God. Hence, while for the Scottish philosophers the metaphorical connection between the landscape of the natural sublime and a creator-God is positive and redemptive, for the French materialists this connection is merely a 'vulgar' illusion.

Indeed, Reid's discussion of the natural sublime effectively confirms the connection that Shelley and Holbach's materialism makes between fear of nature and belief in God. However much Reid refutes Burke's claim that terror is the basis of the sublime, his *Essays* betray the anxiety produced by the defeat of the understanding in the encounter with natural grandeur, and exhibits – as much as it purports to describe – the role of the figurative imagination in resolving that anxiety. 'When we contemplate the earth, the sea, the planetary system, the universe', Reid writes, 'these are vast objects; it *requires* a stretch of the imagination to grasp them in our minds' (*EIPM*, p. 586; emphasis added). But the 'vast objects' of nature only 'appear truly grand, and merit the highest admiration', he concludes, 'when we consider them as the work of God' (*EIPM*, p. 586). As we have seen, it is precisely this anthropomorphic 'stretch of the imagination' that enables Reid and Alison to see natural grandeur 'as the work of God'. The existentially comforting effect of this 'stretch' becomes apparent when Reid explains *why* the 'vast objects' of nature only 'appear truly grand' when considered as the 'work of God':

When we contemplate the world of Epicurus, and conceive the universe to be a fortuitous jumble of atoms, there is nothing grand in this idea. The clashing of atoms by blind chance has nothing in it fit to raise our conceptions, or to elevate the mind. But the regular structure of a vast system of beings produced by creating power, and governed by the best laws which perfect wisdom and goodness could contrive, is a spectacle which elevates the understanding, and fills the soul with devout admiration (*EIPM*, pp. 586–7)

Apparently, then, the Epicurean hypothesis that the universe is nothing more than what Shelley, in the second Note to *Queen Mab*, calls an 'infinite machine', is too terrifying to be 'truly' grand (*Poems*, i, p. 361). Rather, Reid follows the physico-theological tradition going back at least as far as Locke and Newton, offering what amounts to an argument from design. For Reid, the belief that the universe is 'governed' by a benevolent 'creating power', under the auspices of 'the best laws which perfect wisdom and goodness can contrive', is the only possible way to resolve the existential anxiety produced by the defeat of the understanding in the encounter with the natural sublime. 'Religion', Shelley writes, picking up exactly on the existential fear betrayed by Reid, 'is the perception of the relation in which we stand to the principle of the universe. But if the principle of the universe be not an organic being, the model and proto-type of man, the relation between it and human beings is absolutely none' (*Poems*, i, p. 379). The potential inhumanity of the overwhelming power of nature is what Reid finds too terrifying to be 'truly' grand. And this fear of a powerful nature that has no regard for man is the occasion – according to Shelley and Holbach – of the superstitious imaginative response to the natural sublime.

From a materialist or empiricist point of view, then, the imaginative response to the natural sublime is a 'vulgar mistake', a superstitious attempt to overcome the existential terror brought on by the collapse of the understanding when confronted with 'infinite' or 'incomprehensible' natural phenomena. In short, that response is a form of primitivism. Nor indeed is this primitive 'mistake' merely a matter of metaphysics, since the imaginative response to the 'awful' in nature produced and now sustains 'the falsehoods of religious systems', setting up a creator-God who is the legitimating 'prototype of human misrule' (*Poems*, i, p. 360; *Queen Mab* vi, 105). Shelley would certainly have been familiar with the ongoing radical exploration of the political implications of such an aesthetic of terror, implications neatly summed up in Burke's observation that '*we fear God – we look with* AWE *to kings . . . with reverence to priests, and with respect to nobility*'.[11]

In the passage that Shelley quotes from the *Système*, Holbach accordingly formulates an opposition between the imaginative and the rational response to the 'incomprehensible' in nature. Once again, the 'vulgar' anthropomorphic 'mistake' of the imagination is provoked and fuelled by the fear resulting from ignorance of nature. This 'mistake' can therefore be corrected by supplying the defect in the understanding of 'awful' natural phenomena. Man's 'terrors are dissipated in the same proportion as his mind is enlightened', Holbach writes, 'the educated man ceases to be superstitious' (*Prose*, p. 354).[12] Opposed to the falsifying activity of the imagination, then, is the liberating effect of knowledge and reason: knowledge of nature is set up in clear opposition to the fear that provokes the reactionary imaginative response to the natural sublime.

Holbach's opposition between the imaginative and the rational response to the 'incomprehensible' in nature participates in the general distrust of the imagination amongst eighteenth-century empiricists and materialists on both sides of the English Channel. More precisely, despite significant interventions by the likes of Addison and Akenside, in the rationalist-empiricist tradition deriving from Hobbes and Locke, the imagination is repeatedly denigrated as a dangerous source of error.[13] And of course this rationalist tradition formed the epistemological underpinnings of the radical movement from the French *philosophes* and *idéologues* right through to Paine and Godwin, a movement which similarly contrasted the superstitious and reactionary imagination with the socio-politically progressive reason.

Shelley was well aware of the radical, rationalist distrust of the imagination, and it is a notable feature of his early adherence to Locke. His two gothic novels, *Zastrozzi* (1810) and *St. Irvyne* (1810) abound in warnings about the damaging consequences of uncontrolled passion, of imagination indulged without the controlling influence of reason. Indeed, empirical epistemology is valuable to the young Shelley precisely on account of its alignment with radical politics, specifically on account of the ease with which it lends itself to dismantling institutional religion. Whatever the ultimate motivation for Shelley's attacks on Christianity may have been – and it seems likely that, although substantially political, they were also partly personal to begin with – empiricism provided him with an effective weapon for the task. Shelley's first published attack on Christianity, *The Necessity of Atheism*, is little more than an expansion and application to religion of Locke's arguments on sensation and belief, and Hume's arguments on causality. As Angela Leighton notes, however, Shelley's early adherence to empirical philosophy is not unproblematic.[14] Leighton correctly points out that the young Shelley often invokes empirical arguments against 'feeling' in order to establish the 'non-existence' of a creator-God, only to lament the apparent overkill in regard to imagination and individual 'feeling' (*Letters*, i, p. 100).[15] In the same letter to Elizabeth Hitchener which criticises the 'eccentric fancy' as the origin of the idea of God, Shelley goes on to say that the kind of imaginative 'personification' which gives rise to this idea is 'beautiful in Poetry', though 'inadmissable in reasoning' (*Letters*, i, p. 101). There is thus an apparent tension in Shelley's early thought between the demands of a rationalist, empirical epistemology on the one hand, and the pleasures of the imagination on the other. Shelley 'recommend[s] reason' to Hitchener on account of its socio-politically progressive potential, claiming that he has 'rejected all fancy, all imagination' (*Letters*, i, p. 101). This 'rejection', demanded by Shelley's interpretation of empirical epistemology and its attendant politics, is not without cost however: 'since I have devoted myself unreservedly to [reason's] influencing', he writes, 'I have never felt *Happiness* ... I find that all pleasure resulting to self is thereby completely annihilated' (*Letters*, i, p. 101).

The tension in Shelley's thought between the expectations of an empirical epistemology and the 'pleasures' of the imagination is particularly acute in some of his earliest first-hand experiences of the natural sublime. In the summer of 1811, following his expulsion from Oxford, the attendant tension with his family, and the termination of his engagement to Harriet Grove, Shelley accepted an invitation to stay with his cousin Thomas Grove on his estate at Cwm Elan in Wales. Shelley's first reference to the dramatic North Wales landscape is made, almost in passing, in a letter to his friend Thomas Hogg, written around 10 July 1811. 'This is most divine scenery', Shelley writes, 'but all very dull stale flat and unprofitable' (*Letters*, i, p. 118). As Jones notes, 'dull stale flat unprofitable' echoes *Hamlet*, I, ii, 133 (*Letters*, i, p. 118 n. 3). Given the depression that Shelley was experiencing at the time, this echo has an appropriate biographical resonance. However, it also operates as a rationalist-utilitarian qualification of the 'divine scenery', a qualification that not only affirms the *uselessness* of the landscape but also, tellingly, the social and political worthlessness of any affective response it might evoke. Nor would Hogg, Shelley's fellow Oxonian atheist, have missed the irony involved in calling this 'stale' landscape 'divine'.

Around three days later, Shelley wrote to Hitchener, continuing his ongoing attempts to convince her of the 'non-existence' of a creator-God. This second letter not only marks a change in Shelley's appreciation of the Welsh scenery, but also exhibits more fully the tension between the rational-empirical and the imaginative response to natural 'grandeur'. Shelley begins with an appreciative description of the effect of the sublime scenery: 'This country of Wales is excessively grand; rocks piled on each other to tremendous heights, rivers formed into cataracts by their projections, and valleys clothed with woods, present an appearance of enchantment' (*Letters*, i, p. 119). He then acknowledges the difficulties of accounting for this 'enchantment' – the word itself suggests the suspension of reason – within a Lockean framework: 'But *why* do they enchant, *why* is it more affecting than a plain, it cannot be innate, is it acquired?' (*Letters*, i, p. 119). The passage concludes by recognising explicitly the dissipating effect of rational inquiry upon the 'pleasure' derived from the affective response to the natural sublime:

Thus does knowledge lose all the pleasure which invol{un}tarily {ari}ses, by attempting to arrest th{e} fleeting Phantom as it passes – vain al{most}like the chemists aether it evaporates under our observation; it flies from all but the slaves of passion and sickly sensibility who will not analyse a feeling (*Letters*, i, pp. 119–20)

Leighton's claim that Shelley here 'regrets his freedom to reason, and desires to be a slave' is hardly credible.[16] Rather, the passage exhibits the language of the *idéologues* in its concern to 'analyse' the components of experience, a concern echoed by the allusion to the nascent science of chemistry. And again, the epistemological issue has overtly political connotations ('slaves'). Both Alison and Reid had likewise acknowledged the 'involuntary' and irrational basis of the imaginative response to the natural sublime. Alison, too, stressed the dissipative effect of rational inquiry upon that response. 'The mind, in such an employment [i.e. rational or critical thought]', he writes:

instead of being at liberty to follow whatever trains of imagery the composition before it can excite, is either fettered to the consideration of some of its minute and solitary parts; or pauses amid the rapidity of its conceptions, to make them the objects of its attention and review. In these operations, accordingly, the emotion, whether of beauty or sublimity, is lost, and if it is wished to be recalled, it can only be done by relaxing this vigour of attention, and resigning ourselves again to the natural stream of our thoughts (*ENPT*, i, pp. 13–14)

Shelley's reference to the 'fleeting Phantom' and 'sickly sensibility' reminds us of Holbach's critique of the superstitious response to the natural sublime, of the 'anxious imagination' which creates the anthropomorphic 'phantoms' that 'plague' the uneducated mind (*Prose*, p. 354). Appreciation of the natural sublime is tempered by a distrust of the agency of that appreciation; 'enchanting' affective response is irreconcilable with politically responsible, rational inquiry.

A second letter to Hitchener, on 26 July, rehearses this argument. Again, Shelley begins by describing the 'spontaneous', affective response to the natural sublime, and then moves on to acknowledge the incompatibility of that response with rational inquiry:

Nature is here marked with the most impressive character of loveliness and grandeur, *once* I was tremulously alive to tones and scenes – The habit of analysing feelings I fear does not agree with this. It is spontaneous, and when it becomes subjugated to consideration ceases to exist. But you do right to indulge feeling where it does not militate with reason, I wish I could too – This valley is covered with trees, so are partly the mountains that surround it. Rocks piled upon each oth{er t}o an immense height, and clouds intersecting them, in other places waterfalls midst the umbrage of a thousand shadowy trees form the principal features of the scenery. I am not wholly uninfluenced by its magic in my lonely walks, but I long for a thunderstorm (*Letters*, i, pp. 127–8)

The passage – which clearly echoes Alison's severing of reason and imagination – has an almost Wordsworthian dynamic, with Shelley lamenting the loss of 'feeling' for 'tones and scenes' produced by 'the habit of analysing feelings'. The loss is not complete, however, since Shelley acknowledges that he is 'not wholly uninfluenced' by the landscape. Once again, however, the tension between this 'influence' and the empiricist distrust of imagination is evident from Shelley's phrasing: 'feeling', he acknowledges, can and does 'militate' with 'reason'. The passage closes on this problematic note – it is almost as if the scenery is not sublime enough for Shelley, and he longs for a thunderstorm to increase its sublimity.

Another letter to Hogg, written two days later, reveals the same tension. 'This country is highly romantic', Shelley writes, 'here are rocks of

immense height and picturesque waterfalls. I am more astonished at the
grandeur of this scenery than I expected. I do not *now* much regard it.
I have other things to think of' (*Letters*, i, p. 128). These 'other things' –
Shelley's domestic relationships and his concern with Christianity – again
reveal the tension between an affective, 'romantic' response to natural
scenery and the demands of social and political reality. The letter acknowledges an opposition between the astonishment produced by the scenery
and these demands, acknowledges – that is – that 'feeling' can 'militate'
with 'reason'.

One of the Esdaile poems, 'Written on a Beautiful Day in Spring',
confirms that this tension between the affective and the rational response
to nature was an ongoing concern in Shelley's thought at this time. Likely
composed in spring 1812, 'Written on a Beautiful Day' shows the influence of Wordsworth in its acknowledgement of the beneficial effects of
nature on the mind.[17] Shelley's treatment of the response to nature turns
on the Lockean distinction between sensation and reflection, a distinction that will crop up again, four years later, in the opening stanza of
Mont Blanc. In terms that recall Alison's associative 'trains of thought',
'Written on a Beautiful Day' describes the imaginative response to nature
as a 'strange mental wandering' (1). This 'wandering' is a state of unreflective sensation, in which we are 'unpercipient of all other things / Than
those that press around' ('Written on a Beautiful Day', 1, 5–6). This
returns us to Shelley's concern that the imaginative response to nature
militates with the 'other things' that demand the attention of the political
activist. Indeed, the phrase 'mental wandering' itself tellingly suggests
aimlessness and 'Written on a Beautiful Day' reconfirms the unreflective
nature of the imaginative response to nature: 'Sensation all its wondrous
rapture brings, / And to itself not once the mind recurs' ('Written on a
Beautiful Day', 8–9).[18] And yet, for all its awareness of the potential
dangers of the unreflective, 'wandering' imaginative response to nature,
'Written on a Beautiful Day' also places a Wordsworthian emphasis on
the beneficial effects of that response. It is 'a foretaste of Heaven', it
'Cheers the sunk spirits, lifts the languid eye / . . . And to a gorgeous fly
the sluggish worm transforms' ('Written on a Beautiful Day', 10, 13, 18).

In his discussion of the 'mystery' of natural 'grandeur' in the second
Note to *Queen Mab*, Shelley draws an antithesis between the rational and
the imaginative response to the natural sublime similar to that proposed
by Holbach, and reflected in both his 1811 letters from Wales and 'Written
on a Beautiful Day in Spring'. Although the contemplation of the 'awful'
in nature may well lead to a belief in God, Shelley stresses that such

a belief is definitely 'irreconcilable with the *knowledge* of the stars' (*Poems*, i, p. 361; emphasis added). This claim clearly alludes to the history of astronomy: the discoveries of Galileo, Copernicus and Kepler that were instrumental in revising the orthodox, religious conception of the universe. 'The works of his fingers', Shelley quips, 'have borne witness against him' (*Poems*, i, p. 361). In other words, scientific understanding of the universe provides evidence against the existence of its supposed creator, an inference valid as much for early nineteenth-century geology and palaeontology as for the history of astronomy.[19] Again, in Holbach's terminology, 'knowledge' of nature counters the primitive anthropomorphisms provoked by ignorance of nature. But Shelley's reference to astronomical evidence against the existence of creator-God also has a particular resonance for the pious discourse on the sublime formulated by Reid and Alison. As we have seen, both Nicolson and Tuveson argue that the discourse on the sublime arose in seventeenth-century Britain out of a transfer to infinite space of the affective responses previously reserved for God. Shelley's point is that rational understanding of infinite space (the 'knowledge of the stars') inhibits the superstitious reverse of this affective transfer. Indeed, ostensibly rational, *philosophical* arguments employing the nature of infinite space as conclusive evidence for the existence of an immaterial deity can be found in the works of figures as diverse as Locke, Newton, and Berkeley – all of whom Shelley had read by the time he wrote *Queen Mab*. Hence, Shelley's Note also amounts to a direct rebuttal of these arguments since it affirms that accurate 'knowledge of the stars' is 'irreconcilable' with a belief in God.

However, a closer examination of the second Note to *Queen Mab* reveals that it does not in fact turn on the kind of antithesis between the rational and the imaginative response to the natural sublime proposed by Holbach. Shelley confirms that belief in God is 'irreconcilable with the knowledge of the stars', specifically, that scientific understanding of natural phenomena is incompatible with – and effectively contradicts – the theistic configuration of the discourse on the sublime. But at the beginning of the second Note to *Queen Mab*, Shelley asserts that although the pious configuration of the discourse on the sublime is indeed an error, it is an error arising specifically from the failure to '*rightly* feel' the 'mystery' of natural grandeur (*Poems*, i, p. 360; emphasis added). He who 'rightly feels' this 'mystery', Shelley argues, 'is in no danger of seduction from the falsehoods of religious systems'. In other words, Shelley implies that a *correct* affective response to the natural sublime has 'no danger' of leading to a belief in God. In the second Note to *Queen Mab*, then, both the rational *and* the correct imaginative response to the natural sublime point to the same conclusion: that 'There is no God' (*Queen Mab*, vii, 13; *Poems*, i, p. 381). That is, Shelley argues that the correct imaginative response to the natural sublime should be in accord with scientific knowledge of nature, and not antithetical to it: again, in *Mab*'s utopian vision, 'reason and passion cease to combat' (*Queen Mab*, viii, 231). Hence, Shelley has effectively moved beyond the earlier tension in his thought between the rational and the imaginative response to natural grandeur, the tension that Leighton mistakenly identifies as a persistent feature of his work. As this chapter makes clear, however, Shelley's engagement with the discourse on the sublime will remain troublingly conflicted with his radical politics, as the tension between the rational and the imaginative response to the natural sublime gives way to a far more challenging – and ultimately unresolved – tension between a gradualist and a revolutionist interpretation of nature's 'awful' law.

The 'knowledge of the stars' reveals that the universe is an 'infinite machine' (*Poems*, i, p. 361). And the correct ('right') imaginative response to the natural sublime can avoid anthropomorphism and accurately grasp the 'Spirit that pervades this infinite machine' (*Poems*, i, pp. 360–1). More precisely, the 'vulgar' imagination, made 'anxious' by the defeat of the understanding, 'labours' to resolve the existential terror provoked by an inhuman universe through *personifying* the cause of that terror. But the imagination that has the benefit of a rational understanding of the universe does not commit the 'vulgar mistake' of fearing an 'infinite machine'. Rather it looks with 'elevated and dreadless composure upon the links of the universal chain' (*Poems*, i, p. 379). In other words, while those who are ignorant of nature see only 'unlinked contingency and chance' – and we are reminded of Reid's anxious condemnation of Epicurean atomism – the educated recognise that 'No atom of this turbulence fulfils / A vague or unnecessitated task, / Or acts but as it must and ought to act' (*Queen Mab*, vi, 169–73). They are capable, that is to say, of accurately intuiting ('rightly' feeling) the 'spirit' that 'pervades' the universe. And *Queen Mab* explicitly identifies this sublime 'spirit' with philosophical 'Necessity', appropriately rendering the identification in the context of the 'indefinite immensity of the universe':

> Spirit of Nature! here!
> In this interminable wilderness
> Of worlds, at whose immensity
> Even soaring fancy staggers,
> Here is thy fitting temple

> (*Queen Mab*, i, 264–8)

It is thus 'Necessity' and not God that is the true 'mother of the world', and the true object of the 'fancy'-staggering natural sublime (*Poems*, i, p. 375). Necessity shares the traditional, sublime attributes of a creator-God – it is 'eternal' and 'imperishable' – and *Queen Mab*'s apostrophes to Necessity repeatedly invoke the language of the religious sublime (*Queen Mab*, i, 274, 276). In fact, Necessity is synonymous with Shelley's conception of God. In the same letter to Elizabeth Hitchener which denigrates the anthropomorphic tendencies of the imagination, Shelley allows that he does indeed 'acknowledge a God' (*Letters*, i, p. 101). However, it is not a personal creator-God whom he acknowledges, nor is it any kind of neoplatonic world soul, which exists independently of its material mani-festations, nor indeed is it the non-interventionist 'God' of eighteenth-century deism. Rather, Shelley's 'God' is 'a synonime [sic] for the *existing power of existence* . . . the *essence* of the universe'; the word 'god' is 'another *word for* the essence of the universe' (*Letters*, i, p. 101). And again, *Queen Mab* identifies this 'God' – the 'essence of the universe' – as Necessity: 'Necessity' is the 'universal Spirit', the 'Soul of the Universe', the 'all-sufficing Power' of nature (*Queen Mab*, vi, 177, 190, 197).

However, this 'Power' is not necessarily (if I can use the word) bene-volent, a fact which – as we shall see – persistently problematises Shelley's attempt to bring the discourse on the natural sublime in line with a gradualist politics. Indeed, Necessity is a decidedly ambivalent and 'awful' principle in *Queen Mab*. The poem stresses the fact that Necessity is an inhuman, and 'immutable' or deterministic principle, that the 'rela-tion between it and human beings is absolutely none' (*Poems*, i, p. 361, 379). Necessity 'cannot feel' human 'joy or pain', because it has neither 'human sense' nor 'human mind' (*Queen Mab*, vi, 216–19). Necessity's law is 'unappealable' (*Queen Mab*, iii, 218). Necessity is 'the judge beneath whose nod / Man's brief and frail authority / Is powerless as the wind / That passeth idly by' (*Queen Mab*, iii, 219–22). In an attempt to discredit (the idea of) a creator-God in the Notes to *Queen Mab*, Shelley argues that if such an omnipotent being is the origin of good, He must also be the origin of Evil, that 'if he is entitled to our gratitude for the one, he is entitled to our hatred for the other' (*Poems*, i, p. 380). 'It is plain', Shelley writes:

that the same arguments which prove that God is the author of food, light, and life, prove Him also to be the author of poison, darkness, and death. The wide-wasting earthquake, the storm, the battle, and the tyranny, are attributable to this hypothetic being in the same degree as the fairest forms of nature, sunshine, liberty, and peace (*Poems*, i, p. 380)

'Necessity' is an equally Janus-faced 'spirit' of Nature. Shelley recognises that Necessity is just as responsible for 'merciless ambition', 'mad zeal', and 'the tyrant's moody mind' as for any liberty or virtue that may exist in the world – and again, this recognition persistently problematises his engagement with the discourse on the sublime (*Queen Mab*, vi, 178, 183). The only essential difference between the 'all-sufficing Power' of Necessity and a creator-God who is 'the prototype of human misrule' is that Necessity, for all its 'awful' inhumanity – indeed because of this inhumanity – is an essentially neutral principle. Nature's 'harmony' is 'unvarying' and 'impartial' (*Queen Mab*, vi, 203, 216). And this natural harmony – correctly interpreted ('rightly' felt) by the imagination – has profound political implications. 'Nature rejects the monarch, not the man; / The subject, not the citizen', Shelley affirms, and Necessity's 'tribunal' surpasses 'the show of human justice, / As God surpasses man' (*Queen Mab*, iii, 170–1, 223–5). In short, then, the Necessary laws of nature expose the artificiality, the un-naturalness, of the current socio-political order, and provide the blueprint for the utopian society described in *Mab*'s closing cantos: a society, again, that rejects the law of man in favour of the law of nature. 'The doctrine of Necessity', Shelley affirms, 'tends to introduce a great change into the established notions of morality, and utterly to destroy religion' (*Poems*, i, p. 378). Far from supporting reactionary religious ideologies, then, the ability to 'rightly' feel the 'mystery' of natural 'grandeur' has enormous political potential.

The role of the imagination in enabling the mind to realise this potential by 'rightly' feeling the 'mystery' of the 'awful' in nature amounts to a redemption of that faculty from more than a century of distrust in the empirical and radical traditions. How has Shelley effected this redemption? Epistemological support certainly came from David Hume who, like William Godwin many years later, identified Necessity as the animating principle of the universe.[20] Indeed, as Evans notes, Shelley opens his discussion of Necessity in the Notes to *Queen Mab* with an explicitly Humean claim.[21] 'The idea of necessity', he writes:

is obtained by our experience of the connection between objects, the uniformity of the operations of nature, the constant conjunction of similar events, and the consequent inference of one from another (*Poems*, i, p. 375)[22]

However, while for Godwin this 'inference' is an act of reason, Hume affirms that only the imagination is capable of going beyond the limitations of sensation and inferring the Necessitarian principle of nature.[23]

Shelley's debt to Hume's account of the imagination marks the beginning of his rejection of the Scottish Common Sense philosophy, a rejection that he will fully articulate in his 1815 philosophical essays (discussed in chapter 2). But notwithstanding that debt, Shelley's new-found confidence in the imagination was also premised upon his own radical re-theorisation of the faculty. More precisely, the imagination that Shelley claims to be capable of 'rightly' feeling the 'mystery' of natural 'grandeur' is an *educated* or progressive imagination, an imagination – as he will define it in his *Refutation of Deism* – '*considerably tinctured with science, and enlarged by cultivation*' (*PW*, p. 120; emphasis added). Only this 'cultivated' imagination can avoid 'vulgar' anthropomorphism and 'contemplate itself, not as the centre and model of the Universe, but as one of the infinitely various multitude of beings of which it is composed' (*PW*, p. 120). Shelley's theory of the *educated* or *cultivated* imagination – which, as will I show later in this chapter, derives from an unlikely and now little known re-appraisal of the faculty by one of the *idéologues* – forms the central tenet of his ongoing engagement with the discourse on the sublime. Correctly felt by the cultivated imagination, the defeat of the understanding by 'awful' natural phenomena leads not to a reactionary 'seduction from the falsehoods of religious systems', but rather to a revolutionary awareness of nature's law. In short, the contemplation of the natural sublime can have profound political potential if only 'Nature's silent eloquence' – the sceptical equivalent of Alison's 'signs' and 'expressions' of 'Deity' – are interpreted correctly by the imagination (*Queen Mab*, iii, 197).

READING NATURE 'RIGHTLY': REVOLUTION AND THE
NATURAL SUBLIME

Shelley's attempt to revise the British discourse on the sublime along politically radical lines took place against the backdrop of an ongoing debate about the relationship between natural and political history. In the wake of the French Revolution, both sides of the political divide in England appealed to nature as the legitimating prototype for their respective models of society. Burke's *Reflections*, which sparked off the British literary debate about the Revolution, is the classic conservative statement of this strategy. Burke condemns the Revolution itself as something 'out of nature' and identifies the aristocratic basis of British society explicitly as the 'happy effect of following nature'.[24] Following Burke's lead – though certainly not to his conclusions – many of the radical responses to the

Reflections appealed equally to natural law, to the natural rights of man, in
their attempts to praise, justify or defend the Revolution and its aftermath.
'Nature made man equal', Shelley wrote to Elizabeth Hitchener on 25 July
1811, and 'that society has destroyed this equality is a truth not more
incontrovertible' (*Letters*, i, p. 125). A correct reading of nature, then,
became of central importance to the literary debate about political reform,
and ever since Addison's early claim that 'a spacious horizon is an image of
liberty', the discourse on the sublime had been an integral part of this
project.[25]

   In Paine's *Rights of Man* (1791–2), for example, Shelley would have
found an explicit link between political revolution and the imaginative
response to the natural sublime.[26] In the Introduction to Part II of the
Rights, Paine praises the 'Revolution of America' as the beginning of a
general reform in world politics.[27] Part II opens with Archimedes' famous
epigram, also cited by Shelley at the beginning of *Queen Mab*: 'Had
we ... a place to stand upon, we might raise the world' (*Poems*, i, p. 269).
Paine expands on this reference by drawing a parallel between natural law
and political policy, similar to that suggested by *Queen Mab*'s account of
natural processes as the correct model for social institutions: 'the
Revolution of America presented in politics', he notes, 'what was only
theory in mechanics'.[28] Paine then goes on to link the political principles of
the American Revolution directly to the contemplation of the 'awful' in
nature:

As America was the only spot in the political world where the principles of
universal reformation could begin, so also was it the best in the natural world.
An assemblage of circumstances conspired not only to give birth, but to add
gigantic maturity to its principles. The scene which that country presents to the
eye of a spectator has something in it which generates and encourages great ideas.
Nature appears to him in magnitude. The mighty objects he beholds act upon his
mind by enlarging it, and he partakes of the greatness he contemplates.[29]

Paine thus suggests a causal connection between the affective response to
the natural sublime and the promotion of political liberty, proposing a
radical sublime of magnitude that wholly rejects the reactionary leanings of
Burke's aesthetic of terror. The 'enlarging' effect of natural 'magnitude' on
the mind lends 'gigantic maturity' to the 'spectator', Paine affirms, and 'he
partakes of the greatness he contemplates'.[30]

   Paine's claim that the contemplation of the 'awful' in nature can have
revolutionary potential is echoed in *Queen Mab*'s account of the political
potential of 'rightly' feeling the 'mystery' of natural 'grandeur'. In fact,

Queen Mab's emphasis on this potential is the product of Shelley's ongoing attempt to bring the discourse on the sublime in line with radical politics. This attempt is exemplified in another of the Esdaile poems, 'On Leaving London for Wales', which was written in November 1812, and is thus broadly contemporary with *Queen Mab*. 'On Leaving London . . .' opens with Shelley looking forward to leaving the 'miserable city! where the gloom / Of penury mingles with the tyrant's pride' and returning to the mountainous landscape of North Wales ('On Leaving London . . .', 1–2). The poem invokes this landscape as a defence against the deadening effects of the city upon the mind: 'May floods and vales and mountains me divide / From all the taints thy wretched walls contain' ('On Leaving London . . .', 5–6). But the dynamic here is as much public as it is personal. More specifically, the city is identified not only as the locus of emotional or spiritual degradation, but also of an attendant loss of political conviction. London is 'the tomb / Where Freedom's hope and Truth's high courage died' ('On Leaving London . . .', 3–4). By contrast, Shelley praises the sublime landscape of North Wales for its anticipated ability to restore his 'natural sympathies' and heal his 'burdened heart' ('On Leaving London . . .', 11–12). 'Mountain Liberty', he continues, 'alone may heal / The pain which Custom's obduracies bring':

> And he who dares in fancy even to steal
>   One draught from Snowdon's ever-sacred spring
> Blots out the unholiest rede of worldly witnessing
>   ('On Leaving London . . .', 25–7)

To this point, then, the poem is essentially Wordsworthian in tone: the natural sublime can heal the dissipative effects that 'Custom's obduracies' have upon the mind. Immediately after acknowledging these beneficial effects, however, Shelley returns to the ambiguity and distrust that marked his comments on the natural sublime during his first visit to Cwm Elan in the summer of 1811. 'And shall that soul to selfish peace resigned / So soon forget the woe its fellows share?', he asks:

> Can Snowdon's Lethe from the freeborn mind
>   So soon the page of injured penury tear?
> Does this fine mass of human passion dare
>   To sleep unhonouring the patriot's fall,
> Or life's sweet load in quietude to bear
>   While millions famish even in Luxury's hall
> And Tyranny high raised stern lowers over all?
>   ('On Leaving London . . .', 28–36)

The passage immediately recalls the tension in Shelley's 1811 letters between a taste for the 'awful' in nature and those 'other things' which demand the attention of the political reformer, the empiricist distrust of the reactionary and 'eccentric fancy' that 'militates' with the politically progressive 'reason'. Shelley worries if the imaginative response to the 'awful' in nature is a seductive 'Lethe' that causes the mind to forget or abjure its responsibilities to its fellow men in favour of a 'selfish peace'. This concern echoes Coleridge's analogous interrogation of the 'Mount Sublime' in his 1795 'Reflections on Having Left a Place of Retirement' (43). 'Was it right', Coleridge asks, 'while my unnumber'd brethren toil'd and bled, / That I should dream away the entrusted hours / on rose-leaf beds, pampering the coward heart / With feelings too delicate for use?' ('Reflections . . .', 43–8). Having voiced his doubts, however, Shelley proceeds to reformulate them in a manner that was not possible in 1811, a reformulation that Leighton's study – which does not even discuss 'On Leaving London . . .' – fails to recognise. 'No, Cambria!', he responds emphatically, 'never may thy matchless vales / A heart so false to hope and virtue shield, / Nor ever may thy spirit-breathing gales / Waft freshness to the slaves who dare to yield' ('On Leaving London . . .', 37–40). Hence while Shelley's 1811 letters from Wales reveal his concern about the incompatibility of a taste for the 'awful' in nature with the responsibilities of the political activist, 'On Leaving London . . .' confirms the reformulation of this tension:

> . . . the weapon that I burn to wield
> I seek amid thy rocks to ruin hurled,
> That Reason's flag may over Freedom's field,
> Symbol of bloodless victory, wave unfurled
> A meteor-sign of love effulgent o'er the world
>
> ('On Leaving London . . .', 41–5)

In keeping with Shelley's revision of the discourse on the sublime, these lines read the North Wales landscape not as evidence of God but as evidence of Necessity: 'rocks to ruin hurled' being a reference to the visible, geological operations of nature's law.[31] Shelley is thus again suggesting that the *affective* response to the natural sublime can provide an ideological 'weapon' for the political activist (a suggestion bound up, here, with a quasi-Wordsworthian claim that the rejuvenating effects of nature on the mind can supply a renewed vigour for political activity).[32] 'Weapon', however, is a highly ambivalent word to use in such a context, and the next stanza heightens the ambivalence by apparently equating this 'weapon' with a 'dagger' ('On Leaving London . . .', 47). 'Hark to that shriek!', Shelley writes, 'my hand had almost clasped / The dagger that my heart had cast away' ('On Leaving London . . .', 46–7). The only possible inference is that this dagger / weapon refers to political violence (see *Poems*, i, 260). This inference is borne out by continuation of the stanza: 'The storm fleets by and calmer thoughts succeed; / Feelings once more mild reason's voice obey' ('On Leaving London . . .', 51–2). In other words, Shelley now seems to be equating the violent passion produced by the 'awful' in nature – the passion which 'militates' against 'mild reason' – with the impetus to violent revolution. This equation marks a return to the familiar tension in his thought between the affective and the rational response to the 'awful' in nature, but now this tension is mapped in explicitly political terms: no longer a tension between reason and imagination, it has become a troubling tension between gradualism and revolutionism. Shelley wishes 'woe' on 'tyrant's and murderers', but stresses that 'Nature's wound *alone* should make their Conscience bleed' ('On Leaving London . . .', 52–4; emphasis added). In other words, recognition of their unnatural activities should sufficiently trouble the consciences of the corrupt, they should not be literally made to bleed.

In the final analysis, then, 'On Leaving London for Wales' is suspicious of the affective response to the 'awful' in nature, but this suspicion – once epistemological – now has an overtly political resonance. The poem aligns the affective response to the 'awful' in nature with the impetus to violent revolution, and consequently confirms that this response needs to be tempered by 'mild reason' – just as *Queen Mab* affirms and advocates the notion of a *cultivated* imagination. The poem closes with a renewed invocation to 'wild Cambria' along these modified lines: 'Do thou, wild Cambria, *calm* each struggling thought, / . . . I am the friend of the unfriended poor: / Let me not madly stain their righteous cause in gore' ('On Leaving London . . .', 55, 62–3; emphasis added).

Shelley's repeated references – during this period – to his own irrational 'enthusiasm' can only be fully understood within this politicised context (*Letters*, i, pp. 29, 44).[33] Leighton correctly notes the derogatory connotations of 'enthusiasm' within the empiricist and materialist traditions, as a reference to excessive and misguided feeling.[34] She is also correct in pointing out the importance of the word in the discourse on the sublime, particularly in the pious configuration of that discourse. But Leighton wholly fails to acknowledge the overtly political resonance which 'enthusiast' would have had in 1811–12, as a reference to the devotees of the French Revolution – we think, for example, of William

Wordsworth's 1809 account of 'The French Revolution, as it Appeared to Enthusiasts at its Commencement'. Burke coined this usage in the *Reflections*, which identifies the Revolution's leaders as 'warm and inexperienced enthusiasts', and it quickly became a commonplace of the literary debate about events in France.[35] Hence Shelley's description of Godwin as the 'moderator of [his] enthusiasm' needs to be understood not only as a reference to the influence of Godwinian rationalism, but also as an acknowledgement of the quietist, anti-revolutionary basis of Godwin's politics which Shelley saw as a 'moderating' influence on his own more militant sentiments (*Letters*, i, p. 229).[36]

Queen Mab's account of the socio-political ramifications of the Necessity exhibited in the landscape of the natural sublime shares the ambiguity present in 'On Leaving London for Wales': the tension between a gradualist and revolutionist response to the natural sublime. Shelley's discussion of Necessity in *Queen Mab* needs to be contrasted with Godwin's arguments on same in *Political Justice*, arguments which derive in turn from sections IV–VIII of Hume's *Human Understanding*.[37] Godwin's theory of perfectibility is almost entirely premised upon a belief that Necessity will bring about moral and political reform through the passage of time. In other words, Necessity is the *agent* of human perfectibility. But the Necessity in which Godwin places his political faith is an intellectual entity: a community of ideas, or climate of public opinion. *Political Justice* argues that reform will come about gradually, through the continual and inevitable change in opinion engineered by an intellectual élite – that is, through a moral or ideological revolution. Godwin condemns direct political action of any sort, and particularly any appeals to the 'vulgar', to the uneducated poor. *Queen Mab*, however, argues that Necessity will also operate *directly*, through *inhuman* natural processes, to assist in bringing about a political and environmental utopia.[38] *Mab*'s discussion of equinoctial precession exemplifies this conviction. In the Note to *Queen Mab* vi, 45–6, Shelley claims that the earth's 'poles are every year becoming more and more perpendicular to the ecliptic', a theory which had actually already been debunked by Laplace and Euler (*Poems*, i, p. 374).[39] This would have the effect of equalising days and nights throughout the year, 'and probably the seasons also', thereby effectively counteracting any environmental – and specifically, in this regard, any Malthusian – justification for social injustice based upon limited natural resources (*Poems*, i, p. 374).

However, *Queen Mab*'s contention that Necessity will act through inhuman natural processes to match and facilitate the progress of humanity's construction of utopia has a darker, more ambivalent side. While Godwin's discussion of Necessity is couched in quietist and non-interventionist terms, *Queen Mab*'s treatment of the meliorative operations of Necessity through natural processes is often overtly catastrophist and revolutionary. These more violent manifestations of Necessity contribute to making it an 'awful' principle of nature, despite its ultimately meliorative tendencies. 'Earth in itself', *Queen Mab* argues, 'contains at once the evil and the cure; / And all-sufficing Nature can chastise / Those who transgress her law' (*Queen Mab*, iii, 80–3). This conception of punishment marks an advance from Shelley's position in 'On Leaving London for Wales'. In that poem, the transgression of natural law by the corrupt would of itself produce a feeling of remorse ultimately conducive to reform – the operation of Godwinian Necessity. On no account, Shelley argued, should the corrupt be physically punished. But in *Queen Mab*, Shelley argues that 'awful' natural processes will themselves actively 'chastise' the corrupt – and as we shall see, the figurative links between these processes and violent political revolution are inescapable. Hence, Shelley's renewed admonition of those whom he considers the propagators of social injustice is now as much a warning as a plea for conscientious self-analysis: 'Look to thyself, priest, conqueror, or prince! / ... Look to thy wretched self!' (*Queen Mab*, iv, 237–45).

Shelley would have found many metaphorical connections between sublime natural phenomena and political revolution in the literary debate about the French Revolution – and to this extent, again, his engagements with natural grandeur draw upon a pre-existent discourse on the sublime. Mary Wollstonecraft's *Historical and Moral View of the Origins and Progress of the French Revolution* (1794), for example, describes political revolutions as 'violent convulsions', 'like hurricanes whirling over the face of nature'.[40] The metaphor comes in a justification of such action as a last resort, a justification even the pacifist Godwin was prepared to admit. Similarly, as Matthews notes, Abbé Barruel's already cited *Memoirs Illustrating the History of Jacobinism* describes political revolution in terms borrowed directly from contemporary volcanology, likening political conspiracy to the 'subterraneous' build-up of lava and revolution to 'the irruption of the volcano'.[41]

One of the Esdaile poems, 'To the Republicans of North America', draws directly on Barruel's use of the volcano as a metaphor for violent revolution. Though ostensibly addressed to the republicans of 'North America' the poem in fact refers to the revolution in Mexico, ongoing since 1810.[42] In a letter to Elizabeth Hitchener on Valentine's Day 1812 – which included this poem minus, as we shall see, the highly ambivalent fourth stanza – Shelley writes that he has just 'heard that a new republic is set up in Mexico' (*Letters*, i, p. 253; *Esdaile*, p. 201). Another letter, on 10 March, characterises the Mexican revolt as an inaugural step on the road to world reform. 'The Republic of Mexico proceeds and extends', Shelley writes, 'I have seen American papers, but have not had time to read them. I only know that the spirit of Republicanism extends in South America, and that the prevailing opinion is that there will soon be no province which will recognise the ancient dynasty of Spain' (*Letters*, i, 272). Anticipating the thirteenth stanza of the *Ode to Liberty*, 'To the Republicans . . .' likens Mexico's 'new bursting Liberty' to the eruption of Mt. Cotopaxi, an active volcano – in Ecuador, as it happens – which had recently been described by Alexander Von Humboldt in his *Personal Narrative* ('To the Republicans . . .', 36).[43] Drawing explicitly on Barruel's volcanist image of the subterranean activities of political subversives, Shelley exhorts the mountain to spread the revolutionary message throughout the world: 'Cotopaxi! bid the sound / Through thy sister mountains ring' ('To the Republicans . . .', 21–2). The fourth stanza's discussion of the revolutionary struggle itself echoes Wollstonecraft and Godwin's justification of violence as a last resort:

> Blood may fertilize the tree
> Of new bursting Liberty;
> Let the guiltiness then be
>   On the slaves that ruin wreak,
> On the unnatural tyrant brood
> Slow to Peace and swift to blood
>
> ('To the Republicans . . .', 35–40)

These lines confirm a standard position within the radical response to the French Revolution: the idea that the responsibility for any violence lies ultimately with the 'tyrant brood' who have taught violence, by example, to the oppressed. Both Godwin and Wollstonecraft use this line of reasoning in their explanations of the Terror. Shelley's characterisation of the Mexican revolution is more ambivalent, however, since he not only seeks to explain the violence in these terms, but also actively justifies it, or at least portrays it as *natural*. The image of the tree of Liberty draws on the idea of natural cycles, with death providing the material for new life – and again the allusions to the French Revolution are unmissable. As Cameron points out in his editorial commentary, Shelley's claim that 'Blood may fertilize the tree / Of new bursting Liberty' is probably an echo of de Vieuzac's speech at the trial of Louis XVI, during which he called for the death penalty: 'The tree of liberty grows only when watered with the blood of tyrants' (*Esdaile*, p. 203).[44]

'To the Republicans . . .' thus adapts the standard radical response to the Terror by explaining the revolutionary violence provoked by forcible oppression in terms of natural processes. This adaptation betrays a concern that for all the meliorative exertions of reason, violent revolution may be the inevitable agent by which 'awful' Necessity will 'chastise' the oppressors of mankind – and again, this concern will persistently problematise Shelley's engagement with the discourse on the sublime. Tellingly, Shelley excluded the ambivalent fourth stanza of 'To the Republicans . . .' from the version of the text that he sent to Elizabeth Hitchener. Nonetheless, the explicitly revolutionary sentiments it contains are carried over into *Queen Mab* from its opening Voltairean injunction: 'ECRASEZ L'INFAME!' (*Poems*, i, p. 269). In that poem, however, the figurative links between 'awful' natural processes and violent revolution are even more ambiguous in their implications: Shelley confirms that inhuman Necessity will act directly to 'chastise' the '*unnatural* tyrant-brood' who 'transgress her laws' (*Queen Mab*, iii, 82–3; 'To the Republicans . . .', 39; emphasis added). The agency of this 'chastisement' is ostensibly the most pervasive, inescapable, and 'awful' natural process of them all: 'time's unrelaxing grip' (*Queen Mab*, ii, 190). And tellingly, the revolutionary implications of this 'grip' are revealed through 'rightly' feeling the 'mystery' of another commonplace of the discourse on the sublime in Britain: ruin.

RUIN, REVOLUTION AND THE SUBLIME

By 1812, ruin had long been an integral part of the British discourse on the sublime.[45] In an obvious way, ruin figures the essentially transitory nature of human achievement. Early eighteenth-century British ruin-sentiment formulated a moralistic and only partly successful religious resolution to this terrifying fact, denigrating the importance of the earthly in contrast to the eternal hereafter. In other words, ruin was to be interpreted not only as a salutary warning about the vanity of human achievement, but moreover as a potent reminder that humanity could only find permanence through the spiritual values of the Christian religion. In many ways, then, eighteenth-century ruin-sentiment mirrored the pious configuration of the discourse on the sublime: both discourses sought to resolve the existential anxiety produced by a recognition of humanity's essential insignificance by appealing to a benevolent creator-God. As Goldstein puts it:

18th-century ruin sentiment ... asserts that providence controls the course of historical events, a belief both comforting and horrifying. Comforting because it endows structure and meaning to the seemingly random sequence of events in time, but horrifying because it insists on a teleology that dooms all of natural life as we know it.[46]

As the century wore on, however, ruin – and the ruins of empire in particular – took on increasingly obvious political implications, as previously personal angst was consistently mapped onto broader national concerns. If ruin did indeed figure the impermanence of human achievement, what did the fallen empires of the past say about the imperial ambitions of the present? Would England's burgeoning empire go the way of Rome? These political anxieties found an uneasy ideological resolution in a manner broadly analogous on the national scale to the quasi-religious resolution of individual angst. Simply put, the fall of empire could be attributed to the decadence and corruption of the home nation, a view amply borne out by Edward Gibbon's *History of the Decline and Fall of the Roman Empire* (1766–88). Avoid these – by adherence to Christian morality – and empire would prosper.

Precisely this kind of ruin-sentiment – which links the fall of empire to the decadence and corruption of the home nation – lies behind a June 1811 letter from Shelley to Elizabeth Hitchener. Attacking the Prince Regent's recent fête at Carlton house – the ironic antithesis of the French Revolutionary fêtes of the previous decade – Shelley equates the present state of England with the latter days of the Roman Empire. 'How admirably', he writes:

this growing spirit of ludicrous magnificence tallies with the disgusting splendors [sic] of the stage of the roman Empire, which preceded its destruction! Yet here are a people advanced in intellectual improvement, willfully rushing to a Revolution, the natural death of all great commercial Empires, which must plunge them in the barbarism from which they are slowly arising (*Letters*, i, p. 110)

Shelley thus expresses a belief that he would hold throughout his life, and that would remain a central aspect of his engagement with the discourse on the sublime: that England was on the verge of a violent revolution.[47] It is important to recognise, however, the extent to which the passage marks an advance on the conventional, eighteenth-century interpretation of the fall of empire. While eighteenth-century ruin-sentiment linked that fall to decadence and corruption, resolving the terror of ruin through an appeal to moral restraint, Shelley here suggests that the revolutionary 'death' of 'empire' – the vengeful uprising of the oppressed and disenfranchised majority – is '*natural*', and therefore inevitable. France, it seems, proved all too well the causal links between oppression, vengeance, and barbarism. The question of whether or not revolution really *is* the Necessary ('natural') consequence of oppression, of whether or not the cycle of violence can ever be broken, remains the central concern of Shelley's political thought. And while he would like to think that the cycle can be broken by the exertions of a Godwinian Necessity, his engagement with the discourse on the natural sublime – with its far more ambivalent conception of an 'awful' Necessity – repeatedly implies that it cannot.

The quintessential radical revision of eighteenth-century ruin-sentiment came in 1791 with the publication of Constantin Volney's *Les Ruines, ou Méditations sur les Révolutions des Empires*, translated into English shortly thereafter, and again in 1802, 'under the inspection of the author', as the subtitle affirmed. Although Shelley himself never actually mentions Volney, Medwin's biography confirms that he became acquainted with *Les Ruines* shortly after his expulsion from Oxford in 1811, while Hogg's *Life* adds that the book was a favourite with Shelley's first wife.[48] And indeed, in Mary Shelley's *Frankenstein* (1818), it is from *Les Ruines* that the creature learns about human civilisation. Shelley's critics have long noted borrowings from Volney in both *Queen Mab* and *The Revolt of Islam* (1817).[49] In point of fact, however, it would be difficult to over-estimate the impact of *Les Ruines* both upon Shelley's political thought *per se* and upon his politicised engagement with the discourse on the sublime.[50]

The Ruins asks '*by what secret causes do empires rise and fall; from what sources spring the prosperity and misfortunes of nations; on what principles can the peace of society, and the happiness of man be established?*' (*Ruins*, i, pp. 25–6; original emphasis). In effect, the book is an idealised, rationalist rehearsal of the French Revolution (with violence replaced by enlightened discussion), narrating the creation of a socio-political utopia founded on the explicitly *natural* principles of liberty, equality, and fraternity. And this 'rationalist apocalypse' is delivered through the contemplation of ruin.[51]

In his prefatory 'Invocation', Volney apostrophises the sublimity of ruin in terms that directly prefigure, and undoubtedly constitute the source for Shelley's contention – in the second Note to *Queen Mab* – that there is a right and a wrong way to 'feel' the 'mystery' of the sublime. 'Hail solitary ruins', Volney writes, 'while your aspect averts, with secret dread, the *vulgar* regard, it excites, in *my* heart, the charm of delicious sentiments, sublime contemplations' (*Ruins*, i, p. ix; emphasis added). 'Vulgar', we recall, was Shelley's precise term for the primitive failure to 'rightly feel' the 'mystery' of natural 'grandeur'. Volney continues his eulogy to the ruins of empire, confirming this distinction between the 'vulgar' and the correct interpretation of their significance: 'How many useful lessons, how many reflections, affecting and profound, do you suggest *to the mind who knows how to consult you*' (*Ruins*, i, p. ix; emphasis added). That is, unlike the superstitious reaction of the 'vulgar', the ruins of empire can teach revolutionary 'lessons' to 'the mind who knows how to consult' them. 'Oh tombs!', Volney writes, 'what virtues are yours!':

You appal the tyrant's heart, and poison with secret alarm his impious joys. He flies with coward step, your incorruptible aspect, ... You punish the powerful oppressor; you wrest from avarice and extortion their ill-gotten gold; you avenge the feeble whom they have despoiled; you compensate the miseries of the poor by the anxieties of the rich; you console the wretched by opening to him a last asylum from distress; and you give to the soul that just equipoise of strength and sensibility, which constitutes wisdom and the true science of life (*Ruins*, i, pp. x–xi)

Volney thus entirely reconfigures – and re-politicises – the 'appalling' sublimity of the ruins of empire, refusing to resolve the 'anxiety' that ruin provokes in the 'oppressor', but rather transforming that anxiety into a powerful symbol of hope for the historically disenfranchised. The 'awful' political 'lesson' of ruin is that empire will Necessarily fall, and while this explicitly Natural law may well 'appal' those who profit by oppression and corruption, it provides encouragement for the oppressed, 'a last asylum' of hope as much as of literal physical refuge from the elements. The 'vulgar' response to the terror evoked by ruin amounts to a superstitious act of political anthropomorphism: the substitution of the kingdom of God for earthly kingdoms.[52] But the correct, 'wise' interpretation of the Necessity revealed by the ruins of empire not only derives political hope from the transitory nature of earthly power. Rather it also provides guidelines for personal conduct in accordance with justice and benevolence, the true law of Nature: 'Aware that all must be returned to [ruin], the wise man loadeth not himself with the burdens of grandeur and of useless wealth; he restrains his desires within the limits of justice' (*Ruins*, i, p. xi).

The early chapters of *The Ruins* effectively rehearse the theme of the 'Invocation'. The book proper opens with a traveller gloomily contemplating the 'celebrated ruins' of Palmyra, and meditating – in the best eighteenth-century tradition – on the transitory nature of power (*Ruins*, i, p. 3). This traveller, suitably 'appalled' by the implications of the destruction he sees around him, struggles for an adequate explanation, blaming in turn 'a blind fatality', 'a fatal necessity', and 'the justice of heaven' – all familiar tropes of eighteenth-century ruin-sentiment (*Ruins*, i, p. 14). In the midst of his melancholy, the traveller is confronted by the 'Genius' of the Ruins, a local spirit who re-asserts the crucial distinction between the 'vulgar' and the 'wise' interpretation of ruin. 'If, for a moment, you can suspend the delusion which fascinates your senses', the Genius exhorts, 'if your heart is capable of comprehending the language of reason, interrogate these ruins! read the lessons which they offer' (*Ruins*, i, p. 16). Once again, the material-ist analysis of the affective response to the 'awful' distinguishes between the 'delusion' of the 'senses' and 'the language of reason'. As in the second Note to *Queen Mab*, however, Volney's 'Genius' acknowledges that it is possible – and desirable – to 'rightly feel': 'if your *heart* is capable of comprehending the language of reason' (emphasis added). The 'Genius' goes on to stress – in the language of *idéologue* rationalism – that *vulgar* 'passion that mistaketh [and] ignorance which observeth not causes' have led humanity to blame Fate, Chance, or God for its misery (*Ruins*, i, p. 22). The true cause of this misery, the Genius affirms, is humanity's own corruption: empires fall because empire is *inherently* corrupt. The traveller despairs at this conclusion, and in order to relieve his dismay the 'Genius' reveals – in an idealised and explicitly non-violent history of the French Revolution – the establishment, through peaceful rational enquiry, of a utopian society.

Volney's *Ruins* determined Shelley's interpretation of the ruins of empire: the fact that they reveal to the 'wise' the Necessary downfall of tyranny. To take the obvious example, Shelley's most famous engagement with ruin – his 1818 sonnet 'Ozymandias' – is quintessentially Volneyan in its extrapolation of the fate of empire from the ruined statue of the Egyptian monarch.[53] However, despite producing *Mab*'s concept of the cultivated imagination, Shelley's adaptation of Volney is highly problem-atic. More precisely, Shelley's inflection of Volneyan ruin-sentiment feeds directly into a pervasive ambivalence in his thought about the means through which Necessity will bring about political change.

This ambivalence is encapsulated in Shelley's letter to Hitchener on Valentine's Day 1812, the same letter that contained 'To the Republicans ...'. Writing from a politically troubled Dublin, Shelley sets out to re-assure his friend – in clear Volneyan terms – that the ruins of empire figure Necessity as the guarantor of political change. 'I could stand upon thy shores O Erin', Shelley affirms:

and could count the billows that in their unceasing swell dash on thy beach, and every wave might seem an instrument in Time the giant's grasp to burst the barriers of Eternity. Proceed thou giant conquering and to conquer. March on thy lonely way – the nations fall beneath thy noiseless footstep – pyramids that for millen[n]iums have defied the blast, and laughed at lightnings thou dost crush to nought. Yon monarch in his solitary pomp, is but the fungus of a winter day that thy light footstep presses into dust – Thou art a conqueror Time! all things give way before thee *but 'the fixed and virtuous will'*, the sacred sympathy of soul, which was when thou wert not, which *shall* be when thou perishest (*Letters*, i, pp. 251–2; original emphasis)

Once again, the passage is clearly Volneyan in its interpretation of ruin: 'Time', the 'conqueror', will gradually remove the oppositions to political change, sparing only the *idéologue* instrument of that change, 'the fixed and virtuous will'. The most famous of the ruins of empire – the pyramids – prove this fact.

And yet, for all its gradualist confidence in the political potency of the 'virtuous will' – a confidence derived as much from *Political Justice* as from *The Ruins* – the passage is actually markedly ambivalent about the precise manner in which Necessity will effect political change. More precisely, while Shelley – following Godwin and Volney – ostensibly places his political faith in the 'virtuous will', the terms in which he couches his description of Necessity's political agency are anything but gradualist. 'Time' will 'swell', 'dash', 'burst', and 'conquer'. Empire will not be peacefully abandoned or outgrown – as in Volney's 'rationalist apocalypse' – but rather 'crush[ed] to nought', 'pressed into the dust'. In short, this is not the language of Volneyan or Godwinian gradualism; it is the language of Paine, the language of revolution – and the language of the sublime. Shelley's words might well describe the action of a revolutionary crowd. We are returned, then, to Shelley's concern that 'revolution' is the 'natural death of empire', a concern re-enforced here by the use of natural imagery (the crushing of a fungus) to convey the monarch's fate. The ruins of empire – this passage implies – do not merely figure 'Time' as the guarantor of political change. Rather they also affirm – for the 'wise' who know how to read their lessons – that violent revolution is itself an 'awful' agent of Necessity, the 'natural death' of empire. 'Earth in itself', *Mab* reminds us, 'Contains at once the evil and the cure; / And all-sufficing nature can chastise / Those who transgress her law' (*Queen Mab*, iii, 80–3). Necessity is – in a very real sense – 'fatal' to empire.

This ambivalence about the manner in which Necessity will effect political change is expanded in Shelley's approximately contemporary 'To Liberty', another of the Esdaile poems.[54] Like the letter to Hitchener, 'To Liberty' expresses explicitly Volneyan sentiments in its extrapolation of the fate of kings from the ruins of empire. 'The pyramids shall fall', Shelley writes, 'and Monarchs! so shall ye':

> Thrones shall rust in the hall
>   Of forgotten royalty,
> Whilst Virtue, Truth and Peace shall arise
>   And a paradise on Earth
>   From your fall shall date its birth
>
> ('To Liberty', 41–7)

The poem thus anticipates *Mab*'s affirmation that the inauguration of utopia will follow the fall of the present political system. Necessity, through time, will enact this fall. The difficult question, again, is how? Will it be through a Godwinian progressivism, a Volneyan 'rationalist apocalypse', or a violent revolution? 'On Liberty' certainly has overtly revolutionary overtones in the connection it makes between Monarchs and the symbols of their oppression:

> Monarch! sure employer
>   Of vice and want and woe,
> Thou conscienceless destroyer,
>   Who and what art thou? –
> The dark prison house that in the dust shall lie,
>   The pyramid which guilt
>   First planned, which man has built
>
> ('To Liberty', 31–7)

In 1812, the association of a 'monarch' with a 'dark prison house' could hardly fail to suggest Louis XVI and the Bastille, and the poem confirms that both 'in the dust shall lie'. The opening lines of the third stanza gives the poem's only real clue as to how this may come about, and again it is a highly problematic clue:

> Regal pomp and pride
>   The Patriot falls in scorning,
> The spot whereon he died
>   Should be the despot's warning;
> The voice of blood shall on his crimes call down Revenge!
>
> ('To Liberty', 21–5)

'Revenge' – precisely the emotion which Wollstonecraft and Godwin believed to have motivated the French Revolutionary Terror – is a likely candidate for the manner in which Necessity will enact the fall of empire. And the close of the third stanza of 'To Liberty' gives what might well be read as a justification for such 'awful' action:

> And the spirits of the brave
> Shall start from every grave,
> Whilst from her Atlantic throne
> Freedom sanctifies the groan
> That fans the glorious fires of its change
>
> ('To Liberty', 28–30)

Again, Shelley's meaning – however problematic in its political implication – seems clear enough: America, the sublime 'Atlantic throne' of a 'Freedom' won through violent struggle ('fire', 'groan'), 'sanctifies' and legitimates revolutionary violence.

Precisely this same ambiguity about the means in which Necessity will effect political change is carried over into *Queen Mab*, where it is again bound up with a quasi-Volneyan interpretation of ruin.[55] Volney's influence upon the body-text of *Queen Mab* has long been recognised. Since Kellner first marked the relationship – more than a century ago – critics have repeatedly pointed up Shelley's numerous structural, thematic, and verbal borrowings. And yet, despite the clear evidence for a relationship between the two texts, surprisingly little has been written about the impact of Volney's ostensible subject – the connection between the ruin and the fall of empire – upon a poem by Shelley that is explicitly concerned with both. Both *Queen Mab* and Volney's *Ruins* set out to narrate the inauguration of utopia through a gradual, intellectual revolution. Both, similarly, deliver this narrative through the cosmic-voyage trope, where a protagonist is lifted above the earth by a guiding-spirit and given an enlightening, panoramic perspective on human history. In Volney's *Ruins*, the protagonist witnesses, with the help of the Genius, every detail of the process by which rational enquiry replaces the corrupt ancien régime with a new utopian order founded on the French Revolutionary – and again explicitly *natural* – principles of equality, liberty, and fraternity. This is not the case, however, with *Queen Mab*. While Shelley's poem presents a similar historical panorama – describing the past, present, and future within the rubric of the cosmic-voyage – we are significantly not *shown* the means by which the transition from present corruption to future utopia is achieved (a device Shelley consistently repeats in his political narratives). Hence the scope for ambiguity.

On the face of it, *Queen Mab*'s politics are gradualist and rationalist. Canto VI offers an explicitly Volneyan and Godwinian account of Necessity's political agency, rehearsing Shelley's early emphasis on 'the fixed and virtuous will'. 'Some eminent in virtue shall start up, / Even in perversest time', Shelley assures us:

The truths of their pure lips, that never die,
Shall bind the scorpion falsehood with a wreath
Of ever-living flame,
Until the monster sting itself to death

(*Queen Mab*, vi, 31–8)

And again, while Godwin restricts the operations of Necessity to the social and cultural sphere, *Mab* affirms that Necessity will also intervene directly – through inhuman natural processes – to match the intellectual transition from corrupt present to utopian future. More precisely, *Mab* claims that intellectual melioration will go hand in hand with environmental and geophysical melioration, a claim backed up – again – by Shelley's theories about equinoctial precession. However, we are also given to understand that Necessity has a less benevolent aspect, an aspect that is no less essential to the dynamics of political change. 'Earth in itself', *Mab* reminds us, 'contains at once the evil and the cure / And all-sufficing Nature can chastise / Those who transgress her law' (*Queen Mab*, iii, 80–3). The poem ultimately remains ambivalent about the precise manner in which Necessity will chastise the corrupt who 'transgress her law' – the kings, priests, and statesmen critiqued throughout the text – but some suggestive hints are given. These hints derive, in the main, from *Mab*'s quasi-Volneyan engagement with the ruins of power, and they couch Necessity's political agency in explicitly revolutionary terms.

In *Queen Mab* II, the soul of Ianthe is shown the ruins of Palmyra – the same 'celebrated ruins' described by Volney – and exhorted by her guide to learn the lessons they teach (*Ruins*, i, p. 3). 'Behold . . . / Palmyra's ruined palaces', Mab exclaims:

Behold! where grandeur frowned;
Behold! where pleasure smiled;
What now remains? – the memory
Of senselessness and shame –
What is immortal there?
Nothing – it stands to tell
A melancholy tale, to give
An awful warning

(*Queen Mab*, ii, 109–18; emphasis added)

Shelley's account of 'Palmyra's ruined palaces' thus follows Volney in offering a radically politicised critique of sublime monumentality ('What is immortal there? / Nothing'). However, Shelley transforms the 'melancholy tale' of conventional ruin-sentiment not so much – like Volney – into a symbol of hope for the historically disenfranchised, but rather into an 'awful warning' for 'monarchs and conquerors' (*Queen Mab*, ii, 121). And while the meaning of this 'warning' is never made explicit, *Queen Mab*'s closing account of the ruins of power returns us directly to the darker, revolutionary implications of Shelley's 'awful' Necessity.

Mab's final utopian canto describes a landscape dotted with the ruins of empire, a landscape that Necessity has reclaimed from political and environmental corruption. In other words, Canto IX confirms – in terms which directly echo Shelley's letter to Hitchener on 14 February 1812 – the 'awful warning' that the ruins of empire hold for 'monarchs and conquerors': the monarch has been 'pressed to dust' (*Queen Mab*, ix, 33). Telling, too, is the fate of the monarch's residence. This 'gorgeous' palace – described in Canto III – is now 'a heap of crumbling stones' (*Queen Mab*, iii, 22; ix, 96). 'Cathedrals' likewise stand 'lone' and 'roofless', while the 'massy prison' is now 'mouldering' (*Queen Mab*, ix, 103). In short, all the edifices that *Queen Mab* III identifies with political injustice are ruined in Canto IX's utopia. Indeed, they are being *reclaimed* by nature: 'These ruins soon left not a wreck behind: / Their elements, wide scattered o'er the globe, / To happier shapes were moulded, and became / Ministrant to all blissful impulses' (*Queen Mab*, ix, 130–4). The question begged, then – in the absence of an explicit authorial answer – is how such enormous political change has been achieved? How, more precisely, has the 'awful warning' of Palmyra – the ruins of past empire – translated into the ruination of contemporary political institutions?

On the first page of Paine's *Common Sense* (1776), Shelley would have read that 'government, like dress, is the badge of lost innocence; the palaces of kings are built on the ruins of the bowers of paradise'.[56] As David Duff has suggested, this could be taken as confirmation that 'the bowers of paradise' could only be restored by destroying the palaces of kings.'[57] Is this what *Queen Mab* implies, with its vision of 'ruddy children' playing 'fearless and free' within the 'massy prison's mouldering courts', amidst 'the green ivy and red wall-flower' that now 'mock the dungeon's unavailing gloom'? (*Queen Mab*, ix, 114–15, 117–18).

In order to answer this question, we need to realise the extent to which Shelley's account of the ruins of empire in *Queen Mab* IX draws not only on Volney, but also upon the appropriation of ruin-sentiment with the literature of the 'revolution controversy'. For example, the seemingly throwaway reference to the ivy growing on the prison actually invokes a key trope of that appropriation, a trope that Shelley had already invoked directly in a January 1812 letter to Hitchener from Keswick, in which he suggests that he would:

try to domesticate in some antique feudal castle whose mouldering turrets are fit emblems of decaying inequality and oppression, which the ivy shall wave its green banners above like Liberty and flourish upon the edifice that essayed to crush its root (*Letters*, i, p. 239)

Both passages – with their praise for the triumph of the 'ivy' of 'Liberty' over the edifices of 'inequality' and 'oppression' – again use the ruins of power (a 'decaying' 'feudal castle') as an emblem for the explicitly *natural* downfall of political corruption. However, both passages clearly also recall Wollstonecraft's attack – in her 1790 *Vindication of the Rights of Men* – on Burke's attempt to defend the beautiful, aristocratic order of society against the sublime energy of popular violence. 'The ivy is beautiful', Wollstonecraft admits, 'but when it insidiously destroys the trunk from which it receives support, who would not grub it up'.[58] And indeed, Wollstonecraft's ivy image is itself an echo of Paine's quasi-biblical injunction – in the *Rights of Man* – to 'lay the axe to the root of corruption', and this injunction too is explicitly taken up by *Queen Mab*.[59] 'Let the axe / Strike at the root', Canto IV affirms: 'the poison-tree will fall' (*Queen Mab*, iv, 82–3).[60]

These revolutionary echoes are carried through to *Mab*'s final image of the ruins of power, of children playing within a decaying prison, half-reclaimed by nature. Indeed, they effectively identify that image as an 'awful' revolutionary 'warning' to the oppressors of mankind, a warning in marked contrast with the poem's ostensible gradualism. As with 'To Liberty', the mention of a ruined prison in 1812 – especially in so radical a context as *Queen Mab* – could hardly fail to be taken as a reference to the Bastille, the most famous of all the eighteenth-century's ruins of power. And in point of fact, *Mab*'s account of the 'mouldering' prison clearly also draws upon Helen Maria Williams' description – in her *Letters from France* (1790) – of the post-revolutionary 'rejoicings at the Bastille'.[61] 'The ruins of that execrable fortress were suddenly transformed', Williams affirms, 'as if with the hand of necromancy, into a scene of beauty and pleasure'.[62]

Williams' reader, of course, is left in no doubt that the 'wand of necromancy' has been waved by the hand of revolution. Does *Queen Mab*'s identical 'scene of beauty and pleasure' similarly imply that popular violence may be the 'awful' instrument by which Necessity effects political change, the 'natural death' of empire? Ultimately, the poem remains ambivalent, but Shelley's remarks on Nero in Canto III provide a further, telling clue. 'When Rome / With one stern blow hurled not the tyrant down, / Crushed not the arm red with her dearest blood', *Mab* asks, 'Had not submissive abjectness destroyed / *Nature's* suggestions?' (*Queen Mab*, iii, 188–92; emphasis added). Revolutionary vengeance, it would again seem, is the inevitable, *natural* consequence of political oppression. This is the 'awful' truth revealed to the 'wise' by the ruins of empire, Necessity's 'awful warning' to the corrupt.

The darker implications of this 'truth' – the fear that the cycle of political violence may be unbreakable, for all the exertions of the 'wise' – are not fully recognised or articulated until later in Shelley's work. Nevertheless, *Queen Mab* does hint at these implications when Mab points out to the soul of Ianthe that it is not only tyranny that falls with the passage of time:

> Where Athens, Rome, and Sparta stood,
> There is a moral desert now:
> The mean and miserable huts;
> The yet more wretched palaces,
> Contrasted with those ancient fanes,
> Now crumbling to oblivion
>
> (*Queen Mab*, ii, 162–7)

Mab concludes this gloomy exposition of the past with a succinct statement of the 'awful' effects of Necessity through time: 'There's not one atom of yon earth / But once was living man / ... Thou canst not find one spot / Whereon no city stood' (*Queen Mab*, ii, 211–2, 223–4). The whole of the present earth, in other words, is the ruins of a former, a core idea of the geological catastrophism that Shelley would consistently deploy as a figure for, indeed as an equivalent of political catastrophe.[63]

In many important respects, then, the years 1810–12 are paradigmatic of Shelley's ongoing engagement with the discourse on the natural sublime. We see, in the Notes to *Queen Mab*, the genesis of the concept of the imagination that will prove vital not only to that engagement itself, but arguably to the whole of Shelley's thought. Furthermore, we see the emergence of what will become the defining tension in Shelley's 'great revolutionary' writing: the conflict between his gradualist politics and the revolutionism of his engagement with the discourse on the sublime. Shelley would not meet this tension head on, however, for some years. His primary concern in the period immediately following the publication of *Queen Mab* was to refine the concept of the cultivated imagination, and explore in more detail the politics of the secular response to natural grandeur.

CHAPTER 2

Cultivating the imagination, 1813–1815

On the morning of 28 July 1814, Shelley left London for Dover, accompanied by Mary Wollstonecraft Godwin and her stepsister Jane (Claire) Clairmont. Having crossed the Channel, the party proceeded down through France towards Switzerland and the Alps. Shelley and Mary's account of this trip in their co-authored *History of A Six Weeks' Tour* (1817) records that the 'approach to mountain scenery filled [them] with delight', that they 'delighted with every new view that broke upon [them]' (*H6WT*, p. 32). However, they emphasise that it was far 'otherwise' with their French '*voiturier*' (*H6WT*, p. 41). This man 'came from the plains of Troyes', they confirm, 'and these hills so utterly scared him, that he in some degree lost his reason' (*H6WT*, p. 32).

The *Tour's* account of the *voiturier's* terrified response to the 'awful' Alpine landscape returns us to Shelley's early engagement with the eighteenth-century British discourse on the sublime. In the terms of that engagement, the *voiturier's* fear is a primitive failure to 'rightly' feel the 'mystery' of natural 'grandeur' (*Poems*, i, p. 360). Hence, the *Tour's* account of the Frenchman's reaction clearly echoes *Queen Mab's* critique of 'vulgar' wonder at the sublime (*H6WT*, pp. 35, 41). The 'immensity' of the 'snowy Alps' 'staggers the imagination', it confirms, 'and so far surpasses all conception, that *it requires an effort of the understanding* to believe that they indeed form a part of the earth' (*H6WT*, p. 44; emphasis added).[1] The 'stupid' (or uneducated) French *voiturier* is incapable of making this 'effort': hence his fear.

The *Tour's* insistence on the need for an 'effort of the understanding' in response to a landscape 'surpassing imagination' rehearses the central tenet of Shelley's early engagement with the discourse on the sublime: only an imagination 'considerably tinctured with science, and enlarged by cultivation' can avoid the 'vulgar', superstitious response to natural grandeur (*PW*, p. 120). Over the next three years, that engagement continues to explore the politics of this secular response to the natural sublime, always emphasising the need to regulate the 'dizzying' and 'tumultuous' transition from 'sensation to reflection – from a state of passive perception to voluntary contemplation' (*Prose*, p. 186). As we have seen, Shelley had already arrived at a highly problematic statement of those politics in 'On Leaving London for Wales'. On the one hand, the poem worried that the secular response to natural grandeur might prove to be a seductive 'Lethe', capable of causing the political activist to 'forget the woe [his] fellows share' for the sake of a 'selfish peace' ('On Leaving London . . .', 28–9). On the other, the only apparent alternative to this 'selfish peace' was an ambiguous 'weapon' or 'dagger', an *enthusiastic* response to the natural sublime closely aligned with the impetus to violent revolution ('On Leaving London . . .', 41, 47). Hence, while it marked a movement beyond the conventional, pious configuration of the British discourse on the sublime, 'On Leaving London' largely retained rationalist-gradualist distrust of the imagination by suggesting that there is no viable middle ground between a reactionary and a revolutionary response to the 'awful' in nature.

In the years following the publication of *Queen Mab*, Shelley's engagement with the discourse on the sublime remains similarly uncertain about the politics of the imaginative response to natural grandeur. This uncertainty is intimately bound up with his ongoing concern about the efficacy of political gradualism in an age of increasing reaction. In the Postscript to his 1812 *Address to the Irish People*, Shelley had warned against the 'rapidity and danger of revolution' but was also critical of 'the time servingness of temporising reform' (*PW*, p. 37). Similarly, his 1812 *Proposals for an Association of Philanthropists* stressed the 'hazard and horror of Revolutions' while emphasising that the reform movement:

will not be kept alive by each citizen sitting quietly by his own fire-side, and saying that things are going on well, because the rain does not beat on *him*, because *he* has books and leisure to read them (*PW*, pp. 52, 44; original emphasis)

In short, then, Shelley's early political statements repeatedly imply – however uncomfortably – that there may be no tenable middle ground between a largely ineffectual quietism and a violent revolutionary action: for all their gradualism, the *Proposals* recommend the 'annihilation' and 'extermination' of 'bigotry', while the *Address* confirms that 'truth and justice' will 'rise like a Phoenix' from 'the ruin of Governments' (*PW*, pp. 42–3, 35). This tension between quietism and revolution is central to Shelley's engagement with the discourse on the sublime in both *The Assassins* (1814) and *Alastor* (1815). But between these complex and uneven works, Shelley considerably refines the concept of the 'cultivated' imagination itself, thereby laying the foundations not only for his ongoing engagement with the discourse on the sublime, but also for the radical epistemology of the imagination that will find fullest expression – many years later – in the *Defence of Poetry*.

THE ASSASSINS: QUIETISM OR REVOLUTION?

Shelley began writing his unfinished short story, *The Assassins*, on the evening of 25 August 1814, during his stay in Switzerland with Mary and Claire (*MWSJ*, p. 17). Although it is not clear when he actually abandoned the project, Mary refers to it again as late as 8 April 1815 (*MWSJ*, p. 73). The story has not received a great deal of critical attention, and most commentators have been concerned with identifying Shelley's sources.[2] Historically, the Assassins were an eleventh-century Ismaili sect led by Hassan-ben-Sabbah, the original 'old man of the mountains'. They established their stronghold on Alamut in the mountains of Northern Iran, and were responsible for numerous terrorist attacks against both the Crusaders and the leaders of mainstream Sunni Islam. Hassan supposedly advocated intellectual freedom, encouraging advanced members of his sect to reject Islamic doctrine, read Greek philosophy, and accept their own reason as the final arbiter in any decision. He was also reputed to have created a pleasure-garden at Alamut, an earthly paradise where each Assassin could spend the last day before an attack (they were not expected to return). However, this legend more probably recalls the sect's actual use of hashish: the original Arabic name of the Assassins – of which the modern English word is a corruption – means the hashish-smokers. In 1256, the sect suffered a major defeat at the hands of the Mongol prince Hulago, grandson of Ghengis and brother of Kublai Khan; in 1270, it was finally crushed by Baybars I of Egypt.

In 1814, Shelley had two main sources of historical information about the Assassins: Gibbon's *History* and Delisle De Sales' 1799 novel, *Le Vieux de la Montagne*.[3] In the sixty-fourth chapter of his *History*, Gibbon decries the 'odious' Assassins as 'the enemies of mankind', and labels Hulago's 'extirpation' of the sect a 'service' (*D&F*, vii, p. 13). There is no mention of intellectual liberty here: Gibbon's Assassins are religious fanatics, whose 'blind obedience to the vicar of God' made them the 'daggers' by which Hassan's personal 'avarice' and 'resentment' were satiated (*D&F*, vii, p. 13).[4] *Le Vieux de la Montagne* essentially follows Gibbon in portraying the sect as the murderous dupes of the despotic Hassan: the Assassins are 'un peuple purement passif, instrument servile des volontés de son

Souverain'.[5] De Sales is highly critical of the sect's violence and proposes 'l'amour eternel' as the only viable basis of personal and political morality, an idea that would certainly have appealed to Shelley.[6] Equally, as Wu recognises, *Le Vieux de la Montagne* was clearly also intended as an allegorical comment on the Napoleonic invasion of Egypt in the previous year.[7] De Sales' Assassins are committed to liberating the Lebanon from the crusading French king, Louis XI. The novel focuses on a young Assassin named Ariel, whose relationship with the French Bouton-de-Rose brings him to reject violence and recognise the importance of 'eternal love'. Ariel clearly represents Bonaparte: he was born 'dans les îsles obscures de la mer intérieure', is described as 'à la fois petit et grand', and is even called 'Bonih-Phrath' in Egypt.[8] De Sales' point, then, is that Napoleon should eschew mere military and territorial conquest in favour of a kind of benevolent, or culturally liberating colonialism.

Clearly, there is much in De Sales' politicised treatment of the Assassins that one would expect to have struck a chord with Shelley: the gradualist emphasis on love and benevolence, the rejection of political violence, the implicit criticism of Napoleon, the overt critique of tyranny. However, while both De Sales and Gibbon criticise the sect's violence, Shelley wholly re-inflects the *meaning* of that violence. Far from being the murderous dupes of an avaricious despot, Shelley's sect is a revolutionary army, a society of 'tyrannicidal philanthropists'.[9] And Shelley makes it clear that the Assassins' 'singular and memorable' socio-political character is intimately bound up with the 'harrowing sublimity' of the mountain valley that they inhabit (*PW*, pp. 130, 128).

The surviving text of *The Assassins* breaks off after only the fourth chapter. The narrative opens with the flight of 'a little congregation of Christians' from Jerusalem on the eve of the Roman siege in AD 70 (*PW*, p. 124). As Murray notes, Shelley and Mary had been reading 'the description of the siege of Jerusalem in Tacitus' the day before Shelley began *The Assassins*, and this clearly provided the hint for the narrative's initial setting (*MWSJ*, p. 19; *PW*, p. 387). The focus on a 'congregation of Christians' seems somewhat odd at first glance, given Shelley's well-known antipathy to the religion (not to mention the fact that the historical Assassins were Islamic). However, while certainly critical of any *institutional* religion, Shelley always entertained a great deal of respect for Jesus himself, considered not as the Son of God, but as a visionary radical whose philanthropic teachings had been misinterpreted and misrepresented by the church. In February 1812, Shelley told Elizabeth Hitchener that he had 'often thought that the *moral* teachings of Jesus Christ might be very useful if selected from the mystery and immorality which surrounds them' (*Letters*, i, p. 265; emphasis added).[10] His contemporary *Address to the Irish People* confirms this confidence in the radical potential of Christ's message if applied and understood in a secular context, effectively aligning the 'moral teachings' of Jesus with the quietist gradualism of *Political Justice*. The *Address* condemns political and sectarian violence, stressing that 'anything short of unlimited tolerance, and complete charity with all men, on which you will recollect that Jesus Christ principally insisted, is wrong' (*PW*, p. 15). Any political action must, Shelley affirms, be characterised by 'the mildness of benevolence [a familiar Godwinian tag] which Jesus Christ recommended' (*PW*, p. 33).[11]

From the outset, the 'Christianity' of Shelley's Assassins conforms to this secular, politicised construction of the religion, echoing the intellectual liberty legendarily associated with the sect. Although they ostensibly acknowledge 'no laws but those of God', these 'laws' are in fact 'the doctrines of the Messiah concerning *benevolence* and justice for the regulation of ... actions', the same gradualist doctrines recommended by the Godwinian *Address* and *Proposals* (*PW*, pp. 124, 125; emphasis added). And notwithstanding their supposed religious denomination, Shelley's Assassins are also unequivocal rationalists. 'With the devoutest submission to the law of Christ', he writes, 'they united an intrepid spirit of enquiry as to the correctest mode of acting in particular instances of conduct that occur among men' (*PW*, p. 125). More specifically, 'they esteemed the human understanding to be the paramount rule of human conduct' (*PW*, p. 124). Consequently, this 'community of speculators' does not in fact accept the 'laws ... of God' on trust, but subscribes to them only in so far as they passed the test of individual reason (*PW*, p. 125). We are very close here to Godwin's philosophical anarchism: laws are just, and should be followed, only insofar as they are derivable from reason. Given these Godwinian credentials, then, it will come as no surprise to learn that Shelley's Assassins combine a materialist episteme with their rationalism: they reject any 'custom', 'institution', or 'doctrine' that cannot be substantiated by 'arguments derived from the nature of existing things' (*PW*, pp. 124–5). Most significant of all, however, at the point of their departure from Jerusalem, Shelley's Assassins also explicitly share Godwin's *quietism*: they are 'attached from principle to peace' (*PW*, p. 125).

The Assassins leave Jerusalem as the Roman armies arrive. During their residence in the city, Shelley confirms, they had been viewed with increasing 'contempt' by the 'magistracy and priesthood' (*PW*, p. 125). This 'contempt' echoes history's judgement of the Assassins as much as it does

Roman Judea's feelings about Christianity. But whereas both Gibbon and De Sales decry the Assassins on account of their *violence*, it is explicitly the *libertarian* ideals of Shelley's pacifist sect that excite the 'contempt' of the Jewish establishment. Though 'secure and self enshrined in the magnificence and pre-eminence of his conceptions', Shelley affirms, an Assassin 'would be the victim among men of calumny and persecution' (*PW*, p. 131). Hence, the sect leaves Jerusalem on the eve of the siege because 'they had arrived at that precise degree of eminence and prosperity which is peculiarly obnoxious to the hostility of the rich and powerful' (*PW*, p. 125). It would have been 'precarious' for them to remain in 'a city of the Roman Empire', Shelley concludes, whose 'narrow views and . . . sectarian patriotism would not have failed speedily to obliterate' them (*PW*, p. 125).

It is certainly possible to see biographical parallels between the Assassins' flight from persecution in Jerusalem and Shelley's own escape to the continent in 1814. Biographical resonance notwithstanding, however, it is also both tempting and possible to see analogies between the Assassins' situation in Jerusalem and Shelley's understanding of an 1814 British reform movement clearly in danger of being 'obliterated' by 'narrow views . . . and sectarian patriotism'. More specifically, then, given Shelley's already noted qualms about the viability of quietist gradualism in an age of extreme reaction, should we take the Assassins' self-preserving flight from persecution as an allegorical injunction in favour of more direct political action? Shelley's *Refutation of Deism* certainly links *Christian* quietism explicitly to the progress of tyranny. 'The doctrine of acquiescing in the most insolent despotism', he confirms, 'of praying for and loving our enemies; of faith and humility, appears to fix the perfection of the human character in that abjectness and credulity which priests and tyrants of all ages have found sufficiently convenient for their purposes' (*PW*, p. 105). If the Assassins' departure from Jerusalem is an anti-quietist statement, however, then the nature and implications of any alternative political action remain highly ambiguous. The history of the Assassins' departure from Jerusalem returns us directly to Shelley's uncertainty about the middle ground between quietism and revolutionism, and couches that uncertainty explicitly in the terms of his engagement with the discourse on the sublime.

The Assassins flee from Jerusalem to the 'solitudes of Lebanon', where they settle in the valley of 'Bethzatanai' (*PW*, pp. 125, 126). Their new home is unequivocally a landscape of the sublime: an 'awful desolation', filled with Volneyan 'piles of monumental marble and fragments of columns' – which 'spoke, even in destruction, volumes of mysterious import' – and surrounded by 'precipitous mountains' whose 'immensity' 'excluded the sun' (*PW*, pp. 126, 127). Shelley emphasises that the 'harrowing sublimity' of their new environment left 'indelible' 'impressions' upon the Assassins' 'social character', which was 'unalterably ... modelled and determined by its influence' (*PW*, p. 129). This 'influence' encapsulates both the claims and the ambiguities of his engagement with the discourse on the sublime.

Firstly, the sect abandons its former 'religious tenets' (*PW*, p. 130). 'The gratitude which they owed to the benignant spirit by which their limited intelligences had not only been created but redeemed', Shelley writes, 'was less frequently adverted to, became less the topic of comment or contemplation' (*PW*, p. 130). Instead, the Assassins 'learned to identify this ['benignant spirit'] with the delight that is bred among the solitary rocks' of their valley (*PW*, p. 150). In short, they exchange their former belief in a creator-God for a kind of pantheism: no longer the followers of Christ, they become 'the worshippers of the God of Nature' (*PW*, p. 125). This 'Spirit of Nature' – apprehended by the Assassins in the 'immediate and overpowering excitement' of their environment – 'became the unperceived law of their lives and sustenance of their natures' (*PW*, p. 130).

The change in the Assassins' 'religious tenets' returns us directly to Shelley's engagement with the discourse on the sublime. More precisely, that change follows the second Note to *Queen Mab* in rejecting the theistic configuration of the British discourse on the sublime: the idea that natural grandeur is evidence, by design, for the existence of a creator-God. The narrative voice of *The Assassins* recognises this reading of the natural sublime. 'No spectator', Shelley writes of Bethzatanai, 'could have refused to believe that some spirit of great intelligence and power had hallowed these wild and beautiful solitudes to a deep and solemn mystery' (*PW*, p. 128). Again, these lines encapsulate Alison's paradigmatic account of the imaginative response to the natural sublime: the defeat of the understanding prompts an *involuntary* ('no spectator could have refused') act of belief, an associative act of the imagination which reads the 'awful' landscape as the 'signs' and 'expressions' of 'deity'. However, *The Assassins* recognises this conventional discourse on the sublime only to call it into question. 'The *immediate* effect of such a scene', Shelley affirms, 'is *seldom the subject of authentic record*' (*PW*, p. 128; emphasis added). Such an 'authentic record', he continues, would acknowledge that even 'the coldest slave of custom cannot fail to recollect some few moments in which [such 'harrowing sublimity'] has awakened the touch of *nature*' (*PW*, p. 128; emphasis added). *Nature*, not God. Shelley's point, then, is that an 'authentic record' of the natural sublime would acknowledge that the experience – 'rightly' felt by an imagination freed from 'custom' – leads not to a belief in God, but rather to an apprehension of the 'Spirit of Nature'. And this 'Spirit of Nature' is, of course, *Queen Mab*'s eponymous Necessity: nature's amoral law.[12]

The Assassins thus follows *Queen Mab* in formulating a politically progressive revision of the pious discourse on the sublime. Not only does the sect's 'authentic', 'cultivated' (rationalist / materialist) response to its 'harrowing' surroundings convert the Assassins to a Necessitarian atheism. Rather it also leads to the establishment of a utopian republic that Shelley explicitly identifies as the 'practical result' of the Assassins' decision to take the Spirit of Nature revealed by their surroundings as the 'law of their lives' (*PW*, p. 130). Once again, the laws of nature – revealed in the landscape of the natural sublime – provide the blueprint for a radical revision of sociological and political 'custom'. In their natural 'republic', where 'each devoted his powers to the happiness of the other', the Assassins enjoy 'eternal peace', 'securely excluded' from the 'discord, tumult, and ruin' of the 'abhorred world' beyond the valley: Shelley's revisionist take on Hassan's legendary pleasure-garden at Alamut (*PW*, pp. 131, 130, 128).[13]

Shelley's utopian revision of the discourse on the sublime in *The Assassins* is rendered highly problematic, however, by his account of what would happen if the sect *was* to come into contact with the 'perverseness' of the world 'beyond the mountains' (*PW*, p. 131). The same Necessitarian 'Spirit of Nature' by which the Assassins' republican 'social character' was 'modelled and determined', he confirms, would oblige them to 'singular', 'memorable', and 'momentous' action if confronted with the 'calamities' of their 'fellow-men' (*PW*, pp. 130, 131). 'Can the power derived from the weakness of the oppressed or the ignorance of the deceived confer the right in security to tyrannise and defraud?', Shelley asks. 'The subject of regular governments and the disciple of established superstition dares not to ask this question', he affirms, moving close to his 1812 attacks on Godwinian gradualism: 'for the sake of the eventual benefit, he endures what he esteems a transitory evil' (*PW*, p. 132). But 'the religion of an Assassin imposes other virtues than endurance', he continues, in an increasingly open critique of quietism, 'when his fellow men groan under tyranny, or have become so bestial and abject that they cannot feel their chains' (*PW*, p. 132). Rather, the Assassins' newfound utilitarian ethic accepts that 'to produce immediate pain or disorder for the sake of future benefit is consonant ... with the purest religion and philosophy' (*PW*, p. 131). Accordingly, although explicitly 'against their [benevolent] predilections and distastes an Assassin accidentally the inhabitant of a civilised community, would wage unremitting hostility from principle' (*PW*, p. 131). 'No Assassin', Shelley continues, now directly echoing his critique of temporising politics in the *Address to the Irish People*, 'would submissively *temporise* with vice, and in cold charity become a Pandar to falsehood and desolation' (*PW*, p. 132; emphasis added). Rather, 'his path thro' the wilderness of civilised society would be marked with the blood of the oppressor and the ruiner. The wretch whom nations tremblingly adore would expiate in his throttling grasp a thousand licensed and venerable crimes' (*PW*, p. 132). In short, then, the Assassins' Necessitarian 'religion' of 'Nature' – 'modelled and determined' by their 'authentic' response to the 'harrowing sublimity' of their surroundings – would oblige them, if confronted by 'vice', to reject 'temporising', gradualist politics in favour of violent revolutionary action.

Shelley's *Assassins* would thus wholly re-inflect the meaning of the political violence historically associated with the sect. He would present that violence not as the product of a despot's struggle for power, but as the Necessary, violent assertion of natural equality in the face of oppression and – moreover – as the product of the 'authentic' response to the natural sublime. Reversing Gibbon's condemnation of the sect as the enemies of mankind, Shelley would (re)present the Assassins as 'merciful destroyer[s]' whose 'saviour arm' would kill the corrupt in order to facilitate the advancement of liberty (*PW*, p. 132). In place of the quietist, gradualist Christ whom the Assassins formerly followed, then, we have an image of the 'saviour' as a revolutionary who – following the 'law' of the nature – 'would cater nobly for the eyeless worms of Earth and the carrion fowls of Heaven' (*PW*, p. 132).

As long as the Assassins remain secluded in their valley, however – which they do for the entirety of the surviving text – their revolutionary potential remains inert. 'Courage and active virtue', Shelley affirms:

and the indignation against vice, which becomes a hurrying and irresistible passion slept like the imprisoned earthquake, or the lightning-shafts that hang <id>ly in the golden clouds of evening. They were innocent, but they were capable of more than innocence (*PW*, p. 133)

This account of the Assassins' dormant revolutionary potential aligns the impulse to political violence ('a hurrying and irresistible passion') directly with the affective response to the natural sublime, again confirming that the sect would be *obliged* to violence by the 'Spirit of Nature' upon which their society was 'modelled'. And indeed, by likening the sect's dormant revolutionary potential to 'awful' natural phenomena (the 'imprisoned earthquake' or charging 'lightning-shafts') Shelley figures the Assassins – in the most explicit possible terms – as the *agents* of Necessity. Violent revolution, these images imply, is itself an 'awful', *natural* phenomenon – an instance of the *natural* sublime. To return to *Queen Mab*'s terminology, 'all-sufficing nature can chastise / Those who transgress her law', and Shelley's Assassins would be the agents of this 'awful' chastisement (*Queen Mab*, iii, 82–3).

After all, Shelley clearly intended to narrate the activation of the Assassins' revolutionary potential in the unfinished section of his story. The penultimate chapter of the surviving text opens with the arrival of a stranger in the valley, who would almost certainly have been Shelley's version of Hassan-ben-Sabbah, the leader of the Assassins.[14] The stranger announces his intention to use the sect to 'ruin and destroy' some unspecified 'great Tyrant': 'I was thy slave', he exclaims, 'I am thine equal and thy foe. – Thousands tremble before thy throne who at my voice shall dare to pluck the golden crown from thine unholy head' (*PW*, p. 134).

On the face of it, these words recall Gibbon's already quoted account of the Assassins' as the passive instrument of Ben-Sabbah's personal 'avarice' and 'resentment'. However, the portrait of the stranger built up throughout *The Assassins* establishes a broader political context for his speech, albeit doing little to dispel its sinister overtones. The stranger is almost certainly the individual earlier identified as 'the author of [the Assassins'] felicity', the 'one being' whom 'tradition says was seen to linger' among the 'uninhabited' 'ruins of Jerusalem' after the siege (*PW*, pp. 133, 126). As Murray and others have noted, this 'being' clearly recalls *Queen Mab*'s Ahasuerus, or 'Wandering Jew' (*PW*, p. 388; *Queen Mab*, vii, 67–267; *Poems*, i, pp. 392–5). However, his presence among the ruins also makes it possible to see the Stranger as an echo of Volney's enlightening Genius of the Ruins, an association strengthened by the explicitly Volneyan meditation on 'the change of empires and religions' that follows his introduction (*PW*, p. 126; *Ruins*, i, p. 15). In any event, these meditations provide the only real indication of the Stranger's likely role in the text.

Shelley affirms that the 'change of empires and religions' depends 'not on the will of the capricious multitude, nor [on] the constant fluctuations of the many and the weak' (*PW*, p. 126). These 'fluctuations' are rather only 'the mere insensible elements from which a subtler intelligence moulds its enduring statuary' (*PW*, p. 126). 'They that direct the changes of this mortal scene breathe the decrees of their dominion from a throne of darkness and tempest', he concludes: 'the power of man is great' (*PW*, p. 126). Mary Shelley's journal provides the key to this otherwise somewhat obscure and overwrought account of the dynamics of political change: her entry for 23 August 1814 records that she and Shelley had been reading Barruel's *Memoirs* during the composition of *The Assassins* (*MWSJ*, p. 18; *Claire*, pp. 29–31, 49–50). Hence, Shelley's reference to the 'great' 'power' of those who 'direct the changes of this mortal scene' almost certainly echoes Barruel's conspiracy theories about the French Revolution: his claim that Masonic Illuminati had engineered the Revolution, and were continuing to promote political upheaval from their covert 'throne of darkness'. Indeed, as Dawson points out, Barruel tellingly suggests that these Illuminati readily countenanced the assassination of those responsible for 'public crimes which every wise and honest man would wish to suppress', a direct precedent for the Assassins' politically motivated violence.[15] Hence, the strong links between the Stranger who enters the Assassins' valley and Barruel's revolutionary Illuminati confirm that Shelley's Ben-Sabbah would not have been the self-serving despot condemned by Gibbon. Rather – as leader of the Assassins – he would have been the violent antithesis of a Godwinian steward, transforming the dormant sect into precisely the kind of revolutionary secret society that Godwin feared Shelley's *Proposals for an Association of Philanthropists* would establish in Dublin

The implication of the Stranger's arrival in Bethzatanai, then, is Shelley's conviction that the Assassins *need* to be awakened from their seclusion in the valley, that they *ought* to confront the 'unknown and unimagined' 'calamities' of the world 'beyond the mountains' (*PW*, p. 131). In other words, the value of their utopia is made conditional upon its extension onto a world-historical stage. 'Who hesitates to destroy a venomous serpent that has crept near his sleeping friend', Shelley asks, returning to his earlier critique of quietist gradualism, 'but the man who selfishly dreads lest the malignant reptile should turn its fury on himself?' (*PW*, p. 132). The Necessitarian 'religion' of the Assassins demands action in the face of the oppression of their 'fellow-men'; hence, as long as they remain unaware of that oppression, they are failing to fulfil the obligations imposed on them by the 'Spirit of Nature'. Far from being the seat of a reactionary tyrant, then, Shelley's Bethzatanai would become the staging-post of world reform, rehearsing on a much darker level his 1812 hope that reform in Ireland would be 'a flame that may illumine and invigorate the world' (*PW*, p. 28). And the *Six Weeks' Tour* confirms his sense of the propriety of a mountain valley as the base for such an endeavour. Speaking of Switzerland – the mountain valley where *The Assassins* was conceived – the *Tour* affirms that 'these sublime mountains ... seemed a fit cradle for a mind aspiring to high adventure and heroic deeds' (*H6WT*, p. 50). This was, after all, the landscape where William Tell 'matured the conspiracy which was to overthrow the tyrant of his country' (*H6WT*, p. 49).

Given Shelley's apparent confidence in the role of the Assassins as a naturally sanctioned revolutionary army, then, one might well ask why the story remains unfinished. Murray's claim that 'Shelley's millennial penchant for a happy ending would have restored the Assassins' domestic and social tranquillity' fails to recognise the tensions at the heart of the story – or, indeed, to explain in what sense that 'tranquillity' has been lost in the extant text (*PW*, p. 385). The answer is rather that by the end of the surviving text, Shelly had backed himself into a political corner. In other words, we are returned to his concern that there may be no middle ground between quietism and revolution, and again that concern is couched explicitly in the terms of his engagement with the discourse on the sublime. Either the Assassins remain comfortably secluded in their 'awful' valley or they follow the 'law' of their 'harrowing' surroundings and emerge to rid the world of tyranny and oppression. There is no middle ground – no viable alternative between quietism and revolution – and it seems likely that Shelley was either unable or unwilling to make the choice.

For all its political ambiguities, however, *The Assassins'* engagement with the discourse on the sublime does bear clearly upon Shelley's disillusionment with William Wordsworth in the wake of *The Excursion* (1814). After all, while Bethzatanai's utopia may have drawn upon Wordsworth's 'golden age of the Alps', Shelley's intended repudiation of the Assassins' seclusion would certainly have been a 'pointed correction' of the post-*Excursion* Wordsworth – though not, as Wu suggests, of Wordsworth's poem *per se*.[16] Mary's journal records that she and Shelley were 'much disappointed' with *The Excursion*, and labels Wordsworth himself 'a slave' (*MWSJ*, p. 25). Shelley's sonnet 'To Wordsworth' (published in the 1816 *Alastor* volume) explains the grounds for their 'disappointment': in the 'Preface' to this 'portion of *The Recluse*', Wordsworth announced that he had 'retired to his native mountains, with the hope of being enabled to construct a literary Work that might live' (*Wordsworth*, v, pp. 1–2). The work actually enabled by this 'retired' contemplation of 'mountains' was, of course, the highly conservative *Excursion* itself – by no means a defence of solitary retirement, but hardly likely to have been read by Shelley as (the product of) an 'authentic' or 'right' response to the natural sublime. Hence, Shelley's sonnet responds quite specifically to Wordsworth's prefatory announcement. By deciding to live in 'retired' contemplation of his 'native mountains', the 'Poet of Nature' was effectively 'deserting' his former concern with the promotion of 'truth' and 'liberty' in favour of a politically abortive stab at personal fulfilment ('To Wordsworth', 1, 12). The revolutionary emergence of the 'worshippers of Nature' from the seclusion of their mountain valley would indeed have been a resonant – if, again, highly problematic – 'correction' of this solipsistic response to the natural sublime.

IMAGINATION, MORALITY AND THE 'SCIENCE OF MIND': 1815

The Shelley party returned from mainland Europe in September 1814. Two months later, Shelley reviewed Hogg's latest novel, *The Memoirs of Prince Alexy Haimatoff* (1813), for the *Critical Review*.[17] Shelley gives the book suitably qualified praise, noting that it is 'far from faultless' (*PW*, p. 141). He emphasises, however, that he 'hardly ever remember[s] to have seen surpassed the subtle delicacy of imagination, by which the manifest distinctions of character and form, are seized and pictured' (*PW*, p. 141). This praise for the 'seizing' and 'picturing' ability of Hogg's imagination is expanded in terminology by now familiar from Shelley's exploration of the role of the imagination in the theistic configuration of the discourse on the sublime. Shelley confirms that 'the vulgar', who lack Hogg's 'subtlety' of imagination, 'observe no resemblances or discrepancies, but such as are gross and glaring' (*PW*, p. 141). In other words, Shelley's praise is informed by his now-familiar distinction between the 'vulgar' and the discerning, or 'cultivated' imagination. The latter, Shelley affirms, 'distinguishes genius from dullness' (*PW*, p. 141).

The review proceeds – albeit somewhat incongruously – to relate this notion of a discerning imagination directly to what Shelley calls 'the science of mind' (*PW*, p. 141). In fact, a discerning imagination emerges as the fundamental prerequisite for the successful practitioner of this 'science'. Shelley's idea of a 'science of mind' having 'history, poetry, biography' – that is, the products and records of the human mind – as its objects, was by no means an innovation (*PW*, p. 141). Conversely, as Timothy Clark points out, 'the notion of a science of mind analogous in method and certainty to the natural sciences had been a familiar one since the work of John Locke at the end of the seventeenth century'.[18] Contemporary philosophers like Thomas Reid and Dugald Stewart promoted the application of inductive (essentially Baconian) and experimental methods to the study of human nature in the hope of increasing the mind's knowledge of, and thereby command over, its own operations and abilities.[19] And in the radical tradition itself – and particularly within the perfectibilist thought of William Godwin – this nascent 'science of mind' was given an overtly political role as the basis for an attempt to formulate principles of morality akin in their universality to the laws of gravity discovered by Newton.[20]

In 1815, Shelley set out to formulate his own 'science of mind'. This attempt culminated in the 1819 essay *On Life*.[21] Initially, it produced the series of fragmentary and in many respects quite divergent – even on occasion contradictory – essays published by Mary Shelley in 1840 under the title *Speculations on Morals and Metaphysics*.[22] The ostensible aim of Shelley's 'science of mind' is set out in the fragment entitled 'What Metaphysics Are. Errors in the Usual Methods of Considering Them', which Timothy Clark rightly identifies as the 'manifesto' of the *Speculations*.[23] Like Reid and Stewart before him, Shelley placed millennial hopes in his projected conflation of metaphysics and psychology. 'That which the most consummate intelligences that have adorned this mortal scene inherit as their birthright', he enthuses, 'let us acquire (for it is within our grasp)' (*Prose*, p. 185).

What precisely is this 'birthright' that Shelley hopes to 'acquire'? The review of *Prince Alexy* identifies a 'subtle delicacy of imagination' as the mark of 'genius' (surely synonymous with 'consummate intelligence'), confirming that a cultivated imagination allows the mind to 'seize' and 'picture' the 'distinctions' that remain hidden from the 'vulgar'. Hence, if Shelley's 'science of mind' is indeed an attempt to 'acquire' the 'birthright' of 'consummate intelligence', then that 'science' must be an attempt to educate and refine – to *cultivate* – the imagination. Nor indeed – as will by now be obvious – was this attempt solely epistemological in its scope. Rather, in accordance with the radical appropriation of the 'science of mind', Shelley's project is inextricably linked to the promotion of 'virtue' and 'benevolence', progressive morality being a necessary, Godwinian attribute of 'consummate intelligence' (*Prose*, p. 187). In short, Shelley's 'science of mind' is a careful examination of the relationship between epistemology and ethics, an examination in which the 'seizing' and 'picturing' ability of the 'cultivated' imagination plays a central role. Hence, it would be difficult to overestimate the importance of this 'science' to Shelley's thought as a whole, and to his engagement with the discourse on the sublime in particular.

The first fragment of the *Speculations* – the 'Plan of a Treatise on Morals' – is an introductory statement of Shelley's premise and methodology. 'That great science which regards the nature and the operations of the human mind', he begins, 'is popularly divided into morals and metaphysics' (*Prose*, p. 182). 'Metaphysics', he continues, 'relates to a just classification and the assignment of distinct names to [the mind's] ideas' (*Prose*, p. 182). 'Morals' is attendant upon this 'classification' and 'assignment': it regards, Shelley writes in his 'Plan', 'simply the determination of that arrangement of [the mind's ideas] which produces the greatest and most solid happiness' (*Prose*, p. 182).[24]

Having thus established the distinction between 'morals' and 'metaphysics', Shelley's 'Plan' goes on to confirm that 'the design of this little treatise is restricted to the development of the elementary principles of morals' (*Prose*, p. 182). With that 'development' in mind, Shelley concludes, 'metaphysical science will be treated merely so far as a source of negative truth; while morality will be considered as a science respecting which we can arrive at positive conclusions' (*Prose*, p. 182).

As David Lee Clark points out in an editorial footnote to this section of the *Speculations*, Hume's *Enquiry Concerning the Principles of Morals* (1752) contains an approximately equivalent statement of scope and aim (*Prose*, p. 182 n. 3). Not surprisingly, then, Shelley's emphasis on the role of 'metaphysical science' as a source of 'negative truth' is informed by his rejection of materialism in favour of the sceptical philosophy formulated by Hume and defended against the attacks of the Common Sense school by Sir William Drummond.[25] *On Life* provides a clear account of the development of Shelley's philosophical thought from materialism to scepticism. Shelley confirms his early adherence to the materialist position, which he now recognises cautiously as 'a seducing system to young and superficial minds [which] allows its disciples to talk and dispenses them from thinking' (*Prose*, p. 173). *On Life* also confirms the – by now familiar – reasons for Shelley's early materialism. 'The shocking absurdities of the popular philosophy of mind and matter', he writes, 'its fatal consequences in morals, and their violent dogmatism concerning the source of all things, had early conducted me to materialism' (*Prose*, p. 173). Hence, again, Shelley's initial adherence to materialism was informed by its usefulness in combating prejudice or custom ('dogmatism'), and we have been tracing the consequent inseparability of the epistemological and political concerns of his early work.

The 'popular philosophy of mind and matter' that Shelley rejected in favour of materialism was unquestionably the Scottish Common Sense philosophy, without doubt *the* 'popular philosophy' of the early nineteenth century.[26] The principles of the Common Sense school were set out by Reid in his *Inquiry into the Human Mind, on the Principles of Common Sense*

(1764), an attempt to refute Hume's scepticism. Reid found notable followers in, amongst others, Archibald Alison, William Paley, and Dugald Stewart. Common Sense philosophy maintained an empirical dichotomy between 'mind and matter', in which external, objective reality was communicated accurately and immediately to the mind *via* the senses. In other words, Common Sense philosophy rejected what Reid called the 'ideal system': the theory, propounded by Hume and others, that the mind had no direct contact with reality but perceived rather *impressions* derived from the sensory experience of reality. Put differently, while Hume argues that the objects of perception are merely impressions of the world, Common Sense philosophy held that in perception the mind perceives the world directly, without any form of mediation.

The 'fatal consequences in morals' which Shelley attributes to the 'popular philosophy' refers to the conservative leanings of the Common Sense school, to its defence, as Shelley would see it, of custom and prejudice thinly veiled as 'common sense'. The 'dogmatism concerning the source of all things' that Shelley attributes to the school clearly bears upon these 'fatal' moral 'consequences' (and it is worth remembering that from its inception in classical Greece, the stated aim of scepticism was the refutation of 'dogmatism').[27] In an attempt to overcome Hume's critique of personal identity, Reid maintained that the idea of personal identity (along with other ideas incapable of being derived from sense-experience) was innate in the mind's design, placed there by a benevolent creator-God. Shelley's allegations of 'dogmatism concerning the source of all things' respond precisely to this kind of theological determinism.

The fragment entitled 'What Metaphysics Are. Errors in the Usual Methods of Considering Them' confirms Shelley's rejection of the 'popular' Common Sense philosophy. Shelley breaks off a general discussion of metaphysical 'errors' to level an explicit criticism at 'those who are accustomed to profess the greatest veneration for the inductive system of Lord Bacon' but who have nevertheless not 'adhered with sufficient scrupulousness to its regulations' (*Prose*, p. 185). This is clearly an attack on Reid's foremost disciple, Dugald Stewart, whose *Elements of the Philosophy of the Human Mind* (1792, 1814) is, as Clark points out, full of praise for Bacon's inductive method, which Stewart claims to follow.[28]

Shelley's stated rejection of both materialism and the 'popular philosophy of mind and matter' has long led critics to read the development of his philosophical thought as a transition from materialism to the idealism of Berkeley (a reading that informs that standard approach to the 'Shelleyan sublime').[29] Again, Pulos' *Deep Truth* is the seminal refutation of this view, demonstrating conclusively that Shelley abandoned materialism in favour of a sceptical epistemology derived from Hume and mediated through Drummond. One aspect of the sceptical basis of Shelley's 'science of mind' needs to be re-considered, however: namely, the importance that epistemological scepticism assigns to the 'seizing' and 'picturing' ability of the imagination. The extent of this importance is signalled in the fragment of the *Speculations* entitled 'How the Analysis Should be Carried On'. 'Most of the errors of philosophers', Shelley writes, 'have arisen from considering the human being in a point of view too detailed and circumscribed. He is not a moral and an intellectual – but also, and *pre-eminently* an imaginative being' (*Prose*, p. 186; emphasis added).

The later, Italian fragment included by Mary in the *Speculations* – entitled 'The Science of Metaphysics: The Mind' – sets out a solidly empirical framework for Shelley's 'science of mind'. 'It is an axiom in mental philosophy', the fragment begins, 'that we can think of nothing which we have not perceived' (*Prose*, p. 182). In other words, 'all knowledge [is] bounded by perception', and any ideas not apparently derived from the senses are 'no other than combinations which the intellect makes of sensations according to its own laws' (*Prose*, pp. 183, 182).

As David Clark confirms, the epistemology of 'The Science of Metaphysics' effectively re-states that set out by Hume in his *Treatise* and *Enquiries*, although in all fairness it reflects a broad spectrum of eighteenth-century empiricism (*Prose*, p. 182 n. 4). But while empiricism generally, and Common Sense empiricism in particular, argues that the mind perceives the world directly via the senses, Hume – as we have seen – claims that the mind does not perceive phenomenal reality itself, but only *impressions* of that reality derived from the senses. Hence, again, while the empiricist argues that the mind's perception of phenomenal reality is direct, the sceptic argues that perception is indirect, and hence the scope for doubt. The mind does not know the world *per se*, only its impressions of the world.

Accordingly, when Shelley affirms in his essay *On Life* that 'I am one of those who am [sic] unable to refuse my assent to the conclusions of those philosophers who assert that nothing exists but as it is perceived', he is stating his alignment with Humean scepticism and not – as David Clark implies – with Berkeleyan idealism (*Prose*, p. 173 and n. 4). Berkeley had denied the objective, extra-mental existence of the material world: the 'immaterialism' condemned by Shelley in his July 1812 letter to Godwin (*Letters*, i, p. 316). Shelley's essay *On Life* is similarly anti-idealist. 'That the basis of all things cannot be ... mind', he writes, 'is sufficiently evident' (*Prose*, p. 174). 'Mind', he continues, maintaining a sceptical-empiricist stance, 'as far as we have any experience of its properties, and beyond that experience how vain is argument! cannot create, it can only perceive' (*Prose*, p. 174).[30]

Hence, while idealism wholly denies the extra-mental existence of the material world, the sceptic merely argues that there is no possibility of knowing anything about that world (even the fact of its existence) directly – a subtle distinction, but a distinction nonetheless. Accordingly, Shelley's claim that 'nothing exists but as it is perceived' is informed by the sceptical (Humean) conviction that the mind can know nothing of the material world *per se*, but only *via* the impressions of that world derived from the senses. Hence, as Dawson puts it, Shelley's claim that 'nothing exists but as it is perceived' is not a claim 'that all things exist by being perceived, or that they only exist in so far as they are perceived' but rather an assertion that 'the manner in which all things exist is conditioned by the manner in which they are perceived'.[31] 'What Metaphysics Are' confirms that 'our knowledge, sensations, memory, and faith constitute the universe *considered relatively to human identity*' (*Prose*, p. 185; emphasis added).

The impossibility of perceiving the material world directly informs Shelley's conclusion – in the section of the *Speculations* entitled 'How the Analysis Should be Carried On' – that 'it imports little to enquire whether thought be distinct from the objects of thought' (*Prose*, p. 186). 'The use of the words *external* and *internal*, as applied to the establishment of this distinction', he writes, 'has been the symbol and the source of much dispute. This is merely an affair of words' (*Prose*, p. 186; original emphasis). *On Life* similarly affirms that 'the difference is merely *nominal* between those two classes of thought which are vulgarly distinguished by the names of ideas and of external objects' (*Prose*, p. 174; emphasis added). Moreover, *On Life* notes that 'the same thread of reasoning' undermines the concept of 'distinct individual minds' (*Prose*, p. 174). In one of the most discussed (and, paradoxically, misunderstood) passages of Shelley's prose, *On Life* concludes that:

The words *I, you, they* are not signs of any actual difference subsisting between the assemblage of thoughts thus indicated, but are merely marks employed to denote the different modifications of the one mind ... The words *I* and *you* and *they* are grammatical devices invented simply for arrangement, and totally devoid of the intense and exclusive sense usually attached to them (*Prose*, p. 174; original emphasis)

In *Shelley: a Critical Reading*, Earl Wasserman set the trend for reading these lines as evidence of Shelley's adherence to a 'monistic idealism that identifies the One Mind with Existence'.[32] However, seductive as such an idealist reading of the passage may seem, it clearly jars with the unequivocal scepticism of Shelley's 'science of mind' – in fact, it confuses Shelley's 'one mind' with Coleridge's pantheistic 'One Mind' (note Wasserman's silent capitalisation of the *o*). After all, only two paragraphs later, Shelley again affirms that 'the basis of all things cannot be . . . mind' (*Prose*, p. 174).

Accordingly, as Pulos points out, Shelley's 'one mind' certainly refers to 'something less' than 'the basis of all things'.[33] In fact, as Pulos first suggested, the 'one mind' is probably a psychological rather than a meta-physical concept.[34] Pulos usefully compares Jung's idea of a 'collective unconscious' but both Dawson and Timothy Clark have considerably refocused this suggestion.[35] While Dawson – incorrectly – accepts that Shelley's 'one mind' reflects Berkeley's philosophical idealism, he points out that it was probably Godwin's emphasis on Opinion in *Political Justice* that attracted Shelley to the Berkeleyan position.[36] Clark refines this suggestion even further, arguing that the 'one mind' is actually a reference to the 'public mind': the 'atmosphere of common opinion within which all think and act'.[37] The notion of the potentially determining influence of the 'public mind' on an individual mind is a recurrent feature of Shelley's work from 1815 onwards, that is from about four years before the reference to the 'one mind' in *On Life*.[38] The fragment of the 1815 *Speculations* entitled 'Moral Science' confirms that:

None is exempt indeed from that species of influence which affects, as it were, the surface of his being and gives the specific outline to his conduct. Almost all that which is ostensible submits to that legislature created by the general representation of the past feelings of mankind – imperfect as it is from a variety of causes, as it exists in the government, the religion, and domestic habits (*Prose*, p. 192)

Here, then, we have the full political resonance of Shelley's sceptical assertion that 'nothing exists but as it is perceived'. We are close to a (modern) notion of ideology ('that legislature created by the general representation of the past feelings of mankind'): public opinion, institutional ('government', 'religion') conventions determine our perception and understanding of reality.[39] The role of the imagination in shaping ('seizing' and 'picturing') – and thus possibly *re*-shaping – this 'legislature' becomes the fulcrum of Shelley's politicised epistemology, the epistemology that informs his engagement with the discourse on the sublime, and that finds fullest expression in his *Defence of Poetry*. Briefly put, while the 'vulgar' imagination is the agent of prejudice and superstition, of Burke's 'second nature', the 'cultivated' imagination can radically *re-imagine* the 'legislature' upon which society is premised. Indeed, the role of the 'cultivated' imagination consists precisely in this ability to re-imagine the reactionary 'legislature' enacted by the 'vulgar' imagination, a strategy reflected in Shelley's own revision of the pious discourse on the sublime.

Humean scepticism asserts the unknown and essentially unknowable nature of phenomenal reality. Nevertheless, Hume does allow the formulation of practical hypotheses about that reality. And, crucially, the agency of this formulation is the imagination. Through a process of association, the imagination enables the mind to go beyond mere sense-impressions towards the formulation of *ideas*: Shelley's 'combinations which the intellect makes of sensations according to its own laws' (*Prose*, p. 182). According to Hume, ideas such as causation, personal identity – and, most importantly, Necessity – are produced in this way: in short, they are products of the imagination, and reflect the way in which we perceive material reality more than anything about that reality *per se*.

For the Humean sceptic, in other words, the 'seizing' and 'picturing' imagination is the mind's primary ('pre-eminent') faculty, the mind's only putative means of knowing anything *about* the world. Hence, Shelley's definition of the 'human being' as 'pre-eminently an imaginative being'. 'Imagination', he confirms, 'or mind employed in prophetically [imaging forth] its objects is that faculty of human nature on which every gradation of its progress, nay, every, the minutest, change depends' – a clear anticipation of the *Defence* (*Prose*, p. 189).[40] Moreover, Humean scepticism implies that any knowledge we claim to possess over and above immediate sense-impression is the product of the imagination. In other words, any given ontology is an imaginative hypothesis about the nature of material reality, a convention or 'custom' that may or may not be correct.

This conclusion – always uncomfortably close to relativism – explains Shelley's observation, in *On Life*, that 'the relation of *things* remain unchanged by whatever system' one adopts to explain them (*Prose*, p. 174; original emphasis). It also explains his 1815 criticism of those 'philosophers' who have failed to recognise the centrality of the imagination to 'intellectual' and 'moral' issues. Indeed, Shelley's critique of Common Sense philosophy in 'What Metaphysics Are' turns precisely on the school's perceived failure to acknowledge the articulating role of the imagination (although Stewart, at least, pays considerable attention to other aspects of the faculty). 'They have professed', Shelley writes, 'to deduce their conclusions from indisputable facts', the 'facts' of so-called common sense (*Prose*, p. 185). But 'how came many of those facts to be called indisputable?', he asks. 'Their promises of deducing all systems from facts', Shelley concludes, 'have too often been performed by appealing in favour of these pretended realities to the obstinate preconceptions of the multitude', i.e., by appealing to *prejudice* (*Prose*, p. 185). This returns us to the allegations of 'dogmatism' levelled at the Common Sense school in *On Life*, to *Queen Mab*'s critique of 'custom' (*Queen Mab*, iii, 95–100). In short, Shelley recognises that the 'pretended realities' that philosophers like Reid and Stewart called common sense 'facts' are actually little more than conventions of the 'one mind' ('obstinate preconceptions of the multitude'), conventions moreover which Shelley saw to have (literally) 'fatal' moral and political 'consequences'. In other words, Shelley's critique of Common Sense philosophy is based on his awareness that what is called common sense is actually nothing more than the reactionary and superstitious 'legislature' enacted by the 'vulgar' imagination. 'What Metaphysics Are' confirms this awareness that the conventions, the 'obstinate preconceptions of the multitude', on which Common Sense philosophy is premised, are not rationally derived at all. Rather they are the products of the imagination. The passage concludes with an unfinished sentence, suggesting that these 'preconceptions' result from 'the most preposterous mistake of a name for a thing', Shelley's familiar terminology for the erroneous, metaphorical action of the 'vulgar' imagination (*Prose*, p. 185).

Shelley's 'science of mind' aims to reject the 'preposterous' and reactionary dogmatism of the 'popular philosophy' – we might as well say of the popular *imagination* – and to replace it with an epistemologically sound and ethically progressive 'principle'. This agenda explains the 'strict' scepticism of Shelley's 'science of mind', why he views metaphysics primarily as a 'source of negative truth' (*Prose*, p. 185). The fragment entitled 'The Science of Morals' confirms Shelley's awareness that the 'obstinate preconceptions' of the 'one mind', on which the 'popular philosophy' is based, are the products of the imagination rather than the reason. 'The misguided imaginations of men', he begins, 'have rendered the ascertaining of what *is not true* the principal direct service which metaphysical enquiry can bestow upon moral science' (*Prose*, p. 186). 'There is a mass of popular opinion', he continues (explicitly recalling the 'obstinate' ideological 'preconceptions' of the 'one mind'), 'from which the most enlightened persons are seldom wholly free':

[and] into the truth and falsehood of which, it is incumbent on us to inquire before we can arrive at any firm conclusions as to the conduct which we ought to pursue in the regulation of our own minds, or toward our fellow-beings (*Prose*, p. 186)

On Life similarly affirms that sceptical philosophy – the 'intellectual system' embodied in Drummond's *Academical Questions* – 'establishes no new truth, ... gives us no additional insight into our hidden nature, neither its action nor itself (*Prose*, p. 173). Rather, Shelley argues:

Philosophy, impatient as it may be to build, has much work yet remaining as pioneer for the overgrowth of ages. It makes one step towards this object: it destroys error and the roots of error. It leaves, what it is too often the duty of the reformer in political and ethical questions to leave, a vacancy. It reduces the mind to that freedom in which it would have acted but for the misuse of words and signs, the instruments of its own creation (*Prose*, p. 173)

Again, the emphasis here is on the reactionary effects of the 'vulgar' imagination (the 'misuse of words and signs'), effects that the sceptical philosopher must counteract. 'If we would see the truth of things', Shelley confirms, 'they must be stripped of this fallacious appearance' (*Prose*, p. 192). Accordingly, the primary function of 'metaphysical science' is, again, to 'make evident our ignorance to ourselves, and this is much' (*Prose*, p. 172). The role of the scepticism is the critique of dogmatism, the refutation of the 'obstinate preconceptions of the multitude', the 'education of error': the *cultivation of the imagination* (*Prose*, p. 174). Nor indeed is this an easy or a comfortable process. The sceptical argument that knowledge is a – potentially inaccurate – convention had already prompted Shelley to ask Hogg 'What am I to think of a philosophy which conducts to such conclusion?' (*Letters*, i, p. 380). *On Life* confirms explicitly that the 'Intellectual Philosophy has conducted us [to] that verge where words abandon us, and what wonder if we grow dizzy to look down the dark abyss of how little we know' (*Prose*, p. 174). Look down it we must, however, if we are to reform the reactionary 'preconceptions' of the 'one mind' and thereby lay the groundwork for a progressive morality. Hence, the sceptical 'science of mind' becomes itself a kind of discourse on the sublime, an enquiry into the 'dark abyss of how little we know'.

Beyond the role of metaphysics as a 'source of negative knowledge', as a sceptical critique of the 'preconceptions' of the 'vulgar' imagination, however, there remains the possibility for progress. If knowledge is convention – 'the universe considered relatively to human identity' – then the long-term task of the reformer is to reorient, to *re-imagine* the conventions informing the 'one mind' along politically and ethically progressive lines. Shelley's revision of the discourse on the sublime represents precisely such a project. Similarly, the sections of the *Speculations* dealing with ethics acknowledge the integral relationship between the development of 'moral science' and the cultivation of the imagination. To the sceptic, 'virtue' itself is 'a creation of the human mind, or, rather a combination which it has made according to elementary rules contained within itself of the feelings suggested by the relations established between man and man' (*Prose*, p. 189).

Unsurprisingly, then, Shelley's 'science of morals' attacks the supposedly revealed ethics of institutional religion: 'those diversified systems of obscure opinion respecting morals which, under the name of religions, have in various ages and countries obtained among mankind' (*Prose*, p. 190). Rather, in keeping with the sceptical bias of his 'science of mind', Shelley makes the 'seizing' and 'picturing' ability of the imagination the basis of moral action.

By 1815, the concept of the sympathetic imagination had long been a commonplace of British moral philosophy. Shelley was almost certainly familiar with Adam Smith's seminal formulation of the concept in his *Theory of Moral Sentiments* (1759), which Hogg mentions in his account of an 1811 visit to Shelley and Harriet.[41] However, Shelley could easily have come across the concept in a wide range of other sources, including Hume's *Treatise* and, indeed, Dugald Stewart's *Elements* and *Essays*, both of which place a great deal of emphasis on the imagination. As Dawson points out, however, the most likely source for Shelley's account of the connection between the imagination and moral action was William Hazlitt's 1805 *Essay on the Principles of Human Action*.[42]

The fragment of the *Speculations* entitled 'On Benevolence' contains many verbal and argumentative echoes of Hazlitt's 'important metaphysical discovery'.[43] However, while 'On Benevolence' clearly draws heavily on Hazlitt's account of the role of the imagination in moral action, Dawson does not sufficiently examine the extent to which Shelley and Hazlitt part company on the issue of disinterestedness. Both men locate the basis of moral action in the desire to promote pleasure and avoid pain, and both identify the imagination as the agency by which the mind enters into the concerns of another, via its figuration of the conditions of its future self. However, while Hazlitt's *Essay* aims to demonstrate that 'the human mind is naturally disinterested', Shelley argues that the 'seizing' and 'picturing' ability of the imagination – the basis of moral action – needs to be cultivated, and is therefore not the inevitable or natural possession of every mind.[44] 'The only distinction between the selfish man and the virtuous man', Shelley confirms, 'is that the imagination of the former is confined within a narrow limit, while that of the latter embraces a comprehensive circumference' (*Prose*, p. 189). Thus, again, the *cultivation* of the imagination is of paramount importance.

In the early life of the individual, Shelley affirms, the tendency to seek pleasure and avoid pain is largely self-regarding. 'The tendencies of our original sensations', he explains, 'all have for their object the preservation of our individual being' (*Prose*, p. 188). Hence, 'an infant, a savage, and a solitary beast is selfish, because its mind is incapable [of] receiving an accurate intimation of the nature of pain as existing in beings resembling itself' (*Prose*, p. 188). In other words, these 'original' selfish tendencies are 'passive' and 'unconscious' (*Prose*, p. 188). Accordingly, they can – and ought – to be overcome: 'in proportion as the mind acquires an active power', Shelley confirms, 'the empire of these tendencies becomes limited' (*Prose*, p. 188).

The mind's 'active power' is, of course, the imagination. Hence, Shelley's point is that the cultivation of this 'power' is vital to the development of moral sense, since a 'vulgar' or uncultivated imagination is the agent of prejudice and superstition. 'On Benevolence' accordingly emphasises that 'the imagination ... acquires *by exercise* a habit as it were of perceiving and abhorring evil, however remote from the immediate sphere of sensations with which that individual mind is conversant' (*Prose*, p. 189; emphasis added). This 'exercise' of the imagination is facilitated through 'familiarity with the finest specimens of poetry and philosophy' (*Prose*, p. 189). Thus – in an obvious swipe at Rousseauvian primitivism – Shelley affirms that 'the inhabitant of a highly civilised community will more acutely sympathise with the sufferings and enjoyments of others than the inhabitant of a society of a less degree of civilisation (*Prose*, p. 188). Again, this is true because the 'exercise' that the imagination requires is attendant upon the civilising process.[45]

'On Benevolence' accordingly concludes with the Godwinian claim that 'wisdom and virtue may be said to be inseparable and criteria of each other' (*Prose*, p. 189). 'Selfishness', Shelley affirms, repeating the swipe at Rousseau, is 'the offspring of ignorance and mistake; it is the portion of unreflecting infancy and savage solitude' (*Prose*, p. 189). 'Disinterested benevolence', conversely, 'is the product of a *cultivated imagination*': the imagination at the heart of Shelley's engagement with the discourse on the sublime and, now, the fulcrum of his politicised epistemology (*Prose*, p. 189; emphasis added). However, the connection Shelley makes between selfishness and 'savage solitude' does not merely bear upon Rousseauvian primitivism, now presented as another in-'authentic' imaginative response to nature. Rather, it also returns us to Shelley's 'correction' of Wordsworth in *The Assassins*. Nor indeed is this conflation accidental: in *Alastor* Shelley would soon re-assess the work of both Rousseau and Wordsworth – Romanticism's most famous 'worshippers' of Nature – and explain the shortcomings of their thought, explicitly, in terms of the failure of the imaginative response to the natural sublime.

ALASTOR: CRITIQUING THE 'SELFISH' IMAGINATION

It has long been customary to read *Alastor* in relation to the critique of Wordsworth in Shelley's eponymous sonnet (discussed above). Since Mueschke and Griggs first suggested that Wordsworth might be the 'prototype' of the poet-protagonist of *Alastor*, there has been a great deal of critical discussion about the precise nature of the poem's engagement with Wordsworth, and with *The Excursion* in particular.[46] This discussion has tended to read the poet-protagonist of *Alastor* as Shelley's corrective response to *The Excursion*'s misanthropic Solitary. However, this approach tends to miss the point of *Alastor*'s engagement with the 'poet of Nature'. After all, *The Excursion* itself is by no means a defence of the undeniable solipsism of the Solitary. Quite the contrary, in fact, since the poem narrates the efforts of the Wanderer and the Pastor to *convert* the Solitary from his disillusioned retirement and – significantly – to restore his faith. More specifically, then, if *Alastor* is to be read as a critique of *The Excursion*'s Solitary, then Shelley could actually be said to *endorse* Wordsworth's theme, although Mary's journal makes it clear that he, unsurprisingly, disliked the poem. In other words, to follow Blank in reading the poet-protagonist of *Alastor* as 'Shelley's version of *The Excursion*'s Solitary' is to see Shelley either misreading or merely rehearsing Wordsworth.[47] While this interpretation might fuel Bloomian arguments about literary influence, it does little to explain Shelley's engagement with the 'poet of Nature' in *Alastor*.

That said, Shelley's poem clearly does bear upon his disillusionment with Wordsworth in the wake of *The Excursion*, a fact that the numerous intertextual allusions alone would be sufficient to establish (although many of these are to the 1807 'Intimations of Immortality'). In the 'Preface' to *Alastor*, Shelley confirms that the poem 'is not barren of instruction to actual men', and he certainly had Wordsworth – rather than the fictional Solitary – in mind as he wrote (*Poems*, i, p. 463).[48] In 'To Wordsworth', published with *Alastor*, Shelley explains why he felt the 'poet of Nature' to be in need of such 'instruction'. Unsurprisingly, the grounds for *Alastor*'s engagement with Wordsworth are largely identical. 'To Wordsworth', we remember, criticised the 'Poet of Nature' for 'deserting' his former concern with the promotion of 'Truth' and 'Liberty' in favour of an attempt at personal aggrandisement, an attempt premised upon the 'retired' contemplation of the natural sublime (Wordsworth's 'native mountains'). Implicit in that criticism was Shelley's conviction that *The Excursion* – the work enabled by Wordsworth's retirement – hardly constituted an 'authentic' or politically progressive response to the natural sublime. *Alastor* expands and refines this critique, attacking both Wordsworth's self-serving retirement and the ideologically destructive product of that retirement. More precisely, *Alastor* presents Wordsworth's intellectual and political death ('thus having been, that thou shouldst cease to be') not only – in the terms of the *Speculations* – as a failure of the imagination, but as a failure, moreover, of the imaginative response to the natural sublime, to Wordsworth's 'native mountains' ('To Wordsworth', 14). This failure is the 'interesting situation of the human mind' of which – the 'Preface' informs us – *Alastor* 'may be considered as allegorical' (*Poems*, i, p. 462).

It is important to recognise, however, that *Alastor* does indeed explore a 'situation of the human mind' rather than merely describe an individual case study. In *Rousseau in England*, Edward Duffy justly emphasises the need for caution in attempting to identify *Alastor*'s poet-protagonist as any specific 'actual man', arguing that such an identification 'would be merely another fruitless overspecification of Shelley's theme'.[49] 'Instances and personalities are not the focus of Shelley's attention', Duffy affirms: rather he is 'seeking to define a generic morphology'.[50] Wordsworth was clearly an important 'prototype' of this 'morphology', Coleridge another. As Duffy points out, however, there was a further significant 'prototype' for *Alastor*'s poet-protagonist, a figure who would become immensely important in Shelley's thought, and whose 'savage' primitivism he had already criticised in the *Speculations*: Romanticism's other great 'worshipper' of Nature, Jean Jacques Rousseau.

The 'striking congruities' between Shelley's *Alastor* and Rousseau's *Rêveries of the Solitary Walker* (1783) have long been recognised.[51] Both works turn on an ultimately unresolved tension between what Duffy calls 'the powers of vision and the catastrophes of egotism', with Shelley again making the ultimate value of any personal 'vision' (a notion that we will need to refine here) conditional upon its being socialised.[52] Shelley was intensely interested in the *Rêveries* during the composition of *Alastor*, an interest clearly related to the concern with confessional autobiography that Clark identifies in the *Speculations*.[53] Mary's journal confirms that Shelley read the *Rêveries* in 1815, and Duffy establishes that he had set Claire a translation exercise from the book in the same year (*MWSJ*, p. 92).[54]

Despite this intense interest in the *Rêveries*, however, there is little hard evidence to suggest that Shelley was familiar with Rousseau's other writings. Conversely, although he quotes from *De l'Inégalité Parmi les Hommes* (1755) in the Notes to *Queen Mab*, Shelley's early appraisals of Rousseau read more like early nineteenth-century commonplaces than the product of any considered engagement. Take, for example, a May 1811 letter to Hogg which condemns 'the Confessions of Rousseau' as 'either a disgrace to the confessor or a string of falsehoods, probably the latter' (*Poems*, i, p. 365; *Letters*, i, p. 84).[55] On the other hand, the *Rêveries* were consistently published in joint-editions with the *Confessions*, and it is both tempting and possible to detect thematic and even apparent verbal similarities between *Alastor* and a work that must surely also have informed Shelley's sense of the political potency of confessional autobiography in his 'science of mind' essays.[56]

Whatever the extent of Shelley's first-hand familiarity with Rousseau's work may have been in 1815, however, *Alastor*'s engagement with Rousseau was almost certainly also premised upon Wollstonecraft's critique of Rousseau's *imagination* in her 1792 *Vindication of the Rights of Woman*, which Shelley read in August 1812 (*Letters*, i, p. 319). Discussing 'the opinions speciously supported, in some modern publications on the female character and education', Wollstonecraft singles out Rousseau's *Émile* (1762) for especial condemnation – and it may be interesting to note, in this regard, that Claire had been reading *Émile* during the Shelleys' stay in Switzerland in 1814.[57] Speaking of Rousseau himself, Wollstonecraft affirms that:

all [his] errors in reasoning arose from sensibility ... When he should have reasoned he became impassioned, and reflection inflamed his imagination instead of enlightening his understanding ... he debauched his imagination, and reflecting on the sensations to which fancy gave force, he traced them in the most glowing colours, and sunk them deep into his soul.

He then sought for solitude, not to sleep with the man of nature; or calmly investigate the causes of things under the shade where Sir Isaac Newton indulged contemplation, but merely to indulge his feelings.[58]

Wollstonecraft's critique rehearses materialist / empiricist suspicions about the dangers of excessive sensibility, of imagination unrestrained by reason – the same suspicions marking Shelley's early engagement with the discourse on the sublime (it is only fair to say, too, that she draws heavily on aspects of Rousseau's own self-portrait in the *Confessions*). And again – given the popular (Burkean) account of Rousseau's instrumental role in the French Revolution – these epistemological concerns have overtly political implications. Indeed, Shelley's own warning about the 'hazard and horror of Revolutions' in his *Proposals* notes of Rousseau that he 'gave licence by his writings, to passions that only incapacitate and contract the human heart: – so far hath he prepared the necks of his fellow-beings for that yoke of galling and dishonourable servitude, which at this moment, it bears' (*PW*, p. 52). We are thus returned to Shelley's uncertainty about the politics of the imagination, and – given Rousseau's official, post-revolutionary status as the 'homme de la nature et de la verité' – of the imaginative response to natural sublime in particular.[59] The failure of this response is, again, the 'interesting situation' allegorised by *Alastor*.

The first paragraph of *Alastor*'s 'Preface' provides an approximate and important *précis* of the plot – although, as has long been noted, there are some significant divergences between the 'Preface' and the body-text *per se*. *Alastor* is the story of a 'youth' of 'uncorrupted feelings' who is 'led forth by an *imagination inflamed and purified* through familiarity with all that is excellent and majestic, to the contemplation of the universe' (*Poems*, i, p. 462; emphasis added). His initial 'contemplation' of the natural sublime – the 'magnificence and beauty of the external world', of 'objects ... infinite and unmeasured' – leaves him 'joyous, and tranquil, and self-possessed' (*Poems*, i, p. 462). Eventually, however, 'these objects cease to suffice' (*Poems*, i, p. 462). The youth's 'mind is at length suddenly awakened and thirsts for intercourse with an intelligence similar to itself' (*Poems*, i, p. 462). In response to this 'thirst' he 'images to himself the Being whom he loves' (*Poems*, i, p. 462). This 'vision in which he embodies his own imaginations unites all of wonderful, or wise, or beautiful, which the poet, the philosopher, or the lover could depicture' (*Poems*, i, p. 462). The youth – now called a 'Poet' – 'seeks in vain for a prototype of his conception' (*Poems*, i, pp. 462–3). Failing to find one, 'he descends to an untimely grave' (*Poems*, i, p. 463).

Alastor thus centres on the dramatic and eventually fatal change in the poet-protagonist's attitude to *nature*: the moment when the 'contemplation' of the natural sublime 'ceases to suffice'. This change – its origin and consequences – is the 'situation' allegorised in the poem and, again, Shelley presents it explicitly as a failure of the imagination. Hence, the 'Preface's claim that the poet-protagonist's 'imagination' has been 'inflamed' and 'purified' is of paramount importance to any account of the poem.

The notion of an 'imagination' 'purified through familiarity with all that is excellent and majestic' – through 'familiarity', in the terms of the *Speculations*, with the 'finest specimens of poetry and philosophy' – returns us at once to the terminology of Shelley's engagement with the discourse on the sublime. *Alastor*'s body-text confirms that from 'infancy', the poet-protagonist has been 'nurtured' by both the 'choicest impulses' of nature and 'the fountains of divine philosophy', an echo of Wordsworth's account of the Wanderer's education in the first book of *The Excursion* (*Alastor*, 68,

70, 71). Hence, the protagonist undoubtedly bears out Shelley's confidence in the ability of the 'cultivated' or 'purified' imagination to 'seize' politically potent truths from the landscape of the sublime. Witness, for example, his reaction to ruin in lines 107–28, an episode that draws heavily – and unsurprisingly given the context – on Volney. 'Obedient to high thoughts', *Alastor* affirms, the poet-protagonist 'visited / the awful ruins of the days of old' (*Alastor*, 108–9). His extensive tour culminates in the 'desert hills' of 'dark Aethiopia' (*Alastor*, 115). 'Among the ruined temples there', the poem continues:

> Stupendous columns, and wild images
> Of more than man, where marble daemons watch
> The Zodiac's brazen mystery, and dead men
> Hang their mute thoughts on the mute walls around,
> He lingered, poring on memorials
> Of the world's youth, through the long burning day
> Gazed on those speechless shapes, nor, when the moon
> Filled the mysterious halls with floating shades
> Suspended he that task, but ever gazed
> And gazed, till meaning on his vacant mind
> Flashed like strong inspiration, and he saw
> The thrilling secrets of the birth of time
>
> (*Alastor*, 116–28)

These lines, which appropriately echo the researches of the Napoleonic savants sent to Egypt in 1798, describe a quintessentially Volneyan – and indeed by now Shelleyan – situation, with the poet-protagonist seeking to learn the 'thrilling secrets' of 'mute' / 'speechless' ruin.[60] In keeping with Shelley's revision of the discourse on the sublime – and in a reprise of the Assassins' revolutionary interpretation of Bethzatanai's ruins – the poet-protagonist's 'purified' 'imagination' enables him to learn these 'secrets'. And indeed, the 'secrets' that he learns are also lifted straight from Volney. The key to this borrowing is the reference to the 'Zodiac' in line 119, where Shelley doubtless alludes to the famous Zodiac discovered by Napoleon's savants at the temple of Denderah in Upper Egypt ('Aethiopia').[61] In the twenty-second chapter of *The Ruins*, Volney locates the 'origin' of 'religious ideas' in primitive man's anthropomorphic reaction to natural grandeur, an idea now familiar from Shelley's engagement with the theistic configuration of the discourse on the sublime (*Ruins*, ii, p. 61). However, Volney singles out the 'Worship of the Stars' as a particularly important source of these 'ideas', arguing that the 'filiation' of 'religious' imagery stems from its common-source in the constellations (*Ruins*, ii, pp. 77, 61).

Volney proceeds to suggest that by comparing primitive Zodiacs (such as Denderah's) with scientific theory about equinoctial precession, one could date the '*birth*' of the 'first principles' of religion to 'about 17,000 years ago' (*Ruins*, ii, p. 84 and n.; emphasis added). Given the clear verbal and thematic echoes here, the radical 'secret' that the poet-protagonist learns from the Ethiopian temple is undoubtedly the origin of religious belief – '17,000 years ago' (at 'the birth of time') in the 'worship of the stars'.[62]

This successful and politically potent interpretation of the 'secrets' of 'mute' ruin confirms the extent to which – in the terms of Shelley's engagement with the discourse on the sublime – the poet-protagonist's 'imagination' has been 'purified' by the 'fountains of knowledge', a purification that explains the sympathy expressed by both the 'Preface' and body-text in relation to his subsequent fate (*Poems*, i, p. 462). And indeed this sympathy reflects, in turn, the fact that whatever their respective personal shortcomings might have been, the achievements of Wordsworth, Rousseau, and Coleridge – the major prototypes for the poet-protagonist – were not such as could or should be easily written off.[63]

For all his undoubted achievements, however, *Alastor* makes it clear that there is a problem with the poet-protagonist's imaginative response to 'objects . . . infinite and unmeasured'. It has long been customary to assume that *Alastor* condemns the poet-protagonist on account of his solipsism. This assumption is broadly speaking correct, although again the terms of that condemnation are far from unequivocal. The problem with the poet-protagonist's imagination can best be approached through the Narrator who tells his story – and whom we should be wary of too readily identifying with Shelley.[64] The Narrator's relationship to nature functions as the norm in *Alastor*, the standard from which the poet-protagonist departs. However, we need to recognise that the Narrator's relationship to nature is not perfect either. Rather, the poet-protagonist is praise-worthy – and deserving of sympathy – to the extent that his relationship with nature is more 'cultivated' than the Narrator's, and culpable insofar as that relationship – for all its cultivation – is largely self-regarding.

In *Alastor*'s – heavily Wordsworthian – opening invocation, the Narrator aligns himself with 'Earth, ocean, air, beloved brotherhood' in a pantheistic appeal to 'our Great Mother', an alignment which explicitly recalls *Queen Mab*'s invocation of Necessity as the 'mother of the world' (*Alastor*, 1–2; *Queen Mab*, vi, 198; *Poems*, i, p. 375). To begin with, the poet-protagonist shares the Narrator's Wordsworthian 'natural piety', the equivalent of the Assassins' Necessitarian 'religion' of nature (*Alastor*, 3). This is the standard from which he will later depart. The Narrator 'cherishes' the 'bird, insect, or gentle beast' as his 'kindred' (*Alastor*, 13, 15). To begin with, the poet-protagonist is similarly at 'home' in the 'wild' (*Alastor*, 99).

The Narrator's initial invocation describes how he too sought for meaning in Nature, gazing 'on the depth of [its] deep mysteries' and 'hoping' to learn the 'tale / Of what we are', an inquiry echoing not only Shelley's 'science of mind', but also the 'philosophical poem, containing views of Man, Nature, and Society' proposed by Wordsworth in the 'Preface' to *The Excursion* as the product of his 'retired' contemplation of his 'native mountains' (*Alastor*, 23, 26, 28–9; *Wordsworth*, v, p. 2). However, the Narrator's methods have been at best pseudo-scientific, and at worst downright superstitious: he seeks his answers in Gothic landscapes, and alludes to both necromancy and alchemy, disciplines echoed in the researches of Victor Frankenstein (*Alastor*, 23–4, 31). However, while the Narrator never gets an answer to his 'obstinate', Wordsworthian 'questions' ('ne'er yet / Thou [i.e. nature] hast unveiled thy inmost sanctuary'), he learns 'enough' from his researches both to recognise and to 'serenely' *accept* his 'kindred' relationship to the 'Great Parent' (*Alastor*, 26, 37–8, 39, 41, 45).

The poet-protagonist shares the Narrator's desire to understand nature's 'deep mysteries'. The 'Preface' tells us that he 'drinks deeply of the fountains of knowledge, and is still insatiate' (*Poems*, i, p. 462). He then turns to 'the magnificence and beauty of the external world', actively seeking out the natural sublime:

> ... Nature's most secret steps
> He like her shadow has pursued, where'er
> The red volcano overcanopies
> Its fields of snow and pinnacles of ice
> With burning smoke, or where bitumen lakes
> On black bare pointed islets ever beat
> With sluggish surge, or where the secret caves
> Rugged and dark, winding among the springs
> Of fire and poison, inaccessible
> To avarice or pride, their starry domes
> Of diamond and of gold expand above
> Numberless and immeasurable halls,
> Frequent with crystal column, and clear shrines
> Of pearl, and thrones radiant with chrysolite.
> Nor had that scene of ampler majesty
> Than gems or gold, the varying roof of heaven
> And the green earth lost in his heart its claims
> To love and wonder

(*Alastor*, 81–98)

Like the young Narrator, then, *Alastor*'s poet-protagonist seeks out 'objects ... infinite and unmeasured' in the hope of understanding nature's 'deep mysteries', confirmation of Shelley's conviction that the landscape of the sublime has potent 'secrets' to teach. And because his 'imagination' has been 'purified' by the 'fountains of knowledge', he avoids the narrator's quasi-religious approach and does indeed gain some insight into 'the tale of what we are' – witness, again, the 'thrilling secrets' that he learns from the temple of the Zodiac ('the varying roof of heaven'). To this extent, then, his progress is perfectly in accord with Shelley's revision of the discourse on the sublime, and thereby deserving of respect. The over-riding problem, however, is that the poet-protagonist's politically potent 'inspiration' remains fundamentally unsocialised, a shortcoming exemplified in his total neglect of the 'Arab maiden' who tends him during his wanderings.[65] And again, *Alastor* presents this failure, explicitly, as a dysfunction of the imagination.

In order to understand this dysfunction we need to return to the second attribute of the poet-protagonist's imagination: the fact that it is 'inflamed'. The term clearly invokes the idea of an unhealthy 'enthusiasm', and *Alastor* certainly gives the impression that the poet-protagonist's thirst for 'objects ... infinite and unmeasured' is motivated as much by the stimulation of 'love and wonder' as by a more intellectually respectable desire to learn 'the tale / Of what we are'.[66] In other words, 'so long as it is possible for his desires to point towards objects ... infinite and unmeasured, he is joyous, and tranquil, and [significantly], *self-possessed*' (*Poems*, i, p. 462; emphasis added). However, the term 'inflamed' also carries clear sexual connotations: Johnson's *Dictionary*, for example, defines 'to inflame' as 'to kindle desire', 'to fire with passion'.[67] Given these overt sexual connotations, the poet-protagonist's 'inflamed' imagination returns us at once to Wollstonecraft's critique of Rousseau in her *Rights of Woman*, specifically to her claim that the 'man of nature' '*inflamed*' and '*debauched* his imagination', and 'sought for solitude, not to ... calmly investigate the causes of things ... but merely 'to indulge his feelings'.[68] *Alastor*'s poet-protagonist commits a largely similar 'debauch' of the 'imagination', a 'debauch' encapsulated in the much-discussed episode of the 'Arab maiden' and the 'veilèd maid' (*Alastor*, 129, 151).

Appropriately, then, it is at the precise moment when the poet-protagonist's 'contemplation' of 'objects ... infinite and unmeasured' 'ceases to suffice' that he 'thirsts for intercourse [doubtless an intentional pun] with an intelligence similar' to himself. His downfall stems from the solipsistic manner in which he attempts to resolve this 'thirst' through a 'vision' of his 'imagination' (*Poems*, i, p. 462). Ignoring the 'Arab maiden' who has been tending him, the 'Preface' confirms – in a passage laden with anthropomorphic and autoerotic ('self-possessed') overtones – that 'he *images to himself* the being that he loves' in a 'conception' that 'unites the sublimest and most perfect natures' (*Poems*, i, pp. 462–3; emphasis added). The bodytext fills in the details of this 'dream', which takes the form of a 'veilèd maid': a beautiful poetess who sings about 'Knowledge and truth and virtue ... / And lofty hopes of divine liberty' (*Alastor*, 158–9). The Narrator confirms that these 'thoughts' were 'the most dear' to the poet-protagonist – and, we might add, to Shelley himself, to Rousseau, and to the pre-*Excursion* Wordsworth (*Alastor*, 160). The poet-protagonist's union with this visionary 'maid' – in a kind of wet dream – is the key to his downfall: unable to find a 'prototype' of his 'conception' in the real world, he dies broken-hearted.

The psycho-sexual dynamics of the 'veilèd maid' episode have been well documented – by Thomas Weiskel, for example – and I want to explore rather the literary and political resonance of the incident, not least since this resonance feeds directly into Shelley's engagement with the discourse on the sublime.[69] The poet-protagonist's vision of the 'veilèd maid' effectively 'allegorises' Wordsworth's 'retired' contemplation of his 'native mountains' in the hope of being 'enabled', thereby, to write a 'Work that might live', a self-serving ambition, however instructive the 'Work' itself might prove to be. It is certainly no accident, then, that the poet-protagonist's 'debauch' of his 'imagination' culminates in an increasingly self-destructive *excursion*, a journey towards a death-scene borrowed directly from *The Excursion* itself: a telling comment on Wordsworth's own moral and intellectual death.[70] In fact, the poet-protagonist's vision eroticises *nature*: an echo of Wollstonecraft's attacks on Rousseauvian solipsism, and a clear anticipation of Shelley's 1819 account of the 'moral eunuch' Wordsworth's desire to 'touch the hem of Nature's shift' but not 'uplift' her 'all-concealing tunic' (*Peter Bell the Third*, 314–7). Put differently, the 'veilèd maid' represents a solipsistic, self-regarding – and ultimately self-destructive – response to the natural sublime at the expense of the social sympathy available through the 'Arab maiden', the egoistic sublime of a 'recluse' encapsulated in both the *Rêveries* and the 'Preface' to *The Excursion*. In other words, she represents an unsocialised ideology of the natural sublime, an affective response to natural grandeur that avoids primitivism but seeks to make the experience a self-gratifying end in itself, a seductive 'Lethe' that prefers 'selfish peace' to the socio-political responsibilities imposed by nature's Necessitarian law.[71]

The solipsistic desire for nature-as-Lethe embodied in the poet-protagonist's dream of the 'veilèd maid' marks his abnegation of 'kindred' responsibility in nature's 'brotherhood' (just as it does Wordsworth's 'desertion' of 'Truth' and 'Liberty', and Rousseau's love of solitude), a responsibility which the Narrator – by contrast – has learned to recognise and accept.[72] Accordingly, in the wake of his dream, the poet-protagonist's relationship with nature is immediately altered. The 'scene', previously replete with 'meaning', now seems 'empty' (*Alastor*, 201). He is homeless in a landscape that ironically no longer 'echoes' his 'thoughts', alone in the 'wild' that was once explicitly his 'home' (*Alastor*, 290, 99). His relationship to nature – previously pantheistic – is now egoistic and anthropomorphic: 'O stream! / ... Thou imagest my life' (*Alastor*, 502–5). This self-imposed, albeit unwitting exile from nature's 'beloved brotherhood' (the 'bright flowers departed' from his 'steps') – this solipsistic *state of mind* – is *Alastor*'s sub-titular 'spirit of solitude', the cause of the poet-protagonist's 'speedy ruin' (*Alastor*, 536–7; *Poems*, i, p. 463).[73]

In sum, then, the poet-protagonist's quasi-Wordsworthian attempt to learn the 'tale / Of what we are' is noble enough in itself: in the terms of *Alastor*'s 'Preface', he is motivated by a 'sacred thirst of doubtful knowledge' (*Poems*, i, p. 463). To put it another way, the poet-protagonist rejects a Godwinian 'things as they are' in favour of a progressive vision – prompted by 'objects ... infinite and unmeasured' – of 'knowledge and truth and virtue ... / And ... divine liberty', but this vision remains essentially (and tragically) unrealised. Hence, again, his condemnation is equivocal.[74] More precisely, though condemned, he is to be distinguished from the 'morally dead', from 'those meaner spirits' whom *Alastor*'s 'Preface' identifies as 'loving *nothing* on this earth, and cherishing *no* hopes beyond': the 'unforeseeing multitudes who constitute, together with their own, the lasting misery and loneliness of the world' (*Poems*, i, p. 462; emphasis added). Again, the poet-protagonist's shortcoming is rather the *means* by which he pursues his 'sacred thirst': he is 'duped by an *illustrious* superstition', *Alastor*'s 'Preface' affirms, into a '*generous* error' (*Poems*, i, p. 463).

The phrase 'generous error' is purposefully ambiguous: does 'generous' *qualify* the magnitude of the 'error' (i.e. imply reduced culpability) or indicate its *scope* (i.e. a large error). Again, both senses are appropriate. However, the concomitant idea of an '*illustrious* superstition' certainly confirms the extent to which the poet-protagonist's fate is played out within the terms of Shelley's engagement with the discourse on the sublime. His 'purified' imagination avoids the *vulgar* superstition which characterised the Narrator's early relationship with nature, but his 'inflamed' solipsism – exemplified in his self-gratifying pursuit of an eroticised nature at the expense of the 'Arab maiden' – leaves him no less culpable of transgressing the laws of the 'Great Parent'. To return to the terminology of *Queen Mab*, then, 'all-sufficing Nature can chastise / Those who transgress her law', and the poet-protagonist's 'generous error' is – almost paradoxically – avenged by the same Necessitarian 'Power' that he eroticises in his vision of the 'veilèd maid' (*Queen Mab*, iii, 80–3; *Poems*, i, p. 462). In the terms of 'On Leaving London for Wales', his 'selfish', Lethean response to nature transgresses his natural obligations to his 'fellow-men', and for this transgression he is ironically (self-)condemned to a frustrated loneliness. He ignores his place in nature's 'brotherhood' and – again paradoxically – dies from this, albeit unwittingly self-imposed lack of companionship. 'Among those who attempt to exist without human sympathy', *Alastor*'s 'Preface' affirms, 'the pure and tender-hearted perish through the intensity and passion of their search after its communities' (*Poems*, i, p. 462).[75]

Alastor accordingly returns us to Shelley's ongoing concern about the politics of the imaginative response to the natural sublime. The poet-protagonist's fate 'allegorises' and explores the dysfunction of that response. Wordsworth provided Shelley with one telling example of this failure, Rousseau another.[76] Wordsworth's solipsistic desire to live in 'retired' contemplation of his 'native mountains' – a 'desertion' of his socio-political obligations as the 'Poet of nature' – had culminated in the largely conservative *Excursion*; Rousseau's erotic excesses – the enthusiastic 'debauch' of the 'man of nature and truth' – had led indirectly to the debacle of the Revolution. We are thus returned to Shelley's concern – first formulated in 'On Leaving London for Wales' – that there may no viable middle ground between a quietist (and potentially reactionary) and a revolutionist response to the landscape of the sublime.

Less than a year after the completion of *Alastor*, Shelley made a further concerted effort to overcome this tension: *Mont Blanc*, his most famous statement about the natural sublime, which draws together the threads of his early engagement with the British discourse on natural grandeur. The result is a powerful and convincing revision of the conventional 'records' of the Alpine sublime, a revision ironically owing no small amount to one Jean-Jacques Rousseau.

CHAPTER 3

Mont Blanc and the Alps, 1816

On 3 May 1816, Shelley, Mary, and Claire sailed out of Dover *en route* to Switzerland for a second time. Financial and personal motives lay behind the trip. After months of financial wrangling, Shelley certainly wanted to leave London. It seems that his choice of Switzerland was influenced at least in part by Claire's desire to follow Byron, with whom she had been involved for some weeks (Byron had already left for Switzerland on 23 April, following the receipt of his separation papers).[1] The Shelley party would spend the next three months – in the company of Byron – amidst 'scenery of wonderful su{blimity}' on the shores of Lake Geneva (*Letters*, i, p. 475). Shelley and Byron would spend a week sailing around the lake together, visiting Chillon, Lausanne, Meillerie, and Clarens. And shortly before their return to England in August, Shelley, Mary, and Claire would visit the 'famous valley' of Chamonix and see, 'towering far above, in the midst of its snowy Alps, the majestic Mont Blanc' itself (*Letters*, i, p. 494; *H6WT*, p. 94).[2]

Shelley's initial reaction to this 'magnificent valley' was 'astonishment' and 'dizzying wonder' (*Letters*, i, pp. 494, 495, 500). He told Byron that Chamonix 'exceeds and renders insignificant all that [he] had seen before' (*Letters*, i, p. 494). To Peacock he described 'mountains whose immensity staggers the imagination' (*Letters*, i, p. 496). 'I never knew I never imagined what mountains were before', he continued, 'the immensity of these aerial summits excited, when they suddenly burst upon the sight, a sentiment of extatic wonder, not unallied to madness' (*Letters*, i, p. 497).

Shelley's undoubted enthusiasm – I use the word deliberately – for the Savoyard landscape is distinctly qualified in the terms of his early revision of the discourse on the sublime. The old materialist connection between the affective response to natural grandeur ('a sentiment of ecstatic wonder') and the irrational ('not unallied to madness') is clearly present here. Shelley had already tellingly acknowledged to Peacock the difficulty of satisfying his friend's interest in the 'details of all that is majestic or beautiful in nature' (*Letters*, i, p. 495). 'How shall I describe to you the scenes by which I am now surrounded', he asked, 'to exhaust epithets which express the astonishment and admiration … is this to impress upon your mind the images which fill mine now, even until it overflows?' (*Letters*, i, p. 495). There is more to this concern than merely the inexpressibility trope – another commonplace of the discourse on the sublime – discerned by Paul Endo, although that trope was certainly an important part of Shelley's reaction to the Alps.[3] Rather, Shelley's remarks must be seen as expressing dissatisfaction with the conventional discourse on the sublime, that discourse which had failed – as he put it in *The Assassins* – to provide an 'authentic record' of the 'immediate effect of such a scene' (*PW*, p. 128). This dissatisfaction is immediately apparent from the continuation of the letter to Peacock. Shelley confirms pointedly that he 'had read before now the raptures of travellers' (*Letters*, i, p. 495). 'I will be warned by their example', he continues, 'I will simply detail to you, all that I can relate, or all that if related I could enable you to conceive of what we have done or seen' (*Letters*, i, p. 495).

Shelley's preference for clarity ('simply detail') rather than 'rapture' in responding to natural grandeur returns us to his attempts to formulate a philosophically and politically progressive revision of the discourse on the sublime. Moreover, that preference takes on especial resonance when set against the reputation of the 'famous valley of Chamouni' in the late eighteenth and early nineteenth centuries: by the time the Shelley party visited Chamonix in 1816, the region – and Mont Blanc in particular – had become the major European focal point for the pious configuration of the discourse on the natural sublime (*Letters*, i, p. 494).

At the end of this Alpine summer, Shelley set out to replace the religious 'raptures of travellers' with his own, secular discourse on the Savoyard sublime. The result was *Mont Blanc*, a poem informed as much by the preceding three months in Switzerland as by Shelley's experience at Chamonix itself. The attempt was no less than to revise the cultural significance of the mountain away from pious, conservative catastrophism, and to re-engage with the revolutionary symbolism of a tradition deriving from Rousseau's *Julie, ou, La Nouvelle Héloïse* (1761) and passing notably through Wordsworth's 1793 *Descriptive Sketches*. This attempt took place within the context of Shelley's growing understanding of ideology: his sceptical awareness that 'the *records* that are *called* reality' are precisely only 'records' or – to use *Mont Blanc*'s phrase – cultural 'codes' that have become enshrined in the 'one mind' (*Letters*, i, p. 485; emphasis added; *Mont Blanc*, 81).[4] As argued in the previous chapter, the role of the imagination in shaping and determining this cultural 'legislature' becomes an increasingly central feature of Shelley's politicised poetics, finding fullest expression in the *Defence of Poetry*. In the Alps in 1816, Shelley's revision of the conventional discourse on the Alpine sublime is a similarly sceptical critique, a dismantling of the superstitious and reactionary 'records' of natural grandeur produced by the 'vulgar' imagination. But the 'wise' or 'cultivated' imagination – the imagination acting in concert with an 'effort of the understanding' – is capable of forming alternative, politically progressive 'records' (*Mont Blanc*, 82; *H6WT*, p. 41). In Switzerland and Savoy, the work of one man more than any other embodied for Shelley this progressive potential of the imagination: 'the greatest man the world has produced since Milton', none other than Jean-Jacques Rousseau (*Letters*, i, p. 494).

MONT BLANC: THE CULTURAL BACKGROUND

Mont Blanc was composed in the environs of Chamonix around 23 July 1816 and first published in the co-authored *History of a Six Weeks' Tour* in 1817. Since Kapstein's early reading, critical debate about the poem has tended to focus on the alleged 'tensions' and 'equivocations' in its ontology.[5] In general, these epistemological 'ambiguities' have been used to support readings of *Mont Blanc* as a 'great transitional poem': a definitive watershed in the supposed conflict between materialist and idealist strains in Shelley's philosophical thought.[6] In this view, the materialist relationship between the mind and the mountain – 'the secret strength of things / Which governs thought' – that informs the body text is overturned by an apparently idealist climax: 'And what were thou, and earth, and stars, and sea, / If to the human mind's imaginings / Silence and solitude were vacancy?' (*Mont Blanc*, 139–40, 143–5). Accordingly, Kapstein's account of *Mont Blanc* argues that the poem's final lines refute the materialist body-text and imply 'that it is not external necessity, but the mind of man that creates our knowledge and makes a reality of the universe'.[7] Following Kapstein, Earl Wasserman's highly influential account goes so far as to suggest that these lines move towards the belief in a 'transcendent and absolute divine Cause' that he perceives in Shelley's later work.[8] And more recent accounts of *Mont Blanc* have retained this critical bias, despite problematising the ease of the transition between materialism and idealism suggested by the New Critics. We have already noted Ferguson's claim that *Mont Blanc* 'identifies the sublime as the aesthetic operation through which one makes an implicit argument for the transcendent existence of man'.

Angela Leighton's deconstructive reading similarly affirms the apparent priority of mind over mountain in the closing lines. She argues that the landscape is 'a signpost towards some hidden presence that is not named or perceived'.[9] But she denies that this immanent 'Power' is a materialist Necessity. Rather, she concludes that it 'has to do not so much with philosophical or political systems, but with the "human mind's imaginings", and it is in relation to those imaginings that it exists'.[10] And as recently as 1995, Paul Endo's Kantian reading likewise affirmed that 'Shelley dismisses the "secret strength" of things in the poem's final lines, subordinating it to a human and internal power'.[11]

I want to argue against the idealising conclusion of this kind of reading, not least against Leighton's notion that *Mont Blanc*'s 'Power' has 'not so much' to do with 'political systems'. However, the premise of these critics is also subject to doubt. After all, to follow Kapstein's claim that *Mont Blanc*'s 'subject matter is ontology', the 'nature of the mind, the nature of knowledge, the nature of reality, and the relation of the human mind to the universe' is to risk forgetting the poem's ostensible object: the mountain itself.[12] Conversely, a satisfactory account of *Mont Blanc*'s 'ambiguous' ontology can only be provided within the context of Shelley's revision of the discourse on the sublime.[13]

In order to fully re-contextualise *Mont Blanc* in relation to that discourse, the poem's initial publication in the *Six Weeks' Tour* – a volume of travel writing – needs to be remembered. By the time the Shelley party visited Chamonix in 1816, the 'famous valley' was fast becoming one of Europe's main tourist attractions, accessible once again to British travellers after nearly twenty-five years of conflict with France (*Letters*, i, p. 494). The *Tour*'s 'Preface' recognises this popularity, acknowledging that these 'scenes ... are now so familiar to our countrymen, that few facts relating to them can be expected to have escaped the many more experienced and exact observers, who have sent their journals to the press' (*H6WT*, p. iii). The Shelley party participated to some extent in this burgeoning Alpine tourist industry, staying in the tellingly named Hotel de Londres at Chamonix, the alternative to the Hotel d'Angleterre where Byron would later stay (*H6WT*, p. 140; *Letters*, i, p. 495). They visited the Cabinets d'Histoire Naturelle at Servoz and Chamonix, noting their similarity to those they had already seen at Clifton, Keswick, and Matlock (*Letters*, i, pp. 496, 501). And in Chamonix itself they purchased 'a large collection of the seeds of rare Alpine plants ... to colonise [their] garden in England' and 'some specimens of minerals and plants and two or three crystal seals at Mont Blanc to preserve the memory of having approached it' (*Letters*, i, p. 501).

However, both the *Tour* and Shelley's journal letter to Peacock are highly critical of the burgeoning commercialisation of the Alpine sublime, expressing distaste for tourists and locals alike. In fact, Shelley affirms that his guide, Ducree, was 'the only tolerable person [he had] seen in this country' (*H6WT*, p. 157; *Letters*, i, p. 498). In the section of his letter to Peacock written on 25 July, Shelley caustically 'laments' having met with 'some English people' while attempting to picnic in the mountains near Chamonix (*Letters*, i, p. 500). 'I will not detail to you the melancholy exhibitions of tourism', he continues, 'which altho they emanate from the profusion and exigences of these vulgar great corrupt the manners of the people, and make this place another Keswick' (*Letters*, i, p. 500). The comparison with Keswick is instructive, and helps to decipher the tortured syntax here. While staying in Keswick in the winter of 1811, Shelley had written to Elizabeth Hitchener that 'tho the face of the country is lovely, the *people* are detestable' – sentiments exactly anticipating his 1816 reaction to Chamonix (*Letters*, i, p. 223). He went on to explain that 'the manufacturers have crept into this vale and deformed the loveliness of Nature with human taint. The debauched servants of the great families who resort contribute to the total extinction of morality' (*Letters*, i, p. 223).

Reading the 1816 letter to Peacock in the light of these comments, we can see that Shelley considers Alpine tourism to be 'melancholy' on at least two counts. Firstly, the sheer number ('profusion') of wealthy ('great') but 'vulgar' tourists – the type of the 'great families' who 'resort' at Keswick – is lamentable since it overcrowds the region. Secondly, the wealthy tourists have a negative effect on the impoverished Savoyard locals who – understandably enough – attempt to profit by them.[14] Indeed, in this latter respect Shelley affirms that 'the inhabitants of Cumberland are not for a moment to be compared with these people, on whose stupidity, avarice and imposture engenders a mixture of vices truly horrible and disgusting' (*Letters*, i, p. 501). And although Shelley's explicit condemnation of the 'vulgar' English tourists was expediently edited out of the version of the letter that appeared in the *Tour*, it remains implicit in his surviving strictures on the locals. Speaking of the 'proprietor' of the Cabinet d'Histoire Naturelle at Chamonix, the *Tour* confirms verbatim from Shelley's letter to Peacock that he was 'the very vilest specimen, of that vile species of quack that together with the whole army of aubergistes and guides and indeed the entire mass of the population subsist on the weakness and credulity of travellers as leeches subsist on the blood of the sick' (*Letters*, i, p. 501; *H6WT*, pp. 170–1).

Shelley's attack on Chamonix's 'vulgar' tourists certainly reflects the socially – as well as intellectually – active distinction between travel and tourism that James Buzard has identified in early nineteenth-century travel writing.[15] However, Shelley's intellectual élitism also clearly accords with his revision of the discourse on the sublime. As already noted, Chamonix's popularity as a tourist resort was inextricably linked to the pious reading of the natural sublime. Not surprisingly, then, even before expressing his reservations about the 'raptures of travellers' Shelley had observed to Peacock that 'I fear that it will be long before I shall play the tourist deftly' (*Letters*, i, pp. 495, 475). Accordingly, Shelley's critique of Chamonix's tourist industry was not simply a reaction to the negative effects of excessive commercialism. Rather, in the terminology of that critique, we can also trace his distaste for the pious and reactionary 'raptures' of his fellow 'travellers'. Between the *Tour* and the letter to Peacock, Chamonix's tourists are described as 'weak', 'credulous', 'sick', and – most tellingly of all – 'vulgar': Shelley's favourite term for the anthropomorphic tendencies of the reactionary and superstitious imagination.

Mont Blanc itself must have seemed to Shelley a particular focal point of this kind of superstitious primitivism. Indeed, an often-quoted letter to Peacock from Chamonix on 23 July explicitly confirms Shelley's awareness of the causal connection between natural grandeur and the imaginative primitivism of the religious impulse. Peacock was currently writing a Zoroastrian epic – *Ahrimanes* – about the struggle between good and evil spirits for the possession of the world. Following his description of the Bosson and Mer de Glace glaciers, and subsequent account of 'Buffon's sublime but gloomy theory' that these glaciers might perpetually augment, Shelley asks Peacock:

Do you who assert the supremacy of Ahriman imagine him throned among these desolating snows, among these palaces of death and frost, sculptured in this their terrible magnificence by the unsparing hand of necessity, and that he casts around him as the first essays of his final usurpation avalanches, torrents, rocks and thunders – and above all, these deadly glaciers at once the proofs and the symbols of his reign (*Letters*, i, p. 499)

The question – or it may be a *suggestion*, since there is no question mark at the end of the sentence – is informed, explicitly, by Shelley's conviction that religious superstition is the result of a 'vulgar', anthropomorphic response to the natural sublime.[16] Indeed, the 'sublime but gloomy' passage Shelley refers to in Buffon's *Natural History* makes precisely the same claim about the origins of religion in the reaction of primitive man to the catastrophic geological activity marking the earth's early history.[17] 'Even at present', Buffon observes in relation to Chamonix's glaciers, 'men are not entirely emancipated from those superstitious terrors by the experience of time, by the tranquillity which succeeded the ages of convulsions and storms'.[18]

The extent of Shelley's indignation at the conventional, religious reaction to the 'unutterable greatness' of Mont Blanc is notorious from his often-quoted Greek inscriptions in the registers of various inns around Chamonix: 'PB Shelley: Democrat, Philanthropist and Atheist' (*H6WT*, p. 155; *Letters*, i, p. 498).[19] *Mont Blanc's* critics have long taken a hint from these inscriptions, noting that the same indignation informs the poem. *Mont Blanc* is clearly an emphatic rejection of the religious construction of natural grandeur, the poem of an 'atheist in the Alps' to use De Beer's phrase. But in taking Shelley's public avowal of atheism as the grounds for a reading of *Mont Blanc*, critics have tended to overlook the other terms in his inscription, namely 'democrat' and 'philanthropist'. In fact, within Shelley's revision of the discourse on the sublime all three terms are mutually implied, and all three accordingly inform *Mont Blanc*. While the poem is undoubtedly an attempt to secularise the discourse on the sublime, it is also an attempt to revise that discourse along politically progressive lines. The basic premise of Shelley's early revision of the discourse on the sublime was that the correct interpretation of natural grandeur by the 'cultivated' imagination promotes 'democracy' and 'philanthropy'. *Mont Blanc* embodies this conviction that the natural processes revealed in the landscape of the sublime have politically potent lessons to teach. The poem replaces the standard hierarchical notion of Creation with an egalitarian model of 'eternal' natural economy, rejecting a theologically loaded catastrophist reading of natural agency in favour of a secular – and scientifically informed – model of restorative cycles (*Mont Blanc*, 75). And, as an unequivocally public statement – first published in a volume of travel writing about the Alps – *Mont Blanc* is an explicit challenge to the dominant, pious and conservative 'records' of the Alpine sublime. In short, it is nothing less than an attempt to revise, to *re-imagine* the cultural significance of Europe's most famous mountain.

Accordingly, while the *Six Weeks' Tour* ostensibly acknowledges that 'few *facts*' relating to Chamonix 'can be expected to have escaped the many more experienced and exact observers, who have sent their journals to the press', the 'Preface' actually questions the validity of these received 'records' of the Alpine sublime (*H6WT*, p. iii emphasis added). The 'Preface' conjectures that its readers 'have perhaps never *talked* with one who has beheld in the enthusiasm of youth ... the mighty Alps', combining an empirical emphasis on first-hand testimony ('talked') with a Godwinian emphasis on Sincerity, and a Wordsworthian appreciation of uncorrupted 'youth' (*H6WT*, p. v emphasis added). We are told that the *Tour* is addressed precisely to 'those whose youth has been passed as their's ... in pursuing ... the inconstant summer of delight and beauty' (*H6WT*, p. iv). 'They will be interested', the 'Preface' continues, 'to hear of one who has visited Mellerie, and Clarens, and Chillon, and Vevai – *classic ground, peopled with tender and glorious imaginations of the present and the past*' (*H6WT*, p. v emphasis added). The choice of words here is revealing: the Alps are '*classic* ground', classic and not sacred. For a reader in 1817, the word 'classic' was an unmistakable allusion to a Greek, philosophical and republican tradition – and we remember that Shelley's inscriptions in the hotel registers around Chamonix were, pointedly, in Greek because Greek, as Timothy Webb points out, was 'the language of intellectual liberty'.[20] In describing the Alps as 'classic ground', then, the *Tour*'s 'Preface' maintains the same emphasis on a philosophical and politically progressive (as opposed to a superstitious and reactionary) response to the natural sublime that informed Shelley's infamous inscriptions at Chamonix.

Appropriately, then, the 'Preface' goes on to confirm that this 'classic ground' is 'peopled' with '*tender and glorious imaginations*' – the clear antithesis of the 'vulgar' anthropomorphism offered by the theistic account of natural grandeur (*H6WT*, p. v emphasis added). The reference here is to the works of a literary élite, whose 'tender and glorious imaginations' offer a politically potent alternative to the dominant, religious culture of Alpine sublimity. Speaking of her 1814 voyage 'down the castled Rhine, through scenes beautiful in themselves', Mary had already affirmed that 'since she visited them, a great Poet has clothed [them] with the freshness of a diviner nature' – and we note the doubtless intentional pun on the word 'divine' (*H6WT*, p. v). The 'great Poet', of course, is Byron, who described a similar river-voyage in *Childe Harold* III, completed during the Shelley party's stay in Geneva. In a letter to Byron from Chamonix in 1816, which quotes the poet's markedly secular reference to the Alps as the 'palaces of Nature' in the as yet unpublished *Childe Harold* III, Shelley urges Byron to visit the 'magnificent valley' for himself' (*Childe Harold* III, 591; *Letters*, i, p. 494). 'I shall not attempt to describe to you the scenes through which we have passed', he continues, matching the concern he expressed about the 'raptures' of 'travellers' in his letter to Peacock on the same day (*Letters*, i, p. 494). Rather, Shelley states his hope 'soon to see in poetry the feelings with which they will inspire you' (*Letters*, i, p. 494). To Shelley's clear approval, Byron had already cast Mont Blanc as a symbol of the revolutionary sublime in the sixty-seventh stanza of *Childe Harold* III, which Shelley had 'read in MSS' and which, he confirmed to Hogg, 'infinitely surpasses any poem [Byron] has yet published' (*Letters*, i, p. 493). Byron characterises the mountain as an 'immortal', Volneyan monument – 'imperishably pure beyond all things below' – to 'deeds which should not pass away, / And names that must not wither' while 'the earth / Forgets her empires with a just decay' (*Childe Harold* III, 643, 635–7). And to avoid any possible doubt about the identity of his symbol, Byron's note to line 642 confirms that the passage was 'written in the eye of Mont Blanc (June 3rd 1816) which even at this distance dazzles mine' (*Byron*, p. 142).

However, in referring to the 'tender and glorious imaginations' by which the Alps are 'peopled', the *Tour*'s 'Preface' is alluding primarily the work of Jean-Jacques Rousseau, specifically to his long epistolary novel *Julie, ou, La Nouvelle Héloïse: Lettres de Deux Amants, Habitans d'une petite Ville au pied des Alps*. Shelley had been reading *Julie* during his voyage around Lake Geneva with Byron. 'I read *Julie* all day', he told Peacock on 26 June, 'surrounded by the scenes which it has so wonderfully *peopled*' (*Letters*, i, p. 485; emphasis added). In his note to line 927 of *Childe Harold* III, Byron too observes that 'Clarens with the scenes around it . . . has been *peopled*' by Rousseau's novel, precisely the term used by Shelley in the 'Preface' to the *Tour* and the letter to Peacock (*Byron*, p. 144; emphasis added). Mary Shelley's 'Note on the Poems of 1816' points out that this was the 'first time' that Shelley had read the book, although it features on her own reading list for 1815 (*CPW*, p. 536; *MWSJ*, p. 90). This claim is significantly refined by Shelley's observation to Peacock that it was during this voyage that he 'first knew the divine beauty of Rousseau's imagination, as it exhibits itself in *Julie*' (*Letters*, i, p. 480).[21] In a letter to Hogg written six days later, Shelley expands on these sentiments. Having informed Hogg that he has read *Julie* at Clarens, Meillerie, and Vevai, Shelley goes on to confirm that the novel 'tho in some respects absurd and prejudiced, is yet the production of a mighty Genius, and acquires an influence I had not conceived it to possess when giving and receiving influences from the scenes by which it was inspired' (*Letters*, i, pp. 493–4).

There are many reasons while Shelley might have found Rousseau's novel 'absurd and prejudiced': its emphasis on the virtues of obedience to familial – and especially to paternal – wishes, its ostensible defence of chastity and the sanctity of marriage. But clearly, reading *Julie* amidst 'the scenes by which it was inspired' marked a major shift in Shelley's ambivalent understanding of Rousseau. Not content with describing Rousseau as a 'mighty genius', Shelley concludes the letter to Hogg by affirming that this important prototype of *Alastor*'s flawed visionary has become 'in [his] mind the greatest man the world has produced since Milton' (*Letters*, i, p. 494). It is important to remember, however, that – as we have seen in the previous chapter – *Alastor*'s critique of Rousseau was based largely on Wollstonecraft's attacks in her *Rights of Woman*. Shelley's letters to Peacock and Hogg reveal that he has discovered – for himself – a new aspect of Rousseau in *Julie*. And Shelley's claim that *Julie* had acquired for him 'an influence [he] had not *conceived* it to possess' would seem to confirm that his knowledge of the novel prior to 1816 was second-hand (we remember that Mary had read the book in 1815).[22]

The comparison Shelley makes between Rousseau and Milton – England's foremost republican poet – is instructive, and sheds light on the change in his opinion of the Genevan while in the Alps. This change needs to be approached through the extraordinary reputation of *Julie* in the late eighteenth and early nineteenth centuries.[23] On publication in 1761, Rousseau's novel had been an immediate success, quickly becoming one of the most widely read – and widely sought after – novels of the day. The book is set for the most part in Switzerland (at the 'foot of the Alps'), and recounts the life-long love affair between Julie d'Étange and her tutor / lover St Preux, who progresses from conventional sexual desire to an intuition of a more universal, selfless, and unchanging love. Moreover, the novel makes the archetypal Rousseauvian contrast between the virtues of rural community and the decadence of cities, offering a causal link between the enlightened mores of Julie and St. Preux and their Alpine surroundings. As already noted, with the development of the conservative critique of Rousseau – instigated by Burke's *ad hominem* attacks in the *Reflections* and the *Letter to a Member of the National Assembly* – the idea of a causal connection between Rousseauvian sensibility and the French Revolution quickly became a commonplace of the British debate on 1789 and its aftermath.[24] No less a figure than William Hazlitt, for example, considered Rousseau to be 'the founder of Jacobinism, which disclaims the division of the species into two classes, the one the property of the other'.[25] *Julie* became a particular focus of this commonplace: the novel was seen to embody the same egotistical, anti-aristocratic – and ultimately revolutionary – individualism that informed the *Confessions*. Again, Hazlitt's account of the connection between Rousseau and Jacobinism picks up on the centrality of the Genevan's appeal to individualistic passions, confirming that the 'adept' Jacobin 'does not so much consider the political injury as the personal insult. This is the way to put the case to set the true revolutionary leaven, the self-love which is at the bottom of every heart, at work, and this was the way in which Rousseau puts it'.[26] Moreover, the political threat from passionate individualism was construed by commentators in explicitly sexual terms: Rousseau's vaunted preference for ladies of quality in the *Confessions*, and St. Preux's seduction of his socially-superior student, were both figured as evidence of an individualistic sensibility with the power to overthrow social norms.[27] And indeed the second of Mary Shelley's letters in the *Six Weeks' Tour* exhibits precisely the same belief in a causal connection between Rousseau's work and the French Revolution (and given Shelley's contemporary enthusiasm for *Julie*, Rousseau's novel must have been foremost in her mind as she wrote). Speaking of the 'small obelisk erected to the glory of Rousseau' in the Plainpalais at Geneva, Mary notes that 'such is the mutability of human life [that here] the magistrates, the successors of those who exiled [Rousseau] from his native country, were shot by the populace *during that revolution, which his writings mainly contributed to mature*' (*H6WT*, pp. 101–2; emphasis added).

In the section of his journal letter to Peacock written from St Gingoux on 25 June 1816, Shelley himself enthusiastically recounts an anecdote that would seem to confirm *Julie*'s revolutionary potential, and which links that potential directly to Napoleon Bonaparte, a connection that Shelley would later repeat in *The Triumph of Life*. Shelley informs Peacock that no less a person than 'the Empress Maria Louisa had slept at Meillerie', emphasising that this had taken place 'before the present inn was built, and when the accommodations were those of the most wretched village' (*Letters*, i, p. 482). And Marie-Louise – who had become Empress of France and the second wife of Napoleon on 2 April 1810 – had done this, Shelley affirms, 'in remembrance of St. Preux' (*Letters*, i, p. 482).[28] 'A Bourbon dared not even to have remembered Rousseau', Shelley continues, 'she [i.e. Marie-Louise] owed this power to that democracy which her husband's dynasty outraged, and of which it was however, in some sort, the representative among the nations of the earth' (*Letters*, i, pp. 482–3). The passage confirms the revolutionary associations of Rousseau (whom 'a Bourbon dared not even to have remembered'). It also reveals Shelley's highly ambivalent opinion of Napoleon as the initially admirable defender of the revolution against the restorative attempts of foreign monarchs, who ultimately 'outraged' the democratic principles of the revolution he had once defended by making himself emperor of France.[29] But the passage turns on the connection it establishes between Rousseau's novel and 'democracy'. 'How beautiful it is to find', Shelley observes, 'that the common sentiments of human nature can attach themselves to those who are most removed from its duties and its enjoyments, when Genius pleads for their admission at the gate of Power' (*Letters*, i, p. 482). Hence, the real object of Shelley's apostrophe here is the power of Rousseau's imagination ('Genius'), which moved the Empress of France to stay in 'the accommodations of a most wretched village' in 'remembrance' of a virtuous – albeit fictitious – man. In other words, Shelley figures Marie-Louise's stay in Meillerie – ostensibly in 'remembrance' of St. Preux – as actually an homage to the principles of 'democracy' which St. Preux embodies. In short, Rousseau's imagination – 'as it exhibits itself in *Julie*' – had 'pleaded' for 'democracy' at 'the gate of Power', and had been heard. The anecdote encapsulated, for Shelley, the power of the 'cultivated' imagination to effect genuine and lasting political change. 'This little incident', he concludes, 'shows at once how unfit and how impossible it is for the ancient system of opinions, or for any power built upon a conspiracy to revive them, permanently to subsist among mankind' (*Letters*, i, p. 483).

The radical change in Shelley's opinion of Rousseau was accordingly informed by his new awareness (and experience) of the political potency of Rousseau's imagination 'as it exhibits itself in *Julie*'. Shelley's letters from Geneva remain effusive in their praise for the *Nouvelle Héloïse*. Writing to Peacock the following day, Shelley describes the novel as 'an overflowing ... of sublimest genius, and more than human sensibility' (*Letters*, i, p. 485). He even concludes a description of the scenery around Clarens with the advice to 'See *Nouvelle Héloïse*, Lettre 17, Part 4' – the same passage, incidentally, that Byron cites in his note to line 927 of *Childe Harold* III (*Letters*, i, p. 485; *Byron*, p. 143).[30] But there is more to Shelley's intense admiration for Rousseau's 'sublimest genius' than merely his recognition of the political potency of Rousseau's imagination, although it would be difficult to overstate the impact of that recognition upon Shelley's developing sense of the connection between imagination and social progress. Rather, there is also Shelley's awareness of the causal relationship between *Julie*'s potent revolutionary mores and the Alpine landscape 'by which it was inspired' (*Letters*, i, p. 494).

In fact, this relationship is suggested by Rousseau himself in the fourth book of the *Confessions* (1784). Speaking of the *Nouvelle Héloïse*, Rousseau exhorts his readers to 'visit the country' where the novel is set, to 'look over the landscape, take an excursion on the lake, and say whether Nature has not made this fine country for a Julie, a Claire, and a St Preux' (*Rousseau*, v, p. 128).[31] Byron rehearses Rousseau's notion of a determining connection between the Alps and *Julie*'s revolutionary mores in *Childe Harold* III.

'Twas not for fiction chose Rousseau this spot', he writes in stanza 104, 'but he found / It was the scene which passion *must* allot / To the mind's purified beings' (*Childe Harold* III, 966–70; emphasis added). Byron develops this idea in his note to line 927, affirming that Rousseau's claim in the *Confessions* – which he quotes – is 'no exaggeration' (*Byron*, p. 144). 'It would be difficult to see Clarens (with the scenes around it . . .)', he confirms, 'without being forcibly struck with its peculiar adaptation to the persons and events with which it has been peopled' (*Byron*, p. 144). Nor indeed, he continues, is this connection between *Julie* and the Alps merely a matter of 'individual passion' (*Byron*, p. 144). Rather, 'the feeling with which all around Clarens, and the opposite rocks of Meillerie is invested, is of a still higher and more comprehensive order' (*Byron*, p. 144). 'It is as if', he continues, 'the great principle of the universe . . . is there more condensed, but not less manifested' (*Byron*, p. 144). Thus even 'if Rousseau had never written, not lived', he concludes:

the same associations would not less have belonged to such scenes. He has added to the interest of his works by their adoption; he has shown his sense of their beauty by the selection; but they have done that for him which no human being could do for them (*Byron*, p. 144)

Byron's account of the dynamics of inspiration here is firmly empirical: Rousseau's imagination responded to the 'great principle of the universe' as 'manifested' in the Alpine landscape. *Julie* is the embodiment of that response. In short, then, all Rousseau has really done is to embody in a novel the immanent 'principle' that his imagination had discerned in the landscape. This achievement must have appeared to Shelley – and Byron – in stark contrast to *The Excursion*, the 'work' produced by Wordsworth's 'retired' contemplation of his 'native mountains'.

Shelley's understanding of the relationship between *Julie* and the Alps retains Byron's empirical bias, but also emphasises the ongoing dialectical relationship between the novel and the landscape. We have already noted his observation to Hogg that the novel 'acquires an interest [he] had not conceived it to possess *when giving and receiving influences* from the scenes by which it was inspired' (*Letters*, i, pp. 493–4; emphasis added). Six days earlier he had remarked to Peacock that 'it is inconceivable what an enchantment the scene itself lends to those delineations, from which its own most touching charm arises' (*Letters*, i, p. 480). There are two important factors here. First, *Julie*'s revolutionary mores is the product of Rousseau's imaginative response to the natural grandeur of the Alps. This returns us to the central tenet of Shelley's revision of the discourse on the sublime: the idea that natural grandeur – correctly interpreted by a 'cultivated' imagination – has politically potent lessons to teach. Secondly, *Julie* – the embodiment of Rousseau's imaginative response to the Alps – has in turn 'peopled' that landscape, a politically potent act when seen in the light of the Marie-Louise anecdote. In short, then, Shelley sees Rousseau's *Julie* as itself a kind of revision of the discourse on the sublime. Because of *Julie*, Shelley tells Peacock:

Meillerie, the Castle of Chillon, Clarens, the mountains of La Valais and Savoy, present themselves to the imagination as monuments of things that were once familiar, and of beings that were once dear to it. They were created indeed by one mind, but a mind so powerfully bright as to cast a shade of falsehood on the records that are called reality (*Letters*, i, p. 485)

This passage is not an idealist confirmation of the non-existence of extra-mental reality, not proof that 'Shelley no longer distinguishes thoughts of the mind from external things'.[32] Rather, it is a sceptical acknowledgement of ideology: a recognition of the fact that what frequently passes for 'reality' is in fact only a 'record' produced by the 'mind', and which has gained popular acceptance (i.e., is '*called* reality'). In the Alps in 1816, the pious configuration of the discourse on the sublime must have seemed to Shelley a perfect example of such a culturally dominant 'record'. Accordingly he saw *Julie* – the product of Rousseau's 'powerfully bright' imagination – as an explicit, and politically potent challenge to the accepted, religious 'records' of Alpine sublimity; a progressive and instructive 'peopling', with the power to counteract the pervasive anthropomorphism of the theistic discourse on the sublime. Reading the novel amidst 'the scenes by which it was inspired' provided Shelley with a clear example of the political potency of the 'cultivated' imaginative response to natural grandeur. And he went on to apostrophise that potency in the *Hymn to Intellectual Beauty* (1816), a poem in which the example of Rousseau the author of *Julie* looms large.

ROUSSEAU AND THE *HYMN TO INTELLECTUAL BEAUTY*

Mary's 'Note on the Poems of 1816' tells us that 'the *Hymn to Intellectual Beauty* was conceived during [Shelley's] voyage round [Lake Geneva] with Lord Byron' – the 'voyage', that is, during which Shelley discovered Rousseau's 'mighty Genius' in *Julie* (*CPW*, pp. 535–6; *Letters*, i, p. 493). Critics have generally taken the 'intellectual beauty' of the poem's title to be a Platonic reference, and the poem itself as 'a manifesto of Shelley's

Platonism'[33]. As Notopoulos points out, while the term 'intellectual beauty' itself never appears in Plato's *oeuvre* – it apparently derives from Plotinus – there are a number of instances of it in eighteenth-century neo-Platonic texts with which Shelley was familiar.[34] For example, the phrase occurs on three separate occasions in Richardson's 1773 English translation of C. M. Wieland's *Agathon* (1766), which Shelley almost certainly read in 1814 (*MWSJ*, p. 86).[35] And indeed Shelley would later interpolate the phrase 'intellectual beauty' into his own 1818 translation of Plato's *Symposium*, effectively formulating a distinction between 'intellectual beauty' and 'universal beauty' which is not present in Plato's original.[36]

However, there is also a radical, empiricist dimension to the *Hymn* which seems to belie the easy Platonism discerned by most critics. This empiricism – problematic in a Platonic context – can be explained by considering another possible, and far more resonant source for Shelley's knowledge of the term 'intellectual beauty': the first edition of William Godwin's *Memoirs of the Author of a Vindication of the Rights of Woman* (1798).[37]

In fact, Godwin's *Memoirs* are significantly absent from Shelley's reading list, on which almost every other work by both Godwin and Wollstonecraft features. However, it is all but inconceivable that Shelley – married to Wollstonecraft's daughter – would not have been aware of the work. Indeed, not only had Claire read the *Memoirs* during the Shelley party's first trip to mainland Europe in 1814, but there are also significant verbal echoes of it in the sections of the *Speculations on Morals and Metaphysics* written in 1815. Moreover, the term 'intellectual beauty' also appears in Wollstonecraft's *Vindication of the Rights of Woman*, which Shelley certainly had read.[38] During her critique of Rousseau's *Émile* – the critique upon which, as we have seen, *Alastor* drew so heavily – Wollstonecraft contrasts the 'beauty of features' which merely attracts 'sensual homage' to the 'intellectual beauty' which 'inspires more sublime emotions'.[39] And her account of 'intellectual beauty' as the 'beauty' of the mind is later echoed in Amelia Opie's *Adeline Mowbray* (1805), a novel in which both Wollstonecraft and Godwin loom large, and which Shelley had read in July 1811 (*Letters*, i, p. 122). Speaking of his prospects of marrying Adeline, Sir Patrick similarly contrasts the physical 'beauty of his person' to the 'admiration of intellectual beauty', confidently asserting that the latter 'could not, in his opinion, subsist'.[40]

Godwin's account of 'intellectual beauty' in his *Memoirs* retains and develops Wollstonecraft's use of the term as a reference to mental abilities. The phrase occurs close to the end of the *Memoirs*, where Godwin compares his mental development with that of his late wife. 'We had cultivated our powers ... in different directions', Godwin writes:

I chiefly an attempt at logical and metaphysical distinction, she a taste for the picturesque ... I have been stimulated, as long as I can remember, by an ambition for intellectual distinction; but ... discouraged ... by finding that I did not possess, in the degree of some other men, an *intuitive perception of intellectual beauty.* I have perhaps a strong and lively sense of the *pleasures of the imagination*; but I have seldom been right in assigning to them their proportionate value ... What I wanted in this respect, Mary possessed, in a degree superior to any other person I ever knew. The strength of her mind lay in *intuition* ... Her religion, her philosophy ... were ... the pure result of *feeling* and *taste.* She adopted one opinion, and rejected another, spontaneously, by hellip; the force of a *cultivated imagination.*[41]

In short, 'intellectual beauty' is both the product, and the defining characteristic of a 'cultivated imagination'. In this qualified sense, Cameron is correct in asserting that 'intellectual beauty' is 'the beauty of the mind and its creations', and not an attribute of landscape to be distinguished from the sublime vistas of *Mont Blanc.*[42] A 'cultivated imagination' is the prerequisite – that Godwin felt he lacked – of 'an intuitive perception of intellectual beauty'. But 'the force of a cultivated imagination' is also the origin of that 'intellectual beauty' which Godwin felt would have given him the 'intellectual distinction' he sought.

The correlation between Godwin's account of 'intellectual beauty' and the terminology of Shelley's ongoing revision of the discourse on the sublime is immediately apparent. Indeed that correlation is further strengthened by Godwin's reference to Wollstonecraft's 'taste for the picturesque' and 'lively sense of the pleasures of the imagination' – an echo of Addison's seminal account of the sublime and beautiful in *The Spectator.* Shelley's *Hymn to Intellectual Beauty* accordingly takes the hint from Godwin's account of Wollstonecraft's mental character, apostrophising the political potency, 'the force' of a 'cultivated' imaginative response to natural grandeur. The capacity for making and embodying this potent, if transitory, 'intuition' is the 'intellectual beauty' referred to in the title. Thus the *Hymn*, in effect, is an apostrophe to the 'cultivated imagination' and its products. And as Matthews and Everest suggest, Rousseau's *Julie* – a novel which emphasised the connection between revolutionary mores and the natural sublime, and which Shelley was reading at the time he wrote the *Hymn* – was undoubtedly his foremost example of 'intellectual beauty' (*Poems*, i, p. 525). Writing to Peacock from Geneva on 12 July, Shelley had described the '*divine beauty*' of Rousseau's 'imagination as it exhibits itself in *Julie* (*Letters*, i, p. 480; emphasis added). More tellingly, in *Childe Harold* III Byron alludes to Rousseau's 'love' of '*ideal beauty*, which became / In him existence' (*Childe Harold* III, 738–41; emphasis added). This 'ideal beauty', he affirmed, 'breathed itself to life in *Julie*' (*Childe Harold* III, 743).

The opening of the *Hymn to Intellectual Beauty* has proved problematic for Shelley's critics, specifically the relationship between the 'Power' of the opening line, the 'spirit of BEAUTY' addressed at the beginning of the second stanza, and the 'Intellectual Beauty' of the title. In fact, the *Hymn*'s first stanza is an ontological statement similar, as we shall see, to the opening of *Mont Blanc*. 'The awful shadow of some unseen Power', Shelley writes, 'Floats though unseen amongst us, – visiting':

> This various world with as inconstant wing
> As summer winds that creep from flower to flower. –
> Like moonbeams that behind some piny mountain shower,
> It visits with inconstant glance
> Each human heart and countenance
>
> (*Hymn*, 1–7)

As Cameron points out, 'there can be no question but that the "Power" ... is not intellectual beauty'.[43] However, Cameron's claim that the *Hymn*'s title is consequently confusing seems overly harsh. The first stanza of the *Hymn* makes a clear distinction between the 'unseen Power' and its immanent presence ('awful shadow') in the 'various world', the adjective and subsequent similes suggesting that while the 'unseen Power' itself is universal and unchanging, it has 'various' manifestations in natural phenomena. The stanza also makes clear that 'the human heart and countenance' is the agency by which these 'various' manifestations of the 'unseen Power' are perceived, an apparent allusion to eighteenth-century physiological ('countenance') accounts of sensibility ('heart'), very much the tradition from which Rousseau's *Julie* was written.

The 'unseen Power' referred to in the first stanza of the *Hymn* is unquestionably Necessity. From *Queen Mab*, through the *Daemon of the World* and *Alastor*, and on to *Mont Blanc* and the so-called *Essay on Christianity*, 'Power' is Shelley's recurrent term for the sublime ('awful'), immanent ('unseen') law of Nature. Accordingly, the 'spirit of BEAUTY' addressed at the beginning of the second stanza is not the 'unseen Power' (Necessity) itself. Neither is it the 'awful' manifestations of this 'Power' (Necessity) in natural phenomena or works of art. Rather, the 'spirit of BEAUTY' is the experiential apprehension of the visible 'shadow' of this 'unseen "Power"', i.e. the 'awful' apprehension of the 'various' *manifestations* of Necessity in natural phenomena or works of art – again, for the sceptic, Necessity cannot be perceived directly.[44] This explains why the *Hymn*'s final stanza compares the 'spirit of BEAUTY', explicitly, to 'the truth / Of nature'; why the 'spirit of BEAUTY' is described, in terms more redolent of the discourse on the sublime, as an 'awful LOVELINESS'; why Shelley's account of his personal experience of this 'spirit' in the fifth stanza of the *Hymn* draws so directly – albeit histrionically – on the language of the sublime: 'Sudden, thy shadow fell on me; / I shrieked and clasped my hands in ecstasy!' (*Hymn*, 78–9, 71, 59–60).

The 'spirit of BEAUTY' addressed in the second stanza of the *Hymn* is effectively synonymous with the 'intellectual beauty' referred to in the poem's title: accordingly, it is the *Hymn*'s main object of address. The experience of 'intellectual beauty' is the apprehension of the 'awful' visible manifestations of Necessity (the 'truth / Of nature') in natural phenomena.[45] However, following Godwin's *Memoirs*, the term 'intellectual beauty' has a dual reference in Shelley's *Hymn* (which has been the source of a good deal of confusion). The experience of 'intellectual beauty' is the apprehension of the 'truth / of nature'. But the term 'intellectual beauty' also describes the *ability* of the mind both to apprehend *and* to embody this 'truth'. In this qualified sense, Cameron is again correct in claiming that 'intellectual beauty' is 'the beauty of the mind and its creations'. In short, 'intellectual beauty' also functions in the *Hymn* as a synonym for the 'cultivated imagination': the faculty by which the mind makes the experientially potent apprehension of the immanent presence of Necessity in natural phenomena. This is a quintessentially Humean point: it is only the imagination that can go beyond the limits of sensation to an intuition of nature's law. This latter sense of 'intellectual beauty' as a synonym for the cultivated imagination informs the *Hymn*'s address to the 'spirit of BEAUTY' as the 'messenger of sympathies / That wax and wane in lovers' eyes' (*Hymn*, 42–3). As the agency ('messenger') of sympathy, the 'spirit of BEAUTY' is unmistakably the imagination – and we note the mention of 'lovers' eyes', a clear indication that Julie and St. Preux were on Shelley's mind as he wrote.

In keeping with the sceptical bias of Shelley's revision of the discourse on the sublime, then, the 'spirit of BEAUTY' is not created, but only experienced and embodied by the human mind – and we remember Byron's claim that Rousseau had merely embodied in *Julie* the immanent 'principle of the Universe' that he perceived in the Alpine landscape. Hence the *Hymn* uses active verbs to describe the spirit's relationship to the essentially passive mind: the 'spirit' '*visits*' the 'human heart', it '*consecrate*[s]' and 'shine[s] *upon*' human 'thought or form' (*Hymn*, 6, 13–5; emphasis added). Again, the mind is a largely passive, perceptive entity in relation to Nature's active principle. The 'spirit of BEAUTY' is also evanescent. The mind's apprehension of Necessity in the imaginative response to natural grandeur is transitory. In a passage of *The Assassins* with clear bearing upon the *Hymn*, Shelley had already lamented 'that these visitings of the spirit of life should fluctuate and pass away. That the moments when the human mind is commensurate with all that it can conceive of excellent and powerful should not endure with its existence and survive its most momentous change' (*PW*, p. 129). The *Hymn* echoes this lament, asking the 'spirit of BEAUTY' why 'thou dost pass away and leave our state, / This dim vast vale of tears, vacant and desolate?' (*Hymn*, 16–7). And appropriately, since the 'spirit of BEAUTY' is the mind's apprehension of Nature's immanent law, the evanescence of that apprehension is described in similes drawn from natural phenomena: 'Ask why the sunlight not for ever / Weaves rainbows o'er yon mountain river' (*Hymn*, 18–9).

The second and third stanzas of the *Hymn* parallel Shelley's early, materialistically grounded critique of the theistic discourse on the sublime: his claim that fear and ignorance of nature evoke an anthropomorphic response from the imagination. The *Hymn* similarly argues that existential doubt – specifically about natural processes beyond human understanding – is the origin of religious superstition. 'Ask', Shelley writes:

> Why aught should fail and fade that once is shown,
>   Why fear and dream and death and birth
>   Cast on the daylight of this earth
>   Such gloom, – why man has such a scope
>   For love and hate, despondency and hope?
>
>   (*Hymn*, 18–24)

Again, to the sceptic, this kind of existential question is unanswerable – but religion marks the attempt of the 'vulgar' or superstitious imagination to provide an answer. 'No voice', Shelley confirms, 'from some sublimer world hath ever / To sage or poet these responses given – / Therefore the name of God, and ghosts, and Heaven, / Remain the records of their vain endeavour' (*Hymn*, 25–8). But these religious doctrines are 'frail spells' – an explicit example of the 'records that are called reality' – 'whose uttered charm might not avail to sever / From all we hear and what we see, / Doubt, Chance, and mutability' (*Hymn*, 29–31). In short, religion cannot ultimately resolve the mind's existential 'Doubt' about the 'Chance and mutability' it perceives in the universe since religion is not the 'truth / Of nature' only the false product of the mind's attempts to subdue nature.

Conversely, as Shelley first affirmed in *Queen Mab*, only the apprehension of Necessity – Nature's unchanging and deterministic law – resolves the apparent 'Chance and mutability' of natural phenomena into an ordered systematics. Accordingly, the *Hymn* confirms that the evanescent experience of the 'spirit of BEAUTY' – the mind's imaginative apprehension of Necessity (the 'truth / Of nature') – achieves what religion cannot. 'Thy light alone', Shelley affirms, using Coleridgean wind-harp image to figure the action of Necessity on the passive, perceptive mind:

> ... like mist o'er mountains driven,
> *Or music by the night wind sent*
> *Through strings of some still instrument,*
> Or moonlight on a midnight stream,
> Gives grace and truth to life's unquiet dream
>
> (*Hymn*, 32–6; emphasis added)

In the apparently biographical fifth stanza of the *Hymn*, Shelley gives an account of his personal experience of 'the spirit of BEAUTY'. The dynamics of this account are identical with the broader, cultural process we have discerned in the first three stanzas, and in this sense, Tim Webb is correct to highlight the dangers of a strictly biographical interpretation of this section of the *Hymn*.[46] The passage – which echoes the Narrator's account of his education in *Alastor*, and anticipates the 'Dedication' to *Laon and Cythna* – describes how the young Shelley sought for answers to his existential questions about nature and natural agency. Initially, this search was informed by religion and gothic superstition. 'While yet a boy', Shelley writes:

> ... I sought for ghosts, and sped
> Through many a listening chamber, cave and ruin,
> And starlight wood, with fearful steps pursuing
> Hopes of high talk with the departed dead.
> I called on poisonous names with which our youth is fed,
> I was not heard – I saw them not
>
> (*Hymn*, 49–54)

Once again, superstition's 'frail spells' fail to provide satisfactory answers to the mind's existential 'Doubt'. Accordingly, it is only when the young Shelley abandons anthropomorphism in favour of a more philosophical contemplation of nature that the 'passive' imaginative apprehension of 'the truth / Of nature' becomes possible:

> When musing deeply on the lot
> Of life, at that sweet time when winds are wooing
> All vital things that wake to bring

> News of buds and blossoming, –
> Sudden, thy shadow fell on me;
> I shrieked, and clasped my hands in ecstasy!
>
> (*Hymn*, 78–9, 55–60)

Again, it is only through philosophical – as opposed to superstitious – 'musing' on nature that the mind can intuit the immanent presence of Necessity in natural phenomena. Hence, Leighton's claim that the 'deliberate break between "musing deeply" and feeling the sudden shadow fall upon him contradicts the spirit of equanimity and continuity which the poem advocates' seems questionable.[47] Rather, the poem maintains its continuity by presenting the imaginative apprehension of nature's law as the direct consequence of a rejection of superstition in favour of a philosophical 'musing' upon natural phenomena.

This progression from a superstitious to a philosophical contemplation of nature informs the Wordsworthian intertexts that critics have long discerned in the *Hymn*.[48] The last stanza in particular owes much to Wordsworth's *Tintern Abbey* (1798) and *Intimations* ode, two of Shelley's favourite poems. 'The day becomes more solemn and serene', Shelley affirms:

> When noon is past – there is a harmony
> In autumn, and a lustre in its sky,
> Which through the summer is not heard or seen,
> As if it could not be, as if it had not been!
> Thus let thy power, which like the truth
> Of nature on my passive youth
> Descended, to my onward life supply
> Its calm . . .
>
> (*Hymn*, 73–81)

This passage certainly inherits the Wordsworthian distinction between the 'coarser pleasures' of 'boyhood days' and the 'years that bring the philosophic mind' (*Tintern Abbey*, 73; *Intimations of Immortality*, 186). However, Leighton's accusations of 'derivativeness' miss the mark.[49] The passage, she claims, laments a 'loss of intensity', of 'past reverie and ecstasy', and 'celebrates a Wordsworthian compensating tranquillity'.[50] But however accurate this claim might be as an interpretation of Wordsworth's *Intimations* – and one could certainly dispute the accuracy of its value-laden emphasis on 'compensating' – it is by no means an accurate account of the final stanza of Shelley's *Hymn*. Far from a lament for past intensity, Shelley 'celebrates' precisely the *change* in his relationship to the natural world: the shift from superstition to philosophy, the 'cultivation' of the imagination or acquisition of 'intellectual beauty'. The key words here are 'solemn', 'serene', and 'calm'. These are not the tokens of 'resignation' to loss that Leighton perceives, but rather the qualities of Lucretian stoicism: the 'elevated and dreadless composure' that *Queen Mab* recommends as the correct response to natural grandeur.[51]

Hence, while the *Hymn* acknowledges that the actual experience of the 'spirit of BEAUTY' is transitory, the poem affirms that the change in sensibility – the *cultivation* of the imagination – that enables this experience is permanent, positive, and redemptive. Moreover, the *Hymn* emphasises the personal benefits of this change in sensibility. 'Man were immortal, and omnipotent', Shelley affirms, 'Didst thou, unknown and awful as thou art, / Keep with thy glorious train firm state within his heart' (*Hymn*, 39–41).[52] The imaginative apprehension of the 'truth / Of nature', he continues, is 'nourishment' to 'human thought', a curious parallel with the phraseology of Wordsworth's account of the 'spots of time' in the twelfth book of *The Prelude* (1850), which Shelley of course could not have known.

The *Hymn* also recognises the broader political potency of 'intellectual beauty'. The sixth stanza affirms Shelley's 'hope' that the imaginative apprehension of the 'truth / Of nature' will 'free / This world from its dark slavery' (*Hymn*, 69–70). This, of course, is the central tenet of Shelley's revision of the discourse on the sublime: the idea that natural grandeur, correctly interpreted by a cultivated imagination, has politically potent lessons to teach. Accordingly, the *Hymn* goes on to affirm that 'intellectual beauty' has its own 'spells': the politically progressive alternative to the 'frail spells' of religious superstition. These 'spells', which are the 'truth / Of nature', impose democratic, socio-political responsibilities. Firstly, they 'bind' the individual to 'fear himself' – a clear allusion to the dangers of self-love, and an obvious swipe at the solipsistic tendencies of both the Rousseau of the *Rêveries* and the post-*Excursion* Wordsworth (*Hymn*, 83–4).[53] Secondly, subsequent to this abnegation of self-love, they 'bind' the individual to 'love all human kind', an echo of *Alastor*'s assertion that Nature's law imposes on humans a philanthropic duty to 'sympathies with their kind' (*Hymn*, 84; *Poems*, i, p. 463).

In thus asserting the dangers of self-love and the duty of sympathy, the *Hymn*'s closing injunction matches precisely the admirable 'abnegation of self, and . . . worship . . . paid to Love' that Mary's 'Note on the Poems of 1816' attributes to St. Preux (*CPW*, p. 536). And echoing Byron's empirically informed conviction that the revolutionary potency of Rousseau's *Julie* resulted from its embodying this immanent, democratic 'principle of the Universe' (the 'truth / Of nature'), Shelley expresses a 'hope' that 'intellectual beauty' might similarly enrich and empower his own work: 'that thou – O awful LOVELINESS, / Wouldst give whate'er these words cannot express' (*Hymn*, 70–1).[54]

Shelley's intense admiration for *Julie* meant that his voyage around Lake Geneva with Byron quickly became a kind of literary pilgrimage, indeed precisely the kind of pilgrimage recommended by Rousseau in the *Confessions*. But the Swiss locals, at least, had not followed Rousseau's subsequent admonition not to expect to find *Julie*'s characters in the locations where the book is set: 'do not look for them there' (*Rousseau*, v, p. 128). Conversely, Shelley observed that 'the inhabitants of [Clarens] are impressed with an idea, that the persons of this romance had actual existence' (*Letters*, i, p. 486). Accordingly, from the window of their lodging at Clarens, Shelley and Byron's landlady 'pointed out "le bosquet de Julie"': the bower where Julie and St. Preux meet covertly in the fourteenth letter of the first book of the novel, and where they first kiss (*Letters*, i, p. 486). Shelley and Byron visited the site, with Shelley at least affirming that 'it is, indeed, Julia's wood' (*Letters*, i, p. 486). The 'affecting scene' confirmed his sense of the dialectical connection between *Julie* and the 'scenes by which it was inspired': the trees, he told Peacock, 'afford a shade' to the 'worshippers of nature [an echo of the Assassins], who love the memory of that tenderness and peace of which this was the imaginary abode' (*Letters*, i, p. 486).

Shelley and Byron returned to 'Julia's wood' the following day. This time, however, they 'found that the precise spot was now utterly obliterated, and a heap of stones marked the place where the little chapel had once stood' (*Letters*, i, p. 486). While both poets were 'execrating the author of this brutal folly' they learned from their guide that 'the land belonged to the convent of St. Bernard, and that this outrage had been committed by their orders' (*Letters*, i, p. 486). In his note to line 927 of *Childe Harold* III, Byron observes wryly that:

Rousseau has not been particularly fortunate in the preservation of the 'local habitations' he has given to 'airy nothings'. The Prior of Great St Bernard has cut down some of his woods for the sake of a few casks of wine, and Buonaparte has levelled part of the rocks of Meillerie in improving the road to Simplon. The road is an excellent one, but I cannot quite agree with a remark which I heard made, that 'La route vaut mieux que les souvenirs' (*Byron*, pp. 144–5)

Shelley shared Byron's indignation at the apparent triumph of religion and imperialism over the monuments of Rousseau's revolutionary imagination.

His own reaction to the destruction of 'Julia's wood' turns precisely upon the ideological conflict between the 'frail spells' of religion – the false, reactionary 'records that are called reality' – and the 'truth / Of nature' apprehended and expressed by the 'cultivated' few like Rousseau. 'I knew before now', he wrote to Peacock on 27 June:

that if avarice could harden the hearts of men, a system of prescriptive religion has an influence far more inimical to natural sensibility. I know that an isolated man is sometimes restrained by shame from outraging the venerable feelings arising out of the memory of genius, which once made nature even lovelier than itself; but associated man holds it as the very sacrament of his union to forswear all delicacy, all benevolence, all remorse; all that is true, or tender, or sublime (*Letters*, i, pp. 486–7)

Appropriately, then, Shelley's response to the 'outraging' of Rousseau's genius by 'religion' and 'avarice' draws on the quintessentially Rousseauvian conflict between 'natural' and social ('associated') man, the same conflict that informs *Julie*'s praise of Alpine virtue and condemnation of urban decadence.

Shelley's sense of the conflict between 'prescriptive religion' and the 'truth / Of nature', between 'avarice' and the 'intellectual beauty' of 'natural sensibility', came to a head on the final day of his voyage around Lake Geneva. Leaving behind the 'scenes' from *Julie*, Shelley and Byron spent 28 June in Lausanne. In *Childe Harold* III, Byron apostrophised the literary associations of Lausanne and its environs. Unlike Clarens, however, which both Shelley and Byron associated with the revolutionary imagination, Lausanne is connected with an enlightenment, rationalist tradition – although a tradition none the less revolutionary on that account. 'Lausanne! and Ferney!', Byron affirms, 'ye have been the abodes / Of names which unto you bequeath'd a name; / Mortals, who sought and found, by dangerous roads / A path to perpetuity of fame' (*Childe Harold* III, 977–80). These 'Mortals' are Gibbon and Voltaire respectively, the latter – in popular opinion – Rousseau's co-conspirator in instigating the French Revolution.

However, notwithstanding Byron's praise for the revolutionary writings of Lausanne's literati – Voltaire's levelling panegyrics and Gibbon's attacks on Christianity – Shelley seems to have had little time for either while at Lausanne. He makes no mention whatsoever of Voltaire, and offers a highly ambivalent, if ultimately critical portrayal of Gibbon. This is almost certainly because, while Gibbon and Voltaire's politics were akin to Shelley's own, their cynicism ('ridicule', 'sneer') set them apart from the 'natural sensibility' espoused by Rousseau and advocated by Shelley (*Childe Harold* III, 992, 999). Like *Alastor*'s poet-protagonist, who fails to recognise the sympathetic duties imposed by the law of Nature, Gibbon and Voltaire's rationalist 'irony' abnegates the 'truth / Of nature' revealed to the 'cultivated imagination': the individual's obligation to 'fear himself and love all human kind'. Accordingly, Shelley's account of Gibbon and Lausanne turns on precisely the same conflict between 'natural sensibility' and an 'unimpassioned spirit' that informed his response to the destruction of 'Julia's wood'. The passage, though long, needs to be quoted in full. 'We saw Gibbon's house', he wrote to Peacock:

We were shown the decayed summer-house where he finished his History, and the old acacias on the terrace, from which he saw Mont Blanc, after having written the last sentence. There is something grand and even touching in the regret which he expresses at the completion of his task. It was conceived amid the ruins of the Capitol. The sudden departure of his cherished and accustomed toil must have left him, like the death of a dear friend, sad and solitary.

My companion gathered some acacia leaves to preserve in remembrance of him. I refrained from doing so, fearing to outrage the greater and more sacred name of Rousseau; the contemplation of whose imperishable creations had left no vacancy in my heart for mortal things. Gibbon had a cold and unimpassioned spirit. I never felt more inclined to rail at the prejudices which cling to such a thing, than now that Julie and Clarens, Lausanne and the Roman Empire, compelled me to a contrast between Rousseau and Gibbon (*Letters*, i, pp. 487–8)

Although Shelley's first paragraph here is speculative in tone, it actually draws heavily on Gibbon's own account of the completion of the *Decline and Fall*, in both the book itself and in his subsequent *Memoirs* (1796), both of which Shelley had read by 1815 (*Letters*, i, p. 51; *MWSJ*, p. 88). At the end of the *Decline and Fall*, Gibbon informs the reader simply that 'it was among the ruins of the Capitol, that I first conceived the idea of a work which has amused and exercised near twenty years of my life' (*D&F*, vii, p. 325). In his *Memoirs*, however, he provides the background detail upon which Shelley's opening paragraph is based. 'It was on the day, or rather the night, of the twenty-seventh of June', he confirms:

that I wrote the last lines of the last page, in a summer house in my garden. After laying down my pen I took several turns in a *berceau*, or covered walk of Acacias, which commands a prospect of the country, the lake, and the mountains. The air was temperate, the sky was serene; the silver orb of the moon was reflected from the waters, and all Nature was silent. I will not dissemble the first emotions of joy on the recovery of my freedom, and perhaps the establishment of my fame. But my pride was soon humbled, and a sober melancholy was spread over my mind by the idea that I had taken my everlasting leave of an old and agreeable companion.[55]

Having thus rehearsed for Peacock Gibbon's own account of the completion of the *Decline and Fall*, Shelley goes on to draw a 'contrast between Rousseau and Gibbon' which clearly favours the former as the 'greater and more sacred'. The ostensible basis for this contrast is the antithesis between the passionate potency of Rousseau's imagination and Gibbon's rationalism, which Shelley now describes as a 'prejudiced', 'cold and unimpassioned spirit'. However, even Shelley's burgeoning enthusiasm for Rousseau and the imagination is not sufficient to explain such an apparently categorical condemnation of the rationalist Gibbon. After all, Gibbon was – as Byron points out – an enemy of Christianity. Indeed, in a letter to his father on 6 February 1811, Shelley himself had praised Gibbon highly for his advocacy of rational Deism (*Letters*, i, p. 51).

In fact, the contrast Shelley draws between Rousseau and Gibbon is informed not so much by an awareness of their epistemological as of their marked *political* differences (and, by extension, of the different cultural connotations of Clarens and Lausanne). Rousseau, the author of *Julie*, promoted a revolutionary democratic mores: the 'truth / Of nature' revealed by the 'cultivated' imaginative response to the alpine landscape. Gibbon, the author of the *Decline and Fall*, was the century's foremost elegist of empire. Accordingly, Shelley confirms to Peacock that it was the politically resonant contrast between *Julie* / Clarens and Lausanne / the *Decline and Fall* that 'compelled' him to the condemnatory epistemological 'contrast' between Rousseau and Gibbon, between imagination and reason. Ultimately, then, in affirming the supremacy of Rousseau over Gibbon, Shelley is affirming not only the supremacy of imagination over reason, but also the eventual, necessary triumph of virtue (the 'imperishable creation' of the 'cultivated imagination') over empire's 'mortal things'.

Seen in this light, the apparently derivative first paragraph of Shelley's account of Lausanne becomes a potent, Volneyan recasting of Gibbon's *Memoirs*, in which Mont Blanc takes centre stage as a symbol of the revolutionary sublime. Gibbon records that as he completed his *Decline and Fall* he was faced with a 'prospect' of 'mountains'. Shelley's letter to Peacock sharpens the focus. As Gibbon looked nostalgically south from Lausanne towards Italy, he saw not just 'mountains' but Mont Blanc itself, a 'prospect' which he admits 'humbled' his 'pride'. On the first page of his *History* of the humbling of the Roman Empire, Gibbon had described the decline and fall as 'a revolution which will ever be remembered, and is still felt by the nations of the earth' (*D&F*, i, p. 1). On the last – dated 27 June 1787 – he confirmed that the destruction of Rome was 'the greatest, perhaps, and most awful scene, in the history of mankind' (*D&F*, vii, p. 325). The resonance of this statement, written barely two years before the fall of the Bastille, would not have escaped Shelley. Nor would the Volneyan symbolism of the 'imperishably pure' Mont Blanc standing over the 'humbled' 'ruins of the Capitol': a potent emblem of the ultimate, revolutionary triumph of 'the truth / Of nature' over the false 'records that are called reality'.

We have already noted Byron's similar use of Mont Blanc as a Volneyan symbol of the revolutionary sublime in *Childe Harold* III. William Wordsworth had likewise apostrophised the mountain in the 1793 edition of the *Descriptive Sketches*. Immediately after his quasi-Rousseauvian account of the 'golden age of the Alps' – on which Shelley drew in *The Assassins* – Wordsworth proceeds to discuss 'that mountain nam'd of white' which 'towers' 'serene' above an enslaved Savoy (*Descriptive Sketches* (1790), 690, 699). And even earlier, in the twenty-third letter of the first book of *Julie*, Rousseau himself had described the 'inalterable purity' of the Alps in his account of St. Preux's journey through the Upper Valais, linking that environmental 'purity' to the republican mores of the Valais's sparse population (*Rousseau*, vi, pp. 64–6).[56]

Shelley's own poetic account of Mont Blanc at the end of his Alpine summer is firmly in the revolutionary tradition of Rousseau, Wordsworth, and Byron – and indeed it owes a particular debt, as we shall see, to the *Descriptive Sketches*. In the final paragraph of the 'Preface' to the *Six Weeks' Tour*, we are told that *Mont Blanc* was 'composed under the *immediate impression of the deep and powerful feelings* excited by the objects which it attempts to describe; and as an *undisciplined overflowing of the soul*, rests its claim to approbation on an attempt to imitate the untameable wildness and inaccessible solemnity from which those feelings sprang' (*H6WT*, p. vi emphasis added). Mary's 'Note on the Poems of 1816' confirms that this paragraph was written by Shelley (*CPW*, p. 536). The passage is not, as Kapstein and others have suggested, an apology for 'the poem's [ontological] difficulty'.[57] Rather, its language of 'powerful feelings', 'immediate impressions', and an 'undisciplined overflowing of the soul' is the language of the 'Preface' to the *Lyrical Ballads*, the language of the pre-*Excursion* Wordsworth with whom Shelley was 'dosing' Byron 'even to Nausea' at Geneva. It is the language of 'intellectual beauty', the language of 'natural sensibility' – we remember that Shelley had similarly described Rousseau's *Julie* as an '*overflowing* ... of sublimest genius' (*Letters*, i, p. 485; emphasis added). The *Tour*'s emphasis on the passionate spontaneity of *Mont Blanc* accordingly returns us to Shelley's strictures on the conventional discourse on the sublime: his conviction that that discourse had failed to provide an 'authentic record' of the imaginative response to natural grandeur. By stressing the 'immediate' connection between *Mont Blanc* and the 'deep and powerful feelings which it attempts to describe', the *Tour* aims to present the poem as precisely such an 'authentic record', as the revolutionary '*truth* / Of nature'.

MONT BLANC: IMAGINATION, RELIGION AND REVOLUTION

In her journal entry for 22 July 1816, Mary describes the Shelley party's arrival in Chamonix. She notes that 'the summits of the highest [mountains] were hid in Clouds' (*MWSJ*, p. 114). 'But they sometimes peeped out into the blue sky', she continues, 'higher one would think than the safety of God would permit since it is well known that the tower of Babel did not nearly equal them in immensity' (*MWSJ*, p. 114). The unorthodox, antithetical relationship between religion and natural grandeur that informs this passage is by now familiar as the central tenet of Shelley's revision of the discourse on the sublime. Like the *Hymn to Intellectual Beauty*, *Mont Blanc* is informed by his conviction that the 'truth / Of nature' is inimical to religion, that natural grandeur – correctly interpreted by the 'cultivated' imagination – has potent lessons to teach.

Following Harold Bloom, it has long been customary to read *Mont Blanc* as a response to Samuel Taylor Coleridge's *Hymn Before Sun-rise, In the Vale of Chamouni*, published in *The Morning Post* and *Poetical Register* in 1802, and again in the eleventh number of *The Friend* in 1809.[58] Although there is no direct evidence that Shelley read the *Hymn* it has been suggested that he had access to an edition of *The Friend* while in Switzerland in 1816, and numerous verbal echoes imply familiarity.[59] Moreover, *Mont Blanc* clearly responds to the pious, Christian account of the natural sublime that informs Coleridge's *Hymn* (the title of which alone has religious connotations). Indeed, as Matthews and Everest suggest, it is possible that Shelley altered *Mont Blanc*'s subtitle specifically 'in order to point up the poem's implicit address' to Coleridge (*Poems*, i, p. 533).[60]

The *Hymn* – actually an expanded translation of Friederika Brun's 'Chamouni beym Sonnenaufgange' (1795) – is the quintessential poetic statement of the conventional, religious 'records' of natural grandeur, the 'records' that informed Chamonix's burgeoning tourist industry.[61] In a prefatory note to the versions of the text that appeared in *The Morning Post* and *Poetical Register*, Coleridge enthused that 'the whole vale [of Chamonix], its every light, its every sound, must needs impress every mind not utterly callous with the thought – Who *would* be, who *could* be an Atheist in this valley of wonders' (*Coleridge*, p. 362).[62] The *Hymn* itself continues emphatically in this vein, apostrophising the immanently present creator-God presumed to be responsible for Chamonix's overwhelming affective power. The poem opens with an anxious recognition of the 'awful', inhuman silence of the alpine landscape (*Hymn Before Sun-rise*, 3, 5). Mont Blanc itself is an 'awful Form', a 'dread and silent Mount' that rises 'silently' from its 'silent sea of pines' (*Hymn Before Sun-rise*, 5, 13, 6–7). But the poem quickly moves to resolve this anxiety by attributing a 'voice' to the mountain (*Hymn Before Sun-rise*, 60, 62). Paralleling Alison's reading of natural grandeur as the 'signs' and 'expressions' of deity, Coleridge addresses Mont Blanc as one of the 'signs and wonders of the element', which comfortingly 'utter forth God' in response to his troubled questions about natural agency (*ENPT*, ii, p. 423; *Hymn Before Sun-rise*, 68–9).

The re-imagining of the mountain from an 'awful' 'silent' 'form' to a 'sweet' revelatory 'voice' takes place at the end of the *Hymn*'s first stanza – from then on, all doubts resolved, the poem is simply an apostrophe (*Hymn Before Sun-rise*, 17). 'O dread and silent Mount!', Coleridge writes, 'I gazed upon thee':

> Till thou, still present to bodily sense,
> Didst vanish from my thought: entranced in prayer
> I worshipped the Invisible alone
>
> (*Hymn Before Sun-rise*, 13–16)

The passage confirms the defeat of the empirically grounded understanding by the sensory excesses of the natural sublime. The understanding is paralysed: 'entranced' or 'enrapt' (*Hymn Before Sun-rise*, 21). The distinction between 'thought' and 'bodily sense' thus marks the mind's attempts to go beyond the defeat of the empirical understanding by the 'dread and silent Mount', and move towards an intuition of the immanent ('Invisible') power in the landscape. More precisely, that distinction marks the mind's attempts to redress the anxiety of its defeat by *re-imagining* the overwhelming affective power of the mountain in the comforting image of a paternal God. Accordingly, Coleridge confirms that the 'awful', sense-defeating and material Mont Blanc 'vanishes' from his 'thought' while the immanent ('Invisible') presence appears in its place. And he is in absolutely no doubt about the identity of this 'Invisible' power. 'Who made you glorious as the Gates of Heaven', he asks the landscape: 'GOD! let the torrents, like a shout of nations, / Answer! and let the ice-plains echo, GOD' (*Hymn Before Sun-rise*, 54, 58–9).

Shelley's revision of the discourse on the sublime turned precisely upon a rejection of the kind of religious, anthropomorphic response to natural processes embodied in Coleridge's *Hymn*. Shelley follows Coleridge in recognising the 'awful' material silence of the mountain. Mont Blanc is a 'desert peopled by the storms alone', a landscape of 'silent snow' where 'winds contend / Silently', and even the lightning is 'voiceless' (*Mont Blanc*, 67, 74, 134–5, 137). But while the *Hymn* comfortingly transforms this 'awful' material ('bodily') silence into the immaterial 'sign' of God's immanent ('Invisible') presence, the sceptical Shelley is keen to assert that there are no such signs in the landscape, 'none' who can 'reply' to 'unfathomable' questions about natural agency (*Mont Blanc*, 75, 64). Again, while conventionally the metaphorical connection between the sense-defeating landscape of the natural sublime and God is positive and redemptive, Shelley sees this connection as a 'vulgar' illusion of the untutored imagination – an illusion that originated and now sustains 'the falsehoods of religious systems' (*Poems*, i, p. 360).

Mont Blanc accordingly seeks to dispel this 'vulgar' and reactionary illusion of divine presence in the landscape of the natural sublime and reveal the revolutionary 'truth / Of nature'. Hence the poem emphasises the need to *resist* the mind's attempts to re-imagine the sense-defeating power of the mountain in the comforting image of a paternal God, the need to stare unflinchingly – with the sceptic's 'elevated and dreadless composure' – at the 'awful scene' (*Poems*, i, p. 379; *Mont Blanc*, 15). Only by so doing, does the 'truth / Of nature' become apparent.

Like the *Hymn to Intellectual Beauty*, *Mont Blanc* opens with an ontological statement. 'The everlasting universe of things', Shelley writes:

> Flows through the mind, and rolls its rapid waves,
> Now dark – now glittering – now reflecting gloom –
> Now lending splendour, where from secret springs
> The source of human thought its tribute brings
> Of waters, – with a sound but half its own
>
> (*Mont Blanc*, 1–6)

As Timothy Clark and Richard Isomaki have suggested, this passage describes the dynamics of conscious experience in general, a suggestion borne out by the opening of the A-text of *Mont Blanc* which confirms that '*In day*, the everlasting universe [etc.]' (*Mont* Blanc (A-text), 1; emphasis added).[63] As such, the poem's ontology is unequivocally empirical and materialist – Leighton's reading of these lines as evidence that *Mont Blanc* makes 'no hierarchical discrimination between the status of the mind and the everlasting universe of things' is unconvincing.[64] The mind is passive in perception, the 'universe of things' is prior to 'human thought'. But the mind is also capable of limited, active reflection upon the information that it receives from the senses. The products of this active reflection – the mind's contribution ('tribute') to conscious experience – are occasioned by, but also to some extent distinct from the determining information received via the senses. Hence, Shelley likens reflection to the sound of a 'feeble brook', which remains autonomous despite the noise of the 'vast river' (the 'universe of things') nearby (*Mont Blanc*, 7–10).

Having established the ordinary relationship between the 'mind' and the 'universe of things', the second section of *Mont Blanc* examines the dynamics of that relationship in the encounter with the natural sublime. As with the *Hymn to Intellectual Beauty*, *Mont Blanc* refers to an immanent ('secret', 'remote', and 'inaccessible') 'Power' which is manifested in 'awful' natural phenomena (*Mont Blanc*, 17, 97, 16). Hence, for example, Shelley describes an 'athereal waterfall' whose 'veil / Robes some unsculptured image' (*Mont Blanc*, 26–7).[65] Mont Blanc itself functions as the primary symbol of this immanent 'Power'. The 'Power', of course, is material Necessity (the 'truth / of Nature'), what *Mont Blanc* calls the 'secret strength of things / Which governs thought, and to the infinite dome / Of heaven is as a law' (*Mont Blanc*, 139–41). And again as in the *Hymn*, the mind does not perceive this 'remote' 'Power' directly, but only the various 'awful' manifestations of 'Power' in natural phenomena.

Extending the river metaphor used in the poem's opening epistemological statement, the second section of *Mont Blanc* uses the relationship between the river and ravine of Arve to figure the mind's engagement with the 'power' that is manifested in the sublime landscape.[66] 'Thus thou, Ravine of Arve', Shelley writes, 'dark, deep Ravine':

> Thou many-coloured, many-voicèd vale,
> Over whose pines, and crags, and caverns sail
> Fast cloud shadows and sunbeams: awful scene,
> Where Power in likeness of the Arve comes down
> From the ice gulfs that gird his secret throne
>
> (*Mont Blanc*, 12–17)

These lines maintain the epistemology outlined in *Mont Blanc*'s first section, where the 'mind' is the passive receptacle of sensory input from the 'universe' of 'things which governs thought'. The ravine represents the 'mind', and the river – which shapes and determines the ravine – the sensory input from the 'universe of things'. In the encounter with natural grandeur, this input is overwhelming: the mind ('path' / ravine) is 'pervaded' by objective reality (*Mont Blanc*, 33, 32). Accordingly, Shelley confirms that the ravine's 'caverns' are dominated by the Arve's 'commotion': 'a loud, lone sound no other sound can tame' (*Mont Blanc*, 30–31). But Shelley also emphasises that this overwhelming sensory 'commotion' is not the immanent 'Power' of the landscape itself, only a *manifestation* of that 'Power'. Hence, the Arve (the sense data which dominates the mind / ravine) is only the '*likeness*' of the ultimately '*secret*' 'Power' immanent in the landscape (*Mont Blanc*, 16–17; emphasis added).

The role of the ravine and river of Arve as a figure for the experiential relationship between the 'mind' and the 'universe of things' in the encounter with the natural sublime is re-affirmed by the apostrophe to the ravine beginning at line 34. 'Dizzy Ravine!', Shelley writes, emphasising the literal and sensory vertigo produced by the natural sublime:

> And when I gaze on thee
> I seem as in a trance sublime and strange
> To muse on my own separate fantasy,
> My own, my human mind, which passively
> Now renders and receives fast influencings,
> Holding an unremitting interchange
> With the clear universe of things around

> (*Mont Blanc*, 34–40)

This apostrophe is not a Wordsworthian moment, not an instance of the egotistical sublime in which the mind redresses the anxiety of its defeat by re-imagining the agency of that defeat in its own image. Rather, again, Shelley's apostrophe is an epistemological figure – and the epistemology remains consistent with that set out in *Mont Blanc*'s first section. There is a clear empirical dichotomy between the 'mind' and the 'universe of things'; the mind's conscious experience of the universe is an 'unremitting interchange', partly passive (sensation) and partly active (reflection).

Shelley's apostrophe to the ravine concludes with a specific focus on the mind's reaction to the overwhelming sensory input from the 'universe of things' in the encounter with the natural sublime. Still drawing on the sceptical epistemology of Hume and Drummond – in which reality is mediated to the mind via ideas derived from the senses – Shelley outlines the mind's attempts to come to terms with the 'awful scene' by finding internal ideas appropriate to the overwhelming external influence. In the encounter with natural grandeur, the mind is:

> One legion of wild thoughts, whose wandering wings
> Now float above thy darkness, and now rest
> Where that or thou art no unbidden guest,
> In the still cave of the witch Poesy,
> Seeking among the shadows that pass by,
> Ghosts of all things that are, some shade of thee,
> Some phantom, some faint image; till the breast
> From which they fled recalls them, thou art there!
>
> (*Mont Blanc*, 41–8)

The materialist defeat of the mind / 'cave' by the mountain – the defeat of the empirical understanding by the natural sublime – prompts the mind's attempts to re-imagine the 'awful' landscape by finding amongst its ideal 'shadows' / 'ghosts' of reality an adequate or appropriate 'image'. In the theistic configuration of discourse on the sublime, this re-imagining results in an anthropomorphic image of God. Hence, by figuratively locating the mind's imaginative activity in the 'still cave of the witch Poesy' Shelley is more probably recalling Bacon's primitive and reactionary idols of the cave than Plato's famous parable.[67] As already noted, however, Shelley's conception of the 'still cave' was doubtless also influenced by his experience of the 'magnificent vault of ice' at the foot of the Mer de Glace, and his decision to locate the mind's imaginative activity in a cave may well recall Marc Théodore Bourrit's resonant description of this very scene:

an enormous mass of ice, twenty times as large as the front of our cathedral of *St. Peter*, and so constructed, that we have only to change our situation, to make it resemble whatever we please. It is a magnificent palace ... a majestic temple ... It has the appearance of a fortress ... and at the bottom is a grotto, terminating in a dome of bold construction. This fairy dwelling, this enchanted residence, or this *cave of Fancy*, is the source of the Arveron.[68]

Whatever Shelley's source for the 'still cave' passage may have been, however, the conclusion of *Mont Blanc*'s apostrophe to the ravine of Arve evidently describes the mind's superstitious attempts to redress the anxiety of its defeat by *re-imagining* the material agency of that defeat (as in Bourrit's succession of artificial edifices).[69] And crucially, Shelley emphasises the need to resist this anxious, figurative 'labour' of the imagination, the need to 'recall' the mind's attempts to re-figure the 'remote, serene, and inaccessible' 'power' of the landscape. Rather, the 'awful scene' must be left as an 'unsculptured image', as 'the naked countenance of earth' which alone, Shelley affirms, can 'teach the adverting mind' (*Mont Blanc*, 97, 27, 98, 100). In short, it is only by resisting the primitive urge to re-imagine or anthropomorphise the 'awful scene' that the immanent 'Power' manifested in that scene, the 'truth / Of nature', can be apprehended: 'the breast / From which they fled recalls them, thou art there!'. Paradoxically, it is only by accepting Mont Blanc's essential silence that the mountain's true 'voice' can be heard.

Accordingly, in the third section of *Mont Blanc* Shelley re-states the central tenet of his revision of the discourse on the sublime: his conviction that there are two possible imaginative responses to the natural sublime, the primitive and the 'wise' (*Mont Blanc*, 82). 'The wilderness has a mysterious tongue', Shelley writes:

> Which teaches awful doubt, or faith so mild,
> So solemn, so serene, that man may be
> But for such faith with nature reconciled
>
> (*Mont Blanc*, 76–9)[70]

The first of these responses – 'awful doubt' – is the existential anxiety attendant on the defeat of the understanding by the natural sublime, the 'doubt' that prompts the 'vulgar' imagination to attempt to reconfigure the agency of that defeat in the comforting image of a paternal God (and we remember the *Hymn to Intellectual Beauty*'s claim that the 'frail spells' of religion are the product of the primitive mind's attempts to resolve the 'Doubt, Chance, and mutability' it perceives in nature).[71] The alternative to this superstitious reaction to the natural sublime is a 'mild', 'solemn', and 'serene' 'faith' that enables man to be 'reconciled' with 'nature', that replaces a hierarchical model of nature with a democratic, secular organicism. This 'mild' reconciliatory 'faith' – the antithesis of the 'frail' hierarchical 'spells' of religion – is the doctrine of Necessity: the 'truth / Of nature' revealed to the 'cultivated imagination'.[72]

Ultimately, then, *Mont Blanc* affirms that beyond the imaginative primitivism of the pious discourse on the sublime there is another, politically progressive alternative available to the 'cultivated imagination'. We are returned to *Queen Mab*'s seminal claim that it is possible to 'rightly feel' the 'mystery' of natural grandeur, that the natural sublime – correctly interpreted by the 'cultivated' imagination – has politically potent lessons to teach. 'Thou hast a voice, great Mountain', Shelley affirms, 'to repeal':

> Large codes of fraud and woe; not understood
> By all, but which the wise, and great, and good
> Interpret, or make felt, or deeply feel
>
> (*Mont Blanc*, 77–83)

The passage encapsulates Shelley's revision of the discourse on the sublime. On one level, the intellectual elitism of this passage certainly continues Shelley's already-noted indignation at the commercialisation of the Alpine sublime by and for the 'vulgar great'. However, the passage also rehearses the broader – and now familiar – dichotomy in Shelley's thought between the 'vulgar' and the 'cultivated' or 'wise' imaginative response to the natural sublime. While Alison – speaking for more than a century of aesthetic speculation in Britain – had suggested that no man of 'genuine taste' could fail to intuit the presence of God in the sense-defeating landscape of the natural sublime, Shelley now counters with the claim that the true meaning of the mountain's 'voice' is 'not understood / By all' (*ENPT*, ii, p. 442). Opposing Alison's notion of a 'genuine taste' which is the preserve of the moneyed upper-classes, Shelley argues that it is rather only the 'wise, and great, and good' who are able to correctly 'interpret, or make felt, or deeply feel' the radical implications of the natural sublime. In short, for Shelley it is not the propertied aristocracy but a philosophical aristocracy – the few who possess a 'cultivated imagination' – who are able to learn the revolutionary 'truth / Of nature' from the mountain.

The ability of the 'wise' imagination – the imagination 'considerably tinctured with science and enlarged by cultivation' – to go beyond the primitivism of the theistic discourse on the sublime to an intuition of the 'truth / Of nature' informs *Mont Blanc*'s oft-quoted conclusion. 'The secret Strength of things / which governs thought, and to the infinite dome / Of Heaven is as a law, inhabits thee!', Shelley tells the mountain:

> And what were thou, and earth, and stars, and sea,
> If to the human mind's imaginings
> Silence and solitude were vacancy?
>
> (*Mont Blanc*, 139–44)

As noted earlier, this final question is commonly read as signalling the poem's transition from materialism to idealism, as an epistemologically inconsistent refutation of the claim, made only two lines earlier, that the 'Strength of things . . . governs thought'. In fact, quite the contrary is the case. *Mont Blanc*'s closing question is entirely compatible with the scepticism informing the rest of the poem. The final lines are not an idealist affirmation of the non-existence of extra-mental reality, not a subordination of the 'universe of things' to the 'human mind'. Rather, as Leask suggests, *Mont Blanc*'s conclusion is almost certainly a sceptical recasting of Ramond de Carbonnières' apostrophe to the imagination at the end of his 'Observations on the Glaciers' (1782), translated and published as an appendix by Helen

Maria Williams in her 1798 *Tour in Switzerland*.[73] Carbonnières' account of the difficulty that the empirical 'reason' faces in attempting to conceive the enormous time-scale involved in the geological processes exhibited by the Alpine landscape points up the role of the imagination in the encounter with the natural sublime. 'Imagination seizes the reins which Reason drops', Carbonnières confirms, and 'hails' the glimpse of 'eternity' revealed by the landscape with 'religious terror'.[74] Once again, we are returned to the 'vulgar', theistic configuration of the discourse on the sublime. But 'let us forgive [the imagination] its chimeras', Carbonnières continues:

For what would there be great in our conceptions, or glorious in our actions, if finite were not, through its illusions, continually changed into infinite, space into immensity, time into eternity, and fading laurels into immortal crowns![75]

Mont Blanc's conclusion transforms Carbonnières' mediating apology for the 'illusions' of the imagination into an unequivocal vindication of the faculty. The poem's final lines re-affirm the central, sceptical point of Shelley's revision of the discourse on the sublime: only the 'wise' imagination can go beyond the defeat of the understanding by the natural sublime towards an intuition of the Necessity informing the landscape: the 'truth / Of nature'. However, since Necessity is an 'inaccessible' principle, unknown and unknowable, unavailable to reason, any intuition of Necessity must be a product – an 'illusion' if you like – of the imagination. Hence, Shelley has not lost sight of that 'deep abyss' first sighted in his 'science of mind', the unsettling possibility – pointed up again in *Mont Blanc*'s closing question – that 'the deep truth is imageless' (as *Prometheus Unbound* will later put it), that *all* knowledge may be in reality only a 'code', an 'imagining'. 'And what were thou, and earth, and stars, and sea', Shelley asks, 'if to the human mind's imaginings / Silence and solitude were vacancy?'. The question is rhetorical, to an extent even irrelevant since no definitive answer is possible. If all knowledge is a 'code' or an 'imagining' – a 'figure' painted on a 'bubble', as Rousseau himself will later put it in *The Triumph of Life* – then the important task, the crucial responsibility of the 'wise', is to imagine the most politically desirable 'code' (*Triumph of Life*, 249–50).[76] Effectively, then, for all the *Hymn to Intellectual Beauty*'s emphasis on 'truth / Of nature', *Mont Blanc*'s sceptical iconoclasm consciously replaces one 'code' of natural grandeur – the reactionary, religious 'codes of fraud and woe' – with another, politically progressive 'code'.

This progressive 'code' is set out in the fourth section of *Mont Blanc*, which revises the conventional, religious 'records' of nature and the natural sublime. Nature is presented as subject not to divine regulation, but to its

own internal (Necessary) laws. Scientific understanding of natural phenomena reveals that nature is not created in the religious sense. Rather it is
an 'eternal' 'daedal' cycle: 'all things that move and breathe with toil and
sound / Are born and die; revolve, subside, and swell' (*Mont Blanc*, 94–5).

Only Necessity ('Power') – the immutable 'law' governing nature –
'dwells apart' from this cycle (*Mont Blanc*, 96). The existence and operation
of this 'law' is the 'awful' revolutionary 'truth' revealed to the 'wise' by the
'naked countenance of earth'. This 'truth' is figured in the poem – and
ultimately in the landscape itself – by Mont Blanc's glaciers, which Shelley
had already described in a letter to Peacock as explicit evidence of 'the
unsparing hand of Necessity' (*Letters*, i, p. 499). Shelley's apostrophe to the
glaciers effectively relocates catastrophe – the ideological fulcrum of both
conservative earth science and post-revolutionary politics – within a secular
'economy of natural, and by implication political history'. That is, *Mont
Blanc*'s account of the glaciers states the politically potent (re)configuration
of the discourse on the sublime that is available to the 'wise': the mountain's revolutionary 'voice'.

Shelley's account of Mont Blanc's glaciers echoes the Volneyan ruins of
empire tropes associated with Necessity's 'unsparing hand' in early works
like *Queen Mab*. The glaciers are 'a flood of ruin' which overwhelms the
symbols of religious empire: the 'dome, pyramid, and pinnacle' described
in line 104. In other words, the glaciers' inexorable advance on the valley
figures the 'awful', *necessary* destruction of empire, the inevitability – the
naturalness – of revolution. Indeed Shelley's account of how the glaciers
'creep / Like snakes that watch their prey, from their far fountains' is telling
in this regard (*Mont Blanc*, 100–1). The use of snake imagery – while
clearly suggested by the glaciers' form – almost certainly derives from
Wordsworth's 1793 *Descriptive Sketches*, where the same glaciers are likened
to 'two enormous serpents': the revolutionary, Volneyan instruments by
which the 'serene' Mont Blanc 'assails' the enslaved Savoy at its feet
(*Descriptive Sketches* (1790), 696, 699, 694).

In one sense then, the inexorable advance of Mont Blanc's glaciers
represents the inevitable revolutionary destruction wrought by Necessity
upon mankind, the 'awful' destruction that the Shelley party had witnessed
for themselves during their first trip to mainland Europe in 1814.[77] 'The
dwelling-place / Of insects, beasts, and birds, becomes [the glaciers] spoil',
Shelley confirms:

> Their food and their retreat for ever gone,
> So much of life and joy is lost. The race

Of man flies far in dread; his work and dwelling
Vanish, like smoke before the tempest's stream,
And their place is not known

(*Mont Blanc*, 114–20)

This is the conventional, catastrophic account of the natural sublime – and the conventional, post-restoration account of the French Revolution: destruction as the agent of divine retribution. But beyond the apparent destruction of the glaciers, the apparent debacle and failure of the revolution, there is a deeper truth available to the 'wise' or 'cultivated' imagination. Scientific understanding of the 'awful scene' enables the 'wise' imagination to intuit that 'below' the glaciers 'vast caves':

Shine in the rushing torrents' restless gleam,
Which from those secret chasms in tumult welling
Meet in the vale, and one majestic River,
The breath and blood of distant lands, for ever
Rolls its loud waters to the ocean waves,
Breathes its swift vapours to the circling air

(*Mont Blanc*, 120–6)[78]

In short, the 'wise' imagination – the imagination 'considerably tinctured with science, and enlarged by cultivation' – is able to see beyond the immediate destruction caused by the glaciers as they advance towards the valley and intuit the long term benefits immanent in that process: the melt-river which becomes the 'breath and blood of distant lands'. This recognition effectively reconfigures the natural sublime, revealing it as evidence of 'awful' natural processes that – while destructive in the short term – nevertheless produce long-term benefits. Nor, again, is this recognition limited to natural history. Rather it also has potent implications for the interpretation of recent political history in an era of post-Napoleonic reaction. For if Mont Blanc's glaciers represent the natural violence of revolution, then they also affirm the ultimate triumph of revolutionary values despite the apparent destruction which they produced in the short term (seen in this light, Shelley's reference to the 'distant lands' fed by the glaciers is surely an allusion to America). And indeed the *Six Weeks' Tour* sounds precisely this note in defence of the French Revolution in its account of the monument to Rousseau in the Plainpalais at Geneva. 'Notwithstanding the temporary bloodshed and injustice with which it was polluted', the *Tour* affirms, the French Revolution 'has produced enduring benefits to mankind, which all the chicanery of statesmen, nor even the great conspiracy of kings, can entirely render vain' (*H6WT*, p. 102).

In conclusion, then, Shelley's *Mont Blanc* is critical of conventional and ultimately reactionary attempts to re-imagine the defeat of the understanding by the 'awful' mountain in the comforting image of a paternal God. Rather, Shelley argues that it is only by stoically accepting the landscape's emptiness that the mountain's true, revolutionary 'voice' can be heard. The 'truth / Of nature' revealed to the 'cultivated imagination' is not God but Necessity: nature's egalitarian, albeit inhuman law. To read the mountain in the pietist terms proposed by the conventional religious discourse on the sublime is to legitimate and perpetuate 'large codes of fraud and woe', i.e. reactionary, religious ideologies. But to see the 'awful scene' as evidence of nature's law – as evidence of Necessity – is to promote the 'repeal' of those 'codes' by replacing a creationist, catastrophist 'code' of natural grandeur – indeed of nature as a whole – with an egalitarian, progressive 'code'. Thus *Mont Blanc* is concerned to dehumanise, to de-personify the landscape of the natural sublime, to 'repeal' the 'vulgar' mistake that originated and now legitimates a creator-God who is the 'prototype of human misrule'. The poem is an attempt to free the mind from this 'vulgar' 'legislature', an attempt to revise the body of cultural 'code' surrounding natural grandeur. In thus re-asserting the essential inhumanity of the mountain, Shelley is anticipating the reform strategy outlined in his later essay *On Life*: to 'destroy ... error and the roots of error', to 'leave ... what it is too often the task of the reformer in political and ethical questions to leave, a vacancy' (*Prose*, p. 173).

CHAPTER 4

Writing the revolution: Laon and Cythna *(1817)*

Shelley, Mary, and Claire left Geneva at nine in the morning on 29 August 1816, and headed back towards England on a 'shorter route' which avoided Paris, passing instead through Fontainebleu and Versailles (*MWSJ*, p. 132; *Letters*, i, p. 504). Having stopped at Fontainebleu *en route*, they arrived at Versailles just after nine in the evening on 2 September (*MWSJ*, p. 132). The following morning, they visited the 'famous palace' itself (*Letters*, i, p. 154).

Shelley recorded this visit in Mary's journal.[1] His account stresses the 'stupid ... expense' involved in constructing the palace, noting moreover that there was 'something effeminate and royal' in the décor *(MWSJ*, p. 133). He immediately contrasts this 'royal' effeminacy with the classical, republican virtue that he had recently invoked in response to Chamonix's fideist tourist industry. 'Could a Grecian architect have commanded all the labours and money which was expended on Versailles', he observes, 'he would have produced a fabric such as the whole world has never equalled' (*MWSJ*, p. 133). Shelley goes on to explain the bloody course of the French Revolution in terms of the resentment bred in the people by the impact and exhibition of such 'stupid ... expense', echoing his 1812 strictures on the prince regent's fête at Carlton House. 'The present desolation of France', he affirms, 'the fury of the injured people, and all the horrors to which they abandoned themselves ... flowed naturally enough from expenditures so immense' (*MWSJ*, p. 133–4). Shelley complains, however, that 'the people who showed [them] the palace obstinately refused to say anything about the Revolution', an unsurprising obstinacy, perhaps, in post-Restoration France (*MWSJ*, p. 133).[2] Needless to say, Shelley's own account of Versailles is not so hesitant in this respect. The entry in Mary's journal concludes on a resonant, Volneyan note: the 'now vacant rooms of this palace', Shelley affirms, 'imaged well the hollow show of monarchy' (*MWSJ*, p. 134).

The Shelley party arrived back in England on 8 September. Shelley immediately wrote to Byron in Geneva to inform him of the safe arrival of the third canto of *Childe Harold's Pilgrimage*, which he had agreed to deliver to Byron's publisher, John Murray. Shelley's letter also mentions Fontainebleu and Versailles, which he says 'are well worth visiting as monuments of human power; grand, yet somewhat faded' (*Letters*, i, p. 504). He singles out Versailles, in particular, as 'the scene of some of the most interesting events of what may be called the master theme of the epoch in which we live – the French Revolution' (*Letters*, i, p. 504).[3]

Shelley's critics have usually – and quite correctly – situated this definition of the Revolution in the context of Shelley's ongoing attempts to correct the historical pessimism of Byron's recent work.[4] Three weeks after his return to England, Shelley wrote to Byron again, hoping that he might soon 'apply [himself] to the composition of an Epic poem' that would be a 'fountain from which the thoughts of men shall draw strength and beauty' rather than despair (*Letters*, i, p. 507). 'In a more presumptuous mood', Shelley concludes, presumably referring back to a conversation that summer, 'I recommended the Revolution of France as a theme involving pictures of all that is best suited to interest and to instruct mankind' (*Letters*, i, p. 508).

Seen in this context, the point of Shelley's definition seems clear enough; however, we should be wary of overlooking its full significance. After all, by defining the Revolution as 'the master theme of the epoch in which we live', Shelley was not simply identifying it as an appropriate poetic subject ('theme'). Rather, he was identifying the Revolution as *the* appropriate subject because of its status as an *epoch-making* event. In other words, Shelley's recommendation was premised upon a conviction that the Revolution had defined the prevailing attitudes of public opinion or the 'one mind'. To put it more precisely, Shelley recognised that the disastrous collapse of the Revolution meant that historical and political pessimism had become culturally dominant from the 1790s onwards. The pessimism of Byron's work both reflected and perpetuated this broader cultural malaise. Hence, in urging Byron to write an 'Epic poem' about the Revolution – a poem that would be an instructive 'fountain' of 'strength' and 'beauty' – Shelley was not simply attempting to correct the failure of Byron's personal political confidence. Rather, he was also urging Byron to use his 'uncommon powers' to challenge the dominant, catastrophist and reactionary 'records' of the Revolution in the 'one mind' (*Letters*, i, p. 507). Byron, he hoped, would become a kind of latter-day Rousseau: a poet whose 'astonishingly great' imagination could be 'exerted' to reveal '"the truth of things"' about the Revolution (*Letters*, i, p. 507).[5] Writing the Revolution would therefore also be righting the Revolution: correcting public interpretation of what had happened in France.

In spring 1817, Shelley would take up this challenge himself, and make the French Revolution the explicit 'master theme' of his own 'Epic poem'. The attempt was essentially a continuation of the poetico-political project begun the previous summer in *Mont Blanc*'s account of glaciation: an attempt to revise the cultural 'records' surrounding history's foremost *political* catastrophe, to relocate the apparent disaster of the Revolution within a long-term, systematic, *natural* economy of hope. The result was *Laon and Cythna* (1817), written in the shadow of another potential revolution-in-the-making: the Pentridge uprising.[6]

Central to *Laon and Cythna*'s anti-catastrophist understanding of the French Revolution, then, is the notion of a natural history of politics, a history within which the Napoleonic collapse of the Revolution is a natural part of the irresistible, but gradual and long-term process of political change. The idea of a natural history of politics allows Shelley both to challenge public political despondency about the Revolution itself and to promote faith in a gradual, moral and intellectual reform, to offer, in short, a 'wise' interpretation of the Revolution. However, the idea of a natural history of politics is not without cost. For all its apparently unshakeable confidence in the efficacy of gradualist politics, *Laon and Cythna* is scarred by familiar Shelleyan anxieties about the nature and origins of political change, anxieties that are again voiced in the terms of Shelley's engagement with the discourse on the sublime.

THE *BEAU IDÉAL* OF THE FRENCH REVOLUTION?

Laon and Cythna has not received a great deal of attention from Shelley scholars, due in no small part to influential early dismissals by critics like Bloom and White. It is still, to use Lloyd Abbey's summation, 'a poem much maligned and widely ignored'.[7] Criticism of the text has tended to emphasise perceived weakness in structure, largely disregarding Shelley's claim that '*unity* [was] one of the qualifications aimed at', and that the poem was accordingly 'composed' with specific 'attention to the refinement and accuracy of language, and the connexion of its parts' (*Letters*, i, pp. 563, 557; original emphasis).[8] Other critics have argued – more damagingly – that the poem is *thematically* incoherent: Harold Bloom, for example, dismisses *Laon and Cythna* as an 'abortive allegorical epic'.[9]

Charges like Bloom's – and they have often been made – have generally been premised upon the apparent contradiction between *Laon and Cythna*'s ostensible aim of correcting post-Napoleonic political

despondency and the disastrous course of the revolution actually narrated
in the text. Donna Richardson usefully summarises the critical consensus:
'the poem would seem to be a blueprint only for the achievement of
an individual excellence that manifests itself politically in futile self-
sacrifice'.[10] It seems to me that this consensus stems more from a misunderstanding of *Laon and Cythna*'s agenda than from any authorial
incoherence, from a misunderstanding, that is to say, of the *means* by
which Shelley sought to restore public faith in the possibility of political
change. This misunderstanding can be traced to a number of sources.
One such source is undoubtedly the complex ontology laid out in *Laon
and Cythna*'s framing cantos, of which I will say more later. Another
prominent source of confusion, however, has been Shelley's often quoted
claim that *Laon and Cythna* represents 'the *beau ideal* as it were of the
French Revolution'.[11] On the face of it, after all, this claim would seem
to identify the poem as the narrative of an idealised revolution, and hence
the apparent difficulty of squaring this identification with the actual
events narrated. McNiece's reaction typifies critical response: faced with
the 'carnage' of *Laon and Cythna*'s final cantos, it 'becomes difficult to
comprehend what Shelley meant by referring to his revolution as a
beau ideal'.[12]

We can immediately begin to resolve this 'difficulty', however, by
addressing the sense in which Shelley actually intended the phrase *beau
ideal* to qualify his text. *Laon and Cythna*'s critics have uniformly – and
quite understandably – interpreted the phrase in its conventional English
sense: that is, as referring to an idealised version of the French Revolution
(and hence, again, the difficulty in squaring this interpretation with the
events narrated). None of the poem's commentators has, to my knowledge,
pursued the obvious similarity between the term *beau ideal* and the
vocabulary of 'intellectual beauty' developed by Shelley in the summer of
1816, the summer before he began writing *Laon and Cythna*, and during
which he first conceived the idea of an 'Epic poem' about the French
Revolution.[13] Yet it is in this similarity that the key to his problematic
description of the poem can be found.

As we have seen, both Shelley's eponymous *Hymn* and its related writings
repeatedly identify 'intellectual beauty' not only as an attribute of the mind
but also as an experiential category, referring both to the apprehension and to
the embodiment by the cultivated imagination of the Necessitarian 'truth /
Of nature'. In the third canto of *Childe Harold*, Byron had already used the
term 'ideal beauty' – the most literal translation of *beau ideal* – in exactly this
sense, describing Rousseau's 'love' of 'ideal beauty' and affirming that '*This*

breathed itself to life in Júlie' (*Childe Harold* III 738, 740, 743; original emphasis). There are good reasons to suppose, then, that in identifying *Laon and Cythna* as 'the *beau ideal* ... of the French Revolution', Shelley did not intend to identify the poem as the narrative of an idealised French (or other) Revolution.[14] Rather he was confirming – albeit in a vocabulary only fully comprehensible within his own circle – that the poem was an embodiment of the Necessitarian 'truth' about the Revolution, the anti-catastrophist 'truth' only accessible to the 'wise' or cultivated imagination.[15] It is in this sense that *Laon and Cythna* is 'a vision of the nineteenth century' (Shelley's subtitle). The poem is, in other words, what Shelley would later define – in the 'Preface' to *Prometheus Unbound* – as a 'beautiful idealism ... of moral excellence' (*Poems*, ii, p. 475). Referring, in that 'Preface', to his poetic practice prior to the composition of *Prometheus Unbound*, Shelley informs the reader that his:

purpose has hitherto been simply to familiarise the highly refined imagination of the more select classes of poetical readers with beautiful idealisms of moral excellence; aware that until the mind can love, and admire, and trust, and hope, and endure, reasoned principles of moral conduct are seeds cast upon the highway of life, which the unconscious passenger tramples into dust, although they would bear the harvest of his happiness. (*Poems*, ii, p. 475)

The retrospective focus here ('my purpose has hitherto') effectively identifies *Laon and Cythna* as a 'beautiful idealism', and confirms the role of these 'idealisms' – the product and sustenance of the cultivated ('highly refined') imagination – in promoting the moral and intellectual revolution that Shelley, following Godwin, believed to be the necessary pre-requisite of any lasting change in political institutions. Once again, then, we are returned to the concept of 'intellectual beauty', to the ability of the cultivated imagination to challenge, to *re-imagine* the 'records' of the 'one mind', to promote ideological revolution by apprehending and embodying the 'truth / Of nature'.

Laon and Cythna was intended to mount just such a challenge to the reactionary 'records' of the Revolution in the 'one mind', precisely the kind of re-imagining Shelley had first urged Byron to conduct. Shelley therefore never intended to narrate a corrected or idealised version of the French Revolution. Rather, again, *Laon and Cythna* was intended to correct public interpretation of what had *actually* happened in France (and hence the echoes of the historical Revolution in the key episodes of the poem), to re-locate the apparent catastrophe of the Revolution with a long-term, and explicitly *natural* economy of hope.[16]

EXPERIMENTING WITH THE 'PUBLIC MIND'

In the first paragraph of the 'Preface' to *Laon and Cythna*, Shelley describes his poem as:

An experiment on the temper of the public mind, as to how far a thirst for a happier condition of moral and political society survives, among the enlightened and refined, the tempests which have shaken the age in which we live (*Poems*, ii, p. 32)

As Jack Donovan notes in his editorial commentary on this passage, Shelley's 'experiment' echoes both the 'Preface' to the *Lyrical Ballads* and Byron's 'Preface' to Cantos I and II of *Childe Harold*, all of which similarly proclaim the experimental nature of the following text (*Poems*, ii, p. 32 n.).[17] However, *Laon and Cythna*'s target audience is instructive. The poem is not addressed to the 'public mind' *per se* but only to a particular section of that mind: 'the enlightened and refined', those whom the 'Preface' subsequently identifies as the 'worshippers of public good' (*Poems*, ii, p. 37).[18] In other words, *Laon and Cythna* is aimed at the 'wise' (to borrow *Mont Blanc*'s term), at the cultural leaders of the 'one mind', at a Godwinian intellectual aristocracy whose revolutionary aspirations have been dealt a body blow by the disastrous course of events in France.[19] 'Many of the most tender-hearted of the worshippers of public good', Shelley affirms, doubtless with the likes of Wordsworth and Southey in mind, 'have been morally ruined by what a partial glimpse of the events they deplored, appeared to show as the melancholy desolation of all their cherished hopes' (*Poems*, ii, p. 37). Nor is this moral ruination merely a matter of individual political despondency. Conversely, Shelley recognises – with his sense of the reciprocal relationship between the imagination and the ideological 'records' determining the 'public mind' – that the collapse of the French Revolution has produced a *culture* of political despondency, an 'age of despair' (*Poems*, ii, p. 35). 'Gloom and misanthropy', he affirms, in a well known passage from *Laon and Cythna*'s 'Preface', 'have become the characteristic of the age in which we live':

This influence has tainted the literature of the age with the hopelessness of the minds from which it flows. Metaphysics, and enquiries into moral and political science, have become little else than vain attempts to revive exploded superstitions, or sophisms like those of Mr. Malthus, calculated to lull the oppressors of mankind into a security of everlasting triumph. Our works of fiction and poetry have been overshadowed by the same infectious gloom (*Poems*, ii, pp. 37–8)[20]

We are returned, then, to Shelley's account of the French Revolution as 'the master theme of the epoch in which we live': the Revolution has defined the 'spirit of the age', and it is a 'spirit' of 'gloom and misanthropy'.[21]

Laon and Cythna seeks to challenge this pervasive culture of political despondency, to revise the 'records' of the Revolution in the 'public mind'. To this extent, again, it represents Shelley's attempt at the revisionary project he had originally intended for Byron's 'uncommon powers': the task of making the Revolution a 'fountain' of 'hope' rather than 'despair' in 'the thoughts of men'.[22] *Laon and Cythna*'s 'Preface' accordingly makes it clear from the outset that post-Revolutionary political 'gloom' is premised upon a *misinterpretation* of events in France, upon 'what a *partial* glimpse of [these] events ... *appeared* to show' as political truth (*Poems*, ii, p. 37; emphasis added). Against this *apparent* truth, against this ideological 'preconception', the poem sets the actual, Necessitarian truth (the 'truth / Of nature') about the Revolution, explaining its collapse and establishing its long-term, world-historical significance by reference to what is, effectively, a natural history of politics.

Laon and Cythna's 'Preface' sets out this 'truth' succinctly, while still offering an in-depth analysis of the dynamics of revolutionary politics. Shelley's basic point is simple enough: 'such a degree of unmingled good was expected [from the Revolution], as it was impossible to realise' (*Poems*, ii, pp. 35–6). 'Could they listen to the plea of reason', he asks of the French populace:

who had groaned under the calamities of a social state, according to the provisions of which, one man riots in luxury whilst another famishes for want of bread? Can he who the day before was a trampled slave, suddenly become liberal-minded, forbearing, and independent? (*Poems*, ii, p. 36)

The answer, of course, is no. It is wholly unsurprising, Shelley affirms, that 'a nation of men who had been dupes and slaves for centuries, were incapable of conducting themselves with the wisdom and tranquillity of freemen as soon as some of their fetters were partially loosened' (*Poems*, ii, p. 35). By its very nature, he continues, political oppression is not only materially injurious to the populace but is also morally brutalising. 'If the Revolution had been in every sense prosperous', he concludes:

then misrule and superstition would lose half their claims to our abhorrence, as fetters which the captive can unlock with the slightest motion of his fingers, and which do not eat with poisonous rust into the soul (*Poems*, ii, p. 36)

Once again, then, Shelley's point about the Revolution's collapse is clear enough: given the brutalised state of the populace, it was almost inevitable that events should have taken the 'terrible' course that they did (*Poems*, ii, p. 36). Oppression breeds vengeance; tyranny breeds tyranny. Hence, 'the atrocities of the demagogues and the re-establishment of successive tyrannies in France' can be explained in terms of the moral and intellectual depravity of the populace prior to the Revolution, a depravity caused, again, by 'centuries' of 'misrule and superstition'.[23]

But does the collapse of the French Revolution therefore mean that all political optimism is misplaced, that 'generations of mankind ought to consign themselves to a hopeless inheritance of ignorance and misery', to a culture of 'despair'? (*Poems*, ii, p. 35). Of course not. What that collapse 'teaches', Shelley affirms, is that successful and lasting political change cannot be achieved overnight: 'such is the lesson that experience teaches now', such is the 'wise' 'vision of the nineteenth century' (*Poems*, ii, p. 37). Successful political change is, rather:

the consequence of the habits of a state of society to be produced by resolute perseverance and indefatigable hope, and long-suffering and long-believing courage, and the systematic efforts of generations of men of intellect and virtue (*Poems*, ii, pp. 36–7)

Here, then, Shelley makes a crucial, Godwinian point about the dynamics of political change, a point that had informed his thinking since *Queen Mab*, and which underpins his revision of the discourse on the sublime. In order for successful political change to take place, such change must be preceded by a 'long'-term moral and intellectual revolution in the 'one' or 'public mind'. Put differently, lasting political change can only be achieved when the 'obstinate' ideological 'preconceptions' of the 'one mind' have been challenged, when the 'records that are called reality' have been *re-imagined*.

Laon and Cythna was intended to promote this long-term moral and intellectual reform of the 'one mind' by challenging 'public' 'records' about the French Revolution.[24] But the poem also identifies the French Revolution itself as part of this reform. More precisely, *Laon and Cythna* asserts that, while a failure in the short term, the French Revolution has contributed to the 'systematic' progress of humanity towards political liberty – and as such, it should be celebrated not lamented. This is Shelley's anti-catastrophist 'vision of the nineteenth century', the Necessitarian 'vision' of the Revolution apprehended by the cultivated imagination.

'THE LESSON THAT EXPERIENCE TEACHES NOW'

Laon and Cythna proper opens with a narrator plagued by 'visions of despair' after 'the last hope of trampled France had failed' (*Laon and Cythna*, 127–9).[25] His 'despair' clearly mirrors the 'gloom and misanthropy' of the post-Revolutionary 'public mind'. The poem describes the correction of this 'despair': the narrator is told the history of another failed revolution, and its failure is presented to him in the anti-catastrophist terms set out in *Laon and Cythna*'s 'Preface'. His fictional education in the Necessitarian history of revolutionary politics is clearly intended, then, to correct public interpretation of events in France.

From the outset, Shelley links the narrator's political education to the discourse on the sublime. That education begins when the narrator 'scale[s] / The peak of an aerial promontory' and watches an 'irresistible storm' break over the ocean, a clear echo – to use Shelley's image in the 'Preface' – of the recent revolutionary 'tempests' in France (*Laon and Cythna*, 127–9, 154). As the storm abates, the narrator is presented with the 'monstrous sight' of 'an Eagle and a Serpent wreathed in fight', a 'fight' which the 'serpent' eventually appears to lose (*Laon and Cythna*, 191, 193). This 'fight' has received a great deal of attention from *Laon and Cythna*'s commentators since, as Donovan points out, it evidently constitutes 'a major thematic focal point for the entire poem' (*Poems*, ii, p. 64 n). In other words, the 'fight' between the snake and eagle represents some kind of archetypal and *ongoing* conflict, a conflict which provides *Laon and Cythna*'s overall ontological framework, and within which the history of its – and, by extension, the French – Revolution is to be understood.

A number of potential sources for the snake-eagle image have been identified, including passages from the *Iliad*, the *Aeneid*, *Metamorphoses*, and the *Faerie Queene*.[26] Kenneth Neil Cameron has also identified a pertinent contemporary source: a popular cartoon from the American War of Independence, entitled 'The Flight of Congress', which depicts a serpent, labelled 'Independence', struggling with an eagle, which represents British-led Hessian mercenaries.[27] Likewise, many different symbolic connotations have been attached to Shelley's fighting animals. Cameron, for example, points usefully to both the 'use of the snake as a symbol of rebellion' in Volney's *Ruins* and to the opposing, imperialist associations – both Roman and Napoleonic – of the eagle.[28]

This kind of reading is undoubtedly both suggestive and informative. However, it is also problematic to the extent that it tends to assume – as Donna Richardson notes – that the snake and the eagle represent moral absolutes and that the only difficulty, for Shelley's protagonists and critics alike, is to identify which represents good and which evil.[29] Conversely, it is important to recognise that while the snake and the eagle undoubtedly do represent diametrically opposed forces, the multivalence of the snake and eagle imagery throughout *Laon and Cythna* as a whole makes it impossible to reduce their 'fight' to a simple *moral* opposition. That is to say, that the variety of contexts in which snake and eagle imagery features in *Laon and Cythna* makes it impossible to systematically associate either creature with good or evil.

Despite this impossibility, however, Shelley clearly also recognises the temptation to make just such a moralising association, to construct, as it were, a 'record' of the archetypal struggle represented by the 'monstrous' 'fight'. This temptation is examined when the narrator encounters a woman, who tends the injured snake, and who offers what *appears* to be a commentary on the bout that has just taken place.

The woman begins by assuring the narrator that the 'fight' he has witnessed is just one bout in the perpetual struggle between the 'Two Powers', represented by the eagle and the serpent, 'who o'er mortal things dominion hold / Ruling the world with a divided lot' (*Laon and Cythna*, 347–8). These 'Two Powers', she affirms, are 'equal' and archetypal: 'when life and thought / Sprang forth, they burst the womb of inessential Nought' (*Laon and Cythna*, 350–1). This comparison is significant to the extent that it appears to associate the 'Two Powers' with 'life' and 'thought' rather than with any moral category. The woman then goes on to recount a scene which seems to echo, both in terms of its geographical location and in terms of the events witnessed, the 'monstrous sight' already witnessed by the narrator. 'The earliest dweller of the world alone', she says:

> Stood on the verge of chaos: Lo! afar
> O'er the wide wild abyss two meteors shone,
> Sprung from the depth of its tempestuous jar:
> A blood-red Comet and the Morning Star
> Mingling their beams in combat – as he stood,
> All thoughts within his mind waged mutual war,
> In dreadful sympathy – when to the flood
> That fair Star fell, he turned and shed his brother's blood.
>
> Thus evil triumphed, and the Spirit of Evil,
> One Power of many shapes which none may know,
> One Shape of many names; the Fiend did revel
> In victory, reigning o'er a world of woe,
> For the new race of man went to and fro,
> Famished and homeless, loathed and loathing, wild,

And hating good – for his immortal foe,
He changed from starry shape, beauteous and mild,
To a dire snake, with man and beast unreconciled

(Laon and Cythna, 352–69)

This story about the origins of evil clearly contains many elements of the Christian myth: the Fall of Lucifer ('the morning star') from Heaven, the murder of Abel by Cain ('he turned and shed his brother's blood'), the role of the 'dire snake' in the temptation and expulsion from the Garden of Eden, etc. It is, however, only a story, the 'record' of an event witnessed by 'the earliest dweller'. Moreover, it is a story that returns us to familiar territory within Shelley's revision of the discourse on the sublime. After all, the woman's narrative implies fairly unequivocally that this particular (quasi-Christian) 'record' of 'Evil' stems from an anthropomorphic reaction to the natural sublime: from the sight of a 'blood-red Comet and the Morning Star' which the 'earliest dweller' *considers* to be, but which of course are not *actually* in 'combat'. In other words, the 'earliest dweller' projects his inner mental conflict (the 'thoughts within his mind [which] waged mutual war') onto the natural spectacle before him, and hence a religion is born, the religion within which all *Laon and Cythna*'s characters – including, significantly, the narrator's woman-guide herself – largely operate. In sum, then, the 'record' of 'Evil' based on the reaction of the 'earliest dweller' to the Comet and the Morning Star is in fact an imaginative *distortion* of the 'truth / Of nature': in this case, his inner mental turmoil ('the thoughts within his mind [that] waged mutual war').

It is this latter 'war', I would argue – which the 'earliest dweller' misconstrues in anthropomorphic, religious terminology – that Shelley presents as archetypal: as the human experience of the 'immortal' conflict between the two 'equal' 'Powers' that rule 'the world with a divided lot'. This is not, of course, to deny the existence of Good and Evil. But it is to recognise that the religious / Christian framework for morality is a misleading, anthropomorphic construct ('record'). The true nature of the 'immortal' 'war' between the 'two Powers' is, rather, signalled by their already-noted associations with 'life' and 'thought', that is, with general nature and human nature. Hence, as Donna Richardson's excellent reading of the poem makes clear, the central ontological tension in *Laon and Cythna* is between Necessity (represented by the Morning Star and the Serpent) and human desire (represented by the Comet and the Eagle), an opposition in which individuals mistakenly figure Necessity as evil because it restricts and curtails desire.[30] The defeat of the serpent by the eagle amounts, then, not to the triumph of evil over good, but rather to the ascendancy of individual desire over the broader social context within which that desire should be situated and contained.

While the two 'equal' 'Powers' do not therefore represent antithetical *moral* categories, *excessive* adherence to selfhood can certainly have 'evil' consequences and, as Richardson observes, the moral ideal involves striking a balance between them, i.e. between individual desire and the broader social context for and of that desire.[31] We are returned, in other words, to territory already familiar from *Alastor*. The defeat of the serpent by the eagle amounts to the ascendancy of the solipsistic imagination, appropriately identified by Cythna as 'the dark idolatry of self' (*Laon and Cythna*, 3390). What *Laon and Cythna*'s protagonists must learn, then, is to strike a balance between individual desire – however well intentioned – and the duty of the individual to 'fear himself and love all human kind' (to use the terms of *The Hymn to Intellectual Beauty*). And this lesson has both personal and world-historical relevance. After all, the defeat of the serpent by the eagle would seem, allegorically speaking, to attribute the failure of the French Revolution to excessive solipsism, an attribution made all the more resonant when we remember the eagle's Napoleonic associations. Likewise, Shelley's 'Preface' makes it clear that the Terror resulted from the desire for personal vengeance. It is no accident, then, that Cythna's account of 'the dark idolatry of self' links that 'idolatry' directly to 'demands' for 'expiation' (*Laon and Cythna*, 3392–3).[32]

Once again, then, what *Laon and Cythna*'s eponymous revolutionaries must – and do – learn, is to reconcile their personal desires with the broader social context for those desires. This education is vital in enabling them to successfully inaugurate their revolution. Moreover, it plays a crucial role in helping them to understand the failure of that Revolution. It enables them, in short, to avoid both the catastrophist and the solipsistic ('wilful exaggeration of its own despair') responses to that failure which Shelley condemns in the 'Preface', and to apprehend the Necessitarian 'truth' about the dynamics of political change.

While some critics have argued that Laon and Cythna do not develop significantly throughout the course of the text, most now agree that the siblings need to undergo significant moral growth before they are able to inaugurate their revolution. They must learn to reject solipsism, and they must learn to reject political violence, however well intentioned, in favour of a gradualist and bloodless revolution in opinion. What we witness, in effect, is the cultivation of their imaginations.

Appropriately enough, given the ontological context, there are significant and instructive parallels between Laon's education and the history of the *Alastor*-poet; in effect, Laon is a qualified success where *Alastor*'s poet-protagonist was a qualified failure. Like *Alastor*'s poet-protagonist, Laon spends his youth contemplating the literature ('the wondrous fame') of the 'past world', 'the vital words and deeds / Of minds whom neither time nor change can tame' (*Laon and Cythna*, 681–3). He also shares the poet-protagonist's interest in occult 'traditions dark and old, whence evil creeds / Start forth' (*Laon and Cythna*, 683–4). Likewise, Laon repeats the poet-protagonist's journey through the natural world in search of 'food' for his 'many thoughts', and like the *Alastor*-poet, Laon makes this journey alone (*Laon and Cythna*, 746–7).

The most significant – and, at this stage, unsurprising – parallel between the two men's development, however, is the fact that Laon, like the poet-protagonist before him, has a moment of epiphany when confronted by the 'awful' spectacle of ruin. Following in the footsteps, as it were, of the *Alastor*-poet, Laon's quest for mental 'food' eventually leads him – at 'twilight' – to the 'wrecks of days departed', to a Volneyan landscape of 'mountains', 'broken tombs', and 'ruins grey' which clearly recalls not only *Alastor*'s 'Dark Aethiopia' but also the valley of the Assassins (*Laon and Cythna*, 748, 753, 754, 756). Here Laon, again like the poet-protagonist before him, interprets the ruins in quintessentially Volneyan terms. The 'monuments', he affirms, directly echoing the prefatory 'Invocation' of *The Ruins*, in terminology now wholly incorporated within Shelley's revision of the discourse on the sublime, 'tell their own tale to him who *wisely* heeds / The language which they speak' (*Laon and Cythna*, 760–2; emphasis added). Once again, this is the central tenet of Shelley's revision of the discourse on the sublime: only the 'wise' or cultivated imagination can accurately read the 'language' of the sublime. In this now-familiar Shelleyan moment, then, Laon learns the Necessitarian truth about the fall of empire from the sublime spectacle of ruin: 'I felt the sway / Of the vast stream of ages bear away / My floating thoughts', he affirms, echoing Shelley's 1812 apostrophe to Necessity on the 'shores' of 'Erin' (*Laon and Cythna*, 769–71; *Letters*, i, p. 251). 'It shall be thus no more!', he warns the Tyrant's regime, invoking Greece's slumbering republican ideals:

> ... too long, too long,
> Sons of the glorious dead, have ye lain bound
> In darkness and in ruin. – Hope is strong,
> Justice and Truth their wingéd child have found –
> Awake! Arise! until the mighty sound
> Of your career shall scatter in its gust

> The thrones of the oppressor, and the ground
> Hide the last altar's unregarded dust
>
> (*Laon and Cythna*, 775–82)

In short, then, Laon learns the Necessary, historical fate of empire from the sublime spectacle of ruin, and this inspires him, like the Assassins before him, to revolution:

> It must be so – I will arise and waken
> The multitude, and like a sulphurous hill,
> Which on a sudden from its snows has shaken
> The swoon of ages, it shall burst and fill
> The world with cleansing fire: it must, it will –
> It may not be restrained! – and who shall stand
> Amid the rocking earthquake steadfast still,
> But Laon? on high Freedom's desert land
> A tower whose marble walls the leaguèd storms withstand!
>
> (*Laon and Cythna*, 784–92)

The level of violence marking this vision of political change is striking: Laon's politics at this stage are clearly revolutionist rather than gradualist, and to that extent clearly problematic within the terms of Shelley's ostensibly Godwinian political thought. Laon's likening of the revolutionary 'multitude' to an erupting volcano is of course extremely significant in this revolutionist context, and I will examine it in detail in the next section of the chapter.[33] For the time being, however, it is sufficient to recognise that the revolutionist violence attending Laon's vision of political change is a component – an integral component – of the overall solipsism of that vision. Consider, for example, the role he envisions for himself in the overall process: he takes centre-stage as an implacable, phallic 'tower' (an echo, perhaps, of Shelley's image of the 'poet of Nature' as a 'rock built refuge' in 'To William Wordsworth'). Consider also his repeated imperatives: 'I will', 'it must', 'I will'. Taken together, these factors suggest that if the *Alastor*-poet's epiphanic experience of ruin was followed by a solipsistic 'debauch' of the imagination, then so, too, was Laon's.

The solipsism of Laon's initial, revolutionist vision of political change is confirmed when his putsch meets its first serious check: the capture of Cythna by the Tyrant's soldiers at the beginning of Canto III. Laon responds to this setback by attacking and killing some of the Tyrant's men, and by invoking his 'countrymen' to 'death or liberty', a solipsistic and essentially vengeful reaction (since born from anger over the loss of Cythna) which Shelley, through subsequent events, unequivocally condemns (*Laon and Cythna*, 1197). Immediately after this attack, Laon is imprisoned – Prometheus-like – at the summit of a mountain, from whence he is eventually rescued by a Hermit (an intellectual rather than physical Hercules), who has been spreading Laon and Cythna's libertarian doctrines during their captivity.[34]

As a result of a vision he experiences while chained at the summit of the mountain – which presents the killing of the Tyrant's soldiers as an act of cannibalism, possibly of Cythna herself – Laon recognises, in the familiar Shelleyan terms of the 'Preface', that 'love' is 'the sole law which should govern the moral world' (*Laon and Cythna*, 1324–47; *Poems*, ii, p. 47). He learns to abjure solipsism ('the dark idolatry of self') and its social manifestation as revolutionary political violence. He learns to reconcile his desires with the whole within which they must operate and be contained, learns – in the terms of the *Hymn to Intellectual Beauty* – the Necessitarian 'truth' that the individual must 'fear himself and love all human kind'. Having done so, having corrected the well-intentioned but ultimately solipsistic 'error' by which the *Alastor*-poet was self-condemned, Laon's education is complete.

Cythna's imagination, too, must be cultivated before she can co-operate with Laon in inaugurating their bloodless, ideological attempt at reform. As was the case with Laon, her intentions are noble from the outset: the liberation of women from sexual and domestic oppression, an oppression of which the initially solipsistic Laon is 'but coldly' aware (*Laon and Cythna*, 985–98, 982). Again like Laon, however, Cythna's initial vision of the dynamics of political change is flawed. More specifically, she fails to recognise that an ideological reform – the type, in effect, of what she must herself undergo – must take place in the 'public mind' before any lasting change in political institutions can be effected. Cythna initially conceives her 'task' in naively optimistic terms, confident, like Laon, that her vision is irresistible (*Laon and Cythna*, 1001). 'Think'st thou that I shall speak unskilfully, / And none will heed me?', she asks, in response to her brother's initial scepticism (*Laon and Cythna*, 1027–8). 'I remember now', she enthuses:

> How once, a slave in tortures doomed to die,
> Was saved, because in accents sweet and low
> He sung a song his Judge loved long ago,
> As he was led to death. – All shall relent
> Who hear me – tears as mine have flowed, shall flow,
> Hearts beat as mine now beats, with such intent
> As renovates the world; a will omnipotent!
>
> (*Laon and Cythna*, 1028–35)[35]

Like Laon's well-intentioned vision of an irresistible volcanic revolution, then, Cythna's initial confidence in her 'will omnipotent' is both solipsistic and naive. Naive because she fails to recognise that the ideological make-up of the 'public mind' cannot be transformed overnight (and we remember Shelley's questions about the French populace in the 'Preface': 'can he who the day before was a trampled slave, suddenly become liberal-minded, forbearing, and independent?'). Cythna initially fails to recognise, in other words, that a long-term, 'systematic' revolution in opinion must precede any lasting political change.

Cythna learns her mistake harshly: when the Tyrant abducts her, her 'will omnipotent' signally fails to dissuade him from raping her (*Laon and Cythna*, 2856–82). As a result, she becomes pregnant. The child she bears will eventually come, in an obvious way, to symbolise hope for the future. But in the short term, Cythna's child also represents what she learns from her experience with the Tyrant. After her rape, Cythna goes through a period of intense self-analysis. In effect, she practises the kind of 'science of mind' advocated by Shelley in the so-called *Speculations*, the sceptical inflection of which is re-affirmed by Cythna's claim that she acquired the 'key' to 'truths which once were dimly taught / In old Crotona', the seat of the Pythagorean school (*Laon and Cythna*, 3113–34). Shelley's continued confidence in the radical potential of this 'science' as a means of cultivating the imagination is voiced by Cythna in her account of the effect of her self-analysis. 'My mind', she tells Laon:

> became the book through which I grew
> Wise in all human wisdom, and its cave,
> Which like a mine I rifled through and through,
> To me the keeping of its secrets gave –
> One mind, the type of all, the moveless wave
> Whose calm reflects all moving things that are,
> Necessity and love, and life, the grave,
> And sympathy, fountains of hope and fear;
> Justice, and truth, and time, and the world's natural sphere
>
> (*Laon and Cythna*, 3100–8)

Cythna's inquiry into the 'cave' of her 'mind' – the type, in effect, of *Mont Blanc*'s 'still cave of the witch Poesy' teaches her 'all human wisdom'. She learns, as Shelley had argued in *Mont Blanc*, that the mind is partly passive ('moveless', 'calm', reflecting) in relation to external influences ('all *moving* things that are'). But she also learns, again as in *Mont Blanc*, that the mind is capable of imaginative activity, capable of deploying 'a subtler language' (*Laon and Cythna*, 3112).[36] Moreover, since Cythna's individual ('one') mind is 'the type of all' minds, understanding it amounts to understanding all other minds. Her 'one mind', then, is a 'type' of the 'public mind'.[37] And this equivalence ultimately provides her, through the experience of controlling her own mind, with 'the power . . . to frame' the 'thoughts' of other minds 'anew'; with the power, that is, to re-imagine the 'records that are called reality' (*Laon and Cythna*, 3135).

We are returned, then, to the apocalyptic claims Shelley made for the 'science of mind' in his *Speculations*. Cythna's practice of this 'science' enables her to cultivate her imagination, to strike a balance between her 'fancies' and her 'will', and to thereby apprehend the Necessitarian 'truth / Of nature', the need to 'fear' oneself and 'love all human kind' (*Laon and Cythna*, 3126). From hence on, she does indeed speak with 'a subtler language', with a 'strong speech' capable of tearing the ideological 'veil that hid / Nature, and Truth, and Liberty, and Love' (*Laon and Cythna*, 3523–4). In short, she has learned, and now speaks, the Necessitarian 'truth' that is obscured from the masses by the 'obstinate' ideological 'preconceptions' of the 'public mind', appropriately comparing herself to 'one who from some mountain's pyramid, / Points to the unrisen sun!' (*Laon and Cythna*, 3525–6).

Cythna's 'strong', Necessitarian 'speech' takes centre stage in Canto V, when Laon, healed by the Hermit, journeys to the Golden City and hears her speaking from the top of 'The Altar of the Federation' (*Laon and Cythna*, 2072). As critics have long noted, this section of the poem draws clearly and heavily on the actual *Fête de la Fédération*, held on the Champs de Mars on 14 July 1790, the first anniversary of the fall of the Bastille (see *Poems*, ii, p. 148 n.). The details of *Laon and Cythna*'s take on this *fête* are revealing. In the first place, the 'Altar' on which Cythna is seated is described as 'a marble pyramid' (*Laon and Cythna*, 2076). The form of the 'Altar' – and this too has often been noted – echoes Chapters 16 and 17 of Volney's *Ruins*, where the people's newly-elected legislators are seated on a pyramid-shaped throne, before an altar dedicated to Equality (the main subject of Cythna's subsequent speech). Cythna's seat atop the 'pyramid'-'altar' also directly recalls her earlier account of her role as 'one who from some mountain's pyramid, / Points to the unrisen sun!' (and, more generally, *Mont Blanc*'s 'wise' view from the top). Moreover, the movement of the 'multitudes' around the 'base' of the 'Altar' is compared to the 'burst and shiver' of 'Atlantic waves' around the 'base' of 'some mountain islet' (*Laon and Cythna*, 2080–3). On one level, this comparison draws again on the historical *fêtes révolutionaire*, which frequently had artificial mountains or other sublime natural phenomena as their centrepiece.[38] However, the comparison also tellingly casts the 'pyramid'-'mountain'-'Altar' as a *volcanic* peak ('mountain islets' being such by definition). To this extent, then, the 'Altar of the Federation' is another instance of *Laon and Cythna*'s pervasive volcanist imagery (discussed at length in the next section). Specifically, the 'Altar' amounts to a non-violent re-incarnation of Laon's revolutionist 'sulphurous hill'. The point of Cythna's speech from the summit of the 'Altar', in any event, is unequivocally gradualist: no 'death or liberty' here (Laon's earlier injunction), but Equality, Love, and Wisdom (*Laon and Cythna*, 2181–271).[39]

Before Laon and Cythna can seriously challenge the Tyrant, then, they must undergo their own ideological revolutions. Laon must learn that 'love' is the 'sole' valid 'law' of action, and must therefore reject political violence, however well intentioned. Cythna must learn that a successful change in social and political institutions can only take place after the 'public mind' has been reformed. They must, in short, overcome solipsism ('the dark idolatry of self'). They must learn to re-locate their initially solipsistic visions of political change with a broader, Necessitarian framework. When they do this, they are indeed the 'ideal' Shelleyan revolutionaries. But their ideal revolution still fails.

To put it more precisely, Laon and Cythna's attempt at political change collapses because the Tyrant and his subjects have not similarly learned to abjure the 'dark idolatry of self'. Their attempt fails, in other words, because there has been no 'systematic' reform of the 'public mind'. Simply put, that mind is 'unfit' for the 'happy state of equal law' which Laon and Cythna (temporarily) engender. The deposed Tyrant cannot accept his reduced position, despite the compassion of the populace (whom Laon appropriately dissuades from their initially vengeful intentions). Similarly, the people themselves quickly return to their former prejudices and superstitions when struck down by famine and disease in the wake of the Tyrant's bloody restoration. The echoes of France are clear, and like the French Revolution before it, Laon and Cythna's revolution fails because the siblings engineer a drastic change in political institutions before the general populace is ideologically fit to deal with its new state.

Despite the defeat of their Revolution, and the consequent 'fearful overthrow of public hope', however, Laon and Cythna do not 'despair' (*Laon and Cythna*, 2597–8). Cythna affirms that she and Laon 'have survived a ruin wide and deep', an echo of Shelley's claim, in the 'Preface', that 'those who now live have survived an age of despair' (*Laon and Cythna*, 3632; *Poems*, ii, p. 35). Unlike the actual 'public mind' of 1817, however, which the 'Preface' affirms has been hit by an 'epidemic transport' of 'panic' and 'despair' in the wake of events in France, Cythna feels only 'a mighty calmness creep / Over [her] heart' (*Laon and Cythna*, 3637–8). This 'mighty calmness' – the type of the 'elevated and dreadless composure' that Shelley everywhere advocates as the 'wise' response to 'awful' phenomena – stems from her ability to apprehend the systematic operation of Necessity in human history. 'Virtue, and Hope, and Love, like light and Heaven / Surround the world', she affirms:

> – We [i.e. she and Laon] are their chosen slaves.
> Has not the whirlwind of our spirit driven
> Truth's deathless germs to thought's remotest caves?
>
> (*Laon and Cythna*, 3667–70)

Cythna's former rejection of 'the dark idolatry of self' now enables her to accept her position as Necessity's 'slave'. Moreover, she also now voices the same, 'systematic', Necessitarian perspective on political change that Shelley expounds in the 'Preface'. 'Winter comes!', she admits, and '– the grief of many graves', but '*the seeds are sleeping in the soil*' (*Laon and Cythna*, 3671, 3676; emphasis added). 'This is the winter of the world', she continues, speaking of the Tyrant's restoration, 'and here / We die':

> ... even as the winds of Autumn fade,
> Expiring in the frore and foggy air. –
> Behold! Spring comes, though we must pass, who made
> The promise of its birth
>
> (*Laon and Cythna*, 3685–9)

Cythna's evocation of the seasonal cycle at this point echoes Paine's figure of a revolutionary Spring in *The Rights of Man*, and looks forward to the conclusion of Shelley's *Ode to the West Wind*. This evocation voices Cythna's confidence that while their attempt at political change has been defeated in the short term ('winter'), she and Laon have sown the 'seeds' of the inevitable future change in political institutions, of a political 'Spring' to come. In other words, she and Laon have initiated the 'systematic' reform of the 'public mind' that must precede any lasting change in political institutions: they have 'spread' the 'germs' of 'truth' in the 'cave' of the 'mind', where those germs will eventually bear fruit. Moreover, Cythna's evocation of the seasonal cycle confirms that this long-term, 'systematic' political process is *natural*. She offers us, in effect, a *natural history* of political change, and it is an explicitly anti-catastrophist history.

Accordingly, Cythna goes on to identify the agency of this 'systematic' political process – explicitly – as 'Necessity', the 'sightless strength' of which will 'bind' the 'past' to the 'future' in an inevitable causal chain, familiar in Shelley's work from *Queen Mab* onwards (*Laon and Cythna*, 3706–8). Once again, then, the 'systematic' historical operation of Necessity guarantees that while Laon and Cythna's revolution has been defeated, the 'irresistible', long-term process of reform has been initiated. 'The good and the mighty of departed ages / Are in their graves', Cythna explains, 'the innocent and the free':

> Heroes, and Poets, and prevailing Sages,
> Who leave the vesture of their majesty
> To adorn and clothe this naked world; – and we
> Are like to them – such perish, but they leave
> All hope, or love, or truth, or liberty,
> Whose forms their mighty spirits could conceive
> To be a rule and law to ages that survive
>
> (*Laon and Cythna*, 3712–20)

Like the 'mighty spirits' of 'departed ages', then, Laon and Cythna, though defeated, will leave a 'record' of 'hope, or love, or truth, or liberty' in the 'public mind', a 'record' that will determine ('rule and law') the future configuration of the 'public mind'. Although she and Laon must die, Cythna recognises that their 'many thoughts and deeds, our life and love, / Our happiness, and all that we have been, / Immortally must live, and burn, and move, / When we shall be no more' (*Laon and Cythna*, 3730–3).

Hence, while Cythna realises that the Tyrant's post-restoration propaganda machine will construct a false 'record' of their struggle, will heap 'calumny' on their efforts, her understanding of the natural, Necessitarian history of politics allows her to conclude on a triumphant, Volneyan note (*Laon and Cythna*, 3739). Although, for the present, 'none shall dare vouch' what she and Laon have done, their political vision will persist in the 'public mind', and ulti-mately outlive the Tyrant's 'calumny' (*Laon and Cythna*, 3742–3). 'That *record* shall remain', Cythna resonantly affirms, in the terms of Shelley's 1816 praise for Rousseau's 'powerfully bright' imagination, 'when they must pass':

> Who built their pride on its oblivion;
> And fame, in human hope which sculptured was,
> Survive the perished scrolls of unenduring brass
>
> (*Laon and Cythna*, 3744–7; emphasis added)

Defeated revolutionaries as well as poets, then, 'are the unacknowledged legislators of the world'.

This, at least, is very much the point made by the 'mighty Senate' or 'Temple of the Spirit' which features in *Laon and Cythna*'s framing cantos, and within which the narrator eventually sees the poem's eponymous revolutionaries enthroned (*Laon and Cythna*, 606, 4815). This 'Senate' / 'Temple' is not a (quasi) Platonic realm of forms, nor is it any kind of philosophically idealist conception of an ahistorical universal mind. Rather – like the 'abode where the Eternal are' in *Adonais* – it is a figure for the 'public mind' (*Adonais*, 495). More precisely, it figures the persistence in the 'public mind' of those who have beneficially re-imagined its 'records' ('the Great who had departed from Mankind'), and of whom a 'record' therefore remains in that mind (*Laon and Cythna*, 605).[40] Accordingly, *Laon and Cythna*'s 'Senate' / 'Temple' is also – again like 'the abode where the eternal are' – a *temple of fame*, a locus of 'immortality' (Cythna's term) in and through the 'records' of the 'public mind'; it is, in short, the 'native home' of 'Genius' (*Laon and Cythna*, 570). Hence it functions within the poem as a kind of sublime *fête révolutionnaire*, as a means of celebrating Laon and Cythna's true historical achievement, and of enshrining that achievement in the 'public mind'.[41] Once again, although they have been executed, and their revolution defeated in the short-term, they have inaugurated the 'systematic' and 'irresistible' – the *necessary* – moral reform of the 'public mind'.

The keynote of Shelley's '*beau ideal* . . . of the French Revolution' is not therefore the fact that Laon and Cythna's revolution collapses like the French Revolution before it, the fact that so many of *Laon and Cythna*'s critics have had 'difficulty' understanding. Rather it is the way in which Laon and Cythna *react* to the collapse of their revolution. Their insight into the natural, Necessitarian history of politics prevents them from despairing over the course of events. Instead, they recognise that their personal defeat marks a Necessary transitional phase in the broader process of political change. In other words, abjuring 'the dark idolatry of self' allows Laon and Cythna to revise the immediate personal disaster of their revolution into a guarantee of hope for the future. Laon and Cythna avoid a catastrophic conception of events by relocating their personal and political defeat within a 'systematic', long-term natural economy of hope. Their revolution fails because the 'public mind' was 'unfit' for the 'happy state of equal law' that they engendered. In this respect, their defeat was natural, even necessary. But it is equally true that they have initiated a process – the reform of the 'public mind' – that will eventually bring about political change through the 'irresistible' historical operation of Necessity.

As the '*beau ideal* . . . of the French Revolution', *Laon and Cythna* was intended to present this Necessitarian 'truth' about the dynamics of political change to the 'public mind', in order to correct the reactionary 'despair' of that mind in the wake of events in France. Once again, the history and significance of Laon and Cythna's revolution is explained to

Shelley's Narrator in order to correct the 'despair' occasioned by 'trampled France'. So, *Laon and Cythna* was intended to correct the 'despair' of the post-Napoleonic 'public mind', to educate that mind in the natural, Necessitarian history of politics, and, in so doing, to promote the ideological revolution that must precede any lasting change in political institutions. *Laon and Cythna*'s 'lesson' is that while the French Revolution has undoubtedly collapsed, it has not been, and cannot be, reversed because its principles have contributed to the 'systematic' reform of the 'public mind'.

'CLEANSING FIRE'?: THE NATURAL HISTORY OF POLITICS

Until now, I have been painting a fairly positive picture of *Laon and Cythna*. The poem is Shelley's attempt at the revisionary project he had first devised for Byron's 'uncommon powers': the task of re-imagining the reactionary, catastrophist 'records' of the French Revolution in the 'public mind', of making the failed Revolution a 'fountain' of 'hope' rather than 'despair' in 'the thoughts of men'.

As such, *Laon and Cythna* seems to be fairly unequivocally in tune with the gradualist, Godwinian strain in Shelley's political thought. The French Revolution collapsed, Shelley argues in the 'Preface', because the French people had been so brutalised by years of oppression that they were – understandably – unable to 'suddenly become liberal-minded, forebearing, and independent'. Rather, they gave violent vent to the – at least within a Godwinian schema – essentially solipsistic emotions of 'Revenge', 'Envy', and 'Prejudice' (*Poems*, ii, p. 47).[42] Conversely, *Laon and Cythna*'s eponymous protagonists learn to reject this violent, solipsistic response to oppression, and instead place their faith in a 'systematic' ideological reform of the 'public mind'. Both the 'Preface' and the body-text of *Laon and Cythna* fully support this faith by offering a natural history of politics, a Necessitarian history within which lasting political change is presented as an – albeit deferred – historical inevitability.

Despite all this *prima facie* confidence in the politically beneficent operation of Necessity in human history, however, *Laon and Cythna* is actually marked by deep – and now increasingly familiar – Shelleyan anxieties about *where* political change will eventually come from, about *how* that change will eventually come about. And once again, these troubling questions about the nature and origin of political change are broached through Shelley's engagement with the discourse on the sublime.

In order to approach *Laon and Cythna*'s anxieties about political change, we need to examine Shelley's natural history of politics in more detail.

In the 'Preface', Shelley supports the idea of a natural history of politics through the imagery used to describe the processes of political change. We have already noted his (Wollstonecraft inspired) account of French Revolutionary history as 'the tempests which have shaken the age in which we live'. The 'Preface' also describes the Revolution itself as:

One of those manifestations of a general state of feeling among civilised mankind, produced by a defect of correspondence between the knowledge existing in society and the improvement, or gradual abolition of political institutions. The year 1788 may be assumed as the epoch of one of the most important crises produced by this feeling (*Poems*, ii, p. 35)

This definition of revolutionary 'crisis' as the product of a 'defect of correspondence' between the intellectual condition of the 'public mind' and the actual state of 'political institutions' strongly suggests the dynamics of a lightning strike: the result of a critical 'defect of correspondence' in charge between cloud and earth. Indeed, the image clearly looks forward to Shelley's identical, and better-known, account of the impending cultural renovation in and of the 'public mind' in the 'Preface' to *Prometheus Unbound*. 'The cloud of mind is discharging its collected lightning', he argues, 'and the equilibrium between institutions and opinions is now restoring, or is about to be restored' (*Poems*, ii, p. 474). A volcanic interpretation of *Laon and Cythna*'s figure is also possible: revolution is the result of an unstoppable build-up of ideological pressure in the 'public mind'.

At two crucial moments, then, the 'Preface' to *Laon and Cythna* uses *natural* phenomena to image *political* phenomena. And a similar strategy pervades the body-text. We have already noted both the volcanic overtones of Cythna's 'Altar of the Federation' and Laon's violent, volcanic vision of revolution, of the 'multitude' that will sweep away the Tyrant's regime like the 'cleansing fire' from a 'sulphurous hill'. Later in the same canto, Cythna also invokes the notion of 'irresistible' 'cleansing fire' as a figure for revolution. Speaking of the – in this instance ideological – destruction that she and Laon will wreak on the Tyrant's regime, Cythna affirms that:

> ... like the forest of some pathless mountain,
> Which from remotest glens two warring winds
> Involve in fire, which not the loosened fountain
> Of broadest flood might quench, shall all the kinds
> Of evil, catch from our uniting minds
> The spark which must consume them
>
> (*Laon and Cythna*, 1072–7)

Unsurprisingly, then, the eventual outbreak of Laon and Cythna's struggle for 'Liberty' is likened to 'a volcano's voice, whose thunder fills / Remotest skies', a clear echo of Shelley's use of Cotopaxi in 'To the Republicans . . . ' (*Laon and Cythna*, 3498–9).[43] 'Soon bright day will burst', Cythna affirms, 'even like a chasm / Of fire, to burn the shrouds outworn and dead, / Which wrap the world; a wide enthusiasm, / To cleanse the fevered world as with an earthquake's spasm' (*Laon and Cythna*, 3510–14).

Nor does Shelley only use this kind of imagery to figure positive or optimistic moments in the political process. For example, Laon describes the naval bombardment used to support the Tyrant's restoration as 'a killing rain of fire' from 'many a volcano-isle' (*Laon and Cythna*, 2396–7). Nor, for that matter, is the imagery solely volcanic. In Canto V, Laon – sustaining the idea of revolutionary 'cleansing' – tells the narrator that the 'armies' of the people 'through the City's hundred gates / Were poured, like brooks which to the rocky lair / Of some deep lake, whose silence them awaits, / Throng from the mountains when the storms are there' (*Laon and Cythna*, 1855–8). Similarly, after the Golden City is taken, Laon compares the 'mighty crowd' to 'the rush of showers / Of hail in spring' (*Laon and Cythna*, 1974–5). And later, in Canto VI, the 'throng' who attempt (unsuccessfully) to flee ('like waves before the tempest') the Tyrant's returning troops, 'stream' out through the same gates 'like foam-wrought waterfalls / Fed from a thousand storms' (*Laon and Cythna*, 2385, 2366–8).

In sum, then, both the 'Preface' and the body-text of *Laon and Cythna* repeatedly use natural processes – generally, though not exclusively *volcanic* processes – to image political processes. And the overall effect of this imagery is to figure political processes *as* natural processes, to figure political history as a *function* of natural history. In other words, by drawing a figurative equivalence between natural and political history, this kind of imagery lends effective, imaginative support to *Laon and Cythna*'s overarching concept of a natural history of politics. Once again, *Laon and Cythna*'s key idea is that political history is a function of natural history, that political process is a natural process, intelligible to the 'wise' or cultivated imagination.

Appropriately, then, and as will by now be apparent, Shelley does not simply use any natural phenomena to figure political phenomena. Rather, he uses explicitly *sublime* natural phenomena (flood, storm, volcanism, earthquake) to figure political events that are, in effect, equally sublime. *Laon and Cythna* returns us, therefore, to Shelley's revision of the discourse on the natural sublime. In fact, the poem's ideological agenda can only be fully understood within the terms of that revision. After all, the point of *Laon and Cythna*'s 'story of violence and revolution' is precisely to prompt the 'wise' – the 'enlightened and refined' to whom it is addressed – to re-imagine the historical implications of the 'awful' spectacle that was the French Revolution. In other words, the poem's pervasive use of the imagery of natural catastrophe voices Shelley's sense that the reactionary response of the 'public mind' to the collapse of the French Revolution is the cultural equivalent of the individual's terrified response to the natural sublime. By re-locating that collapse within a 'systematic' natural economy of hope, then, Shelley is again challenging the catastrophist 'records' of the Revolution in the 'public mind', a challenge already implicit in *Mont Blanc*'s politically laden account of glaciation. But he is also challenging that 'mind' to stare with 'elevated and dreadless composure', with Cythna's 'mighty calmness', at the 'awful' manifestations of Necessity in human history, challenging it moreover – again as in *Mont Blanc* – to learn the 'lessons' that those manifestations teach.

In this respect, Shelley's summation of *Laon and Cythna*'s agenda is revealing. The 'Preface' affirms that the poem was written with the aim of:

> ... kindling within the bosoms of [its] readers, a *virtuous enthusiasm* for those doctrines of liberty and justice, that faith and hope in something good, which neither violence, nor misrepresentation, nor prejudice, can ever totally extinguish among mankind (*Poems*, ii, p. 32; emphasis added)

In short, the 'awful' spectacle of the French Revolution – allegorised in Laon and Cythna's struggle – should not 'kindle' reactionary 'despair' but rather the 'virtuous enthusiasm' for 'liberty', 'justice', 'faith', and 'hope' that results from the 'wise' or cultivated imaginative response to the sublime. An ideological reform of the 'public mind' must precede any lasting change in political institutions. The 'public mind' must learn, in short, to recognise and accept the Necessitarian 'truth / Of nature', to abjure catastrophism and reaction and embrace the 'wide' philanthropic 'enthusiasm' promoted by Cythna in Canto IX.

There is a problem inherent in *Laon and Cythna*'s guiding idea of a natural history of politics, however, a problem that returns us directly to familiar Shelleyan anxieties about the precise nature and origins of political change. The problem is the tendency of that history to understand and present political violence as itself a *natural* phenomenon, as the inevitable, *necessary* consequence of tyranny. *Laon and Cythna*'s 'Preface' affirms that the solipsistic 'excesses' of the French Revolution were the natural result of 'centuries' of oppression (*Poems*, ii, p. 35). Likewise, by denying the distinction between natural and political history, by using 'awful' natural phenomena to figure 'awful' political phenomena, *Laon and Cythna*'s natural history of politics effectively identifies political violence *as* a natural phenomenon, as an 'awful' manifestation of Necessity in human history, as a kind of sociological volcanism in which the steady build-up of pressure inevitably culminates in eruption. Tyranny naturally breeds vengeance. But if this is the case, how can – or, indeed, *can* – the cycle of oppression and retributive violence be broken? If revolutionary violence is indeed the necessary offspring of a morally and intellectually brutalising regime, (how) can an ideological reform of the 'public mind' ever be successfully effected under such a regime? In the terms of *Laon and Cythna*'s ontology, can the 'fight' between the 'serpent' and the 'eagle' ever really be resolved, or – to put it in Cythna's words – 'must' 'evil with evil, good with good' 'forever' 'wind' in 'bands of union, which no power can sever' (*Laon and Cythna*, 3709–11).[44] This is the question, the anxiety at the heart of *Laon and Cythna*'s ostensibly gradualist natural history of politics: the 'awful' truth is that for all the ideologically reforming exertions of the 'wise', political violence may be inevitable. This, indeed, is the anxiety that has dominated Shelley's political thought from the outset, and it returns to de-rail his most sophisticated attempt at writing the revolution: *Prometheus Unbound*. And there, once again, the seemingly unanswerable question about political change is couched in the terms of Shelley's engagement with the discourse on the natural sublime.

CHAPTER 5

'Choose reform or civil war', 1818–1819

On 6 November 1817, Princess Charlotte – 'the much-loved only daughter of the much-hated Prince Regent' – died in childbirth.[1] Public mourning was immediately declared. Two days later, the leaders of the Pentridge uprising were publicly executed at Derby. Shelley responded to these events with his *Address to the People on the Death of Princess Charlotte*, written on 11 and 12 November. Although ostensibly concerned with Charlotte's death – which dealt, in itself, a significant blow to Radical hopes – Shelley's *Address* is actually a stinging critique of Britain's political institutions.[2] 'A beautiful Princess is dead', Shelley affirms, 'LIBERTY is dead': 'let us follow the corpse of British Liberty slowly and reverentially to its tomb' (*PW*, p. 239). Faced with this 'death', the *Address* identifies the political 'alternatives' available to the British people as 'a despotism, a revolution, or reform' (*PW*, p. 237). Just under three years later, and in the wake of the Peterloo Massacre, Shelley's *Oedipus Tyrannus* (1820) advised the government to 'choose reform or civil war' (*CPW*, p. 389). Continued 'despotism' was no longer an option: Britain, Shelley felt, was on the verge of a violent revolution that could only be avoided if the government allowed the reform of parliament.

Throughout these turbulent years, Shelley's own work – his 'great revolutionary poetry' – was explicitly concerned to forward the *moral* and *intellectual* revolution that he, following Godwin, believed to be the pre-requisite of any 'prosperous' change in 'political institutions' (*Poems*, ii, pp. 36, 35). More precisely, poems like *Laon and Cythna, Rosalind and Helen* (1817–19), and *Prometheus Unbound* were intended to educate the radical leaders of the 'public mind' in the dynamics of political change, to caution against desperation and violence, and to extol the benefits of a long-term revolution in opinion. However, this project was consistently problematised, as I have been arguing, by troubling questions about the nature of political action, questions that are repeatedly couched in the terms of Shelley's engagement with the discourse on the natural sublime.

My purpose in this chapter, then, is to demonstrate the extent to which the ostensibly gradualist politics of Shelley's greatest 'revolutionary' poem – *Prometheus Unbound* – are again inextricably bound up with, and ultimately called into question by, that engagement. Arguably begun at Mont Blanc in 1816, Shelley's mature political poetics found its most powerful – and most problematic – expression in his response to Europe's other famous example of the death-dealing mountain sublime: Vesuvius.

THE PROMETHEAN 'REFORM': REJECTING
THE POLITICS OF DEFIANCE

On 12 March 1818, Shelley sailed out of Dover for the third and final time in his life. Arrived at Este in Northern Italy, he began work on *Prometheus Unbound* – 'the best thing I ever wrote' – in late September 1818 (*Letters*, ii, p. 164).[3] In a letter to Leigh Hunt on 26 May 1820, Shelley noted that *Prometheus Unbound* was 'written only for the elect' (*Letters*, ii, p. 201). This appeal to an 'elect' audience is important since it identifies *Prometheus Unbound* as the culmination of the line that runs from *Queen Mab* through *Laon and Cythna*. In short, Shelley's drama – like *Mab* and *Cythna* before it – is an attempt to educate the 'elect' intellectual leaders of the 'public mind' in the dynamics of political change. Written against the backdrop of an increasingly turbulent political situation in England, *Prometheus Unbound* is an ostensibly gradualist statement, cautioning explicitly against the politics of defiance and extolling the need for a long-term, moral revolution before any 'prosperous' reform of 'political institutions' can take place.[4] For all its ostensible gradualism, however, the poem ultimately remains uncertain about the nature and origin of such reform. In fact, the dénouement of Shelley's drama is dominated by familiar anxieties about the role of popular violence in effecting political change, about the 'awful' relationship between Necessity and revolution. And once again, these anxieties are couched explicitly in the terms of Shelley's engagement with the discourse on the natural sublime. For all the political potential of the 'cultivated imagination', violent revolution emerges once more as 'the natural death' of 'empire', popular vengeance as the inevitable offspring of tyranny.

In a letter to Leigh Hunt on her return journey from Italy in 1823, Mary Shelley suggested that the 'dark high precipices' of the Echelles mountains – through which the Shelley party passed on their way to Italy in 1818 – 'gave S the idea of his Prometheus' (quoted in *MWSJ*, p. 200 n. 2).[5] Mary's claim is important insofar as it points towards the overlap between

Shelley's drama and his engagement with the discourse on the natural sublime. Even more telling in this regard, however, is the topography of the poem's actual composition. In the 'Preface', Shelley affirms that *Prometheus Unbound* was 'chiefly written upon the mountainous ruins of the Baths of Caracalla' in Rome, a quintessentially Volneyan – and again, by now, Shelleyan – landscape of imperial ruin, which provided the 'inspiration' for his revolutionary drama (*Poems*, ii, p. 473).[6] I shall return to the connection between *Prometheus Unbound* and Shelley's reaction to the ruins of Rome later in the chapter. Leaving all topographical 'inspiration' aside for the moment, however, it is also important to recognise that by the time Shelley began composing *Prometheus Unbound*, the Titan had long been – in Stuart Curran's phrase – 'a fundamentally political icon'.[7] Shelley's drama deploys a similarly politicised iconography in an attempt to caution the 'elect' leaders of the radical movement against revolutionary vengeance; hence his discussion of influence in the 'Preface' to *Prometheus Unbound* probably looks as much towards contemporary use of the Titan as towards his ostensible Aeschlyean source.

As Curran notes, in the first decade of the nineteenth century, Prometheus was frequently appropriated as a figure of indomitable libertarian aspiration. After the battle of Waterloo, however, the literary and political appropriation of the Titan became more complex and ambiguous as his bondage was repeatedly used to figure Napoleon's exile on St. Helena, effectively presenting Prometheus as an 'icon' of defeated and/or misguided idealism.[8] One of the most prominent examples of this use of Prometheus occurred – as Curran points out – in Lady Morgan's *France* (1817), which Shelley probably read during the composition of *Laon and Cythna*.[9] Shelley would hardly have warmed to Morgan's broadly sympathetic portrait of Napoleon, however, even though he certainly shared her condemnation of British involvement in the Bourbon restoration. A much more likely source for his engagement with 'the political Prometheus', then, is Byron's use of the Titan as a quasi-Satanic emblem of *defiance* in his *Ode to Napoleon Buonaparte* (1814), *Prometheus* (1817), and – implicitly – in *Childe Harold* IV's infamous 'curse' of 'forgiveness' (*Childe Harold* IV, 1207).[10] To put it more succinctly, Shelley's drama is explicitly concerned to *correct* the defiance embodied in Byron's Titans, to explain that the *politics* of defiance – however well intentioned – will end in revolutionary disaster.

Shelley's *Prometheus Unbound* opens where Aeschylus' *Prometheus Vinctus* left off, with the Titan 'bound' to a 'precipice' in the 'Indian Caucasus' as a result of his attempts to help mankind – against the wishes of Jupiter – by stealing fire from Lemnos (*Prometheus Unbound*, stage direction, I, i). In the 'Preface', Shelley outlines his poem's politically resonant revision of the Titan's subsequent fate. 'The *Prometheus Unbound* of Aeschylus', he notes, 'supposed the reconciliation of Jupiter with his victim as the price of the disclosure of the danger threatened to his empire by the consummation of his marriage with Thetis' (*Poems*, ii, p. 472). 'Had I framed my story on this model', Shelley continues, 'I should have done no more than have attempted to restore the lost drama of Aeschylus' (*Poems*, ii, p. 472). 'But, in truth', he affirms:

I was averse from a catastrophe so feeble as that of reconciling the Champion with the Oppressor of mankind. The moral interest of the fable, which is so powerfully sustained by the sufferings and endurance of Prometheus, would be annihilated if we could conceive of him as unsaying his high language and quailing before his perfidious adversary (*Poems*, ii, p. 472)

Shelley's pun on the dramaturgical term catastrophe – as the dénouement of a play – confirms that it would be a disaster indeed if the 'Champion' of 'mankind' were to surrender his libertarian aspirations in the wake of his defeat by the 'Oppressor'. Such a capitulation would repeat the reactionary response of the 'public mind' to the collapse of the French struggle for liberty: in the 'Preface' to *Laon and Cythna*, Shelley had already affirmed that, from the 1790s onwards, 'hopelessness', 'gloom', and 'misanthropy' had 'become the characteristics of the age' (*Poems*, ii, pp. 35, 37). Hence, Shelley, in the similarly punning words of Mary's 'Note' to the Poem, 'adapted the catastrophe of this story to his peculiar views' (*CPW*, p. 272).

Accordingly, the 'moral interest' of Shelley's revision of the Promethean 'fable' consists not so much in the fact of the Titan's oppression by Jupiter as in his *reaction* to that oppression, and this reaction reflects Shelley's 'peculiar' [i.e. personal] political 'views'. Shelley's Prometheus does not capitulate to Jupiter (the political status quo), as *Laon and Cythna* suggested that many actual 'worshippers of public good' had done in the wake of 'the excesses consequent upon the French Revolution' (*Poems*, ii, p. 35). But neither does he retain his previous – and explicitly Byronic – politics of defiance, the politics that have led, for all their noble intentions, to his present enslavement and mankind's ongoing oppression. Rather, Shelley's Titan abandons the politics of defiance and accepts, in their place, the political efficacy of 'suffering' and 'endurance'.

To this extent, Shelley's revision of Aeschylus almost certainly draws upon Cicero's account of the bound Titan in Book II of his *Tusculan Disputations* (*c.* 45 BC).[11] In his letter to Peacock on 8 October 1818 – the letter that prematurely announced the completion of *Prometheus Unbound* I – Shelley asked his friend to 'tell [him] what there is in Cicero about a drama supposed to have been written by Aeschylus under this title' (*Letters*, ii, p. 43). As Jones notes, the object of Shelley's enquiry was Cicero's *Tusculan Disputations*, II, x, 23–5, in which the Roman both refers to and quotes from Aeschylus' 'lost play' Προμηθεύς Λυομενος, or *Prometheus Delivered* (*Letters*, ii, p. 43 n. 4).[12] Shelley's inquiry is thus at least in part a search for source material.[13] However, the context of Cicero's reference to the Titan is instructive, and points towards *Prometheus Unbound*'s gradualist agenda. 'How', the Roman enthuses, 'does Prometheus in Aeschylus' play bear the pain which he suffers for the theft from Lemnos!'.[14] Cicero then quotes some twenty-eight lines exemplifying the Titan's conduct. These lines show Prometheus stoically enduring his fate without resentment or defiance. Indeed, this stoicism is the point of Cicero's reference: he has been disputing the contention that pain and evil are synonymous, and cites Prometheus as an example of the virtue of an individual suffering pain for the promotion of the greater good.

Armed with this reference, Shelley – in the 'Preface' to *Prometheus Unbound* – draws a clear distinction between his stoic, Ciceronian Titan and Byron's quasi-Satanic figure. Shelley accepts that 'the only imaginary being resembling in any degree Prometheus, is Satan' (*Poems*, ii, p. 472). However, he also affirms that 'Prometheus is ... a more poetical character than Satan' (*Poems*, ii, p. 472). This is because:

in addition to courage, and majesty, and firm and patient opposition to omnipotent force, [Prometheus] is susceptible of being described as exempt from the taints of ambition, envy, revenge, and a desire for personal aggrandisement, which, in the Hero of *Paradise Lost*, interfere with the interest. The character of Satan engenders in the mind a pernicious casuistry which leads us to weigh his faults with his wrongs, and to excuse the former because the latter exceed all measure (*Poems*, ii, p. 472)

In short, then, Shelley's *Prometheus Unbound* rejects Byron's Napoleonic or Satanic Prometheus (characterised precisely by 'ambition', 'envy', 'revenge', and 'a desire for personal aggrandisement') in favour of a Titan who resolutely but calmly ('firm and patient') opposes 'omnipotent force'. To put it more precisely, the unbinding of Prometheus in Shelley's drama coincides with his maturation *from* a Byronic Titan to a Ciceronian one: 'the type of the highest perfection of moral and intellectual nature, impelled by the purest and truest motives to the best and noblest ends' (*Poems*, ii, p. 473). That is to say that Shelley's Titan learns to reject the politics of defiance in favour of a 'firm and patient' gradualism. The chains that bind him are as much ideological as they are physical.

The first act of *Prometheus Unbound* – in which, as critics have long noted, the main *moral* action takes place – accordingly focuses on the Titan's bondage: the reasons for it and his reaction to it. We recall that Prometheus has been bound for rebelling against the will of Jupiter, a rebellion embodied in the Titan's clearly Byronic curse: 'Fiend, I defy thee!' (*Prometheus Unbound*, I, 262). 'Earth' provides a highly instructive history of this rebellion, describing Prometheus's struggle with Jupiter as a global geological upheaval that culminated in environmental disaster. '[A]t thy voice', Earth affirms, 'my pining sons uplifted / Their prostrate brows from the polluting dust, / And our almighty Tyrant with fierce dread / Grew pale' (*Prometheus Unbound*, I, 159–61). 'The sea', Earth continues:

> Was lifted by strange tempest, and new fire
> From earthquake-rifted mountains of bright snow
> Shook its portentous hair beneath Heaven's frown
>
> (*Prometheus Unbound*, I, 165–8)

Like *Laon and Cythna* before it, then, *Prometheus Unbound* uses 'awful' natural phenomena to image the political violence.[15] In this case, nature literally rebels against Jupiter's oppression. Indeed, the choice of volcanic imagery here is highly appropriate given that Lemnos – the island from which Prometheus stole fire – belonged to Vulcan: the fire of revolution is thus explicitly volcanic fire. In fact, Shelley's volcanic imagery becomes even more resonant when we remember that, as Wasserman points out, contemporary mythography frequently suggested that 'the history of the rebellion and punishment of the Titans is nothing else than an allegorical account of volcanic eruptions'.[16] However, Earth's account of the outcome of this volcanic struggle is equally telling. 'Lightning and Inundation vexed the plains', she continues:

> Blue thistles bloomed in cities; foodless toads
> Within voluptuous chambers panting crawled:
> When Plague had fallen on man and beast and worm,
> And Famine, and black blight on herb and tree;
> And in the corn, and vines, and meadow-grass,
> Teemed ineradicable poisonous weeds
>
> (*Prometheus Unbound*, I, 169–75)

Again, Earth's account of the environmental disaster following the defeat of Promethean revolution rehearses the post-restoration plague described in *Laon and Cythna* X – and, by extension, the ideological (and literal)

decimation of post-Napoleonic Europe. Earth's speech uses natural processes to image socio-political processes, and Shelley's point is clear
enough. Earth's speech does not merely participate in a now familiar
Shelleyan concern that violent popular revolution is itself an 'awful' natural
phenomenon. Rather it also reveals a Godwinian conviction that – just as
environmental disaster inevitably follows global geological catastrophe – so
restored despotism is the inevitable outcome of defiant, revolutionary
vengeance.

Accordingly, Prometheus must learn to reject the politics of defiance
before he – and mankind – can be 'unbound' from their ideological chains.
At the opening of Shelley's drama, the Titan's moral education has
already begun. 'Misery', he affirms, has 'made' him 'wise' and 'aught evil
wish / Is dead within' (*Prometheus Unbound*, I, 58–9, 70–1). The Titan's
new wisdom is reflected in his revised attitude to Jupiter, whose 'throne' is
now explicitly unenvied – clear evidence that Shelley's Prometheus has
departed from the Satanic standards of his Byronic counterpart
(*Prometheus Unbound*, I, 17). Unlike Byron's implacably Satanic Titan,
then, Shelley's Prometheus has ceased to 'disdain' Jupiter (*Prometheus
Unbound*, I, 53). Rather, Prometheus now feels 'pity' for his oppressor in
recognition of the eventual 'ruin' that awaits the 'cruel king' of heaven
(*Prometheus Unbound*, I, 53, 60).

Before Prometheus can be wholly 'unbound' from his ideological
chains, however, he must remember and recant the precise curse with
which his rebellion began. It is not sufficient, in short, that he has outgrown his mistake; he must also learn what that mistake was. In order to do
this, he enlists the aid of his 'mother' 'Earth': the feminine principle of
nature (*Prometheus Unbound*, I, 153). Prometheus' dialogue with this
passive principle (the type of *Mont Blanc*'s 'universe of things') anticipates
and parallels Asia's equally crucial later interview with the active 'Power'
informing that 'universe': Demogorgon (of whom more is said below).
Both dialogues are essential in bringing about the downfall of Jupiter.
Hence, Prometheus's relationship with Asia not only rehearses Laon's
relationship with Cythna, but also reflects the crux of Shelley's revision
of the discourse on the natural sublime. The 'truth / Of nature' can only be
grasped by the 'cultivated' imagination, by the mind that harmonises the
rational and the imaginative, figured (or gendered) as masculine and
feminine.

On the advice of 'Earth', and in one of the most complicated passages of
a complicated poem, Prometheus summons the 'Phantasm of Jupiter' and
has it repeat his explicitly Byronic curse: 'Fiend I defy thee!' (*Prometheus*

Unbound, I, 191–207, 262).[17] The fact that it is the 'Phantasm of Jupiter' – rather than Prometheus's 'own ghost' – who repeats the curse not only allows the Titan to distance himself from his former politics of defiance (*Prometheus Unbound*, I, 211). Rather it also emphasises that Prometheus has been bound by moral and ideological as well as by physical chains. Shelley's point, of course, is that Jupiter derives his power *from* Prometheus. In the classical myth, Jupiter gained control of heaven with the aid of Prometheus. In Shelley's revision of the myth, the tyrant who binds and oppresses the human race is empowered by the 'one mind' itself. Oppression and revolution are mutually constitutive; Jupiter (tyranny) is the consequence of Prometheus's former politics of defiance. The Titan's defiance is thus doubly a 'curse'.

When the 'phantasm' finishes speaking, Prometheus immediately recalls his 'curse'. 'It doth repent me', he affirms, 'words are quick and vain; / Grief for awhile is blind, and so was mine. / I wish no living thing to suffer pain' (*Prometheus Unbound*, I, 303–5). 'Earth' immediately interprets these words as evidence that Jupiter has finally triumphed over Prometheus: 'Misery, O Misery to me', she laments, 'that Jove at length should vanquish thee' (*Prometheus Unbound*, I, 306–7). Hence, although she has suffered the disastrous consequences of Prometheus's defiant revolution, 'Earth' has still not learned the Titan's lessons. Conversely, she still considers his 'curse' to be 'a treasured spell' (*Prometheus Unbound*, I, 184). 'We meditate / In secret joy and hope those dreadful words, / But dare not speak them', she affirms (*Prometheus Unbound*, I, 184–6). In short, then, 'Earth' still considers the Titan's former politics of defiance to be the key to Jupiter's downfall, not recognising that those same politics are actually partly responsible for her present condition.

And indeed, for a while it appears as if Earth's interpretation of the Titan's recantation is correct. There is a significant interval – effectively encompassing much of recorded history – between the recall of the curse and the final defeat of Jupiter. Again, Shelley is emphasising the need for political fortitude, for 'firm and patient opposition to omnipotent force'. Immediately after Prometheus recalls his 'curse', the Furies arrive to torment him further. They show the Titan the political catastrophes of the future: the perversion of Christ's teachings by the power hungry and the collapse of the French Revolution (*Prometheus Unbound*, I, 594–615, 648–55). But Prometheus is not swayed by these new, ideological tortures. Although he clearly identifies these further catastrophes as an extension of Jupiter's 'dread revenge' for his rebellion, he now recognises explicitly that 'revenge' leads to 'defeat . . . not victory' (*Prometheus Unbound*, I, 641–2).

Accordingly, the 'sights' which Jupiter intends as tortures in fact 'gird' the Titan's 'soul / With new endurance, till the hour arrives / When they shall be no type of things which are' (*Prometheus Unbound*, I, 643–5). In short, Prometheus recognises that his reform can only prosper through calm 'endurance', through 'firm and patient opposition'.

Hence while 'Earth' and the Echoes believe that the Titan – having abandoned the politics of defiance – now 'lies fallen and vanquished', Panthea alone tellingly observes that Prometheus looks 'firm *not proud*' (*Prometheus Unbound*, I, 312–13, 337; emphasis added).

The relevance of this narrative to an England tottering – after years of political oppression – on the brink of revolution could scarcely be over-estimated. Shelley's revision of Titan's story was clearly intended to caution the 'elect' leaders of the Radical movement against the politics of revolutionary defiance, the politics that was gaining increasing popular support (symbolised here by the fact that 'Earth' and the Echoes still 'treasure' the Titan's defiant 'curse'). Again, this gradualist agenda is best summed up in the already-quoted contrast that the 'Preface' draws between Milton's (Satanic) Titan and Shelley's 'type of the highest perfection of moral and intellectual nature'. *Prometheus Unbound* is explicitly intended to caution against the 'pernicious' political 'casuistry' which would 'excuse' the 'faults' of revolution because the 'wrongs' that it seeks to redress 'exceed all measure'.[18] Shelley's drama sets out to explain that revolution is a 'curse', to affirm that a 'prosperous' reform of 'political institutions' can only be achieved through 'firm and patient opposition to omnipotent power'. The problem, of course, is that it is far from clear how such a gradualist strategy translates into political *action*. At least, when it finally comes, the Promethean 'reform' is far from a gradual, intellectual revolution. Rather, Jupiter's reign is destroyed by an 'awful' – and explicitly volcanic – 'civil war'.[19]

RECALLING THE CURSE: THE RUINS OF ROME
AND THE 'RELIGION OF ETERNITY'

By insisting that the Promethean revolution cannot succeed until the Titan rejects the politics of defiance, Shelley's *Prometheus Unbound* not only advises the 'elect' intellectual leaders of the radical movement against revolutionary hostility, but also corrects the solipsistic and defiant Prometheanism of Byron's *Manfred, Ode to Napoleon Buonaparte*, and *Prometheus*. However, Shelley's decision to embody his Titan's defiance in a *curse* marks a further aspect of the poem's engagement with Byron's

Prometheanism, an aspect that has yet to receive the critical attention it deserves. By the time that Shelley wrote *Prometheus Unbound*, the curse had long been a common motif in Romantic literature, Southey's *Curse of Kehama* (1810) being only one obvious example. By the end of 1818, however, the most prominent instance of this motif was undoubtedly Byron's notorious 'curse' of 'forgiveness' in *Childe Harold* IV.[20] The first act of Shelley's *Prometheus Unbound* demands to be read as (at least in part) a corrective response to this 'curse'.

Byron's famous 'curse' is outlined in stanzas 128–45 of *Childe Harold* IV, which describe the ruins of the Colosseum: that 'long explored but still exhaustless mine / of contemplation' and fit symbol of a Rome – and, by extension, of a *world* – ruined 'past redemption's skill' (*Childe Harold* IV, 1150–1, 1304). 'While stands the Coliseum, Rome shall stand', Byron writes, paraphrasing Gibbon, 'when falls the Coliseum, Rome shall fall; / And when Rome falls – the World' (*Childe Harold* IV, 1297–9; *D&F*, vii, p. 317 and n. 62). The 'curse' itself invokes 'Time' as the ultimate, Volneyan 'Avenger' of human 'wrong' (*Childe Harold* IV, 1169–80). 'A far hour', Byron affirms, 'shall wreak / The deep prophetic fullness of this verse, / And pile on human heads the mountain of my curse!' (*Childe Harold* IV, 1204–6). In other words, Byron invokes Necessity – the 'dread', 'nameless', and 'omnipotent' 'power' whose 'haunts are ever where the dead walls rear / Their ivy mantles' – as the agent of his personal vengeance upon those who have made him suffer: '*thou*', he affirms, 'shalt take / the vengeance' (*Childe Harold* IV, 1234–5, 1238–9, 1194–5). The ruins of power imply – and assure – that vengeance is an 'awful' *natural* process, an assurance reaffirmed in Byron's likening of his revenge to the collapse of a 'mountain' on 'human heads'.

Shelley's dislike for *Childe Harold* IV has long been recognised, and yet the precise reason for that dislike has remained elusive.[21] On 2 January 1818, while still at Marlow, Shelley asked Ollier to 'send' a copy of 'Lord Byron's New Canto the moment' it was published (*Letters*, i, p. 591). However Shelley did not actually read *Childe Harold* IV until the autumn of 1818, while he was writing *Prometheus Unbound* I, and then he reacted angrily. In a letter to Peacock from Naples on 17 or 18 December, Shelley assured his friend that he 'entirely agree[d]' with his strictures on *Childe Harold* IV, both in *Nightmare Abbey* (1818) and in private correspondence (*Letters*, ii, p. 57).[22] 'The spirit in which it is written', Shelley fumed, 'is, if insane, the most wicked and mischievous insanity that was ever given forth' (*Letters*, ii, p. 58). 'It is', he continued, echoing *Laon and Cythna*'s critique of those contemporary poets who promote 'gloom and misanthropy' through 'the wilful exaggeration of [their] own despair', a 'kind of obstinate & *selfwilled* folly in which he hardens himself' (*Poems*, ii, p. 37; *Letters*, ii, p. 58; emphasis added).[23]

Byron's 'curse' of 'forgiveness' seems to have been a particular focal point for Shelley's disappointment. In his 'Lines Written among the Euganean Hills' – composed at Este in October 1818, and thus approximately contemporary with *Prometheus Unbound* I – Shelley describes the 'curse' as a 'mighty thunder fit' ('Euganean Hills', 182).[24] More tellingly, however, Shelley's final strictures on *Childe Harold* IV in his December 1818 letter to Peacock effectively echo the terms of the 'curse' itself in their diagnosis of Byronic disaffection. Byron, Shelley concludes, 'is heartily and deeply discontented with himself, and contemplating in the distorted mirror of his own thoughts, the nature and destiny of man, what can he behold but objects of contempt and despair?' (*Letters*, ii, p. 58).

Byron's 'curse' certainly rehearses the solipsistic Prometheanism of the *Ode to Napoleon Buonaparte* and *Prometheus*. Indeed, Byron effectively figures himself as the Titan of his eponymous 1816 poem: suffering, aligned with (his 'mother') 'Earth' against 'Heaven', and extolling proud, defiant endurance in the certainty of ultimate vengeance (*Childe Harold* IV, 1210, 1208). In *Prometheus Unbound* I, we learn that Shelley's Titan has formulated an effectively equivalent 'sufferer's curse' of defiance, placing his trust in the future 'hour' that would 'wrap' Jupiter in 'a robe of envenomed agony' (*Prometheus Unbound* I, 286, 297, 289). Accordingly, by insisting that the Promethean revolution cannot succeed until the Titan recalls this – explicitly Byronic – 'curse', Shelley's *Prometheus Unbound* is clearly engaging as much with the Prometheanism of *Childe Harold* IV as it is with that of *Prometheus* and the *Ode to Napoleon*. And indeed the terms of Prometheus' recantation are telling in this regard: Shelley's Titan does not self-righteously 'forgive' his oppressor in the certain knowledge of being 'avenged' by 'Time'; rather he 'pities' the 'fierce king' in recognition of his inevitable fall. The 'wicked and mischievous insanity' that Byron was 'giving forth' in *Childe Harold* IV was – at least in part – the promotion of the politics of defiance, the same hazardous politics that Shelley's Aeschylean drama was intended to warn against.

But to reduce Shelley's hostility towards *Childe Harold* IV to his evident distaste for the 'curse' of 'forgiveness' would be to oversimplify the relationship between *Prometheus Unbound* and Byron's poem. Indeed, Shelley's reaction to the 'curse' must have been a good deal more ambivalent than such a reductive reading would allow. After all, on the face of it, Byron's Promethean appeal to 'Time, the Avenger' effectively repeats the problematic overlap between Shelley's own political thought and his revision of the discourse on the natural sublime: the idea that for all the political potency of the 'cultivated' imagination, violent revolutionary retribution may be the 'awful' means by which Necessity will reform the world.[25] Indeed, precisely this same overlap will return to problematise *Prometheus Unbound*'s ostensibly gradualist blueprint for a 'prosperous' reform of 'political institutions'.

In effect, then, Shelley's disapproval of *Childe Harold* IV stemmed not so much from the 'curse' *per se* as from the Prometheanism that informed it, that is, from Byron's pessimistic understanding of the human condition. In short, as his December 1818 letter to Peacock makes clear, what really angered Shelley about *Childe Harold* IV was Byron's 'contempt and despair' for the 'nature and destiny of man' (*Letters*, ii, p. 58). *Childe Harold* IV is explicitly anti-meliorist in its account of this 'nature and destiny'. 'History', Byron famously affirms, 'with all her volumes vast, / Hath but *one* page' and the present is merely a 'rehearsal of the past' (*Childe Harold* IV, 968–9, 965). The 'moral of all human tales' is the essential *unperfectibility* of civilisation: human history is a Polybian cycle of rise and fall: 'first Freedom, and then Glory – when that fails, / Wealth, vice, corruption, – barbarism at last' (*Childe Harold* IV, 964, 966–7). Faced with this – in the words of Byron's *Prometheus* – 'wretched', 'funereal destiny', humanity's only recourse is to the defiant, solipsistic 'resistance' embodied in the 'curse of forgiveness' (*Prometheus*, 24, 50–1).

It is not difficult to see how the perfectibilist Shelley could brand this view of the human condition 'wicked insanity'. Indeed, *Childe Harold* IV must have exemplified the 'gloom and misanthropy' that the 'Preface' to *Laon and Cythna* condemns in the 'literature of the age', the post-Revolutionary culture of despair that Shelley's writing was intended to alleviate (*Poems*, ii, p. 37). After all, Shelley's December 1818 strictures on *Childe Harold* IV not only label the poem 'wicked and mischievous', but also lament that this 'insanity' was being '*given forth*', that is, was determining and perpetuating the reactionary despondency of the 'one mind' (*Letters*, ii, p. 58; emphasis added). To make matters worse, the anti-meliorism of *Childe Harold* IV was both derived from and supported by Byron's interpretation of *ruin*, long a central facet of Shelley's radical – and quintessentially meliorist – revision of the discourse on the sublime!

Appropriately enough, one of 'the first things' that the Shelley party saw as they descended out of the Alps into Italy on 30 March 1818 was 'a ruined arch of magnificent proportions', standing 'in the midst of stupendous mountains' (*Letters*, ii, p. 4). By the time they reached Rome in November, the ruins of the eternal city had long drawn tourists and émigrés from all over Europe. Numerous literary and pictorial representations of the 'marble wilderness' existed alongside the ever-increasing volume of guidebooks.[26] And it is important to recognise that these representations had been *politicised* from the outset: elegy and allegory were inseparable aspects of the British literary engagement with the ruins of Rome.[27]

By the end of 1818, however, *Childe Harold* IV had quickly become the most influential – indeed the *defining* – British representation of the 'marble wilderness'. Byron's Polybian narrative of human history – from 'Freedom', through 'glory', 'wealth, vice, corruption', to 'barbarism' – is obviously premised on the ancient history of Rome: from republic through empire to 'decline and fall'. However his claim that the present was merely a 'rehearsal of the past' had been effectively confirmed by the more recent – and largely analogous – political history of the eternal city. Four days after French Troops entered Rome on 11 February 1798, the pope was exiled and a Roman Republic (re)proclaimed ('Freedom'); two years later the fledgling Republic was overthrown and the papacy restored; ten years later, on 17 May 1809, Napoleon abolished the papacy for a second time and proclaimed Rome a free imperial city ('Glory'); five years later still, after Napoleon's fall, the papacy was restored in an Italy under Austrian rule ('Barbarism') – apparent proof of Byron's claim that Rome was indeed 'ruined past redemption's skill'.

Moreover, the 'marble wilderness' itself – and the Colosseum in particular – had played a central role in the conflicting iconography of this recent political turmoil.[28] When the Republic of Rome was re-proclaimed in 1798, the French Revolutionary armies had 'established', as Carolyn Springer explains, 'the polemical precedent of secularising the monuments and landscape of papal Rome', an ideological (re)possession begun by 'displacing the centre of authority from the Vatican palace to the ancient Forum'.[29] Throughout the city, Republican iconography replaced Christian symbolism, piazzas were renamed, and the Republican Festas drew heavily upon the ruins of the classical city.[30] When the papacy was restored in 1800, Pius VII immediately set about a program of architectural restoration (including the return of the numerous artworks appropriated by the French and sent to Paris) which figured 'the larger political and religious restoration' taking place.[31] Not least amongst these restorations was the addition – in 1807 – of a buttress to the Lateran side of the Colosseum, which had been damaged by an earthquake the previous year (as we shall see later, the ambiguous symbolism of this particular restoration did not escape Shelley). When Napoleon abolished the papacy for the second time (in 1809), the Imperial Armies similarly set about rejuvenating Rome's own imperial past. This rejuvenation went hand in hand with the continuation and expansion of the pope's archaeological activities. Once again, the Flavian amphitheatre took centre-stage: Tournon excavated the ruins in 1813, and had the Stations of the Cross – installed by Benedict XIV – removed. After Napoleon's defeat, Pius VII (restored for the second time in 1814) filled in the excavations and replaced the Stations of the Cross. Hence, by the time of the Austrian occupation of Italy – when Byron and Shelley arrived in Rome – the Colosseum had been effectively 'reclaimed' as 'a strictly religious symbol and site consecrated to the Christian martyrs'.[32]

Thus for Byron, the 'awful' ruins of the capitol – and, again, of the Colosseum in particular – proved humanity to be the victim of 'Circumstance', that 'unspiritual god / And miscreator' who 'makes and helps along / Our coming evils with a crutch-like rod', and 'whose touch turns Hope to dust' (*Childe Harold* IV, 1122–5). In short, the ruins of Rome figure a politically ruined Rome; the 'marble wilderness' is evidence for despair rather than hope, a sign of the ultimate futility of human aspirations and achievements (*Childe Harold* IV, 710). Once again, faced with this futility – this 'funereal destiny' – humanity's only viable response is the solipsistic, defiant Prometheanism of Byron's 'curse' of 'forgiveness'. But even this ambivalent 'curse' – with its ostensibly Shelleyan reading of the ruins of power as evidence of an 'avenging' Necessity – effectively reconfigures that 'awful' agency in reactionary, anti-meliorist terms. Byron's account of the Colosseum – in the 'curse' section of *Childe Harold* IV – alludes to the Dying Gladiator (in the Capitoline Museum) while describing the thousands 'butcher'd to make a Roman holiday' (*Childe Harold* IV, 1267). 'Shall he expire / And unavenged?', Byron asks, rehearsing his own earlier invocation of 'Time, the Avenger' (*Childe Harold* IV, 1268–9). Byron answers this question by (retrospectively) extolling the gladiator's barbarian tribesmen to wreak revolutionary vengeance upon their oppressors: 'arise! ye Goths, and glut your ire!' (*Childe Harold* IV, 1269). Of course Byron is ostensibly referring to the Barbarian invasions of Rome in the fifth century, now re-figured as a noble act of revenge.[33] However, one does not have to go a long way in order to read this Promethean invocation to vengeance as a justification for the *present*, Austrian ('gothic') occupation of Italy. History has come full circle: the vengeful oppressed have become, in their turn, the oppressors; tyranny is the necessary offspring of tyranny.

In his December 1818 letter to Peacock, Shelley acknowledged that he had 'remonstrated in vain with [Byron] on the tone of mind from which

alone such a view of things arises' (*Letters*, ii, p. 58). *Julian and Maddalo* –
composed after Shelley's autumn 1818 visit to Byron in Venice – records
this ultimately unsatisfactory engagement with Byronic despondency.[34]
However, as Robinson notes, 'Shelley was not giving up the argument'.[35]
As we have seen, *Prometheus Unbound* was intended to caution against
Byron's dangerous Promethean politics of defiance, and to extol – in the
face of *Childe Harold* IV's historical pessimism – the possibility of a
'prosperous' reform of 'political institutions' through philanthropic gradualism. In order to successfully refute the 'wicked and mischievous insanity'
of *Childe Harold* IV, however, and demonstrate humanity's perfectibility in
the following acts of *Prometheus Unbound*, Shelley would have to refute the
historical pessimism of the fourth Canto. In other words, Shelley would
effectively have to demonstrate that Rome was not – as Byron had argued –
'ruined past redemption's skill'. More precisely, he would have to correct
Byron's anti-meliorist reading of the 'awful' ruins of power. He would
need to take up the position of a Volneyan 'Genius' in relation to Byron's –
quintessentially – despondent traveller. In short, in order for Shelley to
correct the historical pessimism of *Childe Harold* IV, he would have to
return to his revision of the discourse on the sublime.

Shelley's concern to identify the location in which *Prometheus Unbound*
was composed – 'the mountainous ruins of the Baths of Caracalla' – must
be seen as to some extent an attempt to defend the ruins of Rome against
Byron's pessimistic reading. By citing the ruined Baths as – at least in part –
the 'inspiration' for his revolutionary drama, Shelley was implicitly
asserting the melioristic connotations of the ruins of power (*Poems*, ii,
p. 473). On 25 November 1818, however, during his first visit to Rome,
Shelley broke off work on *Prometheus Unbound* I in order to compose
a more explicit response to Byron's interpretation of the 'marble wilderness': his unfinished and highly problematic short story, *The Coliseum*
(*MWSJ*, p. 239).

Robinson was the first to suggest that Shelley's *Coliseum* responds to 'the
Coliseum sequence in *Childe Harold* IV'.[36] However, Robinson's brief
account of this response needs to be considerably re-focused. Firstly,
while Robinson sketches the relative ethical positions involved, he wholly
fails to examine the most significant factor in both Shelley's and Byron's
response to the Colosseum: namely, their response to the 'vast and wondrous' amphitheatre *as a ruin* (*Childe Harold* IV, 1154). While Byron is
content to identify 'Time' as the '*beautifier* of the dead' and the '*adorner* of
the ruin', Shelley emphasises the fact that the Colosseum is 'sublime' and
'impressive' precisely *because* it is a ruin (*Childe Harold* IV, 1162–3; emphasis

added; *Letters*, ii, p. 59). In his December 1818 description of the amphitheatre to Peacock, Shelley notes that 'a small part of the exterior circumference remains' but that 'the effect of the perfection of its architecture ... is such as to diminish the effect of its greatness' (*Letters*, ii, p. 59). 'The interior is all a ruin', he concludes, noting that he 'can scarcely believe that when encrusted with Dorian marble and ornamented by columns of Egyptian granite its effect could have been so sublime and so impressive as in its present state' (*Letters*, ii, p. 59).[37]

Secondly, we should be wary of too readily following Robinson's reading of *The Coliseum* as merely another skirmish in a private Shelleyan war with Byronic despondency. Rather, when set against the enormous popularity and influence of *Childe Harold* IV, not to mention the long British tradition of writing about the ruins of Rome, Shelley's *Coliseum* demands to be interpreted as an – albeit failed – attempt to make a *public* statement about the 'marble wilderness'. That is to say, that Shelley's story would have marked a return to the kind of project that informed the composition of *Mont Blanc* in 1816. *The Coliseum* was intended to challenge and revise the reactionary public 'record' of Italy's most famous ruin, to replace Byron's historically pessimistic 'code' with a progressive, melioristic interpretation of the 'awful' ruins of power.

While Byron's defiant, Promethean 'curse' figures the ruined amphitheatre as the type of a fallen and irredeemable humanity ('ruined past redemption's skill'), Shelley set out to re-figure the ruin as the 'pledge' of 'all that is to be admirable and lovely in ages yet to come' (*Prose*, p. 226 n. 4). Yet Shelley would have to achieve this re-figuration *without* invoking revolutionary (Byronic and Promethean) defiance as the agency of the 'pledge', that is, *without* reading the amphitheatre in the revolutionary terms of his own revision of the discourse on the sublime. Given this demanding (and uncharacteristic) rubric, it is not surprising that Shelley abandoned the story. However, his failure to complete *The Coliseum* is telling, since the terms of that failure anticipate precisely the ambiguities that would later mark *Prometheus Unbound*'s vision of a gradualist reform. In short, *The Coliseum* comes unstuck on the problematic overlap between Shelley's gradualist political thought and the revolutionism of his revision of the discourse on the sublime.

Mary's journal records that Shelley began writing *The Coliseum* on 25 November 1818, three days after they had visited the amphitheatre for the first time (*MWSJ*, p. 239). It is not clear when he finally abandoned the piece, but the Shelley party visited the Colosseum repeatedly during their second stay in Rome in March-April 1819, and the Easter-tide setting suggests that Shelley was still working on his story at the time.[38] Indeed, the story's Easter setting is thematically central. Like the French Revolutionary (and, later, Imperial) armies before him, Shelley sets up the Colosseum as a secular monument in clear opposition to St. Peter's.[39] That is to say, that Shelley's story rejects the 'strict', religious symbolism accorded to the amphitheatre by the restored papacy.[40] *The Coliseum* opens with 'the great feast of the Resurrection', when 'the whole native populace of Rome, together with all the foreigners who flock from all parts of the earth to contemplate its celebration, were assembled around the Vatican' (*Prose*, p. 224).[41] 'The most awful religion of the world went forth', Shelley writes, re-affirming his sense of its anthropomorphic basis, 'surrounded by emblazonry of mortal greatness, and mankind had assembled to *wonder at and worship the creations of their own power*' (*Prose*, p. 224; emphasis added). *The Coliseum* neglects the religious ceremonies, however, and focuses rather on the visit of an old, blind man and his young daughter (Helen) to the ruined amphitheatre, at 'the hour of noon' on Easter Saturday, the 'feast of the Passover' (*Prose*, p. 224). Unlike the pilgrims to the Vatican, this pair 'sought' the Colosseum 'immediately on their arrival' in Rome (*Prose*, p. 224). Inside the amphitheatre, they are accosted by a strange 'figure' wearing 'an ancient chlamys' and 'ivory sandals' (*Prose*, p. 224). Unaware that the old man is blind, this 'curious' figure berates him for apparently failing to recognise the Colosseum (*Prose*, p. 224). When Helen tells the stranger that her father is blind, he is overcome with remorse for his anger. Helen then proceeds to describe the ruin to her father, who embellishes upon the details she provides. When their dialogue concludes, the stranger, clearly impressed by the old man's speech, desires to make their acquaintance. At this point, the narrative breaks off.

It is not clear what Shelley had in mind for the stranger whom the old man and his daughter encounter in the ruins. Ostensibly, this 'curiosity' – 'only visible at ... night or in solitude, and then only to be seen amid the desolated temples of the Forum or gliding among the weed-grown galleries of the Coliseum' – recalls the numerous accounts of apparitions and/or hermits inhabiting the ruined amphitheatre (*Prose*, p. 224). Hobhouse, for example, records (with suitable scepticism) the reputed apparition of Christian martyrs in the Colosseum, noting that these so-called apparitions were more probably beggars or banditti.[42] Similarly, Forsyth notes that the amphitheatre was 'inhabited by a beadsman'.[43] However, Shelley would hardly have warmed to the superstitious overtones of these anecdotes, and Shelley's 'curiosity' – given his classical attire and explicitly pagan values – seems rather closer to a Volneyan 'genius of the ruins' figure.[44] And indeed the revolutionary overtones of Volney's figure are confirmed when Shelley informs us that the Romans called this stranger – 'with that strange mixture of religious and historical ideas so common in Italy' – '*Il Diavolo di Bruto*' (*Prose*, p. 225; Shelley's emphasis). David Lee Clark's translation of this appellation as 'the devil of a Brute' is unconvincing, not to say mistaken in its Italian (*Prose*, p. 225 n. 2). Rather, Shelley clearly means to identify the figure as the 'daemon of Brutus', Rome's famous republican tyrannicide. This identification is strengthened by Shelley's remark that the stranger could be seen not only in the ruins of the Colosseum, but also 'amid the desolated temples of the Forum', where Julius Caesar was assassinated by Brutus in 44 BC (*Prose*, p. 224). For all his laudable republican credentials however, Shelley's portrait of the stranger is far from flattering. Rather, on his first introduction, he appears rude and arrogant. And indeed his frail, youthful and explicitly feminine appearance also effectively aligns him with the *Alastor*-poet or Laon type: a visionary youth in need of moral education. Indeed, given his express 'contempt' for those whom he believes to be 'blind in spirit', the stranger might well have been intended as a specifically Byronic or Childe Harold figure whose attitudes would be corrected in the body-text (*Prose*, p. 228).

These multiple possibilities effectively reflect the central dilemma of *The Coliseum*: the tension between a revolutionary and a gradualist interpretation of the ruin. And whatever intention Shelley may have had for the stranger, he plays no significant part in the extant text, which focuses rather on the reaction of Helen and her father to the Colosseum.[45] The old man's apostrophe to the amphitheatre conveys Shelley's take on what Hobhouse aptly calls 'the instruction which must be suggested by so awful a memorial of fallen empire'.[46] In other words, his speech 'pictures' the 'truth' that the cultivated imagination 'seizes' in contemplating the 'awful' ruins of power.[47] Accordingly, the means by which the old man arrives at this 'truth' figures the sceptical epistemology of Shelley's revision of the discourse on the sublime. That is to say that the interaction between the father and his daughter figures the mind's engagement with natural grandeur. Since the old man is blind, Helen must describe the physical appearance of the ruin to her father *before* he can extrapolate any speculative 'truth' from the amphitheatre. Helen's blank description of the physical scene figures the mind's (passive) sensory impressions of 'the everlasting universe of things' while her father's extrapolation from that description figures the mind's (active) imaginative reflection upon those impressions. Hence, while Helen acknowledges that her father's blind 'eye has a vision more serene' than her own, she is nevertheless instrumental in the creation of that 'vision' (*Prose*, p. 226). As such, she clearly perpetuates Shelley's attempted (Wollstonecraftian) feminisation of the revolution: Helen is in the line that runs from *Queen Mab*'s Ianthe, through Cythna, to its culmination in Asia.

As noted, the old man's apostrophe to the Colosseum conveys the 'truth' that the cultivated imagination 'seizes' from the 'awful' ruins of power. However, *The Coliseum*'s account of this 'truth' is a good deal less *revolutionary* than one would expect in the light of Shelley's previous engagements with ruin. In short, given the brutal history of the amphitheatre, one would expect Shelley to read the Colosseum as the quintessential Volneyan ruin of power, as the master symbol of the inevitable – of the *necessary* – overthrow of tyranny. Indeed, in a three line 1819 fragment entitled 'Rome and Nature', Shelley interprets the 'marble wilderness' in the explicitly Volneyan terms of his revision of the discourse on the sublime. 'Rome has fallen', the fragment affirms, 'ye see it lying / Heaped in undistinguished ruin / *Nature alone is undying*' ('Rome and Nature', 1–3; emphasis added). In marked contrast to this revolutionary Volneyan sentiment, however, Helen's father affirms that the 'contemplation' of the 'awfulness and beauty' of the 'ruins of human power' – or, for that matter, of 'the ocean, the glacier, the cataract, the tempest, [and] the volcano' – leads to an awareness of a 'Power' which he calls 'Love' (*Prose*, p. 227). He concludes by identifying this sublime ('tingling', 'glorious') awareness of 'power' as 'the Religion of Eternity': the direct, secular, and politically progressive alternative to the institutionalised Christian religion now being celebrated at St Peter's (*Prose*, p. 227).

Thus far, then, *The Coliseum* is on familiar ground: the central tenet of Shelley's radical revision of the discourse on the sublime is that the contemplation of the 'awful' by the 'cultivated imagination' leads not to religious belief, but rather to a politically potent apprehension of Necessity ('power'), nature's inhuman law. And Shelley consistently identifies the moral consequence of this law as 'Love'. In the terms of the *Hymn to Intellectual Beauty*, the apprehension of the Necessitarian 'truth / Of nature' 'binds' the individual to avoid solipsism (to 'fear' himself) and 'love all human kind' (*Hymn to Intellectual Beauty*, 83–4).

The old man's apostrophe to the Colosseum accordingly responds to *Childe Harold* IV's account of the 'vast and wondrous' amphitheatre by setting Shelley's melioristic revision of the discourse on the sublime in opposition to Byron's pessimistic interpretation of the 'marble wilderness' (*Childe Harold* IV, 1154). Ostensibly, Shelley's point is that the contemplation of the 'awful' ruins of power should not be a touchstone for the solipsistic, Promethean defiance 'given forth' by *Childe Harold* IV's account of the Colosseum. Rather, the correct – the *cultivated* – imaginative response to ruin should be the occasion for a politically potent apprehension of ethical responsibility. And indeed, Shelley was apparently not satisfied with merely narrating Helen and her father's apprehension of the philanthropic 'spells' by which Necessity 'binds' the individual. Rather, their contemplation of the amphitheatre also occasions a rational meditation on death, a doubly appropriate meditation given their location: in a ruin, and in Rome during the 'great feast of the Resurrection' (*Prose*, pp. 227, 224).

Having narrated the substance and dynamic of the old man's imaginative response to the Colosseum, however, Shelley's response to *Childe Harold* IV's account of the amphitheatre is essentially complete. This is one reason why *The Coliseum* itself remains incomplete: once Shelley has made his point in the old man's apostrophe he has, in a sense, nothing more to say. The *main* reason why Shelley abandoned his story, however, was the evident difficulty he experienced in constructing and sustaining his response to Byron.

In fact, the apparent confidence of Shelley's narration is belied by the deep ambiguities that mark the old man's apostrophe to the Colosseum. These ambiguities are clearly evident in Shelley's tellingly contradictory footnote to the old man's speech. Helen's father has just identified the Colosseum's historical function as a scene of 'spectacle' and 'sacrifice', Shelley's first and only mention of the amphitheatre's bloody history (*Prose*, p. 226). 'Nor does a recollection of the use to which it [i.e. the Colosseum] may have been destined', Shelley's footnote affirms, 'interfere with these emotions' which the contemplation of the amphitheatre now occasions (*Prose*, p. 226 n. 4). 'Time', he continues, 'has thrown its purple shadow athwart this scene [i.e. amphitheatre's 'use'], and no more is visible than the broad and everlasting character of human strength and genius, that pledge of all that is to be lovely and admirable in ages yet to come' (*Prose*, p. 226 n. 4).

We are certainly close, here, to Byron's notion of 'Time' as the 'beautifier of the dead' and 'adorner of the ruin' (*Childe Harold* IV, 1162–3). But the sentiments are extraordinarily un-Shelleyan. In effect, Shelley's footnote advocates a purely aesthetic – that is a wholly depoliticised – response to the ruin, an aesthetic response which effectively elides both the amphitheatre's historical function and the *process* of its ruination. Such an aesthetic wholly contradicts the terms of Shelley's revision of the discourse on the sublime. Indeed, one need only glance at 'Ozymandias' to realise just how uncharacteristic such an aesthetic is – the only possible explanation is that Shelley was *forced* to adopt this position in order to respond to Byron's defiant, revolutionary reading of the ruin.

Madame De Staël's *Corinne* contains an exact precedent for such an explicitly apolitical and dehistoricised response to the Colosseum. Corinne and Lord Nelvil visit the ruined amphitheatre in chapter IV of Book V. Anticipating Shelley's footnote, Corinne argues that 'there is something supernatural in [its] magnificence, and its origin and purpose are forgotten in its poetic splendour'.[48] Lord Nelvil, however, cannot except this divorce of the aesthetic from the political and neither ultimately, it seems, could Shelley. The remainder of his footnote to the old man's speech describes the 'marble wilderness' in more general terms. The footnote concludes with an account of Titus's triumphant return to Rome after his destruction of Jerusalem in AD 70:

a human being returning in the midst of festival and solemn joy, with thousands and thousands of his enslaved and desolated species chained behind his chariot, exhibiting, as titles to renown, the labour of ages, and the admired creations of genius, overthrown by the brutal force which was placed as a sword within his hand (*Prose*, p. 226 n. 4)[49]

Faced with this 'fearful' and 'abhorred' 'contemplation', the footnote closes with an ominous echo of Byron's appeal to 'Time the Avenger', an echo that wholly contradicts Shelley's earlier formulation of the aesthetic response to the amphitheatre and, moreover, the gradualist tenor of *The Coliseum* per se. 'We do not forget these things . . .', Shelley warns (*Prose*, p. 226 n. 4). Thus a notion of 'Time' which 'elides' history with its 'purple shadow' has given way to Shelley's more familiar, Volneyan notion of 'Time' the agent of inevitable revolutionary vengeance. In effect, time's 'purple shadow' has become Necessity's 'awful', imperial robe.

What Shelley's footnote to *The Coliseum* suggests, then, is that he could only enlist the ruined amphitheatre in support of an anti-Byronic, gradualist ('Love') political agenda by uncharacteristically eliding the *history* of the place. More specifically, Shelley needed to elide both the *process* and the *implications* of ruin. However, he was apparently unable – or unwilling – to sustain this elision and the ambiguity at the heart of his revision of the discourse on the sublime returned to undermine *The Coliseum*'s rejection of Byronic Prometheanism.

Shelley's attempt to elide the history of the Colosseum is apparent from the outset.[50] It is not surprising that in re-figuring the amphitheatre as a secular monument he should choose to ignore the overtly religious symbolism of the Colosseum in 1818, not least the Stations of the Cross which had been restored by Pius VII in 1814. Indeed, Shelley's elision of these objects from his description of the Colosseum can be seen as another, rhetorical blow in the interpretative struggle that had been ongoing since 1798. More significant, however, is the fact that Shelley's reading of the Colosseum as an 'everlasting' 'pledge' of 'human strength and genius' completely ignores contemporary theories – voiced by Hobhouse for one – that the amphitheatre was on the verge of collapse.[51] Even more significantly, Shelley fails to mention the fact that the amphitheatre would have collapsed already had it not been for the restorative interventions of Pius VII who, as already noted, had added a supportive buttress to the Lateran side after it was damaged by an earthquake in 1806. One would ordinarily expect Shelley to *approve* and emphasise the 'awful', natural (earthquake) destruction of the edifices of power and to condemn such a politically resonant act of restoration after the collapse of the 1798–9 Franco-Roman republic. Once again, however, the need to respond to the Byronic politics of defiance apparently forced him into an uncharacteristic elision of historical fact.

Shelley's most significant elision of history from *The Coliseum* marks the story's thematic centre: the old man's apostrophe to the ruined amphitheatre. Again, Shelley could apparently only achieve the gradualist re-figuring of the ruin demanded by his response to Byron by eliding the Colosseum's historical identity as the ruin of an imperial edifice, and a spectacularly bloody edifice at that. This elision is effected by the old man's apostrophe to the amphitheatre, which only reaches its gradualist climax *after* the Colosseum's historical, imperial identity has been obscured. However, the means by which Shelley chose to obscure this identity – by replacing political history with natural history – returns us directly to the problematic overlap between his political thought and his revision of the discourse on the sublime.

As noted, the old man's apostrophe to the Colosseum takes its cue from his daughter's empirical descriptions. The stranger falls silent after he learns that Helen's father is blind. Helen then proceeds to describe to her father the actual scene that the Shelleys themselves would have seen when they entered the ruined amphitheatre for the first time:

a great circle of arches built upon arches, and shattered stones lie around, that once made part of the solid wall. In the crevices and on the vaulted roofs grow a multitude of shrubs ... The stones are immensely massive, and they jut out one from the other. There are terrible rifts in the wall, and broad windows through which you see the blue heaven. There seems to be more than a thousand arches, some ruined, some entire, and they are all immensely high and wide. Some are shattered, and stand forth in great heaps, and the underwood is tufted on their crumbling summits. Around us lie enormous columns, shattered and shapeless – and fragments of capitals and cornice, fretted with delicate sculptures (*Prose*, p. 225)

Helen's account of 'arches built upon arches' echoes Byron's identical 'arches on arches' and, again, her speech describes the actual, sublime ('terrible', 'shattered') ruin, the historical Colosseum, albeit minus the religious shrines (*Childe Harold* IV, 1144). Her father, however, seems uninterested in the specifics of architectural detail and asks only if the amphitheatre is 'open to the blue sky' – a strange question given the Colosseum's original design, not to mention the fact that Helen has already told him that 'the blue heaven' is visible (*Prose*, p. 225). Shelley's elision of the amphitheatre's historical identity has begun. When Helen replies in the affirmative, her father urges her to continue her account of the ruin. She proceeds to describe the amphitheatre in empirical terms, noting the 'bright-green mossy ground, speckled by tufts of dewy clovergrass that run into the interstices of the shattered arches, and round the isolated pinnacles of the ruin' (*Prose*, p. 226). The old man's response to this unequivocally empirical account again seems determined to ignore (and obscure) the fact that Helen is describing a ruined *building*. 'Like the lawny dells of soft short grass which wind among the . . . precipices in the Alps of Savoy?', he enquires. He then proceeds to similarly assert that the 'great wrecked arches' Helen had already described are 'more like chasms rent by an earthquake among the mountains than like the vestige of what was human workmanship' (*Prose*, p. 226).

Shelley's progressive elision of the Colosseum's historical identity reaches its climax immediately before the old man's gradualist apostrophe to 'Love'. The Colosseum, Helen's father affirms, is:

a nursling of man's art, abandoned by his care, and transformed by the enchant-ment of Nature into a likeness of her own creations, and destined to partake their immortality! *Changed into a mountain* cloven with woody dells which overhang its labyrinthine glade, and shattered into toppling precipices. Even the clouds, inter-cepted by its craggy summit, feed its eternal fountains with their rain (*Prose*, p. 226; emphasis added)

Shelley was by no means the first to use the language of the *natural* sublime to describe the ruined amphitheatre. John Dyer's *Ruins of Rome* (1740), for example, describes it as a 'mountainous pile'.[52] And indeed, in his December 1818 letter to Peacock, Shelley himself had already affirmed that the Colosseum had 'been changed by time into the image of an amphitheatre of rocky hills' (*Letters*, ii, p. 59).[53]

However, while 'Time' has changed the Colosseum's *appearance*, Shelley's narrative has effected the *symbolic* transformation upon which the old man's gradualist apostrophe is premised. It is Shelley's narrative, in other words, that has 'changed' this ruin of empire into a 'mountain' capable of symbolising the ethical dimensions of nature's law. In effect, then, the old man's gradualist apostrophe is the product of a rhetorical sleight of hand: he responds not so much to the ruins of empire as to an instance of the natural sublime. As we have seen, however, Shelley's revision of the discourse on the sublime denies such a distinction, implying rather that the ruination of empire *is* an 'awful', *natural* process. And for all his desire to formulate a gradualist response to Byron's account of the amphitheatre, Shelley – it would seem – was either unable or unwilling to sustain this distinction in *The Coliseum* either. After all, if we examine the similes that the old man uses in his attempt to 'change' the ruin into a 'mountain' we find clear echoes of the amphitheatre's historical (imperial) function.[54] When Helen's father describes the 'ruined arches' as 'caves' where an Indian elephant might 'hide her cubs', we recall the fact that real elephants were kept (to kill and be killed) in the Colosseum (*Prose*, p. 226). Similarly, when he compares these 'arches' to the 'caverns' which 'the mightiest monsters of the deep' might inhabit 'were the sea to overflow the earth', we remember that the Colosseum could actually be flooded in order to stage miniature naval battles (*Prose*, p. 226). Again, Shelley is ultimately either unwilling or unable to obscure the history of the Colosseum.

Most telling, in this regard, is Shelley's decision to figure the amphitheatre's ruins as the after-effects of a *natural* catastrophe. When Shelley had Helen's father liken the 'great wrecked arches' of the Colosseum to 'chasms rent by an earthquake among the mountains' he could not have been unaware – as we have seen – that a real earthquake had 'rent' the amphitheatre as recently as 1807. Historically, however, the ruination of the Colosseum was due not so much to natural phenomena as to the defiant Barbarian invasions invoked by Byron. Accordingly, by figuring the historical destruction of the amphitheatre in terms of natural catastrophe, Shelley was returning – albeit implicitly – to the persistent ambiguity at the heart of his revision of the discourse on the sublime: the idea that the ruins of power prove revolutionary defiance to be an 'awful', natural (i.e. *necessary*) phenomenon. He could not have been unaware, either, that the short imperial reign of Titus was marked by natural catastrophes, not the least of which was the eruption of Vesuvius in AD 79. Indeed, as an 'amphitheatre of rocky hills', the ruins of the

Colosseum – Titus's legacy – must have seemed to Shelley like the crater of an extinct volcano. At the heart of his gradualist rejection of *Childe Harold* IV's defiant account of the Colosseum, then, we have Shelley unable to escape Byron's notion of 'Time', of Necessity, as the inevitable Volneyan 'Avenger' of imperial oppression. And precisely this same inability would return to problematise Shelley's vision of a gradualist reform in *Prometheus Unbound.*

THE PROMETHEAN 'CIVIL WAR': DEMOGORGON AND VESUVIUS

When Prometheus rejects the politics of defiance and recalls his Byronic curse at the end of *Prometheus Unbound* I, his moral education is complete and his stalled revolution can be 'prosperously' accomplished as a gradualist reform. Shelley narrates this accomplishment in *Prometheus Unbound* II, which opens with the journey of the Titan's partner Asia and her sister Panthea from 'a lovely vale in the Indian Caucasus' to the 'realm / Of Demogorgon' (*Prometheus Unbound,* stage direction, II, i; II, iii, 1–2). In the opening lines of *Prometheus Unbound,* Shelley's Titan identifies Demogorgon as the 'One' out of all the 'Gods and Daemons, and … Spirits' over whom Jupiter is not 'Monarch' (*Prometheus Unbound,* I, 1–2). The 'Semichorus of Spirits' in Act II refines this claim, describing Demogorgon as the 'mighty law' that 'drives' all other 'Spirits' (*Prometheus Unbound,* II, ii, 43–5). In short, then, Demogorgon 'represents Necessity', and like *Mont Blanc*'s synonymous 'power' that 'dwells apart', he inhabits a 'world unknown' to the rest of the characters (*Poems,* ii, p. 468; *Prometheus Unbound,* II, i, 190).[55]

Asia's meeting with Demogorgon triggers the downfall of Jupiter and the completion of Prometheus's stalled attempt at political reform. As the Titan's partner, Asia effectively reprises Cythna's role in Shelley's 'vision of the nineteenth century': she is the last of Shelley's great female revolutionaries, the most sophisticated statement of his (Wollstonecraftian) concern to feminise the revolution. By extension, as the imaginative complement to Prometheus's rationalism, Asia's role in Jupiter's downfall figures Shelley's conviction that the élite sensibility – the 'cultivated' imagination – is the only viable agent of political change.[56] It is important to remember, however, that Demogorgon is also instrumental in Jupiter's defeat. In fact, Demogorgon's role in *Prometheus Unbound* bears witness to Shelley's conviction that political change is '*necessary*' – to use the terms of his approximately contemporary *Philosophical View of Reform* (1819) – 'not only ... because it is just and ought to be, but necessary because it is *inevitable* and *must* be' (*Prose*, p. 230; emphasis added).

Once again, then, the crucial question is not *whether* political change will take place but *how*. As noted, *Prometheus Unbound* was clearly intended to advise the 'elect' leaders of British Radicalism against the politics of revolutionary defiance and, journeying to the 'realm / Of Demogorgon' in Act II Scene iii, Asia certainly expects the coming political change, which she will help to inaugurate, to be gradual: an ideological reform rather than a violent revolution (*Prometheus Unbound*, II, iii, 1–2). Arrived at 'a pinnacle of rocks among mountains', surrounded by a sublime ('wonderful!') landscape of 'icy spires' and 'cataracts', the Oceanides hear the rumble of a distant avalanche, which Asia immediately deploys as a figure for the coming political change (*Prometheus Unbound*, stage direction, II, iii; II, iii, 17, 28–9). 'Hark!', she says, 'the rushing snow!':

> The sun-awakened avalanche! whose mass,
> Thrice sifted by the storm, had gathered there
> Flake after flake: in Heaven-defying minds
> As thought by thought is piled, till some great truth
> Is loosened, and the nations echo round,
> Shaken to their roots: as do the mountains now
>
> (*Prometheus Unbound*, II, iii, 36–42)

This passage is one of only two instances in Shelley's *oeuvre* where an explicitly sublime natural phenomenon – in this case, the avalanche – is deployed as a figure for *gradual* political change, that is, as a figure for an ideological rather than a violent revolution (the other instance being *Mont Blanc*'s account of glaciation, discussed in chapter 3). Over the original, rough draft of these lines in Bodleian MS. Shelley adds. c. 4, f. 6r, Shelley wrote 'This was suggested by the Xterly Review' (*BSM*, xxi, pp. 2–3). As Tim Webb points out, this inscription identifies the passage as Shelley's riposte to the *Quarterly Review*'s attack on his character in its May 1818 review of Leigh Hunt's *Foliage* (1818).[57] While Shelley is never actually named in the piece, the anonymous reviewer – probably John Taylor Coleridge – clearly blasts his atheistic response to the Alpine sublime in 1816 (discussed in chapter 3), focusing on the now notorious inscriptions in Chamonix's hotel and refuge-registers. 'If we were told', the reviewer writes:

of a man who, placed on a wild rock among the clouds, yet even in that height surrounded by a loftier amphitheatre of spire-like mountains, hanging over a valley of eternal ice and snow, where the roar of mighty waterfalls was at times

unheeded from the hollow and more appalling thunder of the deep and unseen
avalanche, – if we were told of a man who, thus witnessing the sublimest
assemblage of natural objects, should retire to a cabin near and write atheos after
his name in the album, we hope our own feelings would be pity rather than
disgust . . .' (*Quarterly Review*, xvii, pp. 328–9)[58]

Shelley learned about the *Quarterly's* attack from a 14 June 1818 letter from
Peacock, and eventually read the offending article in September or October
of that year. The entire 'pinnacle of rocks' passage from *Prometheus
Unbound* II, iii, 28–42, with its imagery of 'icy spires', 'cataracts' and
'avalanche', clearly echoes the terms of the *Quarterly's* attack. Hence by
having Asia offer such a secular and politically radical interpretation of the
avalanche, Shelley is evidently, and *publicly*, re-affirming his 1816 position
in the face of the *Quarterly's* criticism, re-affirming, in other words, his
radical revision of the conventional, religious configuration of the British
discourse on the natural sublime. Indeed, it is tempting to suspect that
Asia's gradualist avalanche-figure also recasts Byron's Promethean 'curse'
of 'forgiveness' and its image of vengeance: the collapse of a 'mountain' on
'human heads' (*Childe Harold* IV, 206).

Old ambiguities are never far from the surface, however, and we note
even in the midst of Shelley's confident and provocative rendering of Asia's
gradualist account of the natural sublime the idea of 'Heaven-*defying*
minds': defiance, as we have seen, is an enormously loaded concept in
the context, and thus hardly a word that Shelley would have used lightly. In
fact, the now-familiar admixture of gradualism and defiance in Asia's
speech effectively anticipates the fact that *Prometheus Unbound* will offer
a characteristically problematic account of the means by which Necessity
will effect political change.[59] While the poem argues in the most explicit
possible terms against revolutionism, Mary Shelley's 'Note' correctly
affirms that 'the Primal Power of the world *drives* [Jupiter] from his
usurped throne' (*CPW*, p. 272; emphasis added). In other words, when it
finally arrives, the 'catastrophe' of Shelley's 'drama' is far from the gradual,
moral reform advocated by the body text, or envisioned in Asia's account of
the avalanche. Rather, it is an explicitly *geological* catastrophe: a violent,
volcanic 'civil war'. Hence, we are returned to the tension between gradualism and revolutionism at the heart of Shelley's political thought, and
once again, this defining tension is played out within the terms of his
engagement with the discourse on the natural sublime. As the imaginative
complement to Prometheus' rationalism, Asia's meeting with
Demogorgon rehearses Shelley's account of the politically potent interaction between the 'cultivated' imagination and the Necessity manifested in

the 'awful' landscape of the natural sublime. That is to say that Asia's interaction with Demogorgon figures the ability of the 'cultivated' imagination to 'seize' and 'picture' the philanthropic obligations imposed by the law of Nature, the gradualist 'spells' of 'intellectual beauty'. However, as the trigger of a volcanic civil war, Asia's interaction with Demogorgon also voices the ambiguity at the heart of Shelley's engagement with the discourse on the sublime: his concern that violent revolution may be the 'natural death' of empire.

As noted, the 'realm / Of Demogorgon' is unequivocally a landscape of the natural sublime: 'a pinnacle of rocks among mountains' that echoes the pinnacle to which Prometheus himself is bound (*Prometheus Unbound,* stage direction, II, iii). However, Matthews' seminal reading of *Prometheus Unbound* II in 'A Volcano's Voice' has significantly refined our understanding of this landscape. While the setting itself is ostensibly oriental, Matthews justly observes that the lush forest through which Asia and Panthea pass on their way to the 'realm / Of Demogorgon' clearly recalls Shelley's account of the ancient volcanic craters of Agnano and Astroni near the still active Vesuvius.[60] Similarly, the 'pinnacle of rocks' that the Oceanides eventually reach is an unmistakable echo of the 'conical hill' that Shelley observed on the summit of Vesuvius itself (*Letters,* ii, pp. 62–3).[61] In short, then, as Matthews concludes, at the opening of *Prometheus Unbound* II, iii 'Asia and Panthea are conceived as standing in a gigantic *caldera,* the bowl-shaped crater of a quiescent volcano with a tall cinder-cone in the middle' (*Poems,* ii, p. 549 n. 24). Looking down from this 'pinnacle', Panthea locates Demogorgon's 'throne' far beneath them in the 'volcano's meteor-breathing chasm' (*Prometheus Unbound* II, iii, 3, 11).

Before they can descend into the 'chasm', however, the Oceanides are almost overwhelmed by the 'oracular vapour' that is 'hurled up' from Demogorgon's volcanic 'throne' (*Prometheus Unbound,* II, iii, 4). The immediate context for this 'vapour' is, of course, the gas that rises from volcanic craters: the 'heavy white smoke' and 'black bituminous vapour' that was similarly 'hurled up' from Vesuvius during Shelley's visit (*Letters,* ii, pp. 62–3). In classical literature, this gas was frequently identified as a source of prophetic visions, hence the appellation 'oracular' (See *Poems,* ii, p. 548 n. 4). However, Shelley would hardly have warmed to this primitive connection between volcanism and quasi-religious enthusiasm, and indeed his party had already had first-hand experience of the more literally dangerous side effects of such 'vapours'. Shelley would have known that Pliny died after being overwhelmed by volcanic gasses while observing the AD 79 eruption of Vesuvius, and he himself had become ill during his ascent of the summit on 16 December (*MWSJ*, p. 244; *Letters*, ii, p. 63).[62] These already negative connotations of volcanic 'vapours' can only have been re-enforced for Shelley by his subsequent visit to the famous Grotto del Cane, which he describes in a letter to Peacock on 25 February 1819 (*Letters*, ii, p. 78). In the Grotto – one of nineteenth-century Campagna's premier tourist attractions – the level of carbon-monoxide 'vapours' was high enough to kill a dog without harming a human, and this phenomenon was exhibited upon payment for the edification of passing tourists. Shelley informs Peacock that they 'saw' the Grotto because 'other people see it' (*Letters*, ii, p. 78). However he emphasises that they would 'not allow the dog to be exhibited in torture for [their] curiosity' (*Letters*, ii, p. 78). 'The poor little animals stood moving their tails in a slow and dismal manner', he continued, 'as if perfectly resigned to their condition', a 'curlike emblem', he punned, 'of voluntary servitude' (*Letters*, ii, p. 78).

Shelley's politically resonant account of this 'curlike' resignation – surely an allusion to Italian acceptance of Austrian rule – effectively connects with his suspicions about the enthusiastic effects classically attributed to volcanic 'vapours': in both instances, the gasses are causally related to moral or ideological enslavement. Given the predominantly negative associations of volcanic gasses in his thought, then, it is no surprise to find that both Asia and Panthea are wary of the 'vapours' which are 'hurled up' from Demogorgon's volcanic 'cave', a type in fact of the Grotto del Cane. Asia in particular is keen to attract her sister's attention to the 'cave' below them 'ere the vapour dim thy brain' (*Prometheus Unbound* II, iii, 18).

However, Asia's concern for her sister's wellbeing takes on a deeper resonance when read in relation to Shelley's engagement with the discourse on the sublime. More precisely, the relationship between the 'vapours' that are 'hurled up' from Demogorgon's volcanic 'throne' and Demogorgon himself (itself?) effectively figures the relationship between the overwhelming affective power of the landscape of the natural sublime and the immanent 'Power' (Necessity) that is manifested in that landscape. Hence Asia's concern that the volcanic 'vapours' may 'dim' Panthea's 'brain' *before* they can reach Demogorgon's 'throne' might be read as a reflection on the potential dangers of the affective response to the natural sublime. This suggestion is confirmed by Panthea's own account of the 'volcanic vapours' which, she affirms, 'lonely men drink wandering in their youth':

> And call truth, virtue, love, genius, or joy,
> That maddening wine of life, whose dregs they drain

To deep intoxication and uplift,
Like Mænads who cry loud, Evoe! Evoe!
The voice which is contagion to the world
                                   (*Prometheus Unbound* II, iii, 4–10)

These lines clearly subject the classical link between volcanic gas and quasi-religious ('oracular') enthusiasm to characteristically Shelleyan scrutiny: Panthea now affirms the literally 'maddening' effects of the gas. However, her account of the 'vapours' also effectively summarises Shelley's ongoing concerns about the affective response to the natural sublime. To begin with, her allusion to the generic morphology of the solipsistic *Alastor*-poet – a 'lonely' man 'wandering' in 'youth' – is unmistakable, and her speech clearly echoes *Alastor*'s conviction that the imagination can become 'intoxicated' with the affective power of the natural sublime (figured in the 'vapours'). The crucial factor here is her claim that 'lonely' youths 'call' – and, by implication, *mistakenly* 'call' – this 'maddening wine' by the names of 'truth, virtue, love, genius, or joy'. This claim essentially reprises *Alastor*'s conviction that the dysfunctional imagination can sexualise ('love') the affective power of the natural sublime as an end ('joy') in itself, and thereby neglect the philanthropic obligation ('virtue') imposed by the Necessitarian 'truth / Of nature'.[63]

However, Panthea's specific reference to the Bacchic cult is important, and sheds further light on the relationship between Demogorgon's volcanic 'vapours' and Shelley's concerns about the affective response to the natural sublime. As Michael Rossington notes, the Bacchic is a highly ambivalent concept in Shelley's work, figuring a 'radical' and 'subversive' libertarianism that always risks collapse into 'religious excess and collective fervour'.[64] After Jupiter's defeat, Prometheus and Asia retire 'beyond the peak / Of Bacchic Nysa, Mænad-haunted mountain' to a 'cave' which figures the newly liberated 'one mind' (*Prometheus Unbound* III, iii, 154). However Panthea's pre-reform account of the 'wine of life' is much more sinister in its implications, figuring a 'maddening', revolutionary enthusiasm for 'truth' and 'virtue', a literally Mænadic 'intoxication' with nature that can all too easily collapse into French-style 'Bacchanals of Blood' (*Ode to Liberty*, 171–2). In other words, her speech rehearses Shelley's concern – first voiced in 'On Leaving London for Wales' – that the affective response to the natural sublime may be closely aligned with the impetus to violent revolution.[65]

Panthea and Asia – certainly not Mænads – grow 'dizzy' under the influence of the volcanic 'vapours' just as the mind is inevitably overwhelmed by the affective power of the natural sublime. However, they manage to avoid 'intoxication', and descend into Demogorgon's cave. This process is perfectly in keeping with Shelley's revision of the discourse on the sublime: the 'cultivated' imagination can go beyond the defeat of the understanding to 'seize' the Necessity (Demogorgon) that is manifested in the 'awful' landscape. Hence, again, Asia's encounter with Demogorgon himself figures the interaction of the 'cultivated' imagination with the Necessitarian power that is immanent in the landscape of the natural sublime; in fact, it effectively reprises *Mont Blanc's* 'dizzy ravine' episode. In other words, their encounter restates the foundational premise of Shelley's engagement with the discourse on the sublime: the idea that natural grandeur, correctly interpreted by the 'cultivated' imagination, can teach the mind politically potent truths, truths that expose the artificiality of the current social order and provide the blueprint for a 'prosperous', philanthropic reform of 'political institutions'.

As a figure for Shelley's concept of Necessity, Demogorgon is explicitly and appropriately not an anthropomorphic presence. Rather, when the Oceanides enter his 'cave' they see only a 'veilèd form' on the 'ebon throne' of 'power' (*Prometheus Unbound* II, iv, 1, 3). Even when Asia observes that 'the veil has fallen', Panthea can still only see 'a mighty Darkness':

> Filling the seat of power; and rays of gloom
> Dart round, as light from the meridian sun,
> – Ungazed upon and shapeless – neither limb,
> Nor form, nor outline; yet we feel it is
> A living Spirit
>
> (*Prometheus Unbound* II, iv, 3–8)

As Matthews suggests, these lines 'realise' Demogorgon 'in terms of molten magma, the obscure and terrible volcanic agent hidden in the depths of the earth', 'rays of gloom' being a reference – as Grabo was the first to note – to the infrared radiation discovered by William Herschel in 1800.[66] However, Demogorgon's 'mighty darkness' also clearly figures Shelley's sceptical concept of Necessity as an immanent 'Power' in the landscape of the natural sublime, a 'Power' that only the 'cultivated' imagination can 'seize' ('feel') and 'picture'.

Asia converses with Demogorgon in order to learn the identity of the power that 'reigns' in the Universe: 'who made the living world?', she asks (*Prometheus Unbound* II, iv, 8, 29). She wants to learn the identity of this power precisely in order to aid Prometheus in overthrowing it. 'Utter his name', Asia urges, rehearsing Earth's earlier desire for a return to the Titan's former politics of defiance: 'a world pining in pain / Asks but his name: *curses* shall drag him down' (*Prometheus Unbound* II, iv, 28–30; emphasis added). What Asia needs to learn, however, is that the power that actually 'reigns' over the 'living world' is Demogorgon himself (Necessity), whereas the tyrant God (Jupiter) she assumes to 'reign' is actually empowered and sustained by the unreformed condition of the 'one mind'. In short, then, Asia's conversation with Demogorgon represents the efforts of the imagination to figure the power that 'reigns' over the 'living world', the power manifested in the landscape of the natural sublime. As such, again, their encounter reprises *Mont Blanc*'s 'dizzy ravine' episode.

   Accordingly – as critics have frequently suggested – in her 'conversation' with Demogorgon, Asia is effectively talking to *herself*. More precisely, she is refining her imagining of the power she confronts. Hence, her questions become increasingly sophisticated as this analysis proceeds, and as her questions become more sophisticated so Demogorgon's answers become more telling. Initially, Asia assumes the power that 'reigns' is anthropomorphic, but she gradually comes to recognise the metaphorical and imaginative origins of this creator-God (a recognition that parallels the materialist histories of the God-term informing *Queen Mab*'s critique of the theistic discourse on the sublime). More precisely, in the early stages of their conversation, Demogorgon answers Asia's anthropomorphic questions in anthropomorphic terms, apparently affirming the existence of the creator-God she despises (*Prometheus Unbound* II, iv, 11, 18). But when Asia realises the metaphorical origins of this oppressive 'God', she asks Demogorgon what he meant by previously identifying the power that 'reigns' over 'the living world' in such anthropomorphic terms: 'whom calledst thou God?', she asks (*Prometheus Unbound* II, iv, 111). Demogorgon's reply explains that the terms of his answers are dictated by the terms of Asia's questions: 'I spoke but as ye speak', he affirms (*Prometheus Unbound* II, iv, 112). Again, Asia's debate with Demogorgon represents the interaction of the imagination with the inhuman 'Power' manifested in the landscape of the natural sublime. Hence, Demogorgon can only provide answers to the questions that Asia is capable of framing. More precisely, the extent to which the identity and implications of the Necessitarian power that 'reigns' over 'the living world' can be 'seized' and 'pictured' is entirely determined by the extent to which the imagination has been 'cultivated'. Hence – in keeping with Shelley's sceptical epistemology – there are some questions that must remain unanswered, that are in fact unanswerable because they are incapable of being formulated, because 'a voice / Is wanting' (*Prometheus Unbound*, II, iv, 115–6).

In his considerably qualified reply to Asia's final question about the power that 'reigns', Demogorgon affirms that Jupiter is 'the supreme of *living* things' (*Prometheus Unbound* II, iv, 112; emphasis added). Asia now recognises that Jupiter must have a 'master' since she remembers that he 'trembled like a slave' when Prometheus 'cursed him' (*Prometheus Unbound* II, iv, 112, 108–9). Hence she – crucially – concludes by asking Demogorgon not the *identity* of the power that 'reigns', but the means by which this power may be overcome: 'who' is the 'master' of Jupiter (*Prometheus Unbound* II, iv, 113). Given the ostensible politics of *Prometheus Unbound* – and of Shelley's engagement with the discourse on the sublime – we would expect a gradualist answer and that, initially at least, is what we get. 'Love' or imagination – appropriately figured in Asia herself – is the key to political change. 'If the abysm could vomit forth its secrets', Demogorgon replies:

> ... But a voice
> Is wanting, the deep truth is imageless;
> For what would it avail to bid thee gaze
> On the revolving world? What to bid speak
> Fate, Time, Occasion, Chance and Change? To these
> All things are subject but Eternal love
>
> (*Prometheus Unbound* II, iv, 114–20)

As Pulos points out, Demogorgon's much-quoted claim that the 'deep truth is imageless' echoes Democritus' well-known affirmation that 'truth is sunk in an abyss'.[67] As already noted (in chapter 3), however, Shelley's knowledge of this passage was almost certainly mediated through his reading of Bacon, who had translated the Greek philosopher's phrase – more tellingly – as 'the truth of nature lieth hid in certain deep mines and caves'. In any event, Bacon's recasting of Democritus certainly lies behind Demogorgon's speech. Demogorgon literally *is* the 'truth of nature', a truth physically as much as figuratively 'hid' in the 'deep mines and caves' at the heart of the volcano into which the Oceanides descend.

Once again, then, Asia's encounter with Demogorgon encapsulates the political claims of Shelley's engagement with the discourse on the natural sublime: the 'cultivated' imagination learns the politically potent 'truth / Of nature' from the Necessity manifested in the 'awful' landscape. More precisely, Asia learns that 'Eternal love' is the 'master' of oppression, that tyranny can only be overcome by 'the fixed and virtuous will', by 'firm and patient opposition'. Hence, the 'treasured spell' that Asia 'alone' can learn from Demogorgon is the direct antithesis of the defiant, revolutionary 'spell' that Earth still considers to be the basis of political change (*Prometheus Unbound* II, ii, 88). Demogorgon's Necessitarian 'spell' – the 'spells' of 'intellectual beauty' – obliges the individual to reject solipsistic defiance (to 'fear himself') and 'love all human kind'. Accordingly, this 'spell' is repeated in the closing lines of Shelley's drama. In the wake of the Promethean Revolution, Demogorgon reaffirms that 'Gentleness, Virtue, Wisdom, and Endurance' are the key to reform (*Prometheus Unbound* IV, 562). Shelley's message to the 'elect' leaders of post-Peterloo Radicalism – encapsulated in his revision of the Promethean myth – is that they must reject despondency or defiance, and learn 'to hope till hope creates / From its own wreck the thing it contemplates' (*Prometheus Unbound* IV, 562, 572–3).

And yet, in the midst of this final, gradualist apostrophe to 'Hope' and 'Love', Demogorgon also affirms that to '*defy* Power' – explicitly the action of an unreformed, Byronic Titan – also has political potency (*Prometheus Unbound* IV, 572; emphasis added).[68] This is, to put it mildly, something of a mixed-signal on which to conclude an avowedly gradualist drama, but in point of fact Demogorgon's problematic closing words merely hark back to his 'awful' role in Jupiter's earlier defeat. We are, in effect, returned to Shelley's familiar concerns about the viability of gradualism in an age of extreme reaction: how do 'Gentleness, Virtue, Wisdom, and Endurance' translate into *doing* anything, politically speaking? As was the case with *Queen Mab*, the actual moment of political change in *Prometheus Unbound* is – to use Matthews' phrase – 'not staged but reported'.[69] In the closing scene of *Prometheus Unbound* III – originally the final scene – the 'Spirit of the Hour' describes the utopian outcome of the Promethean reform: 'man' is 'sceptreless, free, uncircumscribed', 'equal, unclassed, tribeless and nationless, / Exempt from awe, worship, degree', and 'free from guilt or pain' (*Prometheus Unbound* III, iv, 194, 195–6, 198). In other words, the Spirit seems to affirm that a moral and intellectual revolution has taken place, thereby apparently confirming the validity of Shelley's gradualist emphasis on 'firm and patient opposition'. The 'painted' ideological 'veil' that sustained Jupiter's tyranny has been 'torn aside – / The loathsome mask has fallen' (*Prometheus Unbound*, III, iv, 190, 192, 193). But how has this utopia actually been achieved? Although the Spirit's images clearly imply an *intellectual* revolution, the tearing aside of a veil is hardly an unequivocal figure for a peaceful reform, not least since it clearly recalls Burke's well-known account of the attack on Marie Antoinette in the *Reflections*.[70] Moreover, the utopian landscape of *Prometheus Unbound* III is dotted – like *Queen Mab*'s utopia before it – with the ruins of power: 'thrones, altars, judgement-seats, and prisons' (*Prometheus Unbound* III, iv, 164).

And again, while the 'Spirit of the Hour' affirms that these edifices 'stand' – in contrast to *Queen Mab*'s ruins – 'not o'erthrown, but unregarded now', the reader is ultimately left in no doubt about the violent nature of Jupiter's downfall (*Prometheus Unbound* III, iv, 179).

In fact, the 'fierce king' of Heaven is defeated by the devastating eruption of Demogorgon's 'flaming volcano' (*Prometheus Unbound* I, i, 88).[71] Immediately after Asia has learned that 'Eternal Love' is the key to political change, she asks Demogorgon when the 'destined hour' of the Promethean reform will 'arrive' (*Prometheus Unbound* II, iv, 128). She is – in Matthews' words – 'answered by a volcanic explosion'.[72] The 'rocks' are instantly 'cloven', and Earth warns the 'Spirit of the Hour' that its 'flight must be swifter than fire', swift enough – presumably – to outrun the ensuing lava (*Prometheus Unbound* II, iv, 129; v, 1–6). Asia sees the 'terrible shadow' of this 'dread' 'destiny' arising from Demogorgon's cave to 'wrap in lasting night heaven's kingless throne', a clear allusion to the clouds of ash and debris thrown up by the initial explosion (*Prometheus Unbound* II, 151, 146–7, 149). Indeed, she appropriately compares the ascent of this 'destiny' to the 'lurid smoke / Of earthquake-ruined cities o'er the sea', an equally clear allusion to the destruction of Pompeii and Herculaneum by Vesuvian eruptions (*Prometheus Unbound* II, iv, 153–4; *Poems*, ii, p. 566 n.).[73] Jupiter – still seated confidently in heaven – feels 'the earthquake of [Demogorgon's] chariot thundering up / Olympus' and is 'caught' and overwhelmed by the 'bursting cloud' from the volcano (*Prometheus Unbound* III, i, 50–1; ii, 11).

Jupiter's volcanic defeat by Demogorgon is certainly in line with Shelley's Aeschylean source material: once again, the fire of the Promethean revolution is explicitly volcanic fire (originally stolen from Vulcan's Lemnos).[74] The eruption of Demogorgon's volcano is also scientifically appropriate by the standards of early nineteenth-century geomorphology. As Matthews puts it, 'it is clear what was to be expected, scientifically speaking, if children of Ocean were drawn into contact with the magma of a volcanic cavern'.[75] Early nineteenth-century volcanology frequently echoed the classical hypothesis that volcanic eruptions were caused by lava and seawater coming into contact in magma chambers deep beneath the earth.[76]

Classical and scientific propriety notwithstanding, however, Jupiter's destruction by the pyroclastic flow from Demogorgon's volcano hardly sits easily with the ostensibly gradualist politics of *Prometheus Unbound* per se. Volcanic eruption does not exactly suggest a gradual moral reform ('firm and patient opposition'), and indeed, we have been tracing Shelley's consistent use of volcanism as a figure for popular revolutionary violence. This image-pattern runs from early works like 'To the Republicans of North America', through *Laon and Cythna*, right up to Prometheus's own 'hurling up' of fiery 'insurrection' (*Prometheus Unbound*, III, i, 8). The pattern undoubtedly becomes more prevalent in Shelley's Italian writing, however, due no doubt to his first-hand experience of the 'tremendous and irresistible strength' of Vesuvius (*Letters*, ii, p. 62). We have already noted that the thirteenth stanza of the *Ode to Liberty* describes Europe's ongoing political upheaval in terms of systematic volcanic activity: 'England yet sleeps: was she not called of old? / Spain calls her now, as with its thrilling thunder / Vesuvius wakens Aetna, and the cold / Snow-crags by its reply are cloven in sunder' (*Ode to Liberty*, 181–4). In a March 1821 letter to Peacock, written from a politically troubled Pisa, Shelley similarly affirmed that he was 'surrounded by revolutionary volcanoes', while a letter to Claire Clairmont on the last day of the same year compared the increasingly tense political situation in England to 'a sleeping volcano' (*Letters*, ii, pp. 276, 371).[77]

Reading the revolutionary connotations of volcanism in Shelley's work back into Jupiter's volcanic defeat raises further serious questions about the already ambivalent imagery, an ambivalence again heightened by the fact that Prometheus's former defiance was itself characterised by volcanic activity. These questions are tellingly compounded by Paul Foot's quasi-etymological reading of Demogorgon as the 'people-monster'.[78] The conclusion seems unavoidable: Demogorgon's role in Jupiter's defeat figures the *Necessary* overthrow of tyranny by violent popular uprising. 'So dear is power', Shelley affirms in his *Philosophical View of Reform*, 'that the tyrants themselves neither then, nor now, nor ever, left or leave a path to freedom but through their own blood' (*Prose*, p. 231). The 'catastrophe' of Shelley's drama – the apex of his great revolutionary poetry – thus denies the distinction between natural and political history. Popular violence is as natural a phenomenon as volcanism. For all the gradualist efforts of the 'cultivated' imagination, tyranny makes violence inevitable; oppression breeds revenge; revolution is 'the natural death' of empire. The *Necessity* of revolution: this is the 'awful', 'imageless' truth at the heart of Shelley's ostensibly gradualist vision of reform, the 'deep' political 'truth' that the 'abysm' literally 'vomits forth' at Asia's request.

This 'truth' – however regrettable – is resonantly confirmed by Jupiter's final attempt to hold on to power in the face of what he significantly identifies as the renewed Promethean '*insurrection*' (*Prometheus Unbound* III, i, 8; emphasis added). *Prometheus Unbound* III opens with the 'fierce king' confidently asserting that he has become 'omnipotent', having finally subdued the threat posed to his 'antique empire' by Prometheus' – again tellingly – '*unextinguished* fire' (*Prometheus Unbound* III, i, 4, 9, 5; emphasis added). Jupiter's confidence stems from the 'fatal child' that he has 'begotten' (*Prometheus Unbound* III, i, 18–19). In Aeschylean terms, this 'fatal child' is Jupiter's offspring by Thetis: the 'child' whom the 'fierce king' assumes will become an heir but who will actually overthrow his father. Once again, however, Shelley resonantly adapts his source material. Jupiter informs Thetis and the other deities gathered around his throne that this 'fatal child' will come from Demogorgon's 'vacant throne' (*Prometheus Unbound* III, i, 21). As Pulos points out, Jupiter's 'child' almost certainly represents Malthusian Necessity: the apparently natural laws of population that legitimated – as *Necessary* – the present order of society.[79] In other words, Jupiter's 'fatal' Malthusian 'child' is a reactionary imagining of the Necessitarian 'truth / Of nature', enlisted in support of things as they are, an 'antique empire'. But the 'child' proves to be 'fatal' in a manner that Jupiter does not anticipate. Shelley's point, again, is that Necessity does not support oppression. Rather, it makes the violent downfall of tyranny inevitable. As Jupiter sits confidently awaiting his 'child', he hears Demogorgon's volcanic eruption rising to overwhelm him. At the last moment, when the 'fierce king' identifies this revolutionary uprising as his own 'detested progeny', his now literally 'fatal child', he effectively confirms Shelley's 'awful' conviction that political violence is 'the natural death' of empire (*Prometheus Unbound* III, i, 62).

One final question remains. Asia might well express surprise – 'Thus I am answered: strange!' – at the volcanic response to her query about when the Promethean reform will take place, but what are we to make of her instrumental role in Jupiter's violent defeat? (*Prometheus Unbound* II, iv, 156). We have already noted the scientific propriety of that role. As the imaginative complement to Prometheus's rationalism, Asia's role also undoubtedly voices Shelley's conviction that the 'cultivated' imagination is the only viable agent of political change. The problem, again, is the explicitly violent nature of the change that occurs. Does Asia's role imply that, far from being the agent of a moral reform, Shelley now conceives the 'cultivated' imagination to be the vehicle of revolutionary agitation? The apparent wavering in his political strategy during the Italian years would certainly support such an inference. We have already noted Shelley's claim that *Prometheus Unbound*, like all his 'great revolutionary poetry', was addressed to the 'elect' leaders of British Radicalism. And yet, in a May 1820 letter to Leigh Hunt, Shelley asked his friend if he knew 'of any bookseller who would like to publish a little volume of *popular songs* wholly political, and destined to awaken and direct the imagination of the reformers' (*Letters*, ii, p. 191; original emphasis). The evident conflict here between Shelley's characteristic agenda ('to awaken and direct the imagination of the reformers') and markedly uncharacteristic 'popular' target-audience is compounded by the fact that this 'little volume' would almost certainly have included the highly inflammatory 'Song to the Men of England' (1819) and 'New National Anthem' (1819). We are returned to the dilemma of *The Assassins*: faced with the intransigence of tyranny and apparent necessity of revolution, Shelley himself, it would seem, was ultimately unable or unwilling to choose between 'reform' and 'civil war'.

Conclusion: 'Good and the means of good', 1822

On 15 February 1821, Shelley wrote to Peacock expressing the 'greatest possible desire to break a lance with [him], within the lists of a magazine, in honour of [his] mistress Urania' (*Letters*, ii, p. 261). This 'desire' was prompted by Peacock's 'essay against the cultivation of poetry', which Shelley had just read (*Letters*, ii, p. 244).[1] Drawing heavily on French Enlightenment rationalism, Peacock's *Four Ages of Poetry* links poetry – as the product of the imagination – to primitivism and political reaction. Peacock accepts that 'poetry was the mental rattle that awakened the attention of the intellect in the infancy of civil society', but insists that 'it cannot claim the slightest share in any one of the comforts and utilities of life of which we have witnessed so many and so rapid advances'.[2] 'Poetry' was devised, he maintains, to 'disseminate the fame' of tyrants, and quickly became a vehicle for the 'rude' and 'multifarious' 'chimeras' of the imagination.[3] '[A]s the sciences of morals and of mind advance towards perfection', he continues, 'as reason gains ascendancy in them over imagination and feeling, poetry can no longer accompany them in their progress'.[4] 'A poet in our times', Peacock concludes, is an anachronism: 'a semi-barbarian [whose] ideas, thoughts, feelings, associations, are all with barbarous manners, obsolete customs, and exploded superstitions'.[5]

Shelley responded to these 'anathemas' – which re-deploy much of his own terminology – with his *Defence of Poetry*, composed in February and March 1821 (*Letters*, ii, p. 261). In some of the best-known passages of English Romantic prose, Shelley questions Peacock's easy, rationalist account of 'the march of . . . intellect' and affirms the historical potency of the imagination.[6] But we should be wary of over-simplifying the debate between the *Defence* and *The Four Ages*. To put it more precisely, that debate cannot simply be reduced to the (supposedly) commonplace Romantic dichotomy between reason and imagination, although this kind of reading has frequently been used to support idealising, apolitical conclusions about Shelley's later work. After all, Shelley fully accepts that the efforts of 'reasoners', 'mechanists', and 'the promoters of utility' are 'of the highest value' in correcting 'the aberrations of society', a fact which is more fully articulated in the work from which the *Defence* was quarried: *A Philosophical View of Reform* (*Prose*, pp. 291, 292, 293). In point of fact, then, the *Defence* registers Shelley's disagreement with Peacock over the *scope* – rather than the *validity* – of rationalism. Or, to put it another way, Shelley attacks Peacock's primitivist reading of poetry. Again, Shelley fully accepts that 'the exertions of Locke, Hume, Gibbon, Voltaire, Rousseau, and their disciples ... are entitled to the gratitude of mankind', although he appends a footnote tellingly excluding Rousseau ('essentially a poet') from Peacock's 'classification' of 'mere reasoners' (*Prose*, p. 292 & n. 62).

As such – that is, as an argument over the *scope* rather than the *validity* of rationalism – the debate between the *Defence* and *The Four Ages* effectively rehearses the crucial developmental phase in Shelley's own philosophical thought: the transition from empiricism to scepticism. Like the young Shelley, the Peacock of *The Four Ages* identifies reason as the sole agent of historical perfectibility, and links imagination to superstition and reaction. But Shelley's mature 'science of mind' – formulated under the influence of Hume and Drummond, and discussed in chapter 2 – recognises the epistemological limitations of rationalism and establishes the imagination as the 'pre-eminent' faculty of the human mind (*Prose*, p. 186). In other words, Shelley the sceptic understands that only the imagination can go beyond the accident of sense-impressions to 'seize' and 'picture' the 'relation of things' (*Prose*, p. 174).[7] Accordingly the *Defence* is confident that – while again not *denying* the 'value' of 'reasoners' – 'it exceeds all imagination to conceive what would have been the moral condition of the world if neither Dante, Petrarch, Boccaccio, Chaucer, Shakespeare, Calderón, Lord Bacon, nor Milton had ever existed' (*Prose*, p. 292). 'The human mind could never', Shelley concludes, 'except by the intervention of these excitements, have been awakened to the invention of the grosser sciences and that application of analytical reasoning to the aberrations of society which it is now attempted to exalt over the direct expression of the inventive and creative faculty itself' (*Prose*, p. 293). 'Poetry', in short, is the *condition* of progress, not an obstacle to it.

Effectively, then, Shelley's 'defence' of 'Poetry' ('the direct expression of the inventive and creative faculty') is more properly a defence of that 'faculty' *per se*, i.e. a defence of the *imagination* (although given Shelley's broad definition of 'Poetry', the two terms are effectively cognate). This book has argued that Shelley's concept of an epistemologically and politically progressive imagination – the concept that informs the *Defence of*

Poetry – was worked out during a lifelong engagement with the discourse on the natural sublime. Accordingly, it is not surprising that we find echoes of that discursive context in the *Defence*'s response to *The Four Ages*. Indeed, Peacock himself – following the Enlightenment / materialist tradition described in chapter 1 – had chosen the pious configuration of the discourse on the natural sublime as a prime example of the connection between imagination and 'superstition', enumerating the 'rocks, mountains, seas, unsubdued forests, [and] unnavigable rivers' that 'ignorance and fear have peopled with . . . gods'.[8] Shelley responds quite specifically to this example in the *Defence*. 'While the sceptic destroys *gross superstitions*', he writes, echoing *On Life*'s account of the philosophical reformer's duty, 'let him spare to deface . . . the eternal truths' available to 'the imaginations of men' (*Prose*, p. 292; emphasis added). We are thus returned to the central tenet of Shelley's revision of the discourse on the natural sublime: the opposition between the 'vulgar' or 'gross' imagination (the agent of superstition) and the 'cultivated' imagination, which is capable of 'seizing' and 'picturing' the 'eternal' 'truth / Of nature'.

It is important to recognise, then, that just as the *Defence* does not reject Peacock's rationalism out of hand, neither is it an unqualified defence of the imagination. It is, rather, a defence of the *cultivated* imagination. And hence perhaps the most famous lines in Shelley's *oeuvre*. While *The Four Ages* maintains that primitive 'poets' acquired the role of 'legislators' merely on account of their apparent 'familiarity with the secret history of gods', the *Defence* replies with considerable confidence that 'poets' – those, like Rousseau, who possess a 'cultivated' imagination – are indeed 'the unacknowledged legislators of the world' (*Prose*, p. 297).[9] It was *Julie*, after all, that established beyond doubt for Shelley the power of the 'cultivated' imagination to challenge and re-shape, to *re-imagine*, the 'obstinate' ideological 'preconceptions' of the 'one mind', the 'codes' and 'records that are *called* reality'. The task of the poet, then, like that of the sceptical reformer, is to revise dead metaphor, to 'create afresh' the 'associations' of 'words' and 'thoughts', to inaugurate an ideological revolution (*Prose*, p. 278).

This book has described Shelley's attempt to 'create afresh' the eighteenth-century British discourse on the natural sublime, as part of that ideological revolution. It has rejected conventional and ahistorical attempts to describe Shelley's engagement with the discourse on the natural sublime in terms of a perceived shift from a radical empiricism to an increasingly apolitical philosophical idealism. By extension, it has disputed the validity of reading that engagement alongside Kant's *Critique of Judgement* – and, in so doing, has questioned orthodox critical assumptions about the politics and epistemology of the British Romantic discourse on the natural sublime *per se*. I have argued, rather, that Shelley's engagement with natural grandeur needs to be seen as an attempt to revise the eighteenth-century British discourse on the natural sublime along politically radical and epistemologically sceptical lines, as an attempt to reject the conventional, theistic configuration of that discourse and formulate an alternative, politically progressive 'record' of natural grandeur. This attempt was premised, I have suggested, on the notion of a 'cultivated imagination': an imagination freed from its reactionary tendencies, and capable of going beyond the defeat of the understanding to 'seize' and 'picture' the revolutionary 'truth' about the natural processes revealed in the landscape of the sublime.

However, this book has also shown that Shelley's engagement with the discourse on the natural sublime was far from unambiguously successful. Conversely, I have traced the highly problematic intersection of that engagement with Shelley's ostensibly gradualist politics. Shelley's early qualms about the political ramifications of extreme affect quickly gave way to a confidence in the 'seizing' and 'picturing' ability of the 'cultivated' imagination. But while that imagination is capable of apprehending the philanthropic 'spells' upon which society ought to be premised, Shelley's engagements with natural grandeur consistently betray an anxiety that violent revolution may ultimately be the 'awful', inescapable means by which Necessity will reform the world. To return to the terminology of the *Queen Mab* period, the 'cultivated' imagination recognises that 'all-sufficing nature can chastise / Those who transgress her law' (*Queen Mab*, iii, 82–3). Shelley's revision of the discourse on the natural sublime repeatedly implies that political violence is the agency of this chastisement, the inevitable offspring of tyranny and 'the *natural* death of all great commercial empires' (*Letters*, i, p. 110; emphasis added). Violence breeds violence in a natural – *Necessary* – cycle of creation and destruction.

Shelley's final poem, the unfinished *Triumph of Life* (1822), appears to address this dark and potentially quite reactionary conclusion about the dynamics of political change: the idea that 'good and the means of good' are fundamentally 'irreconcilable' (*Triumph of Life*, 230–1).[10] *The Triumph* is undoubtedly rich in literary and historical allusion: Petrarch, Dante, Goethe, Calderón, Milton, Wordsworth, Southey, and Spenser have all been identified as influences. In closing, I want to examine the most resonant – and, ironically, the least discussed – of *The Triumph*'s historical allusions: namely, its engagement with the history of the French Revolution, the 'times that were / And scarce have ceased to be' (*Triumph of Life*, 233–4; emphasis added).[11] Rousseau (the supposed cause of the

Revolution) and Napoleon (its defender-turned-betrayer) form the major historical poles of the surviving fragment.[12] Indeed it is precisely when Rousseau identifies Napoleon in chains behind the 'chariot' of 'Life' – when he points, that is, to the final defeat of the Revolution – that the narrator becomes convinced that 'good and the means of good' are 'irreconcilable' (*Triumph of Life*, 215–31). Hence, *The Triumph* appears to turn around the anxiety at the heart of Shelley's engagement with the discourse on the natural sublime: the 'awful' spectacle of the defeated Revolution apparently proves that oppression is the necessary offspring of oppression.[13] The key question remains, however, whether or not this cycle can ever be broken and this, I believe, is the question that *The Triumph of Life* would ultimately have addressed.

Critics have long recognised that the 'triumphal pageant' at the centre of the Narrator's vision figures the defeat of almost every human aspiration, whether noble or ignoble, by 'Life' (*Triumph of Life*, 118).[14] More recent scholarship has identified the agency of this defeat as the seemingly inevitable surrender of the imagination to 'vulgar' personal desires or to the 'obstinate' ideological 'preconceptions' of the 'one mind', to what *The Triumph of Life* calls 'thought's empire over thought' (*Triumph of Life*, 211).[15] As John Hodgson puts it, 'the triumph of life is the failure of the imagination'.[16]

There are a number of relevant historical models for *The Triumph's* 'pageant'. One obvious source is the Hindu 'festival' of Rat'ha Jattra, when sacrificial victims were immolated under the chariot of Jaganatha (later Juggernaut), 'the Lord of the Universe'.[17] Shelley would have read about this 'festival' in both Moor's *Hindu Pantheon* (1810) and Southey's *Curse of Kehama* (XVI, v, 5–10).[18] Indeed, as James Mulvihill points out, William Hazlitt apparently anticipated Shelley's echo of Rat'ha Jattra in his December 1816 attacks on the *Times*, comparing 'the spirit of the world' to 'that foul Indian idol, the Jaggernaut' which 'crushes poor upstart poets, patriots, and philosophers (the beings of an hour) and the successive never-ending generations of fools and knaves'.[19] Shelley himself points to a second obvious historical source for *The Triumph's* 'pageant': namely, the triumphs of 'Imperial Rome', which he had already condemned in his note to *The Coliseum* (*Triumph of Life*, 113). However the most resonant historical analogue of *The Triumph's* 'pageant' is surely the 'famous triumph' – described by Burke in the *Reflections* – when Louis XVI and his family were 'moved' from Versailles to the Tuilleries 'amidst ... horrid yells, and shrilling screams, and frantic dances, and infamous contumelies'.[20] Shelley's account of the 'triumphal pageant' of 'Life' echoes Burke's account of 6 October 1789 in many respects – especially in his description of the crowd surrounding the 'chariot' – and Burke himself consistently describes that infamous procession as a 'triumph'. Indeed, in so doing, Burke was merely echoing Richard Price's earlier claim – which he quotes – to have been 'thankful' to 'have lived to see Thirty Millions of People, indignant and resolute, spurning at slavery, and demanding liberty with an irresistible voice. Their King led in triumph'.[21] Hence, it is important to recognise, with Wang, that Shelley's 'triumph' alludes not only to the classical past but also to a more recent political iconography.[22]

To put it more precisely, Shelley's 'triumph' pointedly inverts this contemporary iconography. While Shelley does not show the 'famous triumph' with which the Revolution began, he deliberately invokes that 'triumph' to figure the Revolution's equally infamous collapse. We are not shown Louis XVI led in 'triumph' by his 'people'; rather we are shown Napoleon chained to the 'triumphal' chariot of 'Life'. Shelley's point is a familiar one: just as in the Roman triumphs 'Freedom left those who upon the free / Had bound a yoke', so the seeds of the French Revolution's defeat were inherent in the manner of its beginning (Triumph of Life, 115–16). If Napoleon came to power on the back of the revolutionary 'triumph' of 6 October 1789, then by 1815 that 'triumph' had run its full course and ended with Napoleon himself led in chains under 'a moving arch of victory', after the 'dread war' of Waterloo (Triumph of Life, 439, 436).[23] Like the Dante-esque lovers, the 'maidens and youths' that dance before the chariot of 'Life' until it reaches and destroys them, Napoleon has been defeated by the very impulse on which he rode to power: tyranny breeds tyranny, violence begets violence (Triumph of Life, 149–60).

At the heart of The Triumph of Life's vision of western civilisation, then, is the 'awful' spectacle of the failure of the French Revolution. And it is, undoubtedly, an 'awful' spectacle. Like Burke's and Price's 'triumph' before it, Shelley's 'triumphal pageant' – driven onwards by Necessity (the invisible 'Shape' in the chariot of 'Life') – is explicitly sublime: a terrible proof, for the despairing narrator at least, that 'good and the means of good' are 'irreconcilable' (Triumph of Life, 87). Indeed, Shelley's account of a 'blind' historical process closely echoes Wollstonecraft's earlier description of the Revolution, when 'twenty-five millions of people . . . unable to endure the increasing weight of oppression, . . . rose like a vast elephant terrible in his anger, treading down with blind fury friends as well as foes' – the image of the rampaging 'elephant' anticipating both the Hindu and the Roman analogues of Shelley's destructive chariot (Triumph of Life, 99–106).[24] But would this have been The Triumph of Life's final verdict about the Revolution catastrophe? Shelley's revision of the discourse on the natural sublime turned upon the ability of the 'cultivated' imagination to 'seize' personally and politically potent 'truth' from 'awful' natural and historical processes. Would *The Triumph of Life* have gone on to similarly explore the apparent catastrophe of the French Revolution, in an attempt to correct the narrator's – and, by extension, post-Napoleonic Europe's – 'despair' over the dynamics of political change?[25]

Shelley's narrator certainly interrogates the 'triumphal pageant' he witnesses: indeed, as Quint observes, questions dominate the action of *The Triumph*.[26] However the narrator's initial, general queries about the 'pageant' *per se* merely pave the way – via the introduction of Rousseau – for a more focused examination of the disastrous French struggle for Liberty: the failed product of Rousseau's imagination or, to put it more precisely, the product of the failure of Rousseau's imagination.

Rousseau's dishevelled condition in *The Triumph of Life* appears problematic at first glance. After all, this 'grim Feature' of 'wretchedness' seems a long way from 'the greatest man since Milton', the man recently lauded by the *Defence of Poetry* as 'essentially a poet' (*Triumph of Life*, 190, 181). Despite the seemingly negative connotations of his physical condition, however, Rousseau clearly plays a central role in *The Triumph* as the Dantean narrator's Virgilesque guide through the Inferno of recent history.[27] Indeed, while his Enlightenment peers – Voltaire, Frederick, Catherine, Leopold (and Kant in the MS) – are chained to the 'Chariot' of 'Life', Rousseau himself is not actually *in* the 'triumph', at least not in the poem's narrative present at any rate (*Triumph of Life*, 235–6).[28] In other words, while clearly not one of 'the sacred few' (including Socrates and Jesus) who were never defeated by 'Life', Rousseau – as prophet of reflexive self-analysis ('I / Have suffered what I wrote, or viler pain!') – has dropped out of the 'pageant' and is to some extent capable of *interpreting* his fate to and for the narrator, and by extension for the *reader* (*Triumph of Life*, 278–9). Hence, we should be wary of reducing *The Triumph of Life* to a mere *condemnation* of Rousseau as visionary manqué. Rather, I am suggesting that the poem explores the failure of the French Revolution, and while this failure is undoubtedly traced to the dysfunction of Rousseau's imagination, Shelley never allows us – and never intends us – to lose sight of the Genevan's political achievements as visionary and *philosophe*. 'If I have been extinguished', Rousseau affirms, 'yet there rise / A thousand beacons from the spark I bore' (*Triumph of Life*, 206–7). Hence, while his Revolution has failed, Rousseau's revolutionary ideals have not been defeated by post-Revolutionary history.[29] Indeed, it is Rousseau rather than the narrator who registers the legislating responsibilities enjoined on the individual imagination by Shelley's sceptical epistemology, implications that *The Triumph*'s narrator either eschews or fails to recognise.[30]

The primary significance of Rousseau's physical condition in *The Triumph of Life* is therefore not the extent to which that condition reflects Shelley's personal opinion of the Genevan in 1822 (although, as I show below, the opinion and the appearance are clearly and pointedly related). Rather, as Wang observes, it is the extent to which Rousseau's 'disfigured' appearance reflects *public* commonplaces about his character.[31] That is to say that the 'strange distortion' of Rousseau in *The Triumph of Life* reflects the (reactionary) post-Revolutionary 'records' of Rousseau in the 'public mind': in Wang's terms, Rousseau as 'political radical, nature child, parody of the nature child, monstrous phallus, misunderstood public figure, and Enlightenment dupe' (*Triumph of Life*, 183).[32] Once again, Shelley (re)presents this public conception of Rousseau precisely in order to set up *The Triumph*'s exploration of Rousseauist thought as an exploration of (the failure of) the French Revolution, an exploration informed by Shelley's personal, balanced 'record' of Rousseau. The Rousseau of *The Triumph of Life* certainly subscribes, like Shelley, to the commonplace account of his architectural role in the Revolution: he admits – not altogether ashamedly – that he has 'created ... a world of agony' (*Triumph of Life*, 294–5). In other words, Rousseau the creator of the French Revolution is, in a very real sense, Rousseau the creator of post-Napoleonic Europe. Indeed, in a cancelled passage of the draft, Rousseau confirms this relationship explicitly: pointing to the tyrants chained to the 'chariot' of 'Life' he acknowledges that 'these had their birth / ... from the death of such as I'.[33] Shelley is clearly using the word 'death' in a figurative rather than a literal sense here: the 'birth' of tyrants results not so much from the actual 'death' of people like Rousseau as from the 'death' of their *imagination*, i.e. from the 'triumph of Life', from the kind of despair to which the narrator himself is in danger of succumbing.[34] Hence, Shelley's point is not that a Napoleon will inevitably follow every attempt at political change; rather it is that a Napoleon will inevitably follow every *failure* of the political imagination.

Accordingly, when *The Triumph of Life*'s narrator asks Rousseau to explain how he fell victim to 'Life', he is effectively asking him to explain *why* the Revolution (the product of his imagination) failed, to explain *why* there is a Napoleon chained to the 'chariot' of 'Life'. Thus, while not denying the broader register of *The Triumph*, I am again suggesting that the poem's exploration of Rousseauist thought was intended to explain the failure of the French Revolution in terms of the dysfunction of Rousseau's *imagination*: in terms, that is, of the 'triumph of Life'.

While Rousseau's account of his defeat by 'Life' is undoubtedly the most complex part of *The Triumph*, the broad parameters of his experience are clear enough. Prompted by the narrator's questions, Rousseau recounts how he awoke to find himself in an idyllic valley, beside a 'gentle rivulet' whose 'oblivious melody' causes those who hear it to 'forget / All pleasure and all pain, all hate and love, / Which they had known before that hour of rest' (*Triumph of Life*, 314, 341, 318–20). As Rousseau surveys his surroundings, he is approached by 'A shape all light' (*Triumph of Life*, 343, 352). This 'shape', which carries a cup of 'bright Nepenthe', increases – in fact *embodies* – the explicitly 'Lethean' influence of the landscape: under her influence Rousseau's 'mind' is 'trampled into the dust of death' (*Triumph of Life*, 359, 463, 386, 388). Rousseau asks the 'shape' to explain his current situation – 'shew whence I came, and where I am, and why' – and she responds by telling him to drink from her cup (*Triumph of Life*, 398).[35] When he begins to comply with her request (it is not clear whether he actually drinks from the cup), the vision instantly fades and the Chariot of 'Life' appears.[36] Rousseau is 'swept' among 'the multitude' in its wake, and his account – together with the extant text of *The Triumph* – concludes after a more detailed reprise of the 'pageant' that greeted the narrator at the opening of his vision (*Triumph of Life*, 460–1).

The structural and thematic repetition of Rousseau's story by the frame narrative – where Rousseau becomes, in a sense, the Narrator's 'shape all light' – poses serious problems for any reading of *The Triumph* as an ultimately pessimistic poem and / or as an outright condemnation of Rousseau. After all, that repetition implies the possibility of *progress* – of *interpreting* the historical dynamic at the heart of the text – and re-affirms Rousseau's role as the narrator's instructive guide.

The apparent similarity between Rousseau's encounter with the 'shape all light' and the *Alastor*-poet's dream of the 'veilèd maid' has also prompted many critics to argue that *The Triumph of Life* is a reprise of the 1815 poem.[37] The comparison is valid to the extent that both texts examine 'the failure of the imagination'. As we have seen in chapter 2, the Rousseau of Wollstonecraft's *Rights of Woman* was an important – although by no means the only – 'prototype' of the *Alastor*-poet.[38] However, to reduce Rousseau's 1822 encounter with the 'shape all light' to a rerun of the *Alastor*-poet's dream of the 'veilèd maid' would be to ignore the dramatic shift in Shelley's opinion of Rousseau during the summer of 1816 (described in chapter 3), and reflected in the *Defence of*

Poetry. Moreover, such a reduction again runs the risk of over-simplifying *The Triumph* itself by eliding the nuances of *Alastor*'s exploration of imaginative dysfunction, nuances reflected in *The Triumph*'s balanced attitude to Rousseau.

Critics have long accepted that *Alastor* explores the collapse of the sympathetic imagination into solipsism. However, it is important to recognise – as in chapter 2 – that *Alastor* describes this collapse in terms of the failure of the imaginative response to *nature*, the centrepiece of both Rousseauist and Wordsworthian thought. Accordingly, to reduce Rousseau's fall to his encounter with the 'shape all light' is to assume – all too readily, I think – that Shelley considers Rousseau's initial ('Lethean') existence in the 'oblivious valley' to be ideal (*Triumph of Life*, 539). Conversely, Shelley's politically conscious revision of the discourse on the natural sublime explicitly rejects any affective response to nature which encourages the individual to 'forget' – in the terms of 'On Leaving London for Wales' – the 'woe his fellows share' for the sake of a 'selfish peace'. And yet this is precisely what the Rousseau of *The Triumph of Life*, prior to his encounter with the 'shape all light', appears to do. He even informs the narrator that if he were to find himself in the 'oblivious valley', he too could forget the 'ills' – 'ills' which I have been suggesting are explicitly political – that have kept him awake throughout the night (*Triumph of Life*, 328). Hence Rousseau's condition in the valley arguably looks as much towards the prioritising of the *politically* pre-conscious 'State of Nature' in the *Social Contract* (1762) – the world-historical equivalent of the 'savage solitude' condemned in Shelley's 1815 'science of mind' – as it does towards any merely personal ideology of nature. Once again – within the terms of Shelley's engagement with the discourse on the natural sublime – it is impossible to separate the imaginative from the political. Seen in these terms, then, it is tempting to suggest that Rousseau has been defeated by 'Life' at the moment that he *wakes* in the 'oblivious valley', and that his subsequent narrative is merely intended to reveal how that defeat took place.

The Wordsworthian intertexts in Rousseau's account of the 'oblivious valley' – where the 'scene of woods and waters seemed to keep' a 'gentle trace / Of light diviner than the common sun / Sheds on the common earth' – have long been noted by Shelley's critics (*Triumph of Life*, 336–9).[39] This clear echo of the Intimations *Ode* has prompted many commentators to read Rousseau's defeat by 'Life' as an inevitable (Wordsworthian) decay of the imagination: a transition – figured in his encounter with the 'shape all light' – from preconscious (visionary) childhood into the 'common day' of self-consciousness.⁴⁰ I do not accept this reading for reasons already stated (further objections are set out below). However, it is important to recognise that even *as* a description of childhood, Rousseau's account of his experience in the 'oblivious valley', prior to encountering the 'shape all light', is explicitly 'sceptical' and 'anti-Wordsworthian'.⁴¹ As Quint puts it:

the spell exerted by nature upon the child Rousseau not only blots out consciousness of history – suggested by the similes of the bereft mother and dethroned king (verses 321–6), generational and political images darkly conceived in terms of loss – but it also denies the possibility of the Platonic and Wordsworthian *anamnesis* of a divine origin.⁴²

Although Quint does not pursue the point he makes here, he has hit upon the real significance of the 'oblivious valley'. It is not so much that Rousseau, prior to encountering the 'shape all light', has no consciousness of self. Rather it is that the 'oblivious valley' causes him to *lose* consciousness of *history*: to 'forget all' he 'had known before' (*Triumph of Life*, 319–20). And again, this explicitly 'Lethean' effect is embodied in the 'shape' herself, under whose influence '*all that was seemed as if it had been not*' (*Triumph of Life*, 385; emphasis added). She personifies not so much nature *per se*, but rather nature-as-Lethe.⁴³

Hence, Rousseau's defeat by 'Life' is not a Wordsworthian fading of childhood vision into the light of common day. Nor is it again, as Duffy suggests, that in questioning the 'shape all light' Rousseau betrays the imagination to reason and allows his 'head . . . to poison . . . the gifts of his heart' (*Triumph of Life*, 137).⁴⁴ After all, Rousseau is explicitly 'overcome', as he tells the narrator, 'by [his] *own heart alone*, which neither age, / Nor tears, nor infamy, nor now the tomb / Could temper to its object' (*Triumph of Life*, 240–3; emphasis added).

The narrator's initial vision of the 'triumphal pageant' makes it clear that most of those who have been defeated by 'Life' have either ignored or remained in ignorance of nature. 'Flowers never grew' on the 'public way' they follow, the narrator affirms, and they 'heard not the fountains whose melodious dew / Out of their mossy cells forever burst / Nor felt the breeze which from the forest told / Of grassy paths and wood lawns interspersed' (*Triumph of Life*, 65, 43, 67–70). Indeed, we are given to understand that nature might assuage the 'vain toil' of those caught up in the 'triumph', but again they ignore it and 'pursue . . . their serious folly as of old' (*Triumph of Life*, 66, 73).

Quite the opposite is true of Rousseau: indeed, Rousseau's attitude to nature is one of the major factors differentiating him from the other victims of 'Life'. In short, while they ignore nature, he has become obsessed with it. In other words, Rousseau's defeat by 'Life' is not – as is commonly suggested – that he cannot *remain* in the 'valley of perpetual dream' (*Triumph of Life*, 397). That is actually only the *consequence* of his defeat. The defeat itself – the failure of his imagination ('heart') – is that fact that he is *in* the 'oblivious valley' to begin with, and that he *wants* to remain there rather than 'wake to weep' in 'the sick day' (*Triumph of Life*, 430–1). To put it another way, Rousseau is unwilling to 'temper' his imagination ('heart') to the philanthropic 'spells' imposed by nature's law, and thereby surrender the 'selfish', 'Lethean' 'peace' he derives from the 'oblivious' contemplation of nature in the 'valley'. In short, then, the agency of Life's 'triumph' over Rousseau is the solipsism of his 'own' imagination ('heart'). Hence, Rousseau's physical appearance in *The Triumph of Life* – as an 'old root' – not only figures public commonplaces about Rousseau, but also tellingly encapsulates his moral and imaginative *imprisonment* in nature (*Triumph of Life*, 182).

By asking the 'shape all light' (who, again, embodies nature-as-Lethe) '*not*' to 'pass away upon the passing stream' of time, Rousseau explicitly formulates this 'desire' to remain in the 'oblivious valley', a 'desire' analogous to that informing the *Alastor*-poet's pursuit of the 'veilèd maid' (*Triumph of Life*, 399, 394–5; emphasis added). And indeed the questions Rousseau asks the 'shape' – 'show whence I came, and where I am, and why' – voice the same desire to make a 'Lethean' nature *ontologically* as well as emotionally sufficient: tellingly, Rousseau is not interested in knowing where he should go or what he should do (*Triumph of Life*, 398). Hence, in addressing the 'shape', Rousseau is 'suspended' 'between' 'desire and shame': 'desire' to remain in the 'oblivious valley' and 'shame' at the motivation of that 'desire' (*Triumph of Life*, 394–5). Equally, once he has formulated his 'desire' and been defeated by 'Life', the happiness that Rousseau hoped to *perpetuate* quickly fades and only his 'desire' for that lost happiness remains (a psychological condition figured in the fleeing deer and pursuing wolf imagery of lines 406–10).[45]

In the final analysis, then, Rousseau's defeat by 'Life', the failure of his imagination ('heart'), consists in a solipsistic ('shame') 'desire' to remain in the 'oblivious' 'valley of perpetual dream' and evade the philanthropic 'object' of nature's law, a personal desire reflected equally in the public emphasis on the 'state of nature' in Rousseauvian political thought. In other words, Rousseau's defeat is presented – within the terms of Shelley's engagement with the discourse on the natural sublime – as a failure of the imaginative response to nature. The historical consequences of this failure are tellingly summed up by the transformation of the rainbow that surrounds the 'shape all light' into the 'moving arch of victory' that heralds the 'triumphal' chariot of 'Life' (*Triumph of Life*, 440). But again, Shelley's critique of Rousseau – like *Alastor*'s account of the poet-protagonist – is equivocal. Rousseau's words may have sown 'seeds of misery' in recent history but they were also the 'spark' that lit the still un-extinguished 'beacons' of Liberty (*Triumph of Life*, 280, 207). Rousseau's powerful but ultimately problematic relationship to nature – understood to be voiced as much in the *Social Contract* as in *Julie* and *The Confessions* – is thus Shelley's own take on the egotism that Rousseau's detractors had long since identified as a major cause, not only of the French Revolution itself, but also of its Napoleonic collapse: the failure, through solipsistic excess, of the sympathetic imagination. Shelley's Revolution was not so much – in Burke's terms – a thing 'out of nature'; but its collapse could be attributed to the failure, in *Queen Mab*'s terms, to read nature 'rightly' (*Poems*, i, p. 360).[46]

The *Triumph of Life*'s critics have long sought biographical parallels for Rousseau's account of his experience in the 'oblivious valley'. Matthews, for example, suggests that Shelley's narrative 'owes much to the real Rousseau's situation at Les Charmettes in 1737–8, described in Books V–VI of *The Confessions* as the only idyllic episode in a career that immediately afterwards (Book VII) plunged into the living storm of social and political life'.[47] Reiman – noting that Shelley had apparently been re-reading *Julie* shortly before beginning *The Triumph* in April 1822 – argues that the *Nouvelle Héloïse* rather than the *Confessions* provided the basis of the 'oblivious valley' narrative.[48] However, it seems to me that neither of these suggestions fully encompasses the nuances of Rousseau's defeat by 'Life'.[49] Both Matthews and Reiman identify that defeat as Rousseau's inability – for whatever reason – to cling on to an 'idyllic' existence, be that habitually at Les Charmettes or imaginatively at Clarens. But, again, it is rather Rousseau's *desire* for nature as a source of 'perpetual' 'Lethean' 'dream' that marks his defeat by 'Life' in Shelley's poem. And indeed, seen in these terms, the 'oblivious valley' of *The Triumph of Life* recalls nothing so much as Shelley's highly ambiguous critique of the post-*Excursion* Wordsworth in *The Assassins*. In conclusion, however, and without wishing to add gratuitously to the already lengthy list of potential sources, I will propose another possible biographical parallel for *The Triumph of Life*'s 'oblivious valley' narrative: Rousseau's well-known account, in Book XII of the *Confessions* and Chapter V of the *Rêveries*, of the Lac de Bienne and the Isle St. Pierre.

In September 1765, Rousseau was forced to flee from his house at Môtiers after it had been stoned by a mob, and took up refuge on the Isle St. Pierre near Neufchâtel. Rousseau's account of his brief residence there repeatedly emphasises that the island's scenery is 'interesting for solitary contemplators who like to become intoxicated with the charms of nature at leisure and collect their thoughts in a silence troubled by no noise' (*Rousseau*, viii, p. 41). Shelley's portrait of the solipsistic *Alastor*-poet might well have echoed this description. But the parallels between Rousseau's account of his 'solitary' life on St. Pierre and *The Triumph of Life*'s 'oblivious valley' – which is, similarly, a 'scene of woods and waters' – are unmistakable (*Triumph of Life*, 336).

After moving to the island, Rousseau affirms that he 'in a measure took leave of [his] generation and [his] contemporaries, and said farewell to the world', a possible source for the 'Lethean' seclusion of the 'valley' where Rousseau wakes in *The Triumph of Life*. Indeed, the historical Rousseau explicitly identifies St. Pierre as his 'Papimania, that blessed country where one *sleeps*' (*Rousseau*, v, p. 536; emphasis added). Rousseau further informs the reader that he resumed his study of botany while living on St. Pierre, ostensibly in order to counteract his self-confessed 'delirium of the imagination' (*Rousseau*, v, p. 537). *The Triumph of Life* echoes this claim, and suggests that the attempt was unsuccessful: Shelley's Rousseau notes grimly that 'sweetest flowers delayed not long' his defeat by 'Life' (*Triumph of Life*, 461). The account of St. Pierre in the *Confessions* also records that Rousseau was 'passionately fond of the water', and that 'the sight of it [threw him] into a delightful state of dreaminess, although often without any definite object' (*Rousseau*, v, p. 631). While this notion of dream-without-object certainly brings *Alastor*'s 'veilèd maid' to mind, it surely also informed the appearance of the 'shape all light' over the 'fountain' of a 'gentle rivulet' in *The Triumph of Life* (351, 314).

What I am suggesting, then, is that Rousseau's account of the Isle St. Pierre everywhere reflects the kind of solipsistic imaginative response to nature, the desire for nature-as-Lethe, that is represented in *The Triumph of Life*'s 'oblivious valley' narrative. Indeed, in both the *Confessions* and the *Rêveries*, Rousseau goes so far as to wish that St. Pierre might be made his 'perpetual prison', that he might be 'confine[d]' in this 'refuge' for 'life – so that being unaware of all that went on in the world I might forget its existence and that it might also forget mine' (*Rousseau*, v, p. 541; viii, p. 42). In the *Triumph of Life*, it is precisely this same 'desire' for nature-as-Lethe, this solipsistic failure of the 'heart', which becomes Rousseau's 'prison': the agent of his final defeat by 'Life'. As Rousseau notes of his residence on

St. Pierre, 'the ardent desire to end my days on this Island was inseparable from the fear of being forced to leave it' (*Rousseau*, v, p. 540).

Over and above recording the kind of solipsism explored in *Alastor* and *The Triumph of Life*, however, Rousseau's account of St. Pierre in the *Confessions* reveals another important aspect of his imaginative relationship to nature, an aspect that Shelley must have found particularly difficult to reconcile with his idea of the author of *Julie*. 'When it was fine weather', Rousseau writes of his house on St. Pierre, in a passage that curiously anticipates Gibbon's account of the completion of the *Decline and Fall* at Lausanne:

When the weather was good, when I got up I did not fail to run onto the terrace to breathe in the morning's salubrious and fresh air, and to let my eyes slide over the horizon of that beautiful lake, whose banks and mountains which bordered it enchanted my sight. I find no more worthy homage to the divinity than this mute admiration excited by the contemplation of its works and which is not at all expressed by amplified actions. I understand how it is that the inhabitants of cities who see only walls, streets, and crimes have little faith; but I cannot understand how country folk and above all solitary people can have none whatsoever. How is it that their soul does not raise itself with ecstasy a hundred times a day to the author of the marvels that strike them? For me, it is above all when I get up, worn down by my insomnia, that a long habit carries me to those elevations of heart which do not impose any fatigue of thinking. But that requires that my eyes be struck by the ravishing spectacle of nature (*Rousseau*, v, p. 538)

The 'enchanting' prospect of 'mountains' prompting 'homage to the divinity'? An affective response to 'the ravishing spectacle of nature' that avoids 'any fatigue of thinking' but surrenders to 'habit', to the 'records' of the 'public mind'? And this from 'the greatest man since Milton', the man who had written *Julie*? The revolutionary Valais of the *Nouvelle Héloïse* has indeed become the 'oblivious valley' of *The Triumph of Life*.

Notes

INTRODUCTION: APPROACHING THE 'SHELLEYAN SUBLIME'

1 Thomas De Quincey, 'Percy Bysshe Shelley', in *The Works of Thomas De Quincey*, 16 vols. (Edinburgh: A. and C. Black, 1854–60), v, 7; Matthew Arnold, *Essays in Criticism*, second series, in *The Complete Prose Works of Matthew Arnold*, ed. R. H. Super, 11 vols. (Ann Arbor: University of Michigan Press, 1960–77), ix, 237; George Gilfillan, *A Gallery of Literary Portraits* (Edinburgh, 1854), quoted from De Quincey, v, 28 and n.

2 C. E. Pulos' *The Deep Truth: A Study of Shelley's Poetic Scepticism* (Lincoln, Nebraska: University of Nebraska Press, 1962) remains the seminal account of Shelley's philosophical convictions. Both P. M. S. Dawson's *The Unacknowledged Legislator: Shelley and Politics* (Oxford: Clarendon Press, 1980) and M. H. Scrivener's *Radical Shelley: The Philosophical Anarchism and Utopian Thought of Percy Bysshe Shelley* (Princeton: Princeton University Press, 1982) are vital to any understanding of the poet's politics. For the most recent account of Shelley's political and philosophical thought, see James Chandler, *England in 1819: The Politics of Literary Culture and the Case of Romantic Historicism* (London: University of Chicago Press, 1996), especially pp. 454–83. Kenneth Neill Cameron provides a valuable account of earlier engagements in 'Shelley as Philosophical and Social Thinker: Some Modern Evaluations', *SiR* 21 (1982), pp. 357–66.

3 Peter De Bolla, *The Discourse on the Sublime: Readings in History, Aesthetics and the Subject* (Oxford: Basil Blackwell, 1989), p. 12; Paul Foot, *Red Shelley* (London: Sidgwick and Jackson), p. 274. De Bolla defines the 'discourse on the sublime' as the sustained enquiry, during the eighteenth and early nineteenth centuries, 'into the nature and causes of sublime sensation'; that is, as the attempt 'to describe how an experience is sublime and what caused it' (p. 12). This analytical 'discourse on the sublime' is to be distinguished from what De Bolla calls the 'discourse *of* the sublime': 'a discourse which produces, from within itself, what is habitually termed the category of the sublime and in so doing ... becomes a self-transforming discourse' (p. 12; emphasis added).

4 The phrase is Thomas Weiskel's. See *The Romantic Sublime: Studies in the Structure and Psychology of Transcendence* (Baltimore: Johns Hopkins University Press, 1976).

5 Angela Leighton, *Shelley and the Sublime: An Interpretation of the Major Poems* (Cambridge: Cambridge University Press, 1984).

6 *Ibid.*, vii.

7 *Ibid.*, vii.

8 *Ibid.*, p. 23

9 *Ibid.*, vii.

10 *Ibid.*, vii.

11 Paul Endo, '*Mont Blanc*, Silence, and the Sublime', *English Studies in Canada* 21/3 (Sept. 1995), pp. 283–300; '*The Cenci*: Recognising the Shelleyan Sublime', *Texas Studies in Language and Literature* 38, 3/4 (1996), pp. 379–97.

12 De Bolla, *Discourse of the Sublime*, p. 292

13 *Ibid.*, pp. 33, 292–3. Andrew Ashfield and Peter De Bolla (eds.), *The Sublime: A Reader in British Eighteenth-Century Aesthetic Theory* (Cambridge: Cambridge University Press, 1996), p. 3

14 De Bolla, *Discourse of the Sublime*, p. 293

15 Ashfield and De Bolla, *Reader*, p. 3 Samuel Holt Monk, *The Sublime: A Study of Critical Theories in XVIIIth-Century England*, revised edn (Ann Arbor: University of Michigan Press, 1960).

16 De Bolla, *Discourse of the Sublime*, p. 291

17 *Ibid.*, p. 293. Ashfield and De Bolla, *Reader*, p. 3

18 De Bolla, *Discourse of the Sublime*, p. 293

19 Weiskel, *Romantic Sublime*, p. 38

20 Neil Hertz, *The End of the Line: Essays on Psychoanalysis and the Sublime* (New York: Columbia University Press, 1985). See especially 'The Notion of Blockage in the Literature of the Sublime', which is steeped in Freudian and Kantian terminology, and which cites Monk and Weiskel in support of this methodology (pp. 40–60).

21 De Bolla, *Discourse of the Sublime*, pp. 33–4.

22 *Ibid.*, p. 293. This critique has been carried on by Tom Furniss in *Edmund Burke's Aesthetic Ideology: Language, Gender and Political Economy in Revolution* (Cambridge: Cambridge University Press, 1993). Furniss, 'in contrast to Weiskel', seeks 'to abandon the suggestion that eighteenth-century discussions of the sublime represent early attempts to account for a human condition which Freud has finally allowed us to theorise properly' (p. 28). I return to Furniss's reading of Burke below.

23 Frances Ferguson, 'Legislating the Sublime', in *Studies in Eighteenth-Century British Art and Aesthetics*, ed. Ralph Cohen (California: University of California Press, 1995), pp. 128–47; 'The Sublime of Edmund Burke, Or the Bathos of Experience', *Glyph Textual Studies* 8 (1981), pp. 62–78.

24 Frances Ferguson, *Solitude and the Sublime: Romanticism and the Aesthetics of Individuation* (London: Routledge, 1992), p. x.

25 Ferguson, *Solitude and the Sublime*, vii.

26 *Ibid.*, viii; emphasis added.

27 Frances Ferguson, 'Shelley's *Mont Blanc*: What the Mountain Said', in *Romanticism and Language*, ed. Arden Reed (London: Methuen, 1984), p. 213.

28 Leighton, *Shelley and the Sublime*, p. 22
29 Endo, 'Mont Blanc, Silence, and the Sublime', p. 238; original emphasis. See also Christophe Bode, 'A Kantian Sublime in Shelley: "Respect for our own Vocation" in an Indifferent Universe', in *1650–1850: Ideas, Aesthetics, and Inquiries in the Early Modern Era*, III, ed. Kevin Cope and Laura Morrow (New York: AMS, 1997), pp. 329–58.
30 René Wellek, *Immanuel Kant in England, 1793–1838* (Princeton: Princeton University Press, 1931), p. 182
31 Ashfield and De Bolla, *Reader*, p. 2
32 Leighton, *Shelley and the Sublime*, vii.
33 I. J. Kapstein, 'The Meaning of Shelley's *Mont Blanc*', *PMLA* 62ii (1947), p. 1046. Kapstein's claim that *Mont Blanc*'s 'subject matter is ontology', the 'nature of the mind, the nature of knowledge, the nature of reality, and the relation of the human mind to the universe' set the trend for almost all subsequent readings of the text (p. 1046).
34 Pulos, *The Deep Truth*.
35 *Ibid.*, p. 108.
36 *Ibid.*, p. 107.
37 *Ibid.*, p. 111
38 For a general, if somewhat over schematic history of this commonplace see Marjorie Hope Nicolson, *Mountain Gloom and Mountain Glory: the Development of the Aesthetics of the Infinite* (Ithaca: Cornell University Press, 1959). Nicolson argues that in the wake of the New Astronomy the affective responses previously evoked by the idea of God were gradually extended to the infinite universe which seemed to partake of his attributes, and from hence eventually to all natural phenomena capable of suggesting the infinite (Nicolson, *Mountain Gloom*, p. 143 and *passim*). See also E. L. Tuveson, 'Space, Deity, and the "Natural Sublime"', *MLQ* 12/1 (March 1951), pp. 20–38. For an opposing hypothesis, which suggests that the discourse on the sublime stemmed from the re-discovery, early in the eighteenth century, of Longinus' treatise *On the Sublime*, see Monk, *The Sublime*, p. 10. In fact, a combination of these hypotheses most satisfactorily explains the origins of the British discourse. Longinus can be said to have provided the eighteenth century with a vocabulary adequate for expressing the new affective responses to nature.
39 The phrase 'plurality of worlds' recalls Bernard le Bovier de Fontenelle's 1686 *Entretiens sur la Pluralité des Mondes*, a popularisation of Cartesian astronomical theories, which had been translated into English as *Conversations on the Plurality of Worlds* in 1808 (*Poems*, i, p. 288 n.). The *Entretiens* appear on Mary Shelley's reading list for 1815 (*MWSJ*, p. 88). The Note as a whole echoes Tom Paine's discussion of the 'plurality of worlds' in the *Age of Reason* (1794), which argues that 'though it is not a direct article of the christian system that this world that we inhabit is the whole of the habitable creation, yet it is so worked up therewith, from what is called the Mosaic account of the creation, the story of Eve and the apple, and the counterpart of that story, the death of the Son of God, that to believe otherwise, that is, to believe that God created a plurality of

worlds, at least as numerous as what we call stars, renders the christian system of faith at once little and ridiculous; and scatters it in the mind like feathers in the air. The two beliefs cannot be held together in the same mind; and he who thinks that he believes both, has thought but little of either'. Tom Paine, *The Age of Reason* (London, 1794), p. 40.

40 As early as 1712, Joseph Addison's seminal *Spectator* essays – on the 'pleasures of the imagination' – first identified the faculty as the agency of the mind's response to the 'great, uncommon, or beautiful' (quoted from Ashfield and De Bolla, *Reader*, p. 62).

41 Interest in the imagination continued long into the nineteenth century: Coleridge's *Biographia Literaria* (1817) and Shelley's own *Defence of Poetry* (1821) being only two of the numerous 'romantic' appraisals of the faculty. For a history of the imagination in eighteenth- and early nineteenth-century British thought see James Engell, *The Creative Imagination: Enlightenment to Romanticism* (Cambridge Mass.: Harvard University Press, 1981).

42 Edmund Burke, *Reflections on the Revolution in France*, ed. C. C. O'Brien (Harmondsworth: Penguin, 1982), p. 284, hereafter cited in the text as *Reflections*. As Edward Duffy notes, Burke's harshest critique of Rousseau's influence on the Revolution came after the *Reflections*, and after the National Assembly had itself honoured Rousseau, in his 1791 *Letter to a Member of the National Assembly*, more than one-fifth of which is devoted to attacking Rousseau. Edward Duffy, *Rousseau in England: the Context for Shelley's Critique of the Enlightenment* (Berkeley: University of California Press, 1979), pp. 37–42.

43 For a discussion of the varying political connotations of the term 'enthusiasm' in late eighteenth and early nineteenth-century Britain, see S. I. Tucker, *Enthusiasm: a Study in Semantic Change* (Cambridge: Cambridge University Press, 1972), pp. 98–130.

44 Leighton, *Shelley and the Sublime*, pp. 25–47.

45 Shelley does not seem to have been unduly troubled by the fact that Hume – like those other influential eighteenth-century sceptics Swift and Johnson – was a staunch Tory.

46 Some of the most fruitful readings of Shelley have similarly emphasised his scientific debts. See, for example, Carl Grabo, *A Newton Among Poets: Shelley's Use of Science in Prometheus Unbound* (New York: Cooper Square, 1968). See also G. M. Matthews, 'A Volcano's Voice in Shelley', *ELH* 24 (1957), pp. 191–228; and Nigel Leask, 'Mont Blanc's Mysterious Voice: Shelley and Huttonian Earth Science', in *The Third Culture: Literature and Science*, ed. Elinor S. Shaffer (New York: De Gruyter, 1998), pp. 182–203.

47 *A Refutation* was printed privately in 1814, and appeared again in the March and April 1815 editions of Erasmus Perkins' short-lived *Theological Inquirer* (see *MWSJ*, p. 62 n. 2). For the probable composition date – in late 1813 – see *PW*, p. 365.

48 Edmund Burke, *Reflections on the Revolution in France, and on the Proceedings in Certain Societies in London Relative to that Event, in a Letter Intended to have been*

Sent to a Gentleman in Paris, ed. Conor Cruise O'Brien (Harmondsworth: Penguin, 1982), p. 119; hereafter cited in the text as Reflections. Ironically, in *Edmund Burke's Aesthetic Ideology,* Tom Furniss locates an equally revolutionary sublime at the heart of Burke's own political writing. Furniss suggests that the sublime emerges from Burke's *Philosophical Enquiry* (1757) as precisely that same revolutionary energy that will return to haunt the *Reflections on the Revolution* (1790): as an overpowering and explicitly bourgeois ethos which threatens the beautiful, aristocratic order of society (Furniss, *Aesthetic Ideology,* pp. 115–17, 119–21).

49 A thorough examination of the extent to which Shelley's 'aesthetic ideology' extended to encompass the discourse on the beautiful is regrettably beyond my scope here. This is clearly not the place to explore the extent to which the seminal eighteenth-century dichotomy between the sublime and the beautiful was still operative in early nineteenth-century landscape aesthetics, but Shelley's work certainly makes no obvious or sustained attempt to theorise the beautiful as an aesthetic category. For example – as outlined in chapter 3 – the *Hymn to Intellectual Beauty* (1816) is clearly not an analysis of the beautiful in the sense that *Mont Blanc* is undoubtedly an analysis of the sublime. In fact, Shelley's landscape descriptions frequently blur altogether the distinction between the sublime and the beautiful (a common enough practice in the early nineteenth century, reflected in the development of the picturesque as a median between the rigidly defined eighteenth-century categories). Hence, while a 22 July 1816 letter from Savoy contrasts the 'luxuriant' and 'beautiful' valley of Servoz with the 'immensity' of neighbouring Chamonix, a later letter from Italy recalls the 'immeasurable greatness the overpowering magnificence, [and] above all the radiant beauty of the glaciers' (*Letters,* i, p. 501; ii, p. 62). On the other hand, much of Shelley's work does arguably *politicise* the beautiful: his post-revolutionary utopian landscapes, for example, are often rendered within that category. Indeed it would be tempting – although ultimately, I suspect, impossible – to discern a coherent translation of oppositions like reason / imagination, male / female, revolutionism / gradualism, etc. onto the dichotomy between the sublime and the beautiful. Again, however, such an attempt lies well outside my rubric here.

50 Chloe Chard, 'Crossing Boundaries and Exceeding Limits: Destabilisation, Tourism, and the Sublime', in *Transports: Travel, Pleasure, and Imaginative Geography, 1600–1830,* ed. Chloe Chard and Helen Langdon (London: Yale University Press, *c.* 1996), pp. 117–49. See also Chloe Chard, *Pleasure and Guilt on the Grand Tour: Travel Writing and Imaginative Geography 1600–1830* (Manchester: Manchester University Press, 1999).

51 Furniss sources his use of the term to 'the interrelation between aesthetics and ideology which Paul de Man made the object of his enquiry' (Furniss, *Aesthetic Ideology* p. 266 n.1).

52 *The Monthly Magazine* for April 1797, for example, recorded a proposal put by Tracy before the French National Institute on 15 Nivose (5 January) that 'the science which results from this analysis [i.e. 'the philosophy of mind'], be named

ideology, or the science of ideas, to distinguish it from the ancient metaphysics' (*Monthly Magazine*, iii, p. 285). According to *OED*, the term 'ideology' originally referred specifically to the sensationist philosophy of Condillac.

53 Shelley's debts to Godwin are described at length by Dawson and Scrivener.

54 F. S. Ellis, *A Lexical Concordance to the Poetical Works of Percy Bysshe Shelley* (London, 1892).

55 It is worth noting that the word 'sublime' itself occurs only twenty-three times in Shelley's poetry, and on only three occasions could the immediate context be loosely construed as political (relating to virtuous action).

56 Geoffrey Matthews was the first to point up the importance of volcanism in *Prometheus Unbound* II–III (Matthews, 'A Volcano's Voice', pp. 203–21). Matthews' seminal essay has, inexplicably, been all but ignored by previous critical explorations of the 'Shelleyan sublime'.

57 Ronald Paulson, *Representations of Revolution, 1789–1820* (New Haven: Yale University Press, 1983), pp. 57–88. Matthews similarly traces Shelley's use of volcanic imagery to Abbé Augustin Barruel's account of the Jacobin club in his 1797–8 *Memoirs Illustrating the History of Jacobinism* (Matthews, 'A Volcano's Voice', p. 223). I return to this particular debt in more detail in the next chapter.

58 The phrase 'revolution controversy' comes, of course, from Marilyn Butler's valuable anthology of 1790s political writing, *Burke, Paine, Godwin, and the Revolution Controversy* (Cambridge: Cambridge University Press, 1984).

1. FROM RELIGION TO REVOLUTION, 1810–1813

1 Reid's discussion of the sublime can be found in Chapter III, 'Of Grandeur', in Essay VIII, 'Of Taste'.

2 Addison's 1712 *Spectator* essays identify 'greatness, novelty, or beauty' as the three qualities of matter capable of attracting an affective response from the mind (quoted in Ashfield and De Bolla, *Reader*, p. 62). The eighteenth-century British discourse on the sublime largely retained these categories, although less sustained attention was paid to novelty as the century wore on. As noted, Addison was also the first to identify the imagination as the agency of the mind's affective response to the natural sublime. Shelley ordered the complete *Spectator* from his bookseller, Charles Ollier, at the end of 1817 (*Letters*, i, pp. 568, 591). There is no direct evidence that he read Addison prior to this.

3 Edmund Burke, *A Philosophical Enquiry into the Origin of Our Ideas of the Sublime and the Beautiful* (Dublin, 1757).

4 Anthony Ashley Cooper, Third Earl of Shaftesbury, *Characteristicks of Men, Manners, Opinions, Times*, second edition, 3 vols. (London, 1714); Frances Hutcheson, *An Inquiry into the Original of our Ideas of Beauty and Virtue* (London, 1725).

5 For an account of the publication and reception of Alison's *Essays* see W. J. Hipple, *The Beautiful, The Sublime, and The Picturesque* (Carbondale: Southern Illinois University Press, 1957), p. 158.

6 Shelley cites Stewart's 1793 *Outlines of Moral Philosophy for the Use of Students in Edinburgh University*, for example, in his *Refutation of Deism* (*PW*, p. 122 n. 1). As we shall see in Chapter 2, Shelley had certainly read the *Elements* by 1815, and probably a good deal earlier.

7 Francis Jeffrey, 'Alison on Taste', *Edinburgh Review* (XVIII), pp. 1–46. As Hipple notes, Jeffrey later expanded this review for his entry on 'Beauty' in the *Encyclopaedia Britannica* (Hipple, *The Beautiful, the Sublime, and the Picturesque*, p. 351 n. 5).

8 I use the translation of Holbach given in *Prose*, p. 354. In Shelley's Note, the quotation is given in the original French: 'En un mot, l'homme a toujours respecté les causes inconnues des effets surprenans, que son ignorance l'empêchait de démêler' (*Poems*, i, p. 387).

9 In Shelley's Note, the original French reads 'c'est dans cette obscurité qu'ils ont placé leur Dieu; c'est dans cette abîme ténébreux que leur imagination inquiète travaille toujours à se fabriquer des chimères, qui les affligeront jusqu'à ce que la connaissance de la nature les détrompe des fantômes qu'ils ont tojours si vainement adorés' (*Poems*, i, p. 386).

10 In David Hume's *Dialogues Concerning Natural Religion* – published posthumously in 1799 – Shelley could have found a similar analysis of the relationship between religion and anthropomorphism. Indeed, in his *Natural History of Religion* (1757), Hume locates the origin of religious belief in the 'anxious' response of the 'imagination' to the '*unknown causes*' of natural phenomena 'on which we have so entire a dependence'. 'Convulsions in nature', he continues, 'though the most opposite to the plan of a wise superintendent, impress mankind with the strongest sentiments of religion; the causes of events seeming then the most unknown and unaccountable'. David Hume, *Dialogues and Natural History of Religion*, ed. J. C. A. Gaskin (Oxford: Oxford University Press, 1993), pp. 140, 154. There is no direct evidence that Shelley had read Hume's writings on religion although, as Murray notes, the *Dialogues* were almost certainly a 'major' source for Shelley's 1814 *Refutation of Deism* (*PW*, pp. 367–8). For a full-length discussion of the eighteenth century's exploration of religion, see F. E. Manuel, *The Eighteenth Century Confronts the Gods* (Cambridge Mass.: Harvard University Press, 1959).

11 Burke, *Reflections*, p. 182. Godwin's *Caleb Williams* (1794) – one of Shelley's favourite novels at the time he was writing *Queen Mab* – offers an explicitly politicised investigation of the paralysing effect of the 'wonderful' upon a 'juvenile mind': speaking of his aristocratic master, Caleb affirms that he 'had always been to my imagination an object of wonder, and that which excites our wonder we scarcely suppose ourselves competent to analyse'. William Godwin, *Things as They Are, or, The Adventures of Caleb Williams*, ed. David McCracken (Oxford: Oxford University Press, 1970), p. 297.

12 In the original French: 'ses terreurs se dissipent dans la même proportion que son esprit s'éclaire. L'homme instruit cesse d'être superstitieux' (*Poems*, i, p. 387).

13 Akenside's 1744 *Pleasures of the Imagination*, for example, anticipates much of Shelley's own subsequent theorisation of the faculty by recognising that 'the

influence of the imagination on the conduct of life, is one of the most important points in moral philosophy ... the imagination directs almost all the passions, and mixes with almost every circumstance of action or pleasure' (quoted in Ashfield and De Bolla, *Reader*, p. 86). For a useful overview of other favourable (if qualified) appraisals of the imagination in eighteenth-century British philosophy, empiricist and otherwise, see Engell, *The Creative Imagination*, pp. 33–51.

14 Leighton, *Shelley and the Sublime*, pp. 32ff.

15 *Ibid.*, p. 32. Again, the problem with Leighton's reading is that while it picks up this early tension between a rational and an imaginative response to the natural sublime, it fails to recognise the extent to which Shelley has moved beyond this epistemological crux before the publication of *Queen Mab*.

16 *Ibid.*, p. 34.

17 As Kenneth Neill Cameron points out in *Esdaile*, the Wordsworthian tone of the 'Lines' suggests that the spring referred to is that of 1812. Cameron bases this inference on the assumption that Shelley was first introduced to Wordsworth's poetry by Robert Southey, whom he met in the Lake District in December 1811 (*Esdaile*, p. 188). See also *Letters*, i, p. 210.

18 In this, the 'Lines' anticipate the opening of *Queen Mab*, Canto VI, where the soul of Ianthe is described as 'all touch, all eye, all ear' (*Queen Mab*, vi, 1).

19 Shelley was likely familiar with Adam Smith's *History of Astronomy* – published posthumously in the 1797 *Essays on Philosophical Subjects* – which, incidentally, also points up the links between the natural sublime and the primitive religious impulse.

20 For an account of the extent to which *Mab*'s discussion of Necessity draws as much upon Hume's *Enquiry Concerning Human Understanding* (1748) as it does upon Shelley's more commonly recognised source in Godwin's chapter on 'Free Will and Necessity' in his *Enquiry Concerning Political Justice* (1793), see Frank B. Evans, 'Shelley, Godwin, Hume, and the Doctrine of Necessity', *Studies in Philology* 37 (1940), pp. 632–40.

21 Evans, 'Shelley, Godwin, Hume', p. 636.

22 In his *Refutation of Deism*, Shelley explicitly identifies the source of this idea, noting that 'Hume has shewn, to the satisfaction of all philosophers, that the only idea which we can form of causation is < derivable > from the constant conjunction of objects, and the consequent inference of one from the other' (*PW*, p. 121).

23 In his *Treatise of Human Nature* (1739–40), for example, Hume argues that 'Reason can never shew us the connexion of one object with another, tho' aided by experience, and the observation of their constant conjunction in all past instances. When the mind, therefore, passes from the idea or impression of one object to the idea or belief of another, *it is not determin'd by reason, but by certain principles, which associate together the ideas of these objects, and unite them in the imagination.* Had ideas no more union in the fancy than objects seem to have to the understanding, we cou'd never draw an inference from causes to effects, nor repose any belief in any matter of fact'. David Hume, *A Treatise*

of Human Nature: Being an Attempt to Introduce the Experimental Method of Reasoning into Moral Subjects, ed. L. A. Selby-Bigge, rev. P. H. Nidditch (Oxford: Oxford University Press, 1978), p. 92.

24 Burke, *Reflections*, pp. 92, 119.

25 Quoted in Ashfield and De Bolla, *Reader*, p. 62.

26 Unless otherwise indicated, all quotations from Paine's work are from *Thomas Paine: Rights of Man, Common Sense, and Other Political Writings*, ed. Mark Philp (Oxford: Oxford University Press, 1995).

27 Quoted from Philp (ed.), *Thomas Paine*, p. 210.

28 *Ibid.*

29 *Ibid.*, pp. 210–11.

30 Paine's account of the affective response to the natural sublime has its origins not so much in Burke's *Enquiry* as in Longinus's seminal treatise, *On the Sublime*. Speaking of the rhetorical sublime, Longinus notes that 'the mind is naturally elevated by the true sublime, and so sensibly affected with its lively strokes, that it swells in transport and an inward pride, as if what was only heard had been the product of its own invention'. *Dionysius Longinus on the Sublime*, trans. William Smith (1743), quoted in Ashfield and De Bolla, *Reader*, p. 23.

31 Cameron's suggestion that line 42 refers to the stones which were being taken from the mountain for the nearby Tremadog embankment – a land reclamation project which Shelley supported – is unconvincing (*Esdaile*, pp. 191–2). After all, as Matthews and Everest note, these 'rocks' were 'drawn by railway to the construction site' rather than 'hurled to ruin' (*Poems*, i, p. 260).

32 Matthews and Everest suggest that the lines may include a specific reference to *Queen Mab*, which Shelley 'had been writing among the mountains at Tanyralt' (*Poems*, i, p. 260).

33 Shelley's 1812 claim that *Queen Mab* exemplified his 'constitutional enthusiasm' is thus a deliberate pun (*Letters*, i, p. 342).

34 Leighton, *Shelley and the Sublime*, pp. 29–30.

35 Burke, *Reflections*, p. 100.

36 In a letter on 14 March 1812, Godwin insisted that Shelley was 'reasoning' like 'the French Revolutionists', and that his political activities in Dublin – particularly his planned Association of Philanthropists – were similarly 'preparing a scene of blood' (*Letters*, i, p. 269 n. 6).

37 See Evans, 'Shelley, Godwin, Hume', pp. 633–5.

38 Many of the *idéologue* writings upon which *Queen Mab* drew similarly insist upon the co-incidence of physical, environmental, and moral melioration. See, for example, Pierre Jean Georges Cabanis's *Rapports du Physique et du Moral de l'Homme* (1802), which Shelley ordered on the seventeenth of December 1812, and which he cites in the Notes to *Queen Mab* (*Letters*, i, p. 342; *Poems*, i, p. 374).

39 Early in 1813, Shelley wrote to unknown correspondent – probably his friend and bookseller, Thomas Hookham – asking for information about equinoctial precession (*Letters*, i, p. 349). He clearly was aware of Laplace's – essentially

correct – hypothesis that the earth oscillates on its axis, but chose to disregard it in *Queen Mab* (*Poems*, i, p. 374 and n. 1). Laplace's theory can be found in his *Exposition du Système du Monde* (1796), which Shelley cites in the Note on precession. The references to precession are suppressed, however, in the re-handled sections of *Queen Mab* that Shelley published as *The Daemon of the World* in the 1816 *Alastor* volume.

40 Mary Wollstonecraft, *An Historical and Moral View of the Origins and Progress of the French Revolution*, in *Mary Wollstonecraft: Political Writings*, ed. J. Todd (Oxford: Oxford University Press, 1993), p. 318.

41 Matthews, 'A Volcano's Voice', p. 223. Abbé Augustin Barruel, *Memoirs Illustrating the History of Jacobinism*, trans. R. Clifford, 4 vols. (London, 1797–8), iv, pp. 356–7. The subversive elements responsible for the revolution arose, Barruel affirms, 'from the bowels of the black earth', and hid their intentions like 'the black cloud ... round the summit of the volcano' until eventually 'the eruption denotes the abyss where so great a convulsion was generated' (Barruel, *Memoirs*, i, p. x; iv, 3). And of the Jacobin Club itself, Barruel writes: 'The sect, weakened, may slumber for a while, but such sleep is the calm preceding the irruption of the volcano. It no longer sends forth curling flames; but the subterraneous fire winds its course, penetrates, and preparing many vents, suddenly bursts forth and carries misery and devastation wherever its fiery torrent rolls' (Barruel, *Memoirs*, iv, pp. 356–7).

42 For the dating and context of the poem, including a discussion of Shelley's geographical vagaries, see *Esdaile*, pp. 201–3.

43 Alexander Von Humboldt, *A Personal Narrative of Travels to the Equinoctial Regions of the New Continent During the Years 1799–1804*, trans. H. M. Williams, 7 vols. (London, 1814–29). There is no direct evidence that Shelley read the original text of the *Narrative*, but Humboldt's voyages were well publicised in England before Williams' translation.

44 Cameron further notes Thomas Jefferson's earlier claim that 'the tree of liberty must be refreshed from time to time with the blood of patriots and tyrants. It is its *natural* manure' (*Esdaile*, p. 203 n. 2; emphasis added).

45 For the significance of ruin in the eighteenth- and early nineteenth-century British discourse on the sublime see Anne Janowitz, *England's Ruins* (Oxford: Basil Blackwell, 1990); and Laurence Goldstein, *Ruins and Empire: The Evolution of a Theme in Augustan and Romantic Literature* (Pittsburgh: Pittsburgh University Press, 1977).

46 Goldstein, *Ruins and Empire*, pp. 5–6.

47 Indeed, Shelley's comparison between contemporary Britain and the last days of Rome probably reflects very real fears about the possibility of a French ('barbarian') invasion.

48 Thomas Medwin, *The Life of Percy Bysshe Shelley*, 2 vols. (London, 1847), i, p. 155; Thomas Jefferson Hogg, *The Life of Percy Bysshe Shelley*, 2 vols. only (London, 1858), ii, pp. 183, 266.

49 See L. Kellner, 'Shelley's *Queen Mab* und Volney's *Les Ruines*', *Englische Studien*, 22 (1896), pp. 9–40; Kenneth Neill Cameron, 'A Major Source of

The Revolt of Islam', *PMLA*, 56 (1941), pp. 175–206; and Nigel Leask, *British Romantic Writers and the East: Anxieties of Empire* (Cambridge: Cambridge University Press, 1992), pp. 114–15.

50 For Volney's influence on Shelley's politics of legislation, see Dawson, *Unacknowledged Legislator* pp. 56–7. See also Marilyn Butler, 'Shelley and the Empire in the East', in *Shelley: Poet and Legislator of the World*, ed. Betty Bennet and Stuart Curran (London: Johns Hopkins University Press, 1996), pp. 158–68, especially pp. 158–62.

51 The phrase is Rigby's. See Brian Rigby, 'Volney's Rationalist Apocalypse', in *1789: Reading Writing Revolution; Proceedings of the Essex Conference in the Sociology of Literature, July 1981*, ed. F. Barker et al. (Colchester: University of Essex Press, 1982), pp. 22–37.

52 Shelley singles this strategy out for criticism in his 1812 *Declaration of Rights*, suggesting that 'those who believe that Heaven is, what earth has been, a monopoly in the hands of a favoured few, would do well to reconsider their opinion' (*PW*, p. 59). 'If they find that it came from their priest or their grandmother', he concludes, 'they could not do better than reject it' (*PW*, p. 59).

53 See Ralph A. Nablow, 'Shelley's "Ozymandias" and Volney's *Les Ruines*', *N&Q* (June 1989), pp. 172–3.

54 For the dating of 'To Liberty', see *Esdaile*, pp. 194–5.

55 For a discussion of the verbal echoes of 'To Liberty' in *Queen Mab* see *Esdaile*, pp. 194–5.

56 Thomas Paine, *Common Sense* (Edinburgh, 1776), p. 1.

57 David Duff, *Romance and Revolution: Shelley and the Politics of a Genre* (Cambridge: Cambridge University Press, 1994), p. 40.

58 Quoted from Todd (ed.), *Political Writings*, p. 9.

59 Quoted from Philp (ed.), *Thomas Paine*, p. 108. The borrowing is noted in *Poems*, i, p. 301 n.

60 'Poison-tree' refers as much, of course, to the common Radical image of the Upas Tree, as it does to Wollstonecraft's reactionary 'ivy' (See *Poems*, i, p. 301).

61 Quoted from Butler, *Revolution Controversy*, p. 82.

62 *Ibid.*

63 The geological concept of a ruined earth had been in common circulation since the publication of Thomas Burnet's *Sacred Theory of the Earth* (1681) onwards. Shelley would have encountered it in any one of a number of sources, including James Parkinson's *Organic Remains of a Former World* (1804–11), which he ordered in January 1812 and had received by February (*Letters*, i, pp. 214, 255).

2. CULTIVATING THE IMAGINATION, 1813–1815

1 Compare Mary's description of the Alps in her journal entry for 19 August 1814: 'their immensity staggers the imagination, and so far surpasses all conception that it requ[i]res an effort of the understanding to believe that they are indeed mountains' (*MWSJ*, p. 17).

2 For a valuable analysis of *The Assassins* see Ya-Feng Wu, '*The Assassins*: Shelley's Appropriation of History', *K-SR*, 9 (Spring 1995), pp. 51–62. See also Richard Holmes, *Shelley: the Pursuit* (London: Flamingo, 1994), pp. 243–9 and Nigel Leask, *Anxieties of Empire* (Cambridge: Cambridge University Press, 1992), pp. 76–80.

3 See Wu, '*The Assassins*', pp. 53–4 and Holmes, *Shelley*, p. 243 n. Although there is no direct evidence that Shelley read *Le Vieux de la Montagne* in 1814, the novel appears on Mary's reading list for 1816 (*MWSJ*, p. 94). However, numerous verbal and narrative echoes imply familiarity. For further discussion of these echoes see Kenneth Neill Cameron, *Shelley: the Golden Years* (Cambridge, Mass.: Harvard University Press, 1974), pp. 603–4; and Jean Overton Fuller, *Shelley: a Biography* (London: Jonathan Cope, 1968), p. 159.

4 In a note to his first mention of the sect, Gibbon observes that 'all that can be known of the Assassins of Persia and Syria, is poured from the copious, and even profuse erudition of M. Falconet, in two *Memoires* read before the Academy of Inscriptions' (*D&F*, vii, p. 12 n. 34). Mary Shelley transcribed this note in her journal entry for 8 April 1815 (*MWSJ*, p. 73).

5 Quoted from Wu, '*The Assassins*', p. 54.

6 *Ibid.*

7 *Ibid.*, pp. 53–4.

8 Quoted from Wu, '*The Assassins*', p. 54.

9 Quoting Dawson, *Unacknowledged Legislator*, p. 161.

10 Shelley contemplated and began writing 'a little work' designed to provide such a selection – the lost *Biblical Extracts* (*Letters*, i, p. 265).

11 Shelley continued to see Christ as a misrepresented radical. His 1819 *Philosophical View of Reform*, for example, praises 'the system of liberty and equality ... preached by that great Reformer', and laments its subjugation to 'domination and imposture' (*Prose*, p. 230). This opinion also informs the so-called *Essay on Christianity* (1818), the collection of fragments that David Clark mistakenly identifies as the *Biblical Extracts* (*Prose*, p. 196).

12 As noted in Chapter One, *Queen Mab* i, 264ff. explicitly identifies Necessity as the 'Spirit of Nature'.

13 Critics have proposed a number of possible sources for Shelley's conception of this valley. Newman White, for example, suggests the 'Happy Valley' of Johnson's *Rasselas* (1759), while Cameron proposes Marco Polo's *Travels* (see Wu, '*The Assassins*', pp. 54–5). Another possible source is William Wordsworth's quasi-Rousseauvian account of the 'golden age of the Alps' in his 1793 *Descriptive Sketches*, which describes a liberal community in harmony with nature rather than the negative conceptions of the valley offered by Johnson and Polo (see *Wordsworth*, i, p. 70 n. 1). There is no direct evidence that Shelley had read Wordsworth's poem by 1814 although, as I show in the next chapter, the *Sketches* clearly influenced *Mont Blanc*. I discuss *The Assassins*' engagement with Wordsworth's more recent work – and famous valley residence – below.

14 As Fuller points out, the circumstances of the stranger's arrival in Bethzatanai are taken directly from *Le Vieux de la Montagne* (Fuller, *Shelley*, p. 159).

15 Quoted from Dawson, *Unacknowledged Legislator*, p. 161.
16 See Wu, '*The Assassins*', pp. 59–62. I give a more detailed account of Shelley's engagement with *The Excursion* itself in my reading of *Alastor* below. Suffice it to say, for now, that Shelley's critics have tended to misunderstand that engagement by reading *The Excursion* as a defence of solitude when in fact the poem narrates the efforts of the Wanderer and the Pastor to *convert* the Solitary and restore his faith – in God and the political status quo.
17 Shelley's review, composed in November, was published in the December 1814 number of the *Critical Review*.
18 Timothy Clark, *Embodying Revolution: The Figure of the Poet in Shelley* (Oxford: Oxford University Press, 1989), p. 15. Clark provides a thorough account of both the context and principles of Shelley's 'science of mind' (*Embodying Revolution*, pp. 13–43).
19 The value, indeed the possibility of Stewart's application of inductive and experimental methods to the study of the mind was the subject of a heated debate between the *Edinburgh Review* and the *Quarterly Review* in the first decade of the nineteenth century, with Jeffrey in the *Edinburgh* attacking Stewart's position and Napier in the *Quarterly* defending it. For a full discussion of this debate and its roots in the developing concept of a 'science of mind' see J. C. Robertson, 'A Bacon-Facing Generation: Scottish Philosophy in the Early Nineteenth Century', *Journal of the History of Philosophy* 14/1 (1976), pp. 37–49.
20 For the political implications of the 'science of mind' in *Political Justice* see Clark, *Embodying Revolution*, pp. 18–19, 24–6.
21 There has been a great deal of critical debate about the precise dating of *On Life*, with critics suggesting composition dates anywhere between 1812 and 1818. David Lee Clark opts for a date of approximately 1812–14, believing that 'in thought [the essay] is consistent with material' from that period (*Prose*, p. 171). Internal evidence, however, establishes a date between 1818 and 1819.
22 As with the essay *On Life*, there has been a lot of debate about the dating of the fragments contained in the so-called *Speculations*. These fragments are found in MSS material dating from anywhere between 1815 and 1821. Internal evidence confirms that at least one of the fragments, the 'Catalogue of the Phenomena of Dreams, as Connecting Sleeping and Waking', was composed in 1815 (see Clark, *Embodying Revolution*, pp. 20–1). A notable exception, however, is the fragment entitled 'The Science of Metaphysics: The Mind'. This fragment is found in an Italian notebook, and was thus composed at least three years after the 'Catalogue', Shelley having moved to Italy in 1818 (see Clark, *Embodying Revolution*, pp. 14–15).
23 Clark, *Embodying Revolution*, p. 14.
24 This account of 'morals' is close to Bentham's principle of utility, which the 'Plan' then rehearses as the definition of a moral action. 'It is admitted', Shelley writes, 'that a virtuous or moral action is that action which, when considered in all its accessories and consequences, is fitted to produce the highest pleasure to the greatest number of sensitive beings' (*Prose*, p. 182). The qualificatory note

here ('it is admitted') signals that while Shelley accepts Bentham's definition of a moral action *per se*, his own 'Treatise on Morals' will reject Bentham's account of self-interest as the *basis* of moral action in favour of an ethical disinterestedness premised on the sympathetic imagination.

25 Again, Pulos' *The Deep Truth* is the seminal account of this rejection.

26 Hogg's *Life* records Shelley's early condemnation of some unspecified 'Scotch metaphysicians of inferior ability' whom he had read at Oxford (quoted from Pulos, *The Deep Truth*, p. 60). Given Shelley's contemporary enthusiasm for Hume's *Essays*, this leaves the Scottish Common Sense philosophers as the most likely object of his critique, not least since Shelley was soon to openly reject the theistic configuration of the discourse on the sublime formulated by Reid and Alison.

27 Pulos gives a useful account of the origins and development of the sceptical tradition (*The Deep Truth*, pp. 9–23).

28 Clark, *Embodying Revolution*, p. 34. Clark also cites a review of the second volume of Stewart's *Elements* in the *Quarterly* 24 (January 1815), which observes that: 'the praises which our author bestows upon this very imminent man [Bacon], appear to us, as being not so much exaggerated as injudicious' (*Embodying Revolution*, p. 34 n. 99).

29 This view was maintained despite Shelley's claim that he had 'read Berkeley, and the perusal of his arguments tended more than anything to convince me that immaterialism and other words of general usage deriving all their force from mere *predicates in non* were invented by the pride of philosophers to conceal their ignorance even from themselves' (*Letters*, i, p. 316). The phrasing here notably parallels *Queen Mab*'s critique of the theistic configuration of the discourse on the sublime: 'God is represented . . . under every *predicate in non* that the logic of ignorance could fabricate' (*Poems*, i, p. 385). Ironically, Shelley frequently expresses his own scepticism in terms of negative predicates. See, for example, Timothy Webb, 'The Unascended Heaven: Negatives in *Prometheus Unbound*', in *Shelley Revalued: Essays from the Gregynog Conference*, ed. Kelvin Everest (Leicester: Leicester University Press, 1983), pp. 37–62.

30 In a letter to Leigh Hunt from Livorno on 13 or 14 October 1819, Shelley attributes the phrase 'Mind cannot create; it can only perceive' to Charles Lloyd, a now little-known member of the Wordsworth Circle (*Letters*, ii, p. 122). Shelley says that he came across this phrase in Lloyd's marginalia to 'a copy of Berkeley', which he read in Cumberland in 1812, noting moreover that it 'struck [him] as being the assertion of a doctrine of which even then I had long been persuaded, and on which I had founded much of my persuasions regarding the imagined cause of the Universe' (*Letters*, ii, pp. 122–3).

31 Dawson, *Unacknowledged Legislator*, p. 107.

32 Earl Wasserman, *Shelley: a Critical Reading* (Baltimore: Johns Hopkins University Press, 1971), p. 113. This despite the fact that Wasserman himself reads Shelley's philosophical speculations as deeply informed by a principled scepticism.

33 Pulos, *The Deep Truth*, p. 53.

34 *Ibid.*
35 *Ibid.*
36 Dawson, *Unacknowledged Legislator*, p. 107.
37 Clark, *Embodying Revolution*, p. 40.
38 Clark discusses the concept of the 'public mind' in both Shelley's own work and contemporary literary debate (*Embodying Revolution*, pp. 40–1). This concept is most in evidence in the Prefaces to *Laon and Cythna* and *Prometheus Unbound.*
39 To borrow a phrase from Peter De Bolla, Shelley's 'science of mind' comes close, here, to recognising that 'at any specific historical . . . juncture a discursive network articulates the "real", it allows and controls the possibilities for representation' (De Bolla, *Discourse of the Sublime*, p. 7). For an extended discussion of the relationship between ideology and history in Shelley's work see Chandler, *England in 1819*, pp. 435–55. See also Terence A. Hoagwood, *Scepticism and Ideology: Shelley's Political Prose and its Philosophical Context from Bacon to Marx* (Iowa: University of Iowa Press, 1988).
40 The square brackets indicate David Clark's decision to retain Shelley's first draft of the sentence. In the MS, the words 'imaging forth' are cancelled and replaced by 'delive[ring]'. See Dawson, *Unacknowledged Legislator*, p. 236.
41 Hogg, *Life*, ii, p. 3.
42 Dawson, *Unacknowledged Legislator*, pp. 230–37.
43 Quoted from *The Complete Works of William Hazlitt*, ed. P. P. Howe, 21 vols. (London: J. M. Dent, 1930–4), xvii, 132.
44 *Ibid.*, i, p. 1
45 There are a number of possible sources for Shelley's sense of the reciprocal relationship between imagination and social progress, his conviction – in the terms of the 'Preface' to *Prometheus Unbound* – that 'poets, not otherwise than philosophers, painters, sculptors, and musicians, are, in one sense, the creators, and, in another, the creations of their age' (*Poems*, ii, pp. 474–5). Timothy Clark suggests both David Hume's essay 'On the Rise and the Progress of the Arts and Sciences' and Mme De Staël's 1800 *De la Littérature Considérée dans ses Rapports avec les Institutions Sociales* (Clark, *Embodying Revolution*, pp. 58–9). Another likely source would be Mary Wollstonecraft's *Letters Written During a Short Residence in Norway, Sweden, and Denmark* (1796), which repeatedly emphasises the links between civilisation and moral and intellectual refinement. Shelley read the *Letters* in August 1814 (*MWSJ*, pp. 22, 85).
46 Paul Mueschke and Earl Griggs, 'Wordsworth as the Prototype of the Poet in Shelley's *Alastor*', *PMLA* 49 (1934), pp. 229–45. This debate reached its apex in G. Kim Blank's 1988 study, *Wordsworth's Influence on Shelley* (London: MacMillan, 1988).
47 Blank, *Wordsworth's Influence*, p. 52.
48 In a letter to Robert Southey, Shelley described the poem as his 'first serious attempt to interest the best feelings of the human heart', and Mary too – in her Note to the poem – suggests that *Alastor* 'ought rather to be considered

didactic than narrative' (*Letters*, i, p. 462; *CPW*, p. 31). As Joseph Raben notes, Coleridge is also likely to have been an important 'prototype' of the poet-protagonist of *Alastor*. See 'Coleridge as the Prototype of the Poet in *Alastor*', *RES* 17 (1966), pp. 278–92. Raben's argument is supported by both the Coleridgean intertexts of *Alastor*, and by the strong similarities between *Alastor* and another of its companion-pieces, 'O! there are Spirits of the Air', which Mary Shelley – in her 'Notes on the Early Poems' – claims was 'addressed in idea to Coleridge' (*Poems*, i, p. 448). Significantly in terms of what happens to the *Alastor*-poet, Mary confirms that Shelley 'regarded [STC's] change of [political] opinions as rather an act of will than conviction, and believed that in his inner heart he would be haunted by what Shelley considered the better and holier aspirations of his youth' (*Poems*, i, p. 448).

49 Duffy, *Rousseau in England*, p. 94.
50 *Ibid.*
51 *Ibid.* See also D. L. Maddox, 'Shelley's *Alastor* and the Legacy of Rousseau', *SiR* 9 (Spring 1970), pp. 82–9.
52 Duffy, *Rousseau in England*, p. 94.
53 Clark, *Embodying Revolution*, pp. 25–8. This concern undoubtedly also owed much to Godwin's emphasis on Sincerity in *Political Justice*.
54 Duffy, *Rousseau in England*, p. 93.
55 *Ibid.*, p. 90. What I am suggesting, in other words, is that Shelley's knowledge of Rousseau in 1815 exemplifies what Clifford Siskin – following Carley and Kaufer – calls 'reverse vicariousness': extensive literary 'discourse over objects left unread'. Clifford Siskin, *The Work of Writing: Literature and Social Change in Britain, 1700–1830* (London: Johns Hopkins University Press, 1992), p. 216. Rousseau's public reputation – especially after Burke's attacks – constitutes a prominent instance of this phenomenon.
56 Donald Reiman, for example, suggests that 'Shelley's Preface to *Alastor* parallels very closely *The Confessions*, where Rousseau tells how he embodied his ideals in the character of Julie [from his 1762 novel *La Nouvelle Héloïse*], parallels it so closely, indeed, that one suspects Shelley may have had Rousseau in mind as one of the misled idealists of whom the Youth in *Alastor* was a type'. D. H. Reiman, *Shelley's* The Triumph of Life: *a Critical Study*, Illinois Studies in Language and Literature 55 (Urbana Ill.: University of Illinois Press, 1965), p. 62 n. 106.
57 Quoted from Todd (ed.), *Mary Wollstonecraft*, p. 150. See also Clark, *Embodying Revolution*, p. 206.
58 Quoted from Todd (ed.), *Mary Wollstonecraft*, pp. 164–5.
59 The inscription on Rousseau's tomb in the Pantheon.
60 For a detailed discussion of Shelley's engagement with Napoleon's Egyptian Expedition in *Alastor*, see my '"The Child of a Fierce Hour": Shelley and Napoleon Bonaparte', *SiR* 43 (Fall 2004), pp. 399–416.
61 This Zodiac, now on display in the Louvre, consists of a stone disc adorned with mythological figures arranged after the pattern of the constellations, a probable source for Shelley's 'marble daemons'.

62 For a complementary reading of the 'birth of time' episode in terms of Romanticism's speculation about the origins of civilisation see Nicholas Burns, 'Secrets of the Birth of Time: the Rhetoric of Cultural Origins in *Alastor* and "Mont Blanc"', *SiR* 32/3 (Autumn 1993), pp. 339–65.

63 Shelley would lecture Byron 'even to Nausea' – in the summer of 1816 – about the virtues of the 'Poet of Nature', a 'dosing' which critics have long noted behind Byron's contemporary *Childe Harold* III (See Blank, *Wordsworth's Influence*, p. 42). Indeed, the pairing is significant insofar as Byron, from 1815 onwards, would effectively replace Wordsworth as the major contemporary influence on Shelley's work. Shelley's opinion of Rousseau – and particularly of Rousseau's imaginative engagement with the natural sublime – would also undergo a radical change during the summer of 1816. Both these changes are explored in the next chapter.

64 In *Poems*, for example, Matthews and Everest equate the Narrator with Shelley (*Poems*, i, p. 464 n. 1). This equation tends to occlude the poem's 'allegorical' import. Wasserman first emphasised the need 'to define the Narrator with care' (Wasserman, *Critical Reading*, pp. 15, 17).

65 The poet-protagonist's attitude to the Arab-maiden may well also bear upon the vexed relationship between the members of Napoleon's expedition and the native Egyptians. See my 'Shelley and Napoleon Bonaparte', pp. 412–13.

66 This impression is re-enforced by the epigraph to *Alastor*, taken from St. Augustine's *Confessions*: 'I was not yet in love, and I loved to be in love, I sought what I might love, loving to be in love' (*Poems*, i, 463n.). I quote Everest and Matthews' translation of the Latin cited by Shelley: 'nondum amabam, et amare amabam, quaerebam quid amarem, amans amare'.

67 Samuel Johnson, *A Dictionary of the English Language*, facsimile of first (1755) edition, 2 vols. (New York: AMS Press, 1967). Mathew Lewis's *The Monk* also uses 'inflamed' in this sexual sense, indeed in terms which clearly anticipate the 'Preface' to *Alastor*: 'He [i.e. the Monk, Ambrosio] *inflamed his imagination* by enumerating her [Antonia's] charms'. Matthew Lewis, *The Monk*, eds. H. Anderson and E. McEvoy (New York: Oxford University Press, 1995), p. 273; emphasis added.

68 Quoted from Todd (ed.), *Mary Wollstonecraft*, pp. 164–5; emphasis added.

69 Weiskel, *The Romantic Sublime*, pp. 144–8.

70 For the connection between the death-scene in *Alastor* and *Excursion* vii, 395–400, see Blank, *Wordsworth's Influence*, p. 54. It has also been suggested that the poet-protagonist's itinerary follows Alexander the Great's Indian expedition in 327 BC (see *Poems*, i, p. 461). The poet-protagonist's physical atrophy in the wake of his 'dream' figures his moral decay. For a discussion of *Alastor's* debts to eighteenth- and early nineteenth-century speculation about the physiological aspects of sensibility see Clark, *Embodying Revolution*, pp. 47–53.

71 Indeed, she arguably also represents the dangerous, philosophical 'immaterialism' Shelley had recently condemned in the *Speculations*.

72 As I argue in chapter 5, Shelley will explore the impact of a similar desire upon Rousseau's thought in *The Triumph of Life* (1822), a poem that echoes Shelley's

exploration in *Alastor* of imaginative dysfunction by presenting Rousseau as the victim of his 'own heart alone' (*Triumph of Life*, 241).

73 Everest and Matthews quote Peacock's claim – in his *Memoirs* – to have supplied Shelley with the title of *Alastor, or the Spirit of Solitude*: 'he was at a loss for a title, and I proposed that which he adopted ... The Greek word Αλαστωρ is an evil genius [and] the poem treated the spirit of solitude as a spirit of evil' (*Poems*, i, p. 459). They are right to point out that 'this account has ... led to confusion in its suggestion that the poem's 'Spirit of Solitude' is to be understood as an external supernatural agency' (*Poems*, i, p. 460). However I disagree with their identification of the 'spirit of solitude' with the poet-protagonist's vision; again, the phrase refers rather to his solipsistic state of mind (*Poems*, i, p. 460).

74 Indeed, after his death, the Narrator laments the poet-protagonist's passing in explicitly Wordsworthian terms. Quoting the *Intimations* ode, the Narrator affirms that 'it is a woe "too deep for tears" ... when some surpassing Spirit, / whose light adorned the world around it, leaves/ those who remain behind' (*Alastor*, 713–16). Again, the poet-protagonist may have pursued a solipsistic personal vision, but at least that vision had 'knowledge and truth and virtue ... / And lofty hopes of divine liberty' as its 'theme' (*Alastor*, 158–9).

75 In a letter to Hogg on 8 May 1811, Shelley had informed his friend that he 'cannot endure the horror of the evil which comes to *self* in solitude' (*Letters*, i, p. 77; original emphasis). Shelley goes on to say that, for all his 'bo[a]sted hatred of self', he is 'inconsistent' in his attitude to 'solitude': 'this moment thinking I could so far overcome Nature's law as to exist in complete seclusion, the next shrinking from a moment of solitude, starting from my own company as it were that of a fiend' (*Letters*, i, pp. 77–8). The context for Shelley's 'bo[a]sted hatred of self' is the emphasis on disinterestedness in his ethics: 'hatred of self', in short, is the essence of virtue. Consequently, the impulse to 'exist in complete seclusion' is aligned with self-love, an impulse tellingly identified as a culpable transgression of 'Nature's law'. Two of the Esdaile poems – 'Dark Spirit of the Desart Rude' (1812) and 'Death-spurning rocks!' (1811) – identify a biographical context for 'the horror of the evil which comes to *self* in solitude': the depression Shelley experienced during his first stay in North Wales. For a brief but informative discussion of these poems which have long been recognised as important precursors to *Alastor* – and which explicitly relate the 'evil' of 'solitude' to the landscape of the natural sublime – see *Esdaile*, pp. 207–8, 211–15.

76 Shelley's comparison, in *Alastor*, of Wordsworth and Rousseau was soon echoed by William Hazlitt's essay 'On the Character of Rousseau'. 'The writer who most nearly resembles [Rousseau] in our times', Hazlitt suggests, 'is the author of the *Lyrical Ballads*. We see no other difference between them, than that one wrote in prose and the other in poetry' (*The Complete Works of William Hazlitt*, v, p. 88). Hazlitt's essay was printed in Hunt's *Examiner* on 14 April 1816, barely one month after the publication of *Alastor*. It is no accident that he compares Rousseau to 'the author of the *Lyrical Ballads*' rather than *The Excursion*.

3. MONT BLANC AND THE ALPS, 1816

1 For the biographical context of Shelley's second trip to Switzerland see Holmes, *Shelley*, pp. 319–33.

2 Although the title of the *Six Weeks' Tour* refers to the Shelley party's first trip to mainland Europe in 1814, the published *Tour* also contains four 'Letters, written during a Residence of Three Months in the Environs of Geneva, in the Summer of 1816' (*H6WT*, pp. 85–172). The first two of these 'Letters' are largely Mary's work. The remaining two are edited excerpts from Shelley's long journal-letters to Thomas Love Peacock. These letters – describing Shelley's travels in the Alps – were composed between 12 July and 2 August 1816. For an excellent analysis of Mary's contribution to the *Tour* per se, see Jeanne Moskal's annotations to the text printed in *The Novels and Selected Works of Mary Shelley*, ed. Nora Crook et al., 8 vols. (London: Pickering, 1996), viii, pp. 13–47.

3 Endo, '*Mont Blanc*, Silence, and the Sublime', p. 283.

4 Unless otherwise stated, all quotations from *Mont Blanc* are from the B-text: the version published in the 1817 *History of a Six Weeks' Tour*. The alternative A-text, referred to below, is a fair copy of *Mont Blanc* transcribed by Shelley into the Scrope Davies Notebook, left with Byron in Geneva, and lost until 1976. The A-text MS is reproduced in *MYRS* viii, pp. 143–57, and printed in *Poems*, i, pp. 538–41.

5 Kapstein, 'Shelley's *Mont Blanc*', p. 1046. Kapstein's claim that 'Shelley composed "Mont Blanc" upon the occasion of his first visit to the Swiss Alps' is patently mistaken (p. 1046).

6 *Ibid.* See also Hugo Donnelly, 'Beyond Rational Discourse: The "Mysterious Tongue" of "Mont Blanc"', *SiR* 29/4 (1990), p. 573.

7 Kapstein, 'Shelley's *Mont Blanc*', p. 1058.

8 Wassermann, *Critical Reading*, p. 238.

9 Leighton, *Shelley and the Sublime*, p. 64.

10 *Ibid.*, p. 71.

11 Endo, '*Mont Blanc*, Silence, and the Sublime', p. 296.

12 Kapstein, 'Shelley's *Mont Blanc*', p. 1046.

13 *Ibid.*

14 Mary's journal confirms that a combination of poverty and severity of climate meant that 'in the winter many of the men go to Paris and hire themselves as porters at hotels etc.' (*MWSJ*, p. 120).

15 James Buzard, *The Beaten Track: European Tourism, Literature, and the Ways to Culture, 1800–1918* (Oxford: Clarendon Press, 1993), pp. 1–2, 18–80 *passim*.

16 The passage evidently recalls the local tradition – noted, for example, in Thomas Martyn's *Sketch of a Tour through Switzerland* – by which the 'magnificent vault of ice, at the foot of the glacier on which you look down from the Montanvert [i.e. the Mer de Glace] . . . has been, not unaptly, termed, *the Temple of the God of Frost*'. Thomas Martyn, *Sketches of a Tour through Switzerland* (London, 1788), pp. 89–90; emphasis added. As I suggest later, this

'magnificent vault' probably also influenced Shelley's conception of 'the still cave of the witch of the Poesy' in *Mont Blanc* itself.

17 George Louis Leclerc, Comte de Buffon's hypothesis about glacial augmentation is set out in the *Théorie de la Terre*, part of the first volume of his *Histoire Naturelle Générale et Particulière* (1749–67). Mary's reading lists confirm that she read the *Théorie* in 1817, although there is no mention of Shelley's having read it (*MWSJ*, p. 100).

18 Quoted in Leask, 'Mysterious Voice', p. 195.

19 For a full discussion of these inscriptions and their context see Gavin De Beer, 'An Atheist in the Alps', *K-SMB* ix (1958), pp. 1–15. See also chapter 5, pp. 207–8.

20 Timothy Webb, *Shelley: A Voice not Understood* (Manchester: Manchester University Press, 1977), p. 141.

21 Shelley clearly had some knowledge of *Julie* before 1815 – as is more likely given the novel's unprecedented popularity. In a letter to Hogg, written around 16 November 1811, in the wake of his attempt to seduce Harriet, Shelley assures his friend that 'he is not jealous' (*Letters*, i, p. 184). He goes on to affirm that he 'perfectly understand[s] the beauty of Rousseau's sentiment; yet Harriet is *not* an Heloisa, even were I a St Preux' (*Letters*, i, p. 184). Shelley is referring here to St Preux's selfless love for Julie, which Hogg must have quoted by way of admonitory example. However, the phraseology of the letter suggests a passing acquaintance with the novel's characters and circumstances rather than actual evidence of reading, and may well be another instance of 'reverse vicariousness' – indeed, Shelley may simply have been responding to an instance cited by Hogg.

22 We remember, too, Donald Reiman's suggestion – noted in the previous chapter – that *Alastor*'s 'Preface' was informed, at least in part, by Rousseau's account of Julie in the *Confessions*: *Julie* itself evidently differed from Shelley's expectations.

23 For an informative discussion of this reputation see James Warner, 'Eighteenth-Century English Reactions to the *Nouvelle Héloïse*', *PMLA* 52 (1937), pp. 803–19.

24 For an informative account of British Romanticism's engagement with this commonplace, see Greg Dart, *Rousseau, Robespierre and English Romanticism* (Cambridge: Cambridge University Press, 1999).

25 Quoted from Seamus Deane, *The French Revolution and Enlightenment in England* (London: Harvard University Press, 1988), p. 132.

26 *Ibid.*

27 In contrast to this conservative account of St Preux, Mary's 'Note to the Poems of 1816' suggests that 'there was something in the character of St Preux, in his abnegation of self, and in the worship he paid to Love, that coincided with Shelley's own disposition' (*CPW*, p. 536).

28 In the twenty-sixth letter of the first book of *Julie*, St Preux, unable to see Julie, stays in the mountains at Meillerie across the lake from her home in Clarens. Later in the novel, in the seventeenth letter of the fourth book, St Preux returns

to Meillerie with Julie, shows her his previous retreat, and attempts to describe the feelings he experienced there. This episode was considered one of the most moving parts of the novel, and both Shelley and Byron refer to it directly, the former in a letter to Peacock, the latter in the 'Notes' to *Childe Harold* III (*Letters*, i, p. 485; *Byron*, p. 143).

29 In fact, Shelley's position typifies British Radicalism's opinion of Napoleon. For an informative account of the varied British responses to Napoleon, see Simon Bainbridge, *Napoleon and English Romanticism* (Cambridge: Cambridge University Press, 1995).

30 Again, this is almost certainly also the passage that prompted Marie-Louise's stay in Meillerie, in 'remembrance of St Preux'.

31 Byron quotes the original French: 'allez à Vévay – visitez le pays, examinez les sites, promenez-vous sur le lac, et dites si la Nature n'a pas fait ce beau pays pour une Julie, pour une Claire, et pour un St Preux' (*Byron*, p. 144).

32 Leighton, *Shelley and the Sublime*, p. 51.

33 *The Complete Poetical Works of Percy Bysshe Shelley*, ed. Neville Rogers, 2 vols. to date (Oxford: Clarendon Press, 1972–), ii, p. 344.

34 James Notopoulos, *The Platonism of Shelley* (Durham, NC: Duke University Press, 1949), pp. 196–98. Notopoulos cites Monboddo's reference to 'Plato's intellectual Beauty' in *The Origin and Progress of Language* (1773–6) – which Shelley ordered in 1812 – as evidence that the phrase 'had become a commonplace Platonic formula' in the eighteenth century (Notopoulos, *Platonism*, p. 197; *Letters*, i, p. 344). He further proposes Spenser's *Hymn of Heavenly Beautie* (1596) as an important precursor of Shelley's text (Notopoulos, *Platonism*, p. 196).

35 Hogg's *Life* confirms that Shelley was already familiar with F. D. Pernay's French translation of *Agathon*, in which the phrase 'beauté intellectuelle' occurs on three separate occasions (Hogg, *Life*, ii, pp. 144–5). In his *Discourse on the Manners of the Ancient Greeks Relative to the Subject of Love* (1818), Shelley notes that 'Wieland, in his delightful novels, makes indeed a very tolerable Pagan, but cherishes too many political prejudices and refrains from diminishing the interest of his romances by painting sentiments in which no European of modern times can possibly sympathise' (*Prose*, p. 219).

36 Shelley's translation of the *Symposium* – considered sensitive by his family on account of its discussion of homosexuality – was not published in full until 1931, and then only in a private, limited edition of 100 copies. This text was re-published by Notopoulos in 1949, the edition from which I have quoted here (Notopoulos, p. 449).

37 Shelley's likely debt to Godwin was first pointed out by Burton Pollin in 'Godwin's *Memoirs* as a Source of Shelley's Phrase "Intellectual Beauty"', *K-SJ* 23–5 (1974–6), pp. 14–20.

38 Pollin does not note this additional occurrence.

39 Quoted from Todd (ed.), *Mary Wollstonecraft*, p. 115.

40 Amelia Opie, *Adeline Mowbray* (Woodstock Books: New York, 1995), p. 119.

41 Quoted in Pollin, 'Godwin's *Memoirs*', p. 16; emphasis added.

42 Cameron, *The Golden Years*, p. 238.

43 *Ibid.*, p. 242.
44 In this sense, Shelley's use of the term 'intellectual beauty' in his translation of the *Symposium* is consistent with his earlier usage in the *Hymn*. By effectively introducing a distinction between 'intellectual beauty' and 'universal beauty' into the *Symposium*, Shelley is distinguishing between an objective principle and the subjective apprehension of that principle by the mind.
45 Shelley almost certainly derived the phrase 'truth / of Nature' from Francis Bacon's recasting of Democritus' famous, sceptical epigram as 'the *truth of nature* lieth hid in certain deep mines and cave'. Quoted from William O. Scott, 'Shelley's admiration for Bacon', *PMLA* 73/1, (1958), p. 229; emphasis added. As we shall see in the next chapter, Bacon's phrase also influenced *Prometheus Unbound*'s account of Demogorgon.
46 Webb, *A Voice not Understood*, p. 39.
47 Leighton, *Shelley and the Sublime*, p. 57.
48 For an early account of these intertexts, see Harold Bloom, *The Anxiety of Influence* (Oxford: Oxford University Press, 1973), pp. 108ff. See also Blank, *Wordsworth's Influence*, pp. 167–71; Richard Cronin, *Shelley's Poetic Thoughts* (London: Macmillan, 1981), pp. 224–5; and Judith Chernaik, *The Lyrics of Shelley* (Cleveland: Case Western Reserve UP, 1972), pp. 33–4.
49 Leighton, *Shelley and the Sublime*, p. 52.
50 *Ibid.*
51 *Ibid.* Mary records that Shelley read Lucretius' *De Rerum Nature* in July 1816, shortly after the composition of *Mont Blanc* (*MWSJ*, p. 121). In a July 1817 letter to Hogg, Shelley confirmed that he was 'well acquainted' with the book (*Letters*, i, p. 585). For a discussion Lucretius' impact on Shelley's thought see Paul Turner, 'Shelley and Lucretius', *RES* ns 10 (1959), pp. 269–82.
52 Richard Isomaki notes that the word 'train' recalls the terminology of eighteenth-century associationist psychology, and – significantly – that '"train" suggests the experience of necessity in the succession of ideas or impressions. See 'Interpretation and Value in "Mont Blanc" and "Hymn to Intellectual Beauty"', *Studies in Romanticism*, 30/1 (Spring 1991), pp. 67–8. Isomaki's argument supports my claim that the experience of 'intellectual beauty' is equivalent to the imaginative apprehension of Nature's law. And although Isomaki cites Hume and Drummond as the likely sources for Shelley's awareness of associationism, a more relevant source in this context would of course be Alison's *Essays* (a fourth edition of which appeared in 1815).
53 The injunction on the individual to 'fear himself' is thus certainly not, as critics like Elizabeth Nitchie have suggested on the basis of the medieval meanings of 'fear', an injunction to 'honour' or 'revere' himself (*Poems*, i, p. 531). Shelley may, however, by echoing Wordsworth's closing apostrophe – in his 1798 'Lines Left Upon a Seat in a Yew-Tree … ' – to the individual 'who, in the silent hour of inward thought, / Can still suspect, and still revere himself, / *In lowliness of heart*' (58–60; emphasis added).
54 Shelley's *oeuvre* consistently expresses this 'hope', the best-known instance being the end of the *Ode to the West Wind* (1819). Drawing again on

Coleridge's Aeolian Harp image, Shelley asks the wind – the visible manifestation of the power (Necessity) immanent in nature – to 'make' him its
'lyre' (*West Wind*, 57). The passage reveals Shelley's ongoing conviction that
it is the task of the 'cultivated imagination' to make the revolutionary 'truth /
Of nature' known to the world. The poet is, literally, the instrument of
Necessity.

55 Edward Gibbon, *Memoirs of My Life*, ed. Betty Radice (Penguin: Harmondsworth,
   1990), p. 169.

56 Mary Shelley's journal notes of the same region that 'Napoleon was no great
   favourite here, and they are very indifferent about any government' (*MWSJ*,
   p. 120).

57 Kapstein, 'Shelley's *Mont Blanc*', p. 1046. Matthews and Everest similarly cite
   this passage from the *Tour*'s 'Preface' as an apology for 'a certain intellectual
   irresolution' in *Mont Blanc* (*Poems*, i, p. 537).

58 Harold Bloom, *Shelley's Mythmaking* (Ithaca: Cornell University Press, 1969),
   pp. 11–35.

59 See Charles Robinson, 'The Shelley Circle and Coleridge's *The Friend*', *ELN* 8
   (June 1971), pp. 272–4.

60 The subtitle of the A Text of *Mont Blanc* is 'Scene – Pont Pellisier in the Vale
   of Servox'. This was changed in the B Text – the version published in the *Six
   Weeks' Tour* in 1817 – to 'Lines Written in the Vale of Chamouni'. See *Poems*, i,
   p. 533. A more mundane explanation for the change is the fact that the summit
   of Mont Blanc is not visible from Pont Pellisier.

61 For a full discussion of the relationship between the two texts, see Elinor
   Shaffer, 'Coleridge's Swiss Voice: Frederike Brun and the Vale of Chamouni'
   in *Essays in Memory of Michael Parkinson*, Norwich Papers IV, ed. Christopher
   Smith (Norwich: School of Modern Languages and European Cultures, UEA,
   1996), pp. 67–76.

62 Shelley's inscriptions in the inn-registers around Chamonix can be read as a
   specific response to Coleridge's assertion here – although again this note did
   not accompany the version of the *Hymn* published in *The Friend* (which
   Shelley is presumed to have read).

63 Clark, *Revolution*, p. 112; Isomaki, 'Interpretation and Value', p. 61.

64 Leighton, *Shelley and the Sublime*, p. 63.

65 The entry in Mary's journal for 21 July 1816 – written in Shelley's hand –
   confirms that this 'aethereal waterfall' was the Nant d'Arpenas near Maglans,
   which the Shelley party passed on their way to Chamonix. 'It fell in two
   parts', Shelley notes, 'and struck first on an enormous rock resembling
   precisely … some … colossal Egyptian statue of a female deity. It struck
   the head of the visionary Image and gracefully dividing then fell in folds of
   foam, more like cloud than water, imitating a viel [sic.] of the most exquisite
   woof' (*MWSJ*, p. 113). The 'female deity' is almost certainly Isis, the veiled
   goddess of nature – a resonance encapsulated in Shelley's account of the
   waterfall as a manifestation of the immanent 'Power' of Nature. The use of
   Isis imagery in the context of the natural sublime recalls Kant's similar,

parenthetical reference to the goddess in the third *Critique*, although there is no evidence that Shelley was familiar with the German's work.

66 For an interesting discussion which relates Shelley's word play in this section of *Mont Blanc* to a reading of the poem's epistemological concerns see Ferguson, 'What the Mountain Said', p. 206.

67 Shelley had read Bacon's *Novum Organon*, in which the theory of the idols is set out, in 1815 (*MWSJ*, p. 92). Leask, 'Mysterious Voice', pp. 189ff outlines the extent to which the cave and mountain imagery of this passage draws on conflicting, materialist and idealist, geological theories about earth-formation.

68 Marc Théodore Bourrit, *A Relation of a Journey to the Glaciers in the Dutchy of Savoy*, C. and F. Davy transl. (Norwich, 1775), pp. 129–30; emphasis added. There is no direct evidence that Shelley read Bourrit's *Relation*.

69 *Mont Blanc*'s 'still cave' should also be compared with the cave in Shelley's 1820 *Witch of Atlas* (xiv–xxviii), and with the cave to which Prometheus and Asia retire in *Prometheus Unbound* III iii.

70 A great deal of critical attention has been paid to the textual variant on line 79, which in the A-Text reads 'In such faith' (*Poems*, i, p. 540). See, for example, J. Kinnaird, '"But for such faith": A Controversial Phrase in Shelley's *Mont Blanc*', *N&Q* 15 (1968), pp. 332–4; J. Rees, '"But for such faith": A Shelley Crux', *RES* 15 (1964), pp. 185–6. Most critics agree that the A-Text version is the intended sense of the passage, since even the most torturous explanations have had little success in justifying the B-Text reading as it stands.

71 Bloom suggests that the 'doubt' the wilderness teaches is 'doubt' about the 'orthodox view of nature', i.e. that the phrase refers to geological evidence against the Mosaic chronology (*Shelley's Mythmaking*, p. 32). This is certainly a tempting reading, given *Mont Blanc*'s iconoclastic agenda. However, it is difficult to square Bloom's suggestion with the fact that the 'mild faith' Shelley lauds as the agent of man's reconciliation with nature stands in clear opposition to this – from Bloom's point of view – secularising 'doubt'. In fact, the passage can only be adequately explained within the context of Shelley's revision of the discourse on the sublime.

72 While I have no wish to add gratuitously to the already extensive body of criticism dealing with this key passage in *Mont Blanc*, it is worth recognising that commentators may have been overhasty in assuming that the 'mysterious tongue' of the 'wilderness' (with its Biblical overtones) is analogous with the 'voice' of the 'great mountain'. It is possible, after all, that Shelley meant to identify two possible responses to the 'wilderness' – (sceptical) 'doubt' or (biblical) 'faith' – only one of which, 'doubt', is validated by the 'wise' interpretation of the mountain.

73 *Ibid.*, pp. 197, 201. There is no direct evidence that Shelley read either Carbonnières or Williams, although again numerous verbal echoes imply familiarity. For a discussion of these echoes see Leask, 'Mysterious Voice', pp. 201–2. The 'Observations' originally formed part of the extensive editorial commentary in Carbonnières' 1788 French translation of William Coxe's 1779 *Sketches ... of Swisserland*; an English translation was included, along with

other pertinent extracts from Carbonniéres' commentary, in subsequent editions of Coxe, re-titled *Travels in Switzerland* (a copy of which was used by Wordsworth and Jones during their 1790 walking-tour of the Alps).

74 Ramond de Carbonnières, 'Observations on the Glaciers', in Helen Maria Williams, *A Tour in Switzerland*, 2 vols. (London, 1798), ii, p. 239.

75 *Ibid.*, p. 240.

76 Interestingly, *The Triumph*'s Narrator either fails to recognise or eschews this responsibility: 'the world and its mysterious doom / Is not so much more glorious than it was / That I desire to worship those who drew / New figures on its false and fragile glass' (*Triumph of Life*, 244–7).

77 The Shelleys' account of the post-war France through which they passed while *en route* to Switzerland in 1814 closely anticipates *Mont Blanc*'s account of the destruction wrought by the glaciers.

78 As Everest and Matthews note, these lines seem to be an 'unmistakable echo of Coleridge's *Khubla Khan*', which Shelley might have seen in MS, or learned about from Byron (*Poems*, i, p. 548 n. 122).

4. WRITING THE REVOLUTION: *LAON AND CYTHNA*, 1817

1 The account of the visit is in Shelley's hand.

2 Indeed, as the editors of Mary's journal point out, the Shelley party seems to have laboured under at least one misconception about the role of Versailles in the revolution. Shelley's complaint that they 'could not even find out in which chambre the rioters of 10 August found the King' suggests that he was (surprisingly) unaware that the king and queen were arrested at the Tuilleries – and not at Versailles – on 10 August 1792 (*MWSJ*, p. 133 and n. 2).

3 Although not the 'scene' of the royal family's arrest on 10 August 1792, Versailles did indeed 'witness some of the most interesting events' of the Revolution. On 20 June 1789, the members of the Third Estate swore the historic Tennis Court Oath at Versailles, effectively inaugurating the Revolution proper. On 5 and 6 October 1789, a crowd of Parisians, having heard that a lavish banquet was taking place, marched to Versailles in protest, an event famously condemned by Burke in his *Reflections*, and subsequently defended by Wollstonecraft in her *Vindication of the Rights of Man*. In the wake of these protests, Lafayette removed the royal family to the Tuilleries palace in central Paris on 6 October. Fontainebleu, too, played its part in the Revolution. The palace was ransacked early on, but later restored by Napoleon. Pope Pius VII was imprisoned there for two years during the Napoleonic wars, and it was at Fontainebleu, in 1814, that Napoleon himself abdicated.

4 Charles Robinson first described these attempts in his influential *Shelley and Byron: the Snake and Eagle Wreathed in Fight* (London: Johns Hopkins University Press, 1976). Robinson portrays the personal and creative relationship between the two poets as a struggle between Shelley's political optimism and Byron's worldy cynicism, reading much of Shelley's work from 1816

onwards as in some degree a corrective response to Byron. Robinson's study is valuable to the extent that it points up the creative significance of the relationship, especially for Shelley. However, his straightforward optimist–pessimist dualism is prone to elide some of the nuances of the relationship. For example, as will be made clear in the next chapter, Robinson does not recognise the extent to which Shelley's political thought actually *shares* – however uncomfortably – Byron's pessimism. For a more recent study of the relationship between the two poets see William D. Brewer, *The Shelley-Byron Conversation* (Tampa: University of Florida Press, 1994). Brewer challenges the 'traditional' view of Shelley and Byron 'as two irreconcilable opposites, separated by both temperament and philosophy', and argues rather that 'they have much in common', that their relationship 'resembles a conversation rather than a debate' (p. ix).

5 Jones suggests that Shelley's quotation "the truth of things" is probably a misquotation of line 49 of Wordsworth's *Tintern Abbey* (*Letters*, i, p. 507 n. 5). While this is doubtless the case, both the expression and the context here clearly also recall Shelley's emphasis – in the *Hymn to Intellectual Beauty* – on the 'truth / Of nature' that is accessible to the cultivated imagination.

6 *Laon and Cythna* was composed between April and September 1817. It was published in November of the same year, only to be immediately recalled by the publisher, Charles Ollier, who feared that its radical politics, condemnation of religion, and apparent vindication of incest would render him liable to prosecution. It was re-issued on 10 January 1818, with appropriate changes to the 'Preface' and body-text, as *The Revolt of Islam*. Mary's 1839 note to *The Revolt* confirms that even this revised text was so 'bold in its opinions and uncompromising in their expression' that it met with 'many censurers ... even among those whose opinions were similar to [Shelley's] own' (*CPW*, p. 157). These 'censurers' included William Godwin (see *Letters*, i, p. 577). All quotations here are from the original text of *Laon and Cythna*, as given in *Poems*, ii.

7 Lloyd Abbey, *Destroyer and Preserver: Shelley's Poetic Skepticism* (Lincoln, Nebraska: University of Nebraska Press, 1975), p. 5. From my general agreement with this statement I ought to except a number of constructive and informative readings: Cameron's essay, 'A Major Source'; David Duff's account in *Romance and Revolution*, pp. 154–217; Richard Haswell's 'Shelley's *The Revolt of Islam*: "The Connexion of its Parts"', *K-SJ* 25 (1976), pp. 88–102; and Donna Richardson's "'The Dark Idolatry of Self': the Dialectic of Imagination in Shelley's *Revolt of Islam*', *K-SJ* 40 (1991), pp. 73–98. Nigel Leask's chapter on Shelley in *Anxieties of Empire*, pp. 68–169 provides a valuable account of *Laon and Cythna*'s orientalist dimensions.

8 Haswell provides a useful summary of early critical debate about *Laon and Cythna*, and tackles accusations of structural incoherence. Haswell also suggests that the terminology Shelley uses to describe the structural features of his poem, including the phrase 'connexion of its parts', is derived from Coleridge's *Biographia Literaria*, published in July 1817 (Haswell, 'Shelley's *The Revolt of Islam*', pp. 82, 100–1). This suggestion is convincing despite the fact, acknowledged by Haswell, that there is no direct evidence that Shelley read the

Biographia before 8 December 1817, that is, some two months after the completion of *Laon and Cythna* (*MWSJ*, p. 186).

9 Bloom, *Shelley's Mythmaking*, p. 8

10 Richardson, 'Dark Idolatry of Self', p. 74.

11 Shelley makes this claim in an October 1817 letter to an unidentified, prospective publisher (*Letters*, i, p. 563; original emphasis). Jones suggests that the publisher may have been Longman and Co., 'who had recently published Moore's *Lalla Rookh*' (*Letters*, i, p. 564 n. 1).

12 Gerald McNiece, *Shelley and the Revolutionary Idea* (Cambridge, Mass.: Harvard University Press, 1969), p. 194. *Laon and Cythna*'s revolution is at least 'ideal' to the extent that the conduct of the revolutionaries themselves is largely non-violent.

13 Although Shelley's interest in writing about the French Revolution clearly predates this period. In a January 1812 letter to Elizabeth Hitchener, for example, he claims to have written two hundred pages of 'a tale in which I design to exhibit the cause of the failure of the French Revolution, and the state of morals and opinions in France during the latter years of its monarchy' (*Letters*, i, p. 218). No trace of this 'tale' – entitled *Hubert Cauvin* – has been found.

14 While *Laon and Cythna* certainly does look back to events in France it clearly also looks forward, with its Byzantine setting, Greek protagonists, and oriental despot, to a future Greek 'revolt' against Turkish rule. In his already-cited October 1817 letter to a publisher, Shelley further suggests that the poem is 'a tale illustrative of such a Revolution as might be supposed to take place in an European Nation' (*Letters*, i, p. 563).

15 Donovan suggests that 'Chateaubriand's practical definition of the aesthetic term *beau idéal*, or ideal beauty … as "l'art de choisir et cacher" is apt' for understanding Shelley's claim (*Poems*, ii, p. 21). This suggestion certainly accords with my own reading of the phrase, although it does not uncover the vital link to Shelley's concept of 'intellectual beauty'.

16 Mary's *Journal* confirms that Shelley read a number of key works about the French Revolution during the composition of *Laon and Cythna*. These included C. J. de Lacretelle and J. P. R. St. Etienne's co-authored *Précis Historique de la Révolution Française* (1801–6), Lullin de Châteauvieux's fictional autobiography of Bonaparte, the so-called *Manuscrit Venue de St. Hélène d'une Manière Inconnue* (1817), and Lady Morgan's 1817 *France* (*MWSJ*, pp. 100, 101, 172, 187). Donovan confirms that *Laon and Cythna*'s 'revolution is intended to stand as an image of the French Revolution', but suggests that Shelley 'does not attempt any close approximation of historical events' (*Poems*, ii, p. 21).

17 The result of the experiment was presumably to be judged by *Laon and Cythna*'s reception.

18 Shelley's claim that *Laon and Cythna* is addressed to 'the enlightened and refined' clearly anticipates his already-quoted claim, in the 'Preface' to

Prometheus Unbound, that his writing has 'hitherto' been aimed at 'the more select classes of poetical readers'.

19 Indeed, for most of his career, Shelley's writing was more or less consistently addressed to this élite section of the 'one' or 'public mind'. It was only after the Peterloo Massacre in 1819, and the apparent failure of his writing to reach its intended audience, that Shelley began to address a wider reading public, witness his projected *Popular Songs* project in early 1820 (see *Letters*, ii, p. 131). For a full discussion of Shelley's relationship with his reading public, see Stephen C. Behrendt, *Shelley and his Audiences* (Lincoln, Nebraska: University of Nebraska Press, 1989). See also Kim Wheatley, *Shelley and his Readers* (Columbia: University of Missouri Press, 1999).

20 I discuss Shelley's attitude to Malthus's reactionary spin on the Necessary laws of nature – in his *Essay on the Principle of Population* (1798) – in the next chapter.

21 *OED* cites the surviving fragment of a May 1820 letter from Shelley to Thomas Medwin as the first recorded use of the phrase 'spirit of the age', later popularised by Hazlitt's eponymous collection of essays (*Letters*, ii, p. 189).

22 Indeed, *Laon and Cythna*'s 'Preface' probably has Byron's published work very much in mind when it identifies, in contemporary literature, 'the solace of a disappointment that unconsciously finds relief only in the wilful exaggeration of its own despair' (*Poems*, ii, p. 37). Shelley's later critique of *Childe Harold* IV, discussed in the next chapter, is certainly couched in these terms.

23 As Donovan notes, Shelley's explanation here echoes Paine's account of the early days of the French Revolution in *The Rights of Man* (*Poems*, ii, p. 36 n.). In fact, Shelley is re-stating a fairly standard position in Radical thought about the Terror and its aftermath.

24 Shelley's long account, in the 'Preface', of the 'education peculiarly fitted for a Poet', establishes his personal qualification for promoting this reform of the 'one mind'.

25 Once again, quotations are from the text of *Laon and Cythna* published in *Poems*, ii, which continues the line numbering from the 'Dedication' into the body-text proper.

26 For a thorough overview of these sources, see *Poems*, ii, p. 64 n.

27 Cameron, 'Major Source', pp. 202–3 and n. 131. Cameron's essay significantly identifies Volney's *Ruins* as 'a major source' for Shelley's poem, and I will return to this influence later.

28 *Ibid.*, pp. 202–3. Cameron also points valuably to *Prometheus Unbound* (III, i, 70–4), 'where Jupiter declares that he and Demogorgon will "*sink in the wide waves of ruin,* / Even as *a vulture and a snake outspent*' ('Major Source', p. 203 n. 128; Cameron's emphasis). Again, for a thorough overview of the various critical interpretations of the snake-eagle conflict see *Poems*, ii, p. 64 n.

29 Richardson, 'Dark Idolatry of Self', p. 74.

30 *Ibid.*, p. 75. For a thorough account of the similarities between Shelley's portrayal of the Morning Star and his other major descriptions of Necessity see *Ibid.*, p. 78.

31 *Ibid.*

32 From *Alastor* onward, Shelley's writing comes increasingly to the conclusion that the failure of the French Revolution is attributable to the failure of the imagination, be that of the Revolution's supposed architects (Rousseau, Voltaire), or of its defender-turned-betrayer (Napoleon). The most sophisticated statement of this conclusion, I will argue, is *The Triumph of Life.*

33 Laon's figure is another clear instance of the kind of politicised volcanic imagery that Shelley derived from texts like Barruel's *Memoirs.* Matthews identifies a passage from Humboldt's *Personal Narrative* – which describes the melting of the snows prior to an eruption of Cotopaxi – as the likely source for the image here (Matthews, 'A Volcano's Voice', pp. 199–200). A similar image occurs in *Prometheus Unbound* II, iii, 34–42, where Asia compares 'the sun-awakened avalanche' to the ideological enlightenment of the 'public mind', to the moment when 'thought by thought is piled, till some great truth / Is loosened, and the nations echo round, / Shaken to their roots, as do the mountains now'. I discuss this passage – which is highly significant in terms of Shelley's engagement with the discourse on the natural sublime – in the next chapter.

34 Mary Shelley's 'Note on the Revolt of Islam' identifies the Hermit as 'a memorial of a friend of [Shelley's] youth': Dr James Lind, whom Shelley knew at Eton (*CPW*, p. 157). For an overview of additional, literary sources for the Hermit episode see *Poems*, ii, p. 120 n.

35 As Donovan notes, the story of the condemned slave – later used by Byron in *Childe Harold* IV – is taken from Plutarch's *Life of Nicias* (*Poems*, ii, p. 107 n.) Shelley read Plutarch's *Lives* in Geneva in 1816, and again in May 1817 (*MWSJ*, p. 126; *Letters*, i, p. 541).

36 This 'subtler language' initially takes the (rationalist) form of mathematical or geometrical figures ('clear, elemental shapes'), appropriately enough, as Donovan notes, given 'the Pythagorean conviction that the basis of reality is mathematical' (*Laon and Cythna*, 3111; *Poems*, ii, p. 192 n. 3104). Cythna soon moves from the rationalist to the imaginative mode, however, a transition symbolised in her response to the 'sweet melodies' that she hears in the cave where the Tyrant has imprisoned her (*Laon and Cythna*, 3114).

37 I disagree, therefore, with Donovan's suggestion that these lines are 'underpinned by the idealist conception of a universal mind in which all individual minds participate and which is subject to neither time nor space' (*Poems*, ii, p. 191 n. 3104).

38 Shelley would have known the details of these *fêtes* from a variety of sources. For a thorough account of their imagery see Mona Ozouf, *Festivals and the French Revolution*, A. Sheridan trans. (Cambridge, Mass.: Harvard University Press, 1988).

39 Most critics agree that the sculptures that surround Cythna on the Altar represent Equality, Love, and Wisdom (see *Poems*, ii, p. 152 n. 2156). The echo of the French Revolutionary principles of Liberté, Égalité, et Fraternité is clear, but the primacy of Equality (rather than Liberty) in Cythna's speech derives from *The Ruins* (*Poems*, ii, p. 155 n. 2212).

40 To this extent, the members of both *Laon and Cythna*'s 'Senate' / 'Temple' and *Adonais*'s 'abode where the eternal are', might be said to represent the direct antithesis of those chained to the Chariot of Life in the *Triumph of Life*.

41 The sublime architecture of the 'Senate' / 'Temple' – a 'glorious', 'vast hall' of 'ten thousand columns' and 'labyrinthine aisles' – is appropriately described as 'immortal', in pointed Volneyan contrast with the 'unenduring' monumentality of the Tyrant (*Laon and Cythna*, 586, 595, 597, 4721).

42 I introduce this important caveat to recall – as this study repeatedly emphasises – that Shelley's own political thought, for all its ostensibly Godwinian credentials, certainly cannot be said to easily or systematically dismiss 'Revenge' (at least) as ethically or politically limiting, witness my discussion, in the next chapter, of Shelley's conflicted response to Byron's notorious 'curse' of 'Forgiveness' in the fourth canto of *Childe Harold's Pilgrimage* (1818).

43 This image also looks forward to the thirteenth stanza of the *Ode to Liberty*, discussed in the next chapter.

44 The narrator of the *Triumph of Life* asks a re-formulated version of this same question – 'why God made irreconcilable / Good and the means of good' (230–1) – which I discuss in my final chapter.

5. 'CHOOSE REFORM OR CIVIL WAR', 1818–1819

1 Holmes, *Shelley*, p. 384.

2 Princess Charlotte was known to be much more favourable to parliamentary reform than her father. The leaders of the Pentridge uprising claimed they had been incited and subsequently entrapped by an agent provocateur.

3 In a letter to Peacock on 8 October, Shelley announced – somewhat prematurely – that he had 'finished the first act of a lyric and classical drama to be called "Prometheus Unbound" (*Letters*, ii, p. 43). Yet despite this strong start, it would be over a year before the 'drama' was finished: Acts II and III were written at Rome in March and April 1819, and Act IV was added at Florence in December. Shelley maintained a consistently high opinion of *Prometheus Unbound*, which was finally published in the summer of 1820.

4 Scrivener emphasises the relationship between *Prometheus Unbound* and the deepening political crisis in England (*Radical Shelley*, pp. 140–247).

5 This claim is probably based upon Shelley's entry in Mary's journal for 26 August 1818, which compares the 'scene' at Les Echelles to 'that described in the Prometheus of Aeschylus' (*MWSJ*, p. 200).

6 In point of fact, only Acts II and III of *Prometheus Unbound* were composed at the Baths during Shelley's stay in Rome in March and April 1819.

7 Stuart Curran, 'The Political Prometheus', *SiR*, 25/3 (Autumn 1986), p. 431.

8 *Ibid.*, p. 445.

9 *Ibid.*

10 Charles Robinson identifies *Prometheus*, *Manfred* (1817), and *Childe Harold* IV – all of which figure the Titan as an emblem of defiance – as the important precursors of Shelley's drama (Robinson, *Shelley and Byron*, pp. 81, 114–17,

134–7). Curran adds the *Ode to Napoleon Buonaparte* to the list, albeit suggesting – somewhat misleadingly – that Byron follows Morgan in presenting the Titan as an 'icon of despair' rather than defiance (Curran, 'Political Prometheus', p. 445). There is no direct evidence that Shelley read the anonymous *Ode*, however, and his roughly contemporary 'Feelings of a Republican on the Fall of Bonaparte' (1815) is wholly devoid of Promethean imagery. Conversely, there is strong evidence linking him to Byron's *Prometheus* which, although not published until 1817, was composed during Shelley's stay in Switzerland in 1816 (see Robinson, *Shelley and Byron*, pp. 30–1).

11 Wasserman also points up Cicero's impact on *Prometheus Unbound*. See *Shelley's 'Prometheus Unbound': a Critical Reading* (Baltimore: Johns Hopkins University Press, 1965), p. 80.

12 Marcus Tullius Cicero, *Tusculan Disputations*, trans. J. King, Loeb Classical Library (London: Heinemann, 1960), p. 170 n. 1.

13 As far as I have been able to determine, this passage from Cicero was Shelley's main source of material from the 'lost' third part of Aeschylus's Promethean trilogy – other minor references occur in Ovid and Arrian, both of whom Shelley had read by 1818. Neither Richard Potter's 1777 *Tragedies of Aeschylus* (the only English translation of Aeschylus' surviving works available to Shelley, although there is no direct evidence that he read it) nor Lempriere's *Classical Dictionary* (which Shelley ordered in December 1815) refer to the 'lost play' (*Letters*, i, p. 437). For more on the editions of Aeschylus available to Shelley see Jennifer Wallace, 'Tyranny and Translation: Shelley's Unbinding of Prometheus', *Romanticism*, 1/1 (1995), pp. 15–33. See also Jennifer Wallace, *Shelley and Greece: Rethinking Romantic Hellenism* (London: Macmillan, 1997), pp. 162–6.

14 Cicero, *Disputations*, p. 171.

15 We have already noted *Laon and Cythna*'s account of the French Revolution and its aftermath as 'the tempests that have shaken the age'. The body-text of *Laon and Cythna* frequently uses volcanic imagery to image political violence. See, for example, *Laon and Cythna* 784–790, 2396–7 and 3510–13.

16 Wasserman, *Shelley's 'Prometheus Unbound'*, p. 158 n. 18.

17 The 'Magus Zoroaster' episode from *Prometheus Unbound* I, 191–209 has long defied critical explanation, and potential sources remain elusive (See *Poems*, ii, pp. 488–9). It seems likely that Shelley's notion of the 'two worlds of life and death' is premised upon the Zoroastrian idea of two mutually involved realities, each a reflection of the other, which he might well have come across in the occultist literature he read as a boy. However, such a dualistic account of a second 'world' containing 'the shadows of all forms that think and live' seems unlikely when set against Shelley's mature ontology. Nor indeed does a Platonic realm of Forms fit the bill since the 'world' 'underneath the grave' contains 'shadows' rather than perfect archetypes. However the passage certainly does recall *Mont Blanc*'s account of the *mind* as the 'still cave of the witch Poesy', which contains the 'shadows' and 'ghosts of all things that are'. To this extent, it seems likely that Shelley is re-presenting the Zoroastrian myth of a

world 'underneath the grave' as a kind of public consciousness – or 'one mind' – in which the past 'imaginings of men' persist.

18 Shelley's approximately contemporary drama *The Cenci* (1819) is also explicitly intended to explain that 'revenge, retaliation, atonement, are pernicious mistakes' (*Poems*, ii, p. 730). 'It is in the restless and anatomising casuistry', Shelley affirms, echoing the 'Preface' to *Prometheus Unbound*, 'with which men seek the justification of Beatrice, yet feel that what she has done needs justification … that the dramatic character of what she did and suffered, consists' (*Poems*, ii, p. 731). For a thorough account of the relation between *The Cenci* and English politics, see Stephen Behrendt, 'Beatrice Cenci and the Tragic Myth of History', in *History and Myth: Essays in English Romantic Literature*, ed. Stephen Behrendt (Detroit: Wayne State University Press, 1990), pp. 214–34.

19 Matthews was the first to note the volcanic nature of Jupiter's defeat (Matthews, 'A Volcano's Voice', pp. 216–17). My reading of *Prometheus Unbound* II–III is much indebted to his.

20 For a discussion of the 'curse' and its cultural context, see A. M. Stauffer, 'Romantic Anger and Byron's Curse', in E. Fay and J. Morillo eds., *Romantic Passions* (College Park, MD: University of Maryland Press, 1998), no pagination given.

21 See Robinson, *Shelley and Byron*, pp. 67–77.

22 On 30 May 1818, Peacock had written to Shelley from Marlow, telling him that he had 'almost finished Nightmare Abbey'. 'I think it necessary', Peacock went on, 'to "make a stand" against the "encroachments of black bile". The fourth canto of Childe Harold is really too bad. I cannot consent to be *auditor tantum* of this systematical "poisoning" of the "mind" of the "Reading Public"'. Quoted from *The Letters of Thomas Love Peacock*, ed. A. J. Joukovsky, 2 vols. (Oxford: Clarendon, 2001), v. 2, p. 123.

23 Shelley did except the closing 'address to Ocean' from his condemnation of *Childe Harold* IV, noting that it 'proves' Byron to be 'a great poet' (*Letters*, ii, p. 58).

24 The allusion to Byron's 'curse' in the *Euganean Hills* – originally recognised by Gordon Wilson Knight – is also noted by Robinson, *Shelley and Byron*, p. 77.

25 Hence, again, Shelley's political thought often comes rather closer to Byron's own than Robinson's optimist–pessimist dichotomy allows.

26 The lengthy topographical descriptions in Madame de Staël's *Corinne, or Italy* (translated into English in 1807) frequently provided an itinerary for Italy's tourists. However, the most influential guidebooks properly so-called in the early nineteenth century were Joseph Forsyth's *Remarks on Antiquities, Arts, and Letters, During an Excursion in Italy in the Years 1802 and 1803* (1816), and John Chetwode Eustace's *Classical Tour through Italy* (1815). To this list was added, in 1818, John Cam Hobhouse's *Historical Illustrations to the 4th Canto of Childe Harold's Pilgrimage*. Shelley read *Corinne* throughout December 1818, although Mary had read the novel as early as spring 1815 (*MWSJ*, p. 243; *Letters*, ii, p. 68). He had read Hobhouse, Eustace, and Forsyth by March 1819.

In a letter to Peacock on 23 March, he singled out Forsyth – as 'worth reading' – from the 'shew knowledge' of Eustace and Hobhouse (*Letters*, ii, p. 89).

27 So, for example, James Thomson's pan-historical *Liberty* (1735) uses the ruins of the capitol as the occasion for pointedly lamenting the collapse of republican virtue into imperial corruption. Conversely, John Dyer's 1740 *Ruins of Rome* – which was republished in Chalmers' 1810 *Works of the English Poets* – interpreted that shattered city as a salutary warning of the danger that decadence and excessive commercialism could pose to Britain's nascent imperial ambitions. For a detailed account of British literary engagements with the ruins of Rome see Janowitz, *England's Ruins*, pp. 20–54, and Goldstein, *Ruins and Empire*, pp. 25–43.

28 For a detailed account of the various ideological appropriations of the ruins of Rome during the Revolutionary and Napoleonic wars see Carolyn Springer, *The Marble Wilderness: Ruins and Representation in Italian Romanticism, 1775–1850* (Cambridge: Cambridge University Press, 1987), pp. 64–97.

29 *Ibid.*, p. 68.

30 See *Ibid.*, pp. 68–74.

31 *Ibid.*, p. 75.

32 *Ibid.*, p. 84.

33 Byron's account of Barbarian vengeance ought to be qualified by Gibbon's observation that 'our fancy may create, or adopt, a pleasing romance that the Goths and Vandals sallied from Scandinavia, ardent to … break the chains, and to chastise the oppressors, of mankind … But, in simple truth, the northern conquerors were neither sufficiently savage nor sufficiently refined to entertain such aspiring ideas of destruction and revenge' (*D&F*, vii, pp. 308–9).

34 Robinson discusses this engagement at some length in *Shelley and Byron*, pp. 81–106.

35 *Ibid.*, p. 77.

36 *Ibid.*, p. 79. Brewer's *Shelley-Byron Conversation* curiously makes no mention of *The Coliseum*. Indeed, the story has not generally received a great deal of attention from Shelley's critics. However two excellent studies exist: Timothy Clark's 'Shelley's *The Coliseum* and the Sublime', *Durham University Journal*, 85, 54/2 (July 1993), pp. 225–35 and Kevin Binfield's '"May they be divided never": Ethics, History, and the Rhetorical Imagination in Shelley's *The Coliseum*', *K-SJ*, 46 (1997), pp. 125–49.

37 Byron and Shelley were certainly not the first to prefer the amphitheatre as a ruin: Goldstein quotes John Dyer's observation that 'there is a certain charm that follows the sweep of time, and I can't help thinking the triumphal arches more beautiful now than they ever were' (Goldstein, *Ruins and Empire*, p. 36).

38 The Shelleys visited the Colosseum on 6, 9, and 14 March, and on 5, 9 (Good Friday), 15, and 24 April 1819 (*MWSJ*, pp. 251–3, 256–8, 260). The last visit recorded by Mary took place on 27 May 1819 (*MWSJ*, p. 264).

39 Timothy Clark notes that 'the text turns on the opposition between two colossal works of architecture, St Peter's and the Coliseum itself, which serves as the repository of anti-Christian values' (Clark, 'Shelley's *The Coliseum*', p. 225).

40 Springer, *Marble Wilderness*, p. 84.

41 The Shelleys witnessed the Easter ceremonies at first hand in April 1819. Eustace, Forsyth, and Hobhouse also describe the ceremonies at length, as does *Corinne*.

42 Hobhouse, *Historical Illustrations*, pp. 280–1.

43 Forsyth, *Remarks*, p. 148.

44 The encounter with a mysterious figure in the ruins is, in fact, a standard device of eighteenth- and early nineteenth-century ruin sentiment. For example, both Thomson's and Dyer's poetic personas encounter such figures in Rome. In Thomson, the figure represents Liberty whereas in Dyer the 'seer' warns the poet against mortal vanity, and affirms conventional religious values. See Goldstein, *Ruins and Empire*, pp. 39, 34.

45 Timothy Clark has noted three possible 'literary antecedents' for the relationship between the old man and his daughter: Oedipus and Antigone; Milton and his daughters; and *Frankenstein*'s blind De Lacey and his daughter (Clark, 'Shelley's *The Coliseum*', p. 228). Robinson suggests a fourth possibility: Byron's use of 'the famous story of the Roman daughter' – who fed her imprisoned father from her own breasts – in *Childe Harold* IV, 148–51 (Robinson, *Shelley and Byron*, p. 79). This story is retold by Hobhouse, *Historical Illustrations*, p. 295.

46 Hobhouse, *Historical Illustrations*, p. 286. Clark suggests that the old man's imaginative apostrophe to the amphitheatre is based on Shelley's knowledge of the Italian *improvvisatori*, fictionalised in De Staël's *Corinne* (Clark, 'Shelley's *The Coliseum*', p. 229). The Shelley party made the acquaintance of Italy's most famous living improvvisatore – Tommasso Sgricci – late in 1820 (*MWSJ*, p. 341).

47 Kevin Binfield's essay on *The Coliseum* confirms that 'beyond simply reinterpreting' the amphitheatre, Shelley also outlines 'the potentiality of the imagination to reassemble those ruins in a morally meaningful way' (Binfield, 'Ethics, History, and the Rhetorical Imagination', p. 129). However, Binfield's claim that Helen and her father represent Holbachian materialism and Lockean empiricism (respectively) fails to recognise the epistemological dynamics of their relationship (p. 135).

48 Anne Louise Germaine De Staël, *Corinne, or Italy*, trans. S. Raphael (Oxford: Oxford University Press, 1998), pp. 67–8.

49 Shelley had seen the Triumphal Arch commemorating Titus's destruction of Jerusalem. Shelley describes this arch – in terms which parallel his note to *The Coliseum* – in his 1819 *Notes on the Sculptures in Rome and Florence* (*Prose*, p. 343). The reference to Titus Flavius in *The Coliseum* is highly appropriate since he completed the building of the amphitheatre, the project having been begun by his father Vespasian (hence its alternative appellation: the Flavian amphitheatre).

50 When Helen and her father first enter the amphitheatre, for example, she does not recognise it: hence, they only learn where they are when the stranger berates the old man's apparent ignorance. Furthermore, as Timothy Clark

notes, *The Coliseum*'s historical allusions are primarily to the Greek rather than to the more obviously relevant Roman past ('Shelley's *The Coliseum*', p. 233). Again, the stranger is the exception to this rule but even he, we are told, 'spoke Latin, *and especially Greek*' (*Prose*, p. 224; emphasis added).

51 Timothy Clark likewise notes that 'Shelley's text ignores (or cannot accommodate)' this theory (Clark, 'Shelley's *The Coliseum*', p. 227). He also quotes Hobhouse's remark that 'the most intelligent of our countrymen foresee the speedy dissolution of the whole structure' (Clark, 'Shelley's *The Coliseum*', p. 235 n. 20; Hobhouse, *Historical Illustrations*, p. 284).

52 Quoted in Goldstein, *Ruins and Empire*, p. 38.

53 In a later letter to Peacock, on 23 March 1819, Shelley similarly compared the 'pinnacles and masses' of ruin in the Baths of Caracalla to 'mountains' (*Letters*, ii, p. 85). We remember that the 'Preface' to *Prometheus Unbound* also describes the ruined baths as 'mountainous' (*Poems*, ii, p. 473).

54 Clark points up these historical echoes in the old man's speech (Clark, 'Shelley's *The Coliseum*', p. 233).

55 Mary's 'Note' to *Prometheus Unbound* first identified Demogorgon as 'the Primal Power of the world', and critics have found little reason to dispute her claim (*CPW*, p. 272). For a detailed account of Shelley's likely sources for this identification – in Peacock's *Rhododaphne* (1817), Boccaccio's *Genealogia Deorum*, and Lucan's *Pharsalia* – see *Poems*, ii, pp. 467–8. 'Necessity' also appears in *Prometheus Vinctus* (100–5), where it is identified by the Titan as fate: a power which 'brooketh no resistance'. Quoted from *Aeschylus*, ed. and trans. H. W. Smyth, Loeb Classical Library, 2 vols. (Cambridge Mass.: Harvard University Press, 1922–6), i, 226. See also *Poems*, ii, p. 468.

56 Critics have long noted that – to quote Everest and Matthews – 'the marriage of Asia and Prometheus carries many associations, including the relation of East to West, Oriental to Hellenic cultural traditions, female to male, and also different modes of perception and understanding (Prometheus is locked into a fruitless urge to rational understanding and control, whereas Asia's emotional and intuitive understanding actually leads to change)' (*Poems*, ii, pp. 466–7).

57 Tim Webb, '"The Avalanche of Ages": Shelley's Defence of Atheism and *Prometheus Unbound*', *K-SMB*, 35 (1984), pp. 1–39.

58 Samuel Glover uses this same passage from the *Quarterly* as the epigraph for his *Description of the Valley of Chamouni, in Savoy* (London, 1819). As much an attack on atheism as an account of the Savoyard landscape, the *Description* contains a remarkable, Dante-esque vision of an Alpine hell, in which the punishment for atheists is to be imprisoned in the 'icicles which adorn the spiring rocks ... doomed eternally to behold those magnificent works of nature they ever affected to despise' (Glover, *Description*, p. 19). For a thorough and informative description of the ongoing controversy surrounding Shelley's Alpine inscriptions, see De Beer, 'An Atheist in the Alps'.

59 Webb notes that the avalanche-figure itself 'is by no means a simple metaphor for the inevitability of intellectual progress [but also] carries an unmistakable threat of violence' (Webb, 'The Avalanche of Ages', p. 33).

60 Matthews, 'A Volcano's Voice', pp. 206–7. Shelley describes the scenery around Agnano and Astroni in a letter to Peacock on 25 February 1819 (*Letters*, ii, pp. 77–8).

61 Matthews, 'A Volcano's Voice', p. 211. The Shelley party ascended Vesuvius on 16 December 1818, while it was in 'a slight state of eruption' (*MWSJ*, p. 244; *Letters*, ii, p. 62). Shelley described the volcano to Peacock in a letter from Naples written on 17 or 18 December. He was clearly – and understandably – fascinated: 'Vesuvius is, after the glaciers', Shelley noted, 'the most impressive expression of the energies of nature I ever saw' (*Letters*, ii, p. 62).

62 Madame De Staël describes the circumstances of Pliny's death in *Corinne*, p. 234. She also sets out the 'oracular' associations of the Neapolitan landscape (De Staël, *Corinne*, p. 234).

63 Hence, while I agree with Michael Rossington's suggestion that the 'function' of the 'maddening wine' is 'to counteract the despair which corrupted those idealistic radicals ... whom Shelley associates with post-revolutionary politics, with forgetfulness', I clearly do not agree that this is a positive 'function'. Michael Rossington, '"The Voice Which is Contagion to the World": The Bacchic in Shelley', in *Beyond Romanticism: New Approaches to Texts and Contexts, 1780–1832*, ed. Stephen Copley and John Whale (London: Routledge, 1992), p. 115.

64 *Ibid.*, p. 109.

65 Panthea's 'maddening wine of life' also clearly looks forward to the 'crystal glass' of 'bright Nepenthe' offered to Rousseau by the 'shape all light' in *The Triumph of Life*, (352, 358–9). As I argue in the next chapter, this deadening drink similarly figures the dysfunction of Rousseau's imaginative response to nature, a dysfunction that Shelley links directly to the Napoleonic collapse of the French Revolution. Rossington also notes the anticipation of *The Triumph* in Panthea's speech, although again my reading disagrees with his implicitly favourable interpretation of the 'wine' (Rossington, 'The Bacchic in Shelley', p. 115).

66 Matthews, 'A Volcano's Voice', p. 215; Grabo, *A New Among Poets*, p. 87.

67 Pulos, *The Deep Truth*, p. 9.

68 Robinson notes that Demogorgon's injunction to 'defy power' echoes the conclusion to Byron's *Prometheus* (Robinson, *Shelley and Byron*, p. 116).

69 Matthews, 'A Volcano's Voice', p. 218.

70 As Everest and Matthews note, the Spirit's reference to the 'painted veil' of custom also echoes Shelley's 1818 sonnet 'Lift not the Painted Veil', although – as they correctly emphasise – the implications of the image in the earlier piece are quite different (*Poems*, ii, p. 610 n.).

71 See Matthews, 'A Volcano's Voice', pp. 216–17. Matthews outlines at length the extent to which the imagery of *Prometheus Unbound* II, iv is informed by contemporary – scientific and popular – accounts of volcanism (Matthews, 'A Volcano's Voice', pp. 217–20).

72 *Ibid.*, p. 217.

73 Shelley visited Herculaneum in December 1818 (*MWSJ*, pp. 242, 245).

74 We have already noted Wasserman's observation that late eighteenth-century mythography read the war of the Titans as a volcanic allegory. De Staël's account of Vesuvius in *Corinne* also picks up on the anthropomorphic and mythological associations of volcanism. 'Everything surrounding the volcano', she affirms, 'reminds one of hell, and the poet's descriptions are no doubt borrowed from these places. It is there that one can believe how men have believed in the existence of an evil genius which contradicted the intentions of Providence. In gazing at such a place, people must have wondered whether benevolence alone presided over the phenomena of creation or whether some hidden principle forced nature, like man, into ferocity' (De Staël, *Corinne*, p. 226).

75 Matthews, 'A Volcano's Voice', p. 216.

76 *Ibid.*, pp. 215–16. See also *Poems*, ii, p. 555 n.

77 For an account of Shelley's equally volcanological rendering of the 1820 Neapolitan Revolution see my '"The City Disinterred": the Shelley Circle and the Revolution at Naples', in A. Chapman and J. Stabler (eds.), *'Unfolding the South': Forum for Modern Language Studies Special Edition* 39/2 (April 2003), pp. 152–64.

78 Foot, *Red Shelley*, p. 194. Everest and Matthews render the etymology more accurately – and more revealingly – as a pun on 'the Greek δημος, 'people', and γοργος, 'grim, terrible' (*Poems*, ii, p. 469).

79 C. E. Pulos, 'Shelley and Malthus' *PMLA* 67 (1952), p. 121. Throughout his life, Shelley considered Malthus' 1798 *Essay on the Principle of Population* to be one of the most significant obstacles to the radical agenda. He criticises Malthus explicitly in the 'Prefaces' to *Laon and Cythna* and *Prometheus Unbound*, and in a letter to Peacock from Livorno on 19 or 20 June 1819, he confirmed his sense that Malthus' theories attempted to generate a reactionary configuration of the doctrine of Necessity. He assures Peacock that 'desire never fails to generate capacity', but then proceeds to note that 'that ever present Malthus Necessity has convinced Desire – that even though it generated capacity its offspring must starve' (*Letters*, ii, p. 98). On 15 February 1821, he informed Peacock that he was looking forward to receiving Godwin's 'answer to the apostle of the rich', *Of Population: An Answer to Mr. Malthus's Essay*, which had been published on 1 November 1820 (*Letters*, ii, p. 261 and n. 4).

CONCLUSION: 'GOOD AND THE MEANS OF GOOD', 1822

1 Peacock's 'essay', *The Four Ages of Poetry*, was published in the first and only edition of Ollier's *Literary Miscellany* in 1820. Evidently it did not reach Shelley in Italy until the following January (*Letters*, ii, p. 258).

2 Quoted from *The Works of Thomas Love Peacock*, ed. H. F. B. Brett-Smith and C. E. Jones, 10 vols. (London: Constable and Co., 1934–6), viii, pp. 22, 21.

3 *Ibid.*, pp. 4, 5, 14.

4 *Ibid.*, p. 11.

5 *Ibid.*, p. 20.

6 *Ibid.*, pp. 20–1.

7 Harry White similarly notes that the *Defence* stresses 'the limits of reason in scientific activity' and establishes 'the imagination as the sole source of metaphysical knowledge of some sort'. See 'Shelley's Defence of Science', *SiR*, 16 (Summer 1977), p. 327. Of course this reading 'does not', as Harry White sensibly points out, lead to the conclusion 'that Shelley is describing a Neoplatonic imagination' (White, 'Shelley's Defence of Science', pp. 327–8).

8 Peacock, *The Works*, vii, p. 5.

9 *Ibid.*, p. 6.

10 I sound a (De Manian) note of caution here since we need to be wary of jumping to conclusions about *The Triumph of Life*, that is, of reading the existing fragment through supposition about how it might have ended. See Paul De Man, 'Shelley Disfigured' in *Deconstruction and Criticism*, ed. Harold Bloom et al. (New York: Continuum, 1979), pp. 39–73. All quotations from *The Triumph* are from Donald Reiman's corrected edition of the text in *Shelley's 'The Triumph of Life': A Critical Study* (Urbana Ill.: University of Illinois Press, 1965).

11 Only two studies pay significant attention to the relationship between *The Triumph of Life* and the French Revolution: John Morillo's 'Vegetating Radicals and Imperial Politics: Shelley's *Triumph of Life* as Revision of Southey's *Pilgrimage to Waterloo*', *K–SJ* 43 (1994), pp. 117–40; and Orrin Wang's 'Disfiguring Monuments: History in Paul De Man's "Shelley Disfigured"' and Percy Bysshe Shelley's *The Triumph of Life*', *ELH* 58 (1991), pp. 633–55.

12 Timothy Clark also points up this connection (Clark, *Embodying Revolution*, pp. 223, 236).

13 Hence the full resonance of Morillo's reading of *The Triumph* as a corrective response to Southey's *Pilgrimage to Waterloo* (1816), a response that reveals how – 'despite its anti-war sentiments' – the laureate poem 'participates in a Tory ideology that naturalises imperialism as the necessary result' of England's victory over Napoleon (Morillo, 'Vegetating Radicals', p. 118).

14 See, for example, William Hazlitt's "Shelley's Posthumous Poems" (1824), which famously describes *The Triumph* as 'a new and terrific dance of death' (Hazlitt, *Complete Works*, xvi, p. 273). Only a 'sacred few' – including Jesus and Socrates – escape from the 'triumph' (*Triumph of Life*, 128–37).

15 See, for example, David Quint, 'Representation and Ideology in *The Triumph of Life*', *Studies in English Literature*, 18 (1978), pp. 639–57. Quint identifies *The Triumph*'s 'subject matter' as 'a death-in-life occasioned by man's surrender to ideological representation, whether an ideology shaped by the private imagination or derived ready-made from past thinkers' (p. 642).

16 John Hodgson, 'The World's Mysterious Doom: Shelley's *The Triumph of Life*', *ELH* 42 (1975), p. 619.

17 E. Moor, *The Hindu Pantheon*, ed. W. Simpson (Delhi: Indological Bookhouse, 1968), p. 18.

18 Shelley's familiarity with Southey's *Curse* is well documented. He ordered *The Hindu Pantheon* on 17 December 1812 (*Letters*, i, p. 342). Moor further notes that 'the rising of the moon is the sign for the commencement of the feast', a fact rehearsed in Shelley's (long-recognised) use of the well-known moon-image from Coleridge's *Ode to Dejection* to introduce the 'chariot' of 'Life' (Moor, *Hindu Pantheon*, p. 18; Reiman, *Shelley's 'The Triumph of Life'*, p. 29). The association with the Coleridge poem – which also describes the failure of the imagination – confirms the manner in which 'Life' triumphs over the individual.

19 James Mulvihill, 'Hazlitt, Shelley, and *The Triumph of Life*', *N&Q*, 35/3 (September 1988), p. 306. There is strong evidence that Shelley read Hazlitt's attacks, which were published in Hunt's *Examiner* (Mulvihill, pp. 306–7).

20 Burke, *Reflections*, p. 165; emphasis added. Wang also makes the connection between Burke's account of 6 October 1789 in *The Reflections* and Shelley's 'triumphal pageant', quoting the same passages cited here (Wang, 'Disfiguring Monuments', pp. 646–7).

21 Burke, *Reflections*, p. 157; original emphasis.

22 Wang, 'Disfiguring Monuments', p. 647.

23 As Wang notes, in 1822 *The Triumph*'s 'arch of victory' could not fail to evoke the *Arc de Triomphe* that Napoleon himself had begun in 1806 (Wang, 'Disfiguring Monuments', p. 650).

24 Quoted from Todd (ed.), *Mary Wollstonecraft*, p. 301.

25 Shelley's continued interest in this Godwinian project is evident from *Hellas* (1821). Reiman notes that 'the literary antecedents of *The Triumph* – the *Trionfi*, the *Commedia, Comus, Paradise Lost, Julie* – end in the protagonist's salvation through love' (Reiman, *Shelley's 'The Triumph of Life'*, p. 78).

26 Quint, 'Representation and Ideology', p. 642.

27 Rousseau's role as guide is consolidated – as I suggest below – through the repetition of his story in *The Triumph*'s frame-narrative.

28 See Reiman, *Shelley's 'The Triumph of Life'*, p. 166.

29 Edward Duffy likewise argues that 'Rousseau is to be placed at the imaginative source of the French Revolution' (Duffy, *Rousseau in England*, p. 132). However, my reading here disagrees with his subsequent claim that *The Triumph* 'goes on to describe the failure of the revolution as a consequence of Rousseau's prototypical *apostasy* from imaginative vision' (Duffy, *Rousseau in England*, p. 132). Duffy argues for the separation, in Shelley's thought, of the public from the private Rousseau, of the political *philosophe* from the imaginative visionary. The extent to which such a distinction was made in the wake of the Revolution is debatable, but it is not a distinction allowed by *The Triumph* (or by Shelley's politicised epistemology generally). Moreover, the Rousseau of *The Triumph of Life* does not, as Duffy suggests, sacrifice imagination to reason (Duffy, *Rousseau in England*, pp. 135ff). His defeat consists rather – as I argue below – in the dysfunction of his imagination.

30 Donald Reiman affirms that 'one implication' of Rousseau's 'retort' to the Narrator's relativistic pessimism about 'those who drew / New figures on

[the world's] false and fragile glass' is 'that if the virtuous cease to devote their energies to the molding of philosophical attitudes and political actions, the state of the world can become even worse than it is' (Reiman, *Shelley's 'The Triumph of Life'*, p. 49; *Triumph of Life*, 246–7).

31 Wang, 'Disfiguring Monuments', p. 644.

32 Ibid.

33 See Reiman, *Shelley's 'The Triumph of Life'*, p. 177.

34 To this extent, again, Rousseau differs from the 'few' who have escaped defeat by 'Life', those who – while their teachings were posthumously perverted – never compromised their *personal* moral and imaginative integrity.

35 Rousseau's questions clearly recall the 'obstinate', quasi-Wordsworthian 'questions' asked by *Alastor's* narrator (Alastor, 26).

36 This uncertainty was first noted by Bloom, *Shelley's Mythmaking*, p. 269.

37 Edward Duffy, for example, suggests that 'In *The Triumph of Life* Shelley once again takes up the theme of *Alastor*' (Duffy, *Rousseau in England*, p. 105).

38 It is certainly no accident that Wordsworth – Rousseau's co-prototype in 1815 – also looms large in The *Triumph*.

39 These intertexts are discussed by F. Melian Stawell in 'Shelley's *The Triumph of Life*', *Essays and Studies by Members of the English Association* (Oxford: Oxford University Press, 1914), p. 5, 104ff. See also Bloom, *Shelley's Mythmaking*, p. 222 and n. 4.

40 See, for example, Hodgson, 'The World's Mysterious Doom', p. 606; Bloom, *Shelley's Mythmaking*, pp. 263ff. This Wordsworthian reading is apparently strengthened by the links that Duffy draws between the 'oblivious valley' episode of *The Triumph* and Shelley's definition of 'reverie' in his essay *On Life* (Duffy, *Rousseau in England*, p. 109; *Prose*, p. 174). While Duffy notes that this definition is drawn from Rousseau's *Rêveries*, Shelley introduces a distinctly Wordsworthian element into the equation, linking 'reverie' to childhood and lamenting the 'decay' of this 'power' as 'men grow up' (Duffy, *Rousseau in England*, p. 109; *Prose*, p. 174).

41 Reiman, *Shelley's 'The Triumph of Life'*, p. 61; Quint, 'Representation and Ideology', p. 646 n. 8.

42 Quint, 'Representation and Ideology', p. 646; original emphasis.

43 Bloom suggests that the 'shape' represents Nature (*Shelley's Mythmaking*, pp. 265ff).

44 Once again, Edward Duffy reads the historical Rousseau as a Shelleyan visionary manqué, who failed to overcome his early rationalist leanings (Duffy, *Rousseau in England*, pp. 133ff and passim). However accurate this may be as a diagnosis of Rousseau, it misconceives both Shelley's epistemology and his understanding of Rousseau: after all Shelley's *Defence of Poetry* excludes Rousseau – 'essentially a poet' – from Peacock's list of 'reasoners'.

45 Quint, among others, notes that the wolf and deer imagery of these lines symbolises a desire that outlasts its object (Quint, 'Representation and Ideology', p. 652). Cp. Orsino's account of his desire for Beatrice in *The Cenci* I, ii, 11–13: 'Because I am a priest do you believe / Your image, as the

hunter some struck deer, / Follows me not whether I wake or sleep'. This imagery ultimately derives from the myth of Actaeon, also deployed by Shelley his self-portrait in *Adonais* 271–9.

46 Burke, *Reflections*, p. 92.

47 Geoffrey Mathews, 'Shelley's *The Triumph of Life*', *Studia Neophilologica*, 34/5 (1962–3), p. 108. Matthews' claim is considerably strengthened by both verbal and descriptive echoes, as well as by the fact that the centrepiece of the Les Charmettes episode takes place on 11 April, a possible source for the 'April-prime' in which *The Triumph of Life*'s Rousseau wakes in the 'oblivious valley' (Matthews, 'Shelley's *The Triumph of Life*', pp. 108–9; *Triumph of Life*, 308).

48 Reiman, *Shelley's 'The Triumph of Life'*, pp. 19–20, p. 59 and n. 96, pp. 73–5. Reiman suggests that Shelley interpreted the 'story of St. Preux' as 'an idealised picture of Rousseau's interior experience', as narrated in the pre-1761 sections of *The Confessions* (*Shelley's 'The Triumph of Life'*, pp. 59–60). In a letter written on 10 April 1822, Shelley refers John Gisborne to 'the 54th letter of the 1st part of the *Nouvelle Héloïse*' – which suggests that he may have been re-reading the novel at this time (*Letters*, ii, p. 407).

49 It is worth noting that the geography of the 'oblivious valley' resembles Petrach's Fontaine de Vaucluse as much as anything in *Julie or The Confessions*.

Bibliography

WORKS BY SHELLEY

The Poems of Shelley, ed. Kelvin Everest and Geoffrey Matthews, 2 vols. to date (London: Longman, 1989, 2000–).

The Esdaile Notebook, ed. Kenneth Neill Cameron (London: Faber and Faber, 1964).

The Letters of Percy Bysshe Shelley, ed. Frederick L. Jones, 2 vols. (Oxford: Clarendon Press, 1964).

Shelley's The Triumph of Life: A Critical Study Based on a Text Newly Edited from the Bodleian Manuscript, ed. Donald H. Reiman, Illinois Studies in Language and Literature (Urbana Ill.: University of Illinois Press, 1965).

Shelley's Prose, or, The Trumpet of a Prophecy, ed. David Lee Clark, corrected edn (Albuquerque: University of New Mexico Press, 1966).

The Complete Poetical Works of Percy Bysshe Shelley, ed. Thomas Hutchinson, 2nd edn, updated and corrected by Geoffrey Matthews (Oxford: Oxford University Press, 1970).

The Complete Poetical Works of Percy Bysshe Shelley, ed. Neville Rogers, 2 vols. to date (Oxford: Clarendon Press, 1972–).

The Prose Works of Percy Bysshe Shelley, ed. E. B. Murray, 1 vol. to date (Oxford: Clarendon Press, 1993–).

Manuscripts of the Younger Romantics: Shelley, ed. D. H. Reiman et al., 9 vols. (New York, Garland: 1985–1996).

The Complete Poetry of Percy Bysshe Shelley, ed. D. H. Reiman and N. Fraistat, 1 vol. to date (Baltimore: Johns Hopkins University Press, 2000–).

The Bodleian Shelley Manuscripts, ed. D. H. Reiman et al., 23 vols. (New York, Garland: 1986–2002).

Shelley's Poetry and Prose, ed. D. H. Reiman and N. Fraistat, 2nd edn (New York: Norton, 2002).

PRIMARY SOURCES

Addison, Joseph, *The Spectator*, 8 vols. (London, 1712–15).

Aeschylus, *The Tragedies of Aeschylus*, trans. Richard Potter (London, 1777).

  Prometheus Bound, in *Aeschylus*, ed. and trans. H. W. Smyth and H. Lloyd-Jones, Loeb Classical Library, 2 vols. (London: Heinemann, 1922–6), i, pp. 211–315.

Alison, Archibald, *Essays on the Nature and Principles of Taste*, 3rd edn, 2 vols. (Edinburgh, 1812).

Arnold, Matthew, *The Complete Prose Works of Matthew Arnold*, ed. R. H. Super, 11 vols. (Ann Arbor: University of Michigan Press, 1960–77).

Bacon Francis, *The Works of Francis Bacon, Baron of Verulam, Viscount St. Alban, and Lord High Chancellor of England*, ed. James Spedding, Robert Leslie Ellis, and Douglas Denon Heath, 14 vols. (London, 1857–74).

Barruel, Abbé (Augustin), *Memoirs Illustrating the History of Jacobinism*, trans. R. Clifford, 4 vols. (London: 1797–8).

Bentham, Jeremy, *Utilitarianism, On Liberty, Considerations on Representative Government*, ed. G. Williams (London: Dent, 1993).

Berkeley, George, *Philosophical Works*, ed. M. R. Ayer (London: Dent, 1980).

Blair, Hugh, *A Critical Dissertation on the Poems of Ossian* (London, 1763).
Lectures on Rhetoric and Belles Lettres, 2 vols. (London, 1783).

Buffon, Georges Louis Leclerc, Comte de, *Histoire Naturelle Générale et Particulière* (Paris, 1749–67).

Burke, Edmund, *A Philosophical Enquiry into the Origin of Our Ideas of the Sublime and the Beautiful*, ed. J. T. Boulton (London: Routledge, 1958).
A Letter to a Member of the National Assembly (Paris, 1791).
Reflections on the Revolution in France, and on the Proceedings in Certain Societies in London Relative to that Event, in a Letter Intended to have been Sent to a Gentleman in Paris, ed. Conor Cruise O'Brien (Harmondsworth: Penguin, 1982).

Burnet, Thomas, *The Sacred Theory of the Earth* (London, 1681).

Byron, Lord, *Byron: A Critical Edition of the Major Works*, ed. Jerome J. McGann (Oxford: Oxford University Press, 1986).

Cabanis, Pierre Jean Georges, *Rapports du Physique et du Moral de l'Homme*, 2 vols. (Paris, 1802).

Chalmers, A., (ed.), *Works of English Poets from Chaucer to Cowper* (London, 1810).

Cicero, Marcus Tullius, *Tusculan Disputations*, trans. J. E. King, Loeb Classical Library (London: Heinemann, 1960).

Clairmont, Jane (Claire), *The Journals of Claire Clairmont*, ed. Marion Kingston Stocking (Cambridge Mass.: Harvard University Press, 1968).

Clarke, Edward Daniel, *Travels in Various Countries in Europe, Asia, and Africa*, 6 vols. (London, 1810–23).

Coleridge, Samuel Taylor, *Biographia Literaria; or, Biographical Sketches of my Literary Life and Opinions*, ed. Nigel Leask (London: Everyman, 1997).
The Complete Poems of Samuel Taylor Coleridge, ed. William Keach (Harmondsworth: Penguin, 1997).

Cooper, Anthony Ashley, Third Earl of Shaftesbury, *Characteristicks of Men, Manners, Opinions, Times. The Second Edition Corrected*, 3 vols. (London, 1714).

Cuvier, Georges, *Leçons d'Anatomie Comparée*, 2 vols. (Paris, 1797).
Recherches sur les Ossemens Fossiles de Quadrupèdes, ou l'On Rétablit les Caractères de Plusieurs Espèces d'Animaux que les Révolutions du Globe Paroissent avoir Détruites, 4 vols. (Paris, 1812).

Darwin, Erasmus, *The Botanic Garden* (London, 1792).

Zoonomia, or the Laws of Organic Life, 2 vols. (London, 1794–6).

The Temple of Nature, or the Origin of Society. A Poem with Philosophical Notes (London: 1803).

Dennis, John, *The Grounds of Criticism in Poetry* (London, 1704).

De Quincey, Thomas, *The Works of Thomas De Quincey*, 16 vols. (Edinburgh: A. and C. Black, 1854–60).

De Staël, Anne Louise Germaine (Madame), *Corinne, or Italy*, trans. S. Raphael (Oxford: Oxford University Press, 1998).

De la Littérature Considérée dans ses Rapports avec les Institutions Sociales, 2 vols. (Paris, 1800).

Drummond, Sir William, *Academical Questions* (London, 1805).

Eustace, John Chetwode, *A Classical Tour through Italy, Anno MDCCCII*, 3rd edn, 4 vols. (London, 1815).

Ferguson, Adam, *An Essay on the History of Civil Society* (Edinburgh, 1767).

Fontenelle, Bernard le Bovier de, *Conversations on the Plurality of Worlds*, trans. Elizabeth Gunning (London, 1808).

Forsyth, Joseph, *Remarks on Antiquities, Arts, and Letters, During an Excursion in Italy in the Years 1802 and 1803*, 2nd edn (London, 1816).

Gibbon, Edward, *History of the Decline and Fall of the Roman Empire*, 6 vols. (London, 1766–88).

Memoirs of my Life, ed. Betty Radice (London: Penguin, 1984).

Godwin, William, *An Enquiry Concerning Political Justice and its Influence on General Virtue and Happiness*, 2 vols. (London, 1793).

Things as They Are, or, The Adventures of Caleb Williams, ed. David McCracken (Oxford: Oxford University Press, 1970).

Hartley, David, *Observations on Man: His Frame, his Duty and his Expectations*, 2 vols. (London, 1749).

Hazlitt, William, *The Complete Works of William Hazlitt*, ed. P. P. Howe, 21 vols. (London: J. M. Dent, 1930–4).

Hobhouse, John Cam, *Historical Illustrations to the 4th Canto of Childe Harold: Containing Dissertations on the Ruins of Rome; and an Essay on Italian Literature* (London, 1818).

Hogg, Thomas Jefferson, *The Life of Percy Bysshe Shelley*, 2 vols. only (London, 1858).

Holbach, Baron Paul Henri d', *La Système de la Nature* (London, 1770).

Home, Henry (Lord Kames), *Essays on the Principles of Morality and Natural Religion* (Edinburgh, 1751).

Elements of Criticism, 3rd edn, 2 vols. (Edinburgh, 1765).

Humboldt, Alexander Von, *A Personal Narrative of Travels to the Equinoctial Regions of the New Continent During the Years 1799–1804*, trans. H. M. Williams, 7 vols. (London, 1814–29).

Hume, David, *Enquiries Concerning Human Understanding and Concerning the Principles of Morals*, 3rd edn, ed. L. A. Selby Bigge, rev. P. H. Nidditch (Oxford: Clarendon Press, 1975).

A Treatise of Human Nature: Being an Attempt to Introduce the Experimental Method of Reasoning into Moral Subjects, ed. L. A. Selby-Bigge, rev. P. H. Nidditch (Oxford: Oxford University Press, 1978).

Dialogues Concerning Natural Religion and *The Natural History of Religion,* ed. J. C. A. Gaskin (Oxford: Oxford University Press, 1993).

Hutcheson, Frances, *An Inquiry into the Original of our Ideas of Beauty and Virtue* (London, 1725).

Hutton, James, *The Theory of the Earth, with Proofs and Illustrations, in Four Parts,* 2 vols. (Edinburgh, 1795).

Johnson, Samuel, *A Dictionary of the English Language,* facsimile of 1st (1755) edn, 2 vols. (New York: AMS Press, 1967).

The History of Rasselas, Prince of Abissinia, ed. Geoffrey Tillotson and Brian Jenkins (Oxford: Oxford University Press, 1977).

Laplace, Pierre Simon de, *Exposition du Système du Monde* (Paris, 1798).

Lempriere, John, *A Classical Dictionary,* 8th edn (London, 1812).

Lewis, Matthew, *The Monk: A Romance,* ed. Howard Anderson (Oxford: Oxford University Press, 1995).

Locke, John, *Essay Concerning Human Understanding,* ed. Roger Woolhouse (London: Penguin, 1994).

Longinus, Dionysius, *Dionysius Longinus on the Sublime,* trans. William Smith, 2nd edn (London, 1743).

Lowth, Robert, *Lectures on the Sacred Poetry of the Hebrews,* 2 vols. (London, 1787).

Lucretius Caro, Titus, *On the Nature of the Universe,* trans. Sir. Ronald Melville, ed. D. and P. Fowler (Oxford: Clarendon, 1997).

Malthus, Thomas, *An Essay on the Principle of Population as it Affects the Future Improvement of Society* (London, 1798).

Martyn, Thomas, *Sketch of a Tour Through Switzerland: With an Accurate Map. A New Edition, to Which is Added a Short Account of an Expedition to the Summit of Mont Blanc, by M. De Saussure, of Geneva* (London, 1788).

Medwin, Thomas, *The Life of Percy Bysshe Shelley,* 2 vols. (London, 1847).

Moor, Edward, *The Hindu Pantheon,* ed. W. Simpson (Delhi: Indological Bookhouse, 1968).

Opie, Amelia, *Adeline Mowbray,* facsimile of 1805 London edition (New York: Woodstock Books, 1995).

Owenson, Sydney (Lady Morgan), *France* (London, 1817).

Parkinson, James, *Organic Remains of a Former World,* 3 vols. (London, 1804–11).

Paine, Thomas, *The Age of Reason; Being an Investigation of True and of Fabulous Theology* (London, 1794).

Rights of Man, Common Sense, and Other Political Writings, ed. Mark Philp (Oxford: Oxford University Press, 1995).

Payne Knight, Richard, *An Analytical Enquiry into the Principles of Taste,* 4th edn (London: 1808).

Peacock, Thomas Love, *The Works of Thomas Love Peacock,* ed. H. F. B. Brett-Smith and C. E. Jones, 10 vols. (London: Constable and Co., 1934–6).

The Letters of Thomas Love Peacock, ed. A. J. Joukovsky, 2 vols. (Oxford: Clarendon, 2001).

Petrarch, Francesco, *The Triumphs of Petrarch*, trans. E. H. Wilkins (Chicago: University of Chicago Press, 1962).

Price, Richard, *A Discourse on the Love of Our Country, Delivered on November 4, 1789, at the Meeting-House in the Old Jewry, to the Society for Commemorating the Revolution in Great Britain* (London, 1790).

Radcliffe, Ann, *The Italian, or The Confessional of the Black Penitents: A Romance*, ed. Frederick Garber (Oxford: Oxford University Press, 1981).

Reid, Thomas, *An Inquiry into the Human Mind: On the Principles of Common Sense* (Edinburgh, 1764).

Essays on the Intellectual Powers of Man (Edinburgh, 1785).

Essays on the Intellectual Powers of Man, ed. D. Brookes and K. Haakonssen (Edinburgh: Edinburgh University Press, 2002).

Rousseau, Jean Jacques, *The Collected Writings of Jean Jacques Rousseau*, ed. C. Kelley, R. Masters, and P. Stillman, 8 vols. to date (London: University of New England Press, 1990–).

Schlegel, August Wilhelm, *A Course of Lectures on Dramatic Art and Literature*, trans. John Black, 2 vols. (London, 1815).

and Percy Bysshe Shelley, *A History of a Six Weeks Tour* (London, 1817).

The Journals of Mary Shelley: 1814–1844, ed. Paula R. Feldman and Diana Scott-Kilvert, softshell edn, 1 vol. (London: Johns Hopkins University Press, 1987).

Shelley, Mary Wollstonecraft, *The Novels and Selected Works of Mary Shelley*, ed. Nora Crook et al., 8 vols. (London: Pickering, 1996).

Smith, Adam, *The Theory of Moral Sentiments* (London, 1759).

An Enquiry into the Nature and Causes of the Wealth of Nations (Edinburgh, 1776).

Essays on Philosophical Subjects (London: 1795).

Southey, Robert, *Poems of Robert Southey*, ed. M. H. Fitzgerald (Oxford: Oxford University Press, 1909).

Stewart, Dugald, *Elements of the Philosophy of the Human Mind*, 3 vols. (London 1792–1827).

Philosophical Essays (Edinburgh, 1810).

Thomson, James, *Liberty, The Castle of Indolence, and Other Poems*, ed. James Sambrook (Oxford: Clarendon, 1986).

Volney, Constantin François, *A New Translation of Volney's Ruins, Made Under the Inspection of the Author*, facsimile of 1802 Paris edn, 2 vols. (New York: Garland, 1979).

Williams, Helen Maria, *A Tour in Switzerland; or A View of the Present State of the Governments and Manners of those Cantons: With Comparative Sketches of the Present State of Paris*, 2 vols. (London, 1798).

Wollstonecraft, Mary, *Letters Written During a Short Residence in Sweden, Norway, and Denmark*, in *A Short Residence in Sweden and Memoirs of The Author of 'The Rights of Woman'*, ed. Richard Holmes (Penguin: Harmondsworth, 1987).

Political Writings, ed. Janet Todd (Oxford: Oxford University Press, 1994).

Wordsworth, William, *The Poetical Works of William Wordsworth*, ed. E. De Selincourt and Helen Darbishire, rev. Helen Darbishire, 5 vols. (Oxford: Oxford University Press, 1952–9).

SECONDARY SOURCES

Abbey, Lloyd, *Destroyer and Preserver: Shelley's Poetic Skepticism* (Lincoln, Nebraska: University of Nebraska Press, 1979).

Albrecht, W. P., *The Sublime Pleasures of Tragedy: A Study of Critical Theory from Dennis to Keats* (Kansas: University Press of Kansas, 1975).

Allen, L. H., 'Plagiarism, Sources, and Influences in Shelley's *Alastor*', *MLR* 18 (1923), pp. 133–51.

Ashfield, Andrew, and De Bolla, Peter (eds.), *The Sublime: A Reader in British Eighteenth-Century Aesthetic Theory* (Cambridge: Cambridge University Press, 1996).

Baker, Carlos, *Shelley's Major Poetry: The Fabric of a Vision* (Princeton: Princeton University Press, 1948).

Baker, J. J., 'Myth, Subjectivity, and the Problem of Historical Time in Shelley's *Lines Written Among the Euganean Hills*', *ELH* 56/1 (Spring 1989), pp. 149–72.

Bainbridge, Simon, *Napoleon and English Romanticism* (Cambridge: Cambridge University Press, 1995).

Bean, John C., 'The Poet Borne Darkly: The Dream-Voyage Allegory in Shelley's *Alastor*', *K-SJ* 23 (1974), pp. 60–76.

Behrendt, Stephen C., *Shelley and his Audiences* (Lincoln Nebr.: University of Lincoln Press, 1989).

'Beatrice Cenci and the Tragic Myth of History', in *History and Myth: Essays in Romantic Literature*, ed. Stephen Behrendt (Detroit: Wayne State University Press, 1990), pp. 214–34.

Bennett, Betty T., and Curran, Stuart (eds.), *Shelley: Poet and Legislator of the World* (Baltimore: Johns Hopkins University Press, 1996).

Binfield, Kevin, ' "May they be divided never": Ethics, History, and the Rhetorical Imagination in Shelley's *The Coliseum*', *K-SJ* 46 (1997), pp. 125–47.

Birns, N., ' "Secrets of the Birth of Time": The Rhetoric of Cultural Origins in *Alastor* and *Mont Blanc*', *SiR* 32/3 (Autumn 1993), pp. 339–65.

Black, Jeremy, *The British Abroad: The Grand Tour in the Eighteenth Century* (New York: St Martins, 1992).

Blank, G. Kim, *Wordsworth's Influence on Shelley* (London: Macmillan, 1988).

(ed.), *The New Shelley: Later Twentieth-Century Views* (New York: St Martins, 1991).

Bloom, Harold, *Shelley's Mythmaking* (Ithaca: Cornell University Press, 1969).

The Anxiety of Influence: A Theory of Poetry (Oxford: Oxford University Press, 1973).

Bode, Christophe, 'A Kantian Sublime in Shelley: "Respect for our own Vocation" in an Indifferent Universe', in *1650–1850: Ideas, Aesthetics, and*

Inquiries in the Early Modern Era, III, ed. Kevin Cope and Laura Morrow (New York: AMS, 1997), pp. 329–58.

Brewer, William D., *The Shelley–Byron Conversation* (Tampa: University Press of Florida, 1994).

Butler, Marilyn, *Romantics, Rebels, and Reactionaries: English Literature and its Background 1760–1830* (Oxford: Oxford University Press, 1981).

(ed.), *Burke, Paine, Godwin, and the Revolution Controversy* (Cambridge: Cambridge University Press, 1984).

'Shelley and the Empire in the East', in *Shelley: Poet and Legislator of the World*, ed. B. T. Bennet and S. Curran (Baltimore: Johns Hopkins University Press, 1996), pp. 158–68.

Butter, Peter, *Shelley's Idols of the Cave* (Edinburgh: Edinburgh University Press, 1954).

Buzard, James, *The Beaten Track: European Travel, Tourism and the Ways to 'Culture', 1800–1918* (Oxford: Oxford University Press, 1994).

Cameron, Kenneth Neill, 'A Major Source of *The Revolt of Islam*', *PMLA* 56 (1941), pp. 175–206.

Shelley: The Golden Years (Cambridge Mass.: Harvard University Press, 1974).

'Shelley as Philosophical and Social Thinker: Some Modern Evaluations', *SiR* 21 (1982), pp. 357–66.

Campbell, William Royce, '*Shelley's Philosophy of History: A Reconsideration*', *K-SJ* 21 (1972), pp. 43–63.

Chandler, James, *England in 1819: The Politics of Culture and the Case of Romantic Historicism* (London: University of Chicago Press, 1996).

Chard, Chloe, *Pleasure and Guilt on the Grand Tour: Travel Writing and Imaginative Geography 1600–1830* (Manchester: Manchester University Press, 1999).

Chard, Chloe and Helen Langdon (eds.), *Transports: Travel, Pleasure, and Imaginative Geography, 1600–1830* (London: Yale University Press, *c.* 1996).

'Crossing Boundaries and Exceeding Limits: Destabilisation, Tourism, and the Sublime', in *Transports: Travel, Pleasure, and Imaginative Geography, 1600–1830*, ed. Chloe Chard and Helen Langdon (London: Yale University Press, *c.* 1996), pp. 117–49.

Chernaik, Judith, *The Lyrics of Shelley* (Cleveland: Case Western Reserve University Press, 1972).

Clark, David Lee, '*Shelley and Bacon*', *PMLA* 48 (1933), pp. 529–46.

Clark, Timothy, *Embodying Revolution: The Figure of the Poet in Shelley* (Oxford: Clarendon Press, 1989).

'Shelley's *The Coliseum* and the Sublime', *Durham University Journal*, 85, 54/2 (July 1993), pp. 225–35.

Clark, Timothy and Mark Allen, 'Between Flippancy and Terror: Shelley's *Marianne's Dream* (1817)', *Romanticism* 1/1 (1995), pp. 90–105.

Cooper, Bryan, '*Shelley's Alastor: The Quest for a Vision*', *K-SJ* 19 (1970), pp. 63–76.

Cronin, Richard, *Shelley's Poetic Thoughts* (London: Macmillan, 1981).

'Peter Bell, Peterloo, and the Politics of Cockney Poetry', in *Essays and Studies 1992: Percy Bysshe Shelley Bicentenary Essays*, ed. Kelvin Everest (Cambridge: D. S. Brewer, 1992), pp. 63–87.

Crook, Nora, and Guiton, David, *Shelley's Venomed Melody* (Cambridge: Cambridge University Press, 1986).

Crucefix, Martin, 'Wordsworth, Superstition, and Shelley's *Alastor*', *Essays in Criticism* 33 (1983), pp. 126–47.

Curran, Stuart, *Shelley's Annus Mirabilis: The Maturing of an Epic Vision* (California: Huntington Library, 1975).

'The Political Prometheus', *SiR* 25/3 (Autumn 1986), pp. 429–55.

Dart, Greg, *Rousseau, Robespierre and English Romanticism* (Cambridge: Cambridge University Press, 1999).

Dawson, Paul M. S., *The Unacknowledged Legislator: Shelley and Politics* (Oxford: Clarendon Press, 1980).

Deane, Seamus, *The French Revolution and Enlightenment in England* (London: Harvard University Press, 1988).

De Beer, Gavin, '*An Atheist in the Alps*', *K-SMB* 9 (1958), pp. 1–15.

De Bolla, Peter, *The Discourse of the Sublime: Readings in History, Aesthetics and the Subject* (Oxford: Basil Blackwell, 1989).

De Man, Paul, 'Shelley Disfigured', in *Deconstruction and Criticism*, ed. Harold Bloom et al. (London: Routledge and Kegan Paul, 1979), pp. 39–73.

Donnelly, Hugo, '*Beyond Rational Discourse: The "Mysterious Tongue" of Mont Blanc*', *SiR* 29/4 (1990), pp. 571–81.

Dowden, Edward, *The Life of Percy Bysshe Shelley*, 2 vols. (London, 1886).

Duerksen, Roland A., '*Shelley's "Deep Truth" Reconsidered*', *ELN* 13 (1975), pp. 25–7.

Duff, David, *Romance and Revolution: Shelley and the Politics of a Genre* (Cambridge: Cambridge University Press, 1994).

Duffy, Cian, 'Mont Blanc's Revolutionary "Voice": Shelley and Archibald Alison', *Bulletin of the British Association for Romantic Studies* 17 (March 2000), pp. 8–11.

'Shelley and the Discourse on the Sublime', in F. L. Price and S. J. Masson (eds.), *Silence, Sublimity and Suppression* (Lampeter: E. Mellen, 2001), pp. 15–36.

'"The City Disinterred": The Shelley Circle and the Revolution at Naples', in A. Chapman and J. Stabler (eds.), '*Unfolding the South*': *Forum for Modern Language Studies Special Edition* 39/2 (April 2003), pp. 152–64.

'*Revolution or Reaction? Shelley's Assassins and the Politics of Necessity*', *K-SJ* 52 (September 2003), pp. 77–93.

'"The Child of a Fierce Hour": Shelley and Napoleon Bonaparte', *Studies in Romanticism*, 43 (Fall 2004), pp. 399–416.

'"One draught from Snowdon's ever-sacred spring": Shelley's Welsh Sublime', in Lynda Pratt and Damian Walford-Davies (eds.), *Wales and the Romantic Imagination* (Lampeter: University of Wales Press, 2005), pp. 15–41.

Duffy, Edward, *Rousseau in England: The Context for Shelley's Critique of the Enlightenment* (Berkeley: University of California Press, 1979).

Ellis, F. S., *A Lexical Concordance to the Poetical Works of Percy Bysshe Shelley: An Attempt to Classify Every Word Found therein according to its Signification* (London, 1892).

Endo, Paul, '*Mont Blanc*, Silence, and the Sublime', *English Studies in Canada* 21/3 (September 1995), pp. 283–300.

'*The Cenci*: Recognising the Shelleyan Sublime', *Texas Studies in Literature and Language* 38, 3–4 (Autumn–Winter 1996), pp. 379–97.

Engell, James, *The Creative Imagination: Enlightenment to Romanticism* (Cambridge Mass.: Harvard University Press, 1981).

Evans, F. B., 'Shelley, Godwin, Hume, and the Doctrine of Necessity', *Studies in Philology* 37 (1940), pp. 632–40.

Everest, Kelvin (ed.), *Shelley Revalued: Essays from the Gregynog Conference* (Leicester: Leicester University Press, 1983).

(ed.), *Essays and Studies 1992: Percy Bysshe Shelley Bicentenary Essays* (Cambridge: D. S. Brewer, 1992).

Ferguson, Frances, 'Shelley's *Mont Blanc: What the Mountain Said*', in *Romanticism and Language*, ed. Arden Reed (Ithaca: Cornell University Press, 1984), pp. 202–14.

Solitude and the Sublime: Romanticism and the Aesthetics of Individuation (London: Routledge, 1992).

'Legislating the Sublime', *Studies in Eighteenth-Century British Art and Aesthetics*, ed. Ralph Cohen (Berkeley: University of California Press, 1995), pp. 128–47.

Foot, Paul, *Red Shelley* (London: Sidgwick and Jackson, 1980).

Fuller, Jean Overton, *Shelley: A Biography* (London: Jonathan Cape, 1968).

Furniss, Tom, *Edmund Burke's Aesthetic Ideology: Language, Gender and Political Economy in Revolution* (Cambridge: Cambridge University Press, 1993).

Gibson, Evan K., '*Alastor: A Reinterpretation*', *PMLA* 62 (1947), pp. 1022–42.

Goldstein, Laurence, *Ruins and Empire: The Evolution of a Theme in Augustan and Romantic Literature* (Pittsburgh: University of Pittsburgh Press, 1977).

Grabo, Carl, *A Newton Among Poets: Shelley's Use of Science in Prometheus Unbound* (New York: Cooper Square, 1968).

Haley, B., '*Shelley, Peacock, and the Reading of History*', *SiR* 29/3 (Fall 1990), pp. 439–61.

Hamblyn, Richard, 'Private Cabinets and Popular Geology: The British Audience for Volcanoes in the Eighteenth-Century', in *Transports: Travel, Pleasure, and Imaginative Geography, 1600–1830*, ed. Chloe Chard and Helen Langdon (London: Yale University Press, *c.* 1996), pp. 179–205.

Haswell, Richard H., '*Shelley's The Revolt of Islam: "the Connexion of its Parts"*', *K-SJ* 25 (1976), pp. 88–102.

Hertz, Neil, *The End of the Line: Essays on Psychoanalysis and the Sublime* (New York: Columbia University Press, 1985).

Hipple, Walter John, *The Beautiful, the Sublime, and the Picturesque in Eighteenth-Century British Aesthetic Theory* (Carbondale: Southern Illinois University Press, 1957).

Hoagwood, Terence A., *Scepticism and Ideology: Shelley's Political Prose and its Philosophical Context from Bacon to Marx* (Iowa City: University of Iowa Press, 1988).

Hodgson, John A., '*The World's Mysterious Doom: Shelley's Triumph of Life*', *ELH* 42(1975), pp. 595–622.

Hogle, Jerrold E. '*Shelley's Fiction: The "Stream of Fate"*', *K-SJ* 30 (1981), pp. 78–99.

Shelley's Process: Radical Transference and the Development of his Major Work (New York: Oxford University Press, 1988).

'Shelley as Revisionist: Power and Belief in *Mont Blanc*', in *The New Shelley: Later 20th-Century Views*, ed. G. K. Blank (Basingstoke: Macmillan, 1991), pp. 108–27.

Holmes, Richard, *Shelley: The Pursuit* (London: Weidenfeld and Nicholson, 1974).

Houston, Ralph, 'Shelley and the Principle of Association', *Essays in Criticism*, 3(1953), pp. 45–59.

Isomaki, Richard, 'Love as Cause in *Prometheus Unbound*', *Studies in English Literature*, 29(1989), pp. 655–73.

'Interpretation and Value in *Mont Blanc* and *Hymn to Intellectual Beauty*', *SiR* 30/1(Spring 1991), pp. 57–69.

Janowitz, Anne, '*Shelley's Monument to Ozymandias*', *PQ* 63/4 (August 1984), pp. 477–91.

England's Ruins: Poetic Purpose and the National Landscape (Oxford: Basil Blackwell, 1990).

Kallich, Martin, *The Association of Ideas and Critical Theory in Eighteenth-Century England* (The Hague: Mouton, 1970).

Kapstein, Israel James, '*Shelley and Cabanis*', *PMLA* 52 (1937), 238–43.

'The Meaning of Shelley's *Mont Blanc*', *PMLA* 62 (1947), pp. 1046–60.

Keach, William, *Shelley's Style* (New York: Methuen, 1984).

Keller, L., 'Shelley's *Queen Mab* und Volney's *Les Ruines*', *Englische Studien*, 22 (1896), pp. 9–40.

King-Hele, Desmond, *Shelley: His Thought and Work*, 2nd edn (London, Macmillan, 1971).

'Shelley and Erasmus Darwin', in *Shelley Revalued: Essays from the Gregynog Conference*, ed. Kelvin Everest (Leicester: Leicester University Press, 1983), pp. 129–46.

Kinnaird, J., '*"But for such faith": A Controversial Phrase in Shelley's Mont Blanc*', *N&Q* 15 (1964), pp. 332–4.

Kipperman, M., '*History and Ideality: The Politics of Shelley's Hellas*', *SiR* 30/2 (Summer 1991), pp. 147–68.

Knapp, Stephen, *Personification and the Sublime: Milton to Coleridge* (London: Harvard University Press, 1985).

Leask, Nigel, *British Romantic Writers and the East: Anxieties of Empire* (Cambridge: Cambridge University Press, 1992).

'Mont Blanc's Mysterious Voice: Shelley and Huttonian Earth Science', in *The Third Culture: Literature and Science*, ed. Elinor S. Shaffer (New York: De Gruyter, 1998), pp. 182–203.

Leighton, Angela, *Shelley and the Sublime: An Interpretation of the Major Poems* (Cambridge: Cambridge University Press, 1984).

McCosh, James, *The Scottish Philosophy from Hutcheson to Hamilton* (London, 1875).

McGann, Jerome J., *The Romantic Ideology: A Critical Investigation* (Illinois: Chicago University Press, 1983).

' "The Secrets of an Elder Day": Shelley after *Hellas*', *K-SJ* 15 (1966), pp. 25–41.

McNiece, Gerald, *Shelley and the Revolutionary Idea* (Cambridge, Mass.: Harvard University Press, 1969).

Maddox, Donald L., 'Shelley's *Alastor* and the Legacy of Rousseau', *SiR* 9 (1970), pp. 82–98.

Manuel, F. E., *The Eighteenth Century Confronts the Gods* (Cambridge, Mass.: Harvard University Press, 1959).

Marshall, Linda E., 'The "Shape all Light" in Shelley's *The Triumph of Life*', *English Studies in Canada* 5 (1979), pp. 49–55.

Matthews, G., 'On Shelley's *The Triumph of Life*', *Studia Neophilologica* 34 (1962), pp. 102–34.

'A Volcano's Voice in Shelley', *ELH* 24 (1957), pp. 191–228.

Monk, Samuel Holt, *The Sublime: A Study of Critical Theories in Eighteenth-Century England* (Ann Arbor: University of Michigan Press, 1960).

Monteiro, J. P., 'Hume's Conception of Science', *Journal of the History of Philosophy*, 19 (1981), pp. 327–42.

Morillo, John, 'Vegetating Radicals and Imperial Politics: Shelley's *Triumph of Life* as Revision of Southey's *Pilgrimage to Waterloo*', *K-SJ* 43 (1994), pp. 117–40.

Morillo, J. and Fay, E. (eds.), *Romantic Passions* (College Park, MD: University of Maryland Press, 1998).

Morton, Timothy, *Shelley and the Revolution in Taste: The Body and the Natural World* (Cambridge: Cambridge University Press, 1994).

Murphy, J. F., 'Time's Tale: The Temporal Poetics of Shelley's *Alastor*', *K-SJ* 45 (1996), pp. 132–55.

Mueschke, Paul, and Griggs, Earl L., 'Wordsworth as the Prototype of the Poet in Shelley's *Alastor*', *PMLA* 49 (1934), pp. 229–45.

Mulvihill, James, 'Hazlitt, Shelley, and *The Triumph of Life*', *N&Q* 35/3 (September 1988), pp. 305–7.

Munro, Hector, 'Coleridge and Shelley', *K-SMB* 21 (1970), pp. 35–8.

Nablow, Ralph A., 'Shelley's "Ozymandias" and Volney's *Les Ruines*', *N&Q* (June 1989), pp. 172–3.

Nair, S., 'Poetic Constitutions of History: The Case of Shelley', *Textual Practice*, 8/3 (Winter 1994), pp. 449–66.

Nicolson, Marjorie Hope, *Mountain Gloom and Mountain Glory: The Development of the Aesthetics of the Infinite* (Ithaca: Cornell University Press, 1959).

Notopoulos, James A., '*The Dating of Shelley's Prose*', *PMLA* 58 (1943), pp. 447–98.

The Platonism of Shelley: A Study of Platonism and the Poetic Mind (Durham, NC: Duke University Press, 1949).

O'Neill, Michael, 'Shelley's *The Triumph of Life*: Questioning and Imagining', in *An Infinite Complexity: Essays on Romanticism*, ed. J. R. Watson (Edinburgh: Edinburgh University Press, 1983), pp. 161–80.

The Human Mind's Imaginings: Conflict and Achievement in Shelley's Poetry (Oxford: Clarendon Press, 1989).

Mona Ozouf, *Festivals and the French Revolution*, A. Sheridan trans. (Cambridge, Mass.: Harvard University Press, 1988).

Paulson, Ronald, *Representations of Revolution, 1789–1820* (London: Yale University Press, 1983).

Pollin, Burton R., 'Godwin's *Memoirs* as a Source of Shelley's Phrase "Intellectual Beauty"', *K-SJ* 23/5 (1974–6), pp. 14–20.

Pulos, C. E., '*Shelley and Malthus*', *PMLA* 67(1952), pp. 113–24.

The Deep Truth: A Study of Shelley's Poetic Scepticism, 2nd edn. (Lincoln, Nebr.: University of Nebraska Press, 1962).

Quinn, Mary A., '"Ozymandias" as Shelley's Rejoinder to Peacock's *Palmyra*', *ELN* 21/4 (June 1984), pp. 48–56.

Quint, David, 'Representation and Ideology in *The Triumph of Life*', *Studies in English Literature 1500–1900* 18 (1978), pp. 639–57.

Raben, Joseph, 'Coleridge as the Prototype of the Poet in Shelley's *Alastor*', *RES* ns 17 (1966), pp. 278–92.

Rees, J., '"But for such faith": A Shelley Crux', *RES* 15 (1964), pp. 185–6.

Reiman, Donald H., 'Shelley's *The Triumph of Life*: The Biographical Problem', *PMLA* 78 (1963), pp. 536–50.

Shelley's The Triumph of Life: *A Critical Study Based on a Text Newly Edited from the Bodleian Manuscript* (Illinois Studies in Language and Literature; Urbana Ill.: University of Illinois Press, 1965).

Reisner, Thomas A., 'Some Scientific Models for Shelley's "Multitudinous Orb"', *K-SJ* 23/5 (1974–6), pp. 52–9.

Richardson, Donna, '"The Dark Idolatry of Self": The Dialectic of Imagination Shelley's *Revolt of Islam*', *K-SJ* 40 (1991), pp. 73–98.

Rieger, James, *The Mutiny Within: The Heresies of Percy Bysshe Shelley* (New York: George Brazillier, 1967).

Rigby, B., 'Volney's Rationalist Apocalypse', in *1789: Reading, Writing, Revolution; Proceedings of the Essex Conference in the Sociology of Literature, July 1981*, ed. F. Barker et al. (Colchester: University of Essex Press, 1982), pp. 22–37.

Robertson, Charles J., 'A Bacon-Facing Generation: Scottish Philosophy in the Early Nineteenth Century', *Journal of the History of Philosophy* 14 (1976), 37–49.

Roberts, Hugh, *Shelley and the Chaos of History: A New Politics of Poetry* (Pennsylvania: Pennsylvania State University Press, 1997).

Robinson, Charles E., 'The Shelley Circle and Coleridge's *The Friend*', *ELN* 8 (1971), 269–74.

Shelley and Byron: The Snake and Eagle Wreathed in Fight (Baltimore: Johns Hopkins University Press, 1976).

Rogers, Neville, *Shelley at Work: A Critical Inquiry* (Oxford: Clarendon Press, 1956).

Rossington, Michael, '"The Voice Which is Contagion to the World": The Bacchic in Shelley', in *Beyond Romanticism: New Approaches to Texts and Contexts 1780–1832*, ed. Stephen Copley and John Whale (London: Routledge, 1992), pp. 101–17.

Ruff, James Lynn, *Shelley's 'The Revolt of Islam'* (Salzburg Studies in English Literature, Romantic Reassessment, 10, Salzburg: Institut für Englische Sprache und Literatur, 1972).

Schaffer, Simon, 'Natural Philosophy and Public Spectacle in the Eighteenth Century', *Journal of the History of Science* 21 (1983), pp. 1–43.

Scott, William O., 'Shelley's Admiration for Bacon', *PMLA* 73 (1958), pp. 228–36.

Scrivener, Michael Henry, *Radical Shelley: The Philosophical Anarchism and Utopian Thought of Percy Bysshe Shelley* (Princeton: Princeton University Press, 1982).

Shaffer, Elinor (ed.), 'Coleridge's Swiss Voice: Frederike Brun and the Vale of Chamouni', in *Essays in Memory of Michael Parkinson*, Norwich Papers IV, ed. Christopher Smith (Norwich: School of Modern Languages and European Cultures, University of East Anglia, 1996), pp. 67–76.

The Third Culture: Literature and Science (New York: De Gruyter, 1998).

Shelley, B. K., 'The Synthetic Imagination: Shelley and Associationism', *The Wordsworth Circle* 14/1 (Winter 1983), pp. 68–73.

Siskin, Clifford, *The Work of Writing: Literature and Social Change in Britain, 1700–1830* (London: Johns Hopkins University Press, 1998).

Sperry, Stuart, *Shelley's Major Verse* (Cambridge, Mass.: Harvard University Press, 1988).

Springer, Carolyn, *The Marble Wilderness: Ruins and Representation in Italian Romanticism, 1775–1850* (Cambridge: Cambridge University Press, 1987).

Stawell, F. M., 'Shelley's *The Triumph of Life*', *Essays and Studies* 5 (1914), pp. 104–31.

Tetreault, Ronald, 'Shelley and Byron Encounter the Sublime: Switzerland, 1816', *Revue des Langues Vivantes* 41 (1975), pp. 145–55.

Tucker, Susan I., *Enthusiasm: A Study in Semantic Change* (Cambridge: Cambridge University Press, 1972).

Turner, Paul, '*Shelley and Lucretius*', *RES* ns 10 (1959), pp. 269–82.

Tuveson, E. L., '*Space, Deity, and the "Natural Sublime"*', *MLQ* 12/1 (March 1951), pp. 20–38.

Imagination as a Means of Grace: Locke and the Aesthetics of Romanticism (Berkeley: University of California Press, 1960).

Vivian, Charles H., 'The One *Mont Blanc*', *K-SJ* 4 (1955), pp. 55–65.

Wallace, Jennifer, 'Tyranny and Translation: Shelley's Unbinding of Prometheus', *Romanticism*, 1/1 (1995), pp. 15–33.

Shelley and Greece: Rethinking Romantic Hellenism (London: Macmillan, 1997).

Wang, Orrin, 'Disfiguring Monuments: History in Paul De Man's "Shelley Disfigured" and Percy Bysshe Shelley's *The Triumph of Life*', *ELH* 58 (1991), pp. 633–55.

Warner, James H., 'Eighteenth-Century English Reactions to the *Nouvelle Héloïse*', *PMLA* 52 (1937), pp. 803–19.

Wassermann, Earl R., *Shelley's* Prometheus Unbound: *A Critical Reading* (Baltimore: Johns Hopkins University Press, 1965).

Shelley: A Critical Reading (Baltimore: Johns Hopkins University Press, 1971).

Webb, Timothy, 'Coleridge and Shelley's *Alastor*: A Reply', *RES* ns 18 (1967), pp. 402–11.

The Violet in the Crucible: Shelley and Translation (Oxford: Clarendon Press, 1976).

Shelley: A Voice not Understood (Manchester: Manchester University Press, 1977).

'The Unascended Heaven: Negatives in *Prometheus Unbound*', in *Shelley Revalued: Essays from the Gregynog Conference*, ed. Kelvin Everest (Leicester: Leicester University Press, 1983), pp. 37–62.

' "The Avalanche of Ages": Shelley's Defence of Atheism and *Prometheus Unbound*', *K-SMB* 35 (1984), pp. 1–39.

Weiskel, Thomas, *The Romantic Sublime* (Baltimore: Johns Hopkins University Press, 1976).

Wellek, René, *Immanuel Kant in England, 1793–1838* (Princeton: Princeton University Press, 1931).

Wertz, S. K., 'Hume, History, and Human Nature', *Journal of the History of Ideas* 36 (1975), pp. 481–96.

White, Harry, 'Shelley's Defence of Science', *SiR* 16 (Summer 1977), pp. 319–30.

White, Newman Ivey, *Shelley*, 2 vols. (London: Secker and Warburg, 1947).

Woodings, E. B. (ed.), *Shelley: Modern Judgements* (London: Macmillan, 1968).

Wu, Y. F., '*The Assassins*: Shelley's Appropriation of History', *K-SJ* 9 (Spring 1995), pp. 51–62.

Index

CAMBRIDGE STUDIES IN ROMANTICISM

GENERAL EDITORS
MARILYN BUTLER *University of Oxford*
JAMES CHANDLER *University of Chicago*